EDITORS' LETTER

There is still life
    …in print
    …in art
        …in storytelling
        …in L.A.
            …all around you

Welcome to *Slake*, a handcrafted selection of deeply reported journalism, essay, memoir, poetry, fiction, painting, and photography from an embarrassment of talented contributors. We expect you'll find a lot of your city and yourself in these pages.

Joe and Laurie

WE DROPPED A BOMB ON YOU

The Best of Slake I-IV

WE DROPPED A BOMB ON YOU

THE BEST OF SLAKE I-IV

Edited by
JOE DONNELLY and **LAURIE OCHOA**

A CITY AND ITS STORIES

LOS ANGELES

RARE BIRD BOOKS
Los Angeles, Calif.

THIS IS A GENUINE RARE BIRD BOOK

A Rare Bird Book | Rare Bird Books
453 South Spring Street, Suite 531
Los Angeles, CA 90013
rarebirdbooks.com

FIRST PAPERBACK EDITION

All of these works have been previously published.

Set in Goudy Old Style
Printed in the United States
Distributed in the U.S. by Publishers Group West
Interior Photo by Shannon Donnelly

10 9 8 7 6 5 4 3 2 1

Publisher's Cataloging-in-Publication data

We dropped a bomb on you : a city and its stories : the best of Slake
I-IV, Los Angeles/ edited
    by Joe Donnelly and Laurie Ochoa.
    p. cm.
    ISBN 978-0-9889312-0-6

1. Los Angeles (Calif.)—Social life and customs. 2. Creative nonfiction.
3. Reportage literature, American—California—Los Angeles. 4. City and
town life—California—Los Angeles. 5. Popular culture—California—Los
Angeles. 6. Arts and society—California—Los Angeles. I. Donnelly, Joe
James. II. Ochoa, Laurie. III. Title.

F869.L85 W33 2013
979.4/94—dc23

Contents

INTRODUCTION

Joe Donnelly

L IKE GOOD WRITING, SHANNON Donnelly's photograph on the cover of *Slake*'s first issue, "Still Life," says a lot with a little. It's full of familiar cues and mysterious questions. Even if the cover didn't have any words, those two palm trees, poking their heads into a denuded landscape of endless blue, interrupted only by wispy cirrus clouds that appear to be getting sucked off the page into a vast unknown, would give you a sense of the book's geography and its contents' psychology.

That image captured so much of how we were feeling back in the Spring of 2010, and those palm trees became sort of talismanic for us, declaring our embrace of all the perils and the possibilities of those uncertain times. Signaling a willful tilt into the next moment and the moment after that, just out of frame.

With that, we started *Slake: Los Angeles*.

The first issue was nothing if not bold. It weighed in at more than 230 four-color pages, some of which stacked three columns of type next to each other. Our amazing art director, Alex Bacon, and his colleague, Dan Peterka, handcrafted every page, sometimes layering a dozen textures on top of each other to get just the right feel. We ran 11,000-word pieces, sixteen-page photo essays, put poems up on walls of abandoned houses and sandwich boards. Editors, art directors, copyeditors, and proofreaders lovingly attended to each and every detail.

We did everything they said you shouldn't or couldn't do anymore.

It was a lot to ask of everybody, readers included.

As if to double-down on our bet, we made the second issue, "Crossing Over," even more sprawling, commissioning and curating original art, debuting the epic *Survivor's Guild* graphic novel, breaking new voices, and urging more familiar ones to explore new terrain.

Our goal was to raise expectations.

We didn't know how any of this would be received, but we had a sense we were making something that spoke to, of, and for Los Angeles when people came to our launch parties in the hundreds. And when readings backed out the doors at Skylight, Stories, and Vromans. And when our first two issues spent more than a dozen weeks on the *Los Angeles Times* bestsellers list. And when honors and awards started piling up for work featured in *Slake*.

Things slowed down, of course. They had to. We had no sustainable business practices or practitioners. *Slake* operated mostly on personal investments and the dedication of volunteers and underpaid staff such as irrepressible associate editor Craig Gaines and the incredible artist, Anne McCaddon, who not only ran our offices but recruited artist Michael Dopp to paint original iconography for "War and Peace" and crafted, with Alex Bacon, the conceptual art collages for "Dirt."

Though we were working with a sense that we were on borrowed time, "War and Peace" and "Dirt" were confident efforts, the alignment of intention and aesthetic becoming more and more seamless. I like to think we were getting better all the time, and often wonder where we may have gone from where we left things.

Our four-issue run may have been too short, but it was certainly sweet. Together, *Slake* issues I-IV total nearly a thousand pages comprised of 140 beautiful works of fiction, poetry, long-form journalism, essay, art, and photography. Each piece had something essential to say about who we were and how we were living.

There are so many people to thank for making *Slake* special—the volunteers, interns, the bookstores, the subscribers, donors and advertisers who believed in us, and especially the writers and artists. It would be unfair to start naming names knowing we couldn't get to everyone, but you know who you are. Please know that we thank you from the bottom of our hearts.

Meanwhile, how to say thanks to Tyson Cornell and Rare Bird for recognizing the special moment of *Slake: Los Angeles* and collecting a meaningful testament that will last into the next moment and the moment after that?

Not sure. Will have to think about it while enjoying *The Best of Slake I-IV*.

INTRODUCTION

Laurie Ochoa

SLAKE BEGAN IN A Guadalajara taxi cab headed toward a mescal bar called Para de Sufir, "to suffer," when the Los Angeles writer Yxta Maya Murray told me she'd been a child beauty queen in suburban Lakewood. It began on Saturday-morning walks, in foothills at the base of Southern California's San Gabriel Mountains, when novelist Michelle Huneven and I talked about the tough parts of writing and life over hot tea she'd brought to share at the top of the trail.

It began with an all-night reading binge, stuck in a hotel room without a book in my bag, when I went through every Aimee Bender short story I could find online and decided *Slake* needed a Bender short story we could call our own. It began with an afternoon macchiato at Little Dom's deli, just below *Slake*'s first office in Los Feliz, when the guy behind the counter turned out to be not just an actor but a writer, David Schneider, with a very funny story about the long reach of celebrity.

Every encounter with a writer or artist became a fresh beginning for *Slake*, with potential in each conversation for a new story, photo essay or picture to be imagined.

My co-editor, Joe Donnelly, has a hundred other *Slake* beginnings. Some are his alone, for in truth, one beginning is a prototype, long before I joined the project, for a glossy magazine called *Slake* created by Joe with Rob Hill, who is now editor of the magazine *Treats*.

Many beginnings Joe and I shared, like the time we walked into the studio of the artist Matjames. Filled with books and ink pots and remarkable assemblage sculptures, some no bigger than a matchbook, others taller than a basketball player and fitted with secret doors, looking glasses and intriguing figures, the light-drenched space revealed a busy, creative mind. Neatly stacked piles of journals held drawings and words that told the story of Matjames' journey to Los Angeles from a devastated New Orleans after Katrina, and how he discovered the daughter he never knew he had. We'd already been impressed with his graphic novel in the making, but with the studio visit we realized one of *Slake*'s important missions: to make sure that artists like Matjames would have a place to publish, a place to call his creative home.

Slake also began in a gritty east Melrose Avenue design studio, best suited as a rehearsal space for extremely loud bands, where art directors Alex Bacon and Dan Peterka explored many ways to express the curves of the letter "S" on their way to a logo for *Slake* and where they rejected easy computer fonts and came up with a design template to match our idea for *Slake* as a spark for a slow-journalism movement.

Slake began around a glass-topped dining table we bought at Ikea, and assembled with one mismatched leg, in a one-room office where Joe, Simone Kredo, Craig Gaines, and I planned our first stories and tried to figure out how you get an ISBN.

It began when we picked up the first boxes of *Slake* from our book distributor and Joe, Simone, and

Introduction

I celebrated at Pasadena's Pie 'N Burger. It began with Craig's executive decision as *Slake's* copy chief that his beloved Chicago Manual of Style would be our grammar guide.

It began with Anne McCaddon, a fine artist on the rise, who for not enough money took on the role of *Slake's* head of operations, and for our fourth issue, created a series of collages and other original art pieces for our title pages, some of which hang on the wall of my Los Angeles Times office today.

It began with the persistence of a woman named Ava Bromberg, an urban planning pied piper, who brought *Slake's* growing office and live-event programming to the then-nascent creative hub called Atwater Crossing. It began, as we prepared to move into our new office, with exchanged glances of love in bloom between Joe and his future wife, artist Ingrid Allen, whose painting of boxing gloves became the cover of our third issue, "War and Peace."

It began with a recurring cast of characters, writers, and interns who joined us during our many public readings and were just as important to the life of *Slake* as Joe or me. Hank Cherry, Joseph Mattson, Jerry Stahl, John Albert, Jervey Tervalon, Luke Davies, Jamie Brisick, Lauren Weedman, Dave White, Iris Berry, John Tottenham, Cindy Carcamo, Sandow Birk, Erica Zora Wrightson, Erin Aubry Kaplan, Melissa Chadburn, Lynell George, Arty Nelson, Natasha Vargas Cooper, and many, many others joined us at the mic.

It began, again in Guadalajara, when Mark Z. Danielewski, one of the world's finest novelists and thinkers, found himself sitting on the floor of a packed convention hall and lent his shoulder to a beer-toting man who was angrily sobbing during a panel discussion of Charles Bukowski's writing because the participants from Los Angeles weren't, in his opinion, showing proper respect.

Most of all, *Slake* started in a window booth at Vic's, more properly known as Victor's Square Restaurant, when, over an eggplant-parm sandwich and order of fries, Joe asked me to join his adventure, funded generously from money he had after selling a house.

Four issues later, the money was gone. A Kickstarter campaign helped us finish the last issue, but it wasn't enough to keep going.

We now have all-consuming jobs that have taken us away from *Slake*, Joe as head of the news and narrative journalism website Mission and State in Santa Barbara, me as arts and entertainment editor of the *Los Angeles Times*. In time, we may get the band back together again, but until then, we are grateful to have this chance to collect some of *Slake*'s strongest writing and images.

I wouldn't go so far as to call these stories "the best of *Slake*." If the choices were left to me alone, this collection would have many more pages. But the stories that Tyson Cornell and Rare Bird's Alice Marsh-Elmer and Julia Callahan have brought to you in this volume give a glimpse of what we were trying to do with *Slake: Los Angeles*—or as we said on every cover, "A City and Its Stories."

Consider it another beginning.

THE PROMISE OF MEANING

Mark Z. Danielewski

1. Writers who do not read poetry cannot be taken seriously.

Which goes (self-evidently) for poets, (just as evidently) for novelists, philosophers, historians and (perhaps less evidently) for jotters of laws, judgments, appraisals, prescriptions, blogs, tweets, text messages, menus, directions and grocery lists.

Without a slow and careful consideration of how words move, form, diminish, connect, enact, deceive, sway, detach, destroy, allude, reattach, imply, fail, obscure, seduce, reveal, relax, undo, hold, tease, estrange and clash, achieved through the patient sounding out of meter and sense, the watchful measuring of what inheres and what escapes, writers can no more know what they mean than what they intend. They will not understand how in what they are writing they are already written and therefore have as yet written nothing at all.

Words are just words. Poetry is something else.

Because poetry is at the heart of the matter.

Because poetry is the heart of the matter.

Because poetry depends on what we cannot do without.

Because poetry defines what we are without.

Because poetry defends why without still matters when we're no longer around.

2. QUESTION: How is it possible to write something and not write anything at all?

ANSWER: The same way it is possible to say "Let there be peace" or "I love you" over and over and not convey a thing.

QUESTION: Are you serious about devaluing writers who don't read poetry?

ANSWER: What might indicate any answer to the contrary?

QUESTION: Grocery lists?

ANSWER: Without knowing how to read closely we cannot say adequately and therefore can never heed accurately what we need.

QUESTION: So people who read poetry eat better?

ANSWER: Suddenly the possibility is there.

QUESTION: And lawmakers?

ANSWER: They will write better grocery lists too. Not to mention laws. After all, how can anyone conceive a directive on behavior without a thorough understanding of the material that comprises the very design of that directive? Furthermore, how can the consequences of such a mandate even be effectively assessed? Can the great enterprise of justice on behalf of the living succeed if the potentials and limitations of its own construction go unrecognized?

QUESTION: Is poetry then merely the particle physics of expression?

ANSWER: That is the matter. But not the heart of.

3. "I cannot imagine having written *House of Leaves* without Rilke (*You must change your life* — **Archaic Torso of Apollo**) or *Only Revolutions* without Dickinson (*For I have but the power to kill, / Without — the power* to die — **My Life had stood**) and Stevens (*It is cold to be forever young, / To come to tragic shores and flow* — **Variations on a Summer Day**).

"I may have loved but would I have understood love's consequences without Vergil (*omnis et una / dilapsus calor atque in ventos vita recessit* — **Aeneid IV**) or love's hope without Apollinaire (*Comme la vie est lente / Et comme l'Espérance est violente* — **Le Pont Mirabeau**) or love's denial without Donne (*For thou art not so* — **Holy Sonnet X**)?

"I would have fallen for her anyway but doubt I would remember her so eidetically without Crane (*And so it was I entered the broken world / To trace the visionary company of love* — *The Broken Tower*) or know her still so intimately without Graham (*They're flowers because they stop where they do* — *The Strangers*).

"I cannot see sustaining the reckless engagement with life's infinite propositions without Milton (*in the lowest deep a lower deep / Still* — **Paradise Lost IV**) or endure its dereliction without Whitman (*I too am but a trail of drift and debris* — **As I Ebb'd**) or greet its vicissitudes with anything close to a smile without Chaucer (*and in he throng* — *The Merchant's Tale*) let alone suffer its misreadings without Keats (*forget / What thou among the leaves hast never known* — **Ode to a Nightingale**).

"To experience the intense requires a language confident in its calmness. While to live without language is to forfeit life's gift. As to live without awareness is to forfeit life's meaning.

"Meaning, after all, is what survives but what survives only offers the promise of meaning if it can perish.

"Or fail.

"Or at least fall.

"During that blur of time before I turned eight, when the outdoors increasingly offered the chance of unrestricted investigation, my father's recitations of Shakespeare still intrigued me most (*for in the very torrent, tempest, and, as I may say, whirlwind of your passion, you must acquire and beget a temperance that may give it smoothness.* — **Hamlet III 2**).

"During my freshman year when music blared loud it was Eliot in a black-lipstick scrawl on a dorm-room wall who proved loudest (*I will show you fear in a handful of dust* — **The Waste Land**).

"And of those days between desks and debt, requirement and request, whether at a bus station or park or coffee shop or encampment on a friend's sofa, Hollander (*Are you done with my shadow* — **Kitty**), Bishop (*This is the house of Bedlam* — **Visits to St. Elizabeths**), Merrill (*A new voice now?* — T**he Changing Light at Sandover**), Rimbaud (*Je me suis armé contre le justice.* — **Une Saison en Enfer**), Tennyson ('*The Gods themselves cannot recall their gifts*' — **Tithonus**), Blake (*immediately Go out* — **Auguries of Innocence**), Auden (*dismantle the sun* — **Stop all the clocks**), and Wordsworth (*Was it for this* — **The Prelude**) gave voice to what thirst and hunger nightly threatened to digest.

"And now in years more recently traversed when political challenges increasingly demand the philosophical and the pedestrian scheduling of taxes and travels encounters the unanticipated shocks of death and solitude, Hill (*To have lost dignity is not the same / as to be humble* — **The Triumph of Love**), Szymborska (*The panther wouldn't know what scruples mean* — **In Praise of Feeling Bad about Yourself**), Stanford (*Blood come out like hot soda* — **The Singing**

Knives), Oliver (*hurrying* / *day after day, year after year* / *through the cage of the world* — **Mountain Lion on East Hill Road, Austerlitz, N.Y.**) and Telford (*What bores an angel more — violence or beauty? — **At the Theatre***) grant prominence to that miracle limit where even the expected conclusion is unended by a rarer and revitalized retelling."

4. What was that all about?

5. Scene: Lucques. Time: After closing. Cast: Your usual strangers.

GUSTAV: Writers who don't read poetry can't be taken seriously. That goes for poets, novelists, jotters of laws, grocery lists and —
IVAN: Text messages?
OCTAVIO: Menus?
LORRAINE: Eviction notices?
VANESSA: Dear Gustav, what about love letters?

Vanessa and Gustav are falling in love but they will never get together in a play or a novel. If only they could live in a poem.

But who will write it?
Not I.

A fast rattle of dialogue ensues defending and denouncing the value of various poets ranging from Plath, Lowell, Byron, Frost, Millay, Baudelaire, Pound, Cummings, Milosz, Paz, Williams, Yang, and Mallarmé to Hughes, Shelley, Nash, Wilbur, Sappho, Hix, Neruda,

Herrera, Yeats, Basho, Perillo, Ashbery and Kees along with splashes of lines like: — If truth is beauty what of an ugly truth? — I will show you love in a handful of dust. — I will show you an allergen!

> MAN AT THE BAR: Who are you people?
> VANESSA: Good question.

Finally —

> IVAN: And what of writers who don't read poetry at all but still manage to produce volumes of verse? Should they be taken seriously?
> GUSTAV: They should be shot.

Man at the Bar runs away. Lorraine takes advantage and finishes his drink. She is drunk again.

> LORRAINE: Is serious even so important?
> GUSTAV: Without it levity also departs.
> IVAN: Always so clever.
> LORRAINE: Clever isn't funny. I'm not smiling, Gustav. I'm leaving and I'm not smiling. And I haven't laughed once. Seriously.

But Lorraine doesn't leave. Gustav and Vanessa do. Lorraine gulps down their unfinished drinks. Octavio laughs and falls off his stool. He's drunk as well. Lorraine's laughter turns to snorts. They both end up on the floor.

Lorraine and Octavio are not in love, but they get together all the time. They don't need to live in a poem. They are happy. Tomorrow morning they won't remember a thing. Well, that's not true. They will remember things but only vaguely. Meanwhile Ivan's fast asleep dreaming of Russian faces.

8

VANESSA: And how will we say good night this time?

GUSTAV: As we always do.

VANESSA: But will they be the same words?

GUSTAV: Never.

VANESSA: Promise me.

GUSTAV: I promise you.

CISCo KID

Luke Davies

2011 Entertainment Reviews/Criticism/Column,
Los Angeles Press Club, Finalist

"How's the ol' universe?"

I AM EIGHT YEARS old. I'm given a book of children's
poetry. I hurry past the poems. It's the photos that I
study, that I want to enter. There's a girl stamping in a
puddle, and I feel a terrific yearning for her, so terrific
as to be painful. It's that preadolescent anticipation
of falling in love, and it's the foreknowledge of the
mysteries of sex. In that single image, in that barefoot
girl stomping so joyfully in a puddle, there lies
the possibility of eternal contentment, possession,
surrender, sublimation.

But what else about that photo? It's not the girl; it's
not the foreground that matters so much. It's the house
behind her that draws my attention, a house distinctly and
completely American, the likes of which I've never seen in
my own quiet neighborhood. It's a two-story gabled house
with a deep front porch. The vernacular of American
suburban architecture works as a great, entrancing,
hypnotic force in my life. I obsess for hours about all the
perfection of form in my mother's *House and Gardens*.

An inconceivable mystery: from where I stood as
a youngster, the people all around me appeared to be
more or less satisfied with the notion that they were

living in Australia. They seemed, in fact, to embrace the idea! For me, Australia was a pale simulacrum of what reality should surely have been offering. The thought never crossed my mind that a physical continent—a country, flesh and stone, citizens and states, events taking place with or, more extraordinarily, without me present—could in any way be disentangled from the imagination. It was all one world. It was all one country, and it was called America: this place I was living in, in every way except the physical. The way to this land, this America, was television.

I wasn't insane, not at all. I didn't think I lived inside television shows. But television stood for that which was even more real than that which was. Television showed the way. It was a design for living. It was an aid to the imagination. It was the bridge of metaphor, or the metaphor of the bridge. It led me to the promised land.

I could understand, at thirteen, understand in some abstract intellectual fashion, that something altogether BBC-ish like *Doctor Who* was a show worth following; these episodes were smart. They contained story, in a way that *Gilligan's Island* didn't, not really: *Gilligan's Island* was situation. Yet I couldn't stomach *Doctor Who*, whereas *Gilligan's Island* was like a nightly religious ritual. The *Doctor Who* sets were so cheap; sometimes you saw them shake. My imagination was no help here. I never wanted to be reminded of the stage machinery. Americans had budget! There was no stage machinery in America. It was the reality beyond artifice. *The Brady Bunch*, or better still *The Partridge Family*: now those interiors looked real, and solid. You could live somewhere like that and be happy.

"Real" life in Australia was messier. I felt I was on the wrong planet. Ceilings got moldy, and cupboard doors came loose. Something essential and perfect was missing from life. But the puddle girl: surely back in that house behind her, there would be a kitchen filled with all the wonders of the world, all the products in the advertisements in the American magazines. What on Earth was a Hershey's bar? Its unattainability was like a heavy weight on my soul.

"I'm a simple cat, man."

I'M TWELVE, THIRTEEN. I'VE lost interest now in Gilligan's Island and Lost in Space. I've come to recognize their locales as sets. I've become more spatially aware. Now, I need shows shot largely on location. Thus, reruns of *Room 222* or a new show called *Chico and the Man* are mostly only good for the opening credits. I watch *The Streets of San Francisco*. It's a bipolar viewing experience: whenever the action is inside, on a set, my attention wanders; outside, when the show is on location, I'm all eyes, devouring backgrounds, cars, shopfronts, extras. Where might I live? How will my life turn out? America becomes a slant of light.

I'm allowed to take the train to the cinema on Saturdays. With film, everything is different. With film, you can spend ninety minutes sinking into the "real" America as you might sink into a warm bath. I see *Jaws, Macon County Line, Dirty Mary Crazy Larry*. Now everything coalesces at once. I discover masturbation. I leapfrog from Steinbeck to *On the Road*. I seem to literally make a decision to become obsessed with drugs, and then I do. And a certain kind of drifting, American B-movie becomes my bible. For a while *Billy Jack* seems like the most important film ever made. *Little Fauss and Big Halsy* makes a kind of existential poetry of the motocross circuit in the Southwestern states. I decide I want to live in a trailer in Arizona after seeing *Electra Glide* in Blue.

One summer holiday, I'm with my mother at a mall in Surfers Paradise on Queensland's Gold Coast, and I scan the movies and I know from the poster alone that *Alice Doesn't Live Here Anymore* is the one we need to see. I'm intrigued by Kris Kristofferson for the first time. More and more I am coming to like rootlessness, Arizona, New Mexico.

On the one hand there's this child still in me: I spend hours buried in the final volume, W-X-Y-Z-and-Atlas, of the old set of encyclopedias my father has picked up from a school fete. It's a very American set, an American atlas: there are fifty beautiful, detailed double-page spreads for the fifty states, then about ten pages for the rest of the world. I continually invent the places where I will live. I invent entire networks of high schools, the team colors, team names. I work out obsessive methodologies of gathering quarterback statistics and game scores via a complex system of darts thrown at a target from three feet away. Every time I "move," every time I create a new life (a different double page, a different state), the fantasy begins again. New notebooks get filled with statistics. It's the OCD phase of my life: decisions within my imaginary world are made with obscure, rule-based alphabetical and numbering systems, and a 1970 pro football yearbook I find becomes, for many years, as talismanic as the *I Ching*.

When we travel north to the Gold Coast for those yearly family holidays, leaving Sydney behind us, the Pacific Ocean is always to the right. So I invert my world and imagine we are traveling south, from San

Francisco, through Los Angeles (Brisbane) to warmer climes in San Diego (Surfers Paradise). The east coast of Australia replicates the west coast of America. The ocean remains on the right and, so long as I ignore the fact that we drive on the left-hand side of the road, a kind of plausibility is achieved.

On the other hand: there's the continually frustrating fact that I long to be an adult and yet I have no control over the glacial speed of the passage of time. I've leapfrogged again, now from Kerouac to Faulkner, then on to poetry, and everything has changed, and yet nothing at all. I see myself as a poet from now on. I feel like an adult. I'm only thirteen. I want older friends. I desperately want to have sex.

The Partridge Family has long receded into the past. I discover Bob Dylan. Then, in *Pat Garrett and Billy the Kid* there's Kris Kristofferson again. I want to be handsome, and soulful, and laconic, like him. When girls take a mysterious liking to me or kiss me, or let me finger them, I don't feel lucky or blessed for all that long; I don't know how to take things in stride. Hovering behind my heightened yearning is the sense that this kissing or this fingering must surely only be some temporary malfunction in the workings of the universe, and that regular anguish will shortly resume. But if I were handsome and soulful and laconic like Kristofferson, then I would not be living in a world of malfunction. The future is waiting for me but not arriving fast enough.

Kristofferson is in *Pat Garrett and Billy the Kid* because Peckinpah cast him after seeing him in *Cisco Pike*, the 1971 B. L. Norton film about a dealer/ex-rock star who gets out of prison and tries to go straight. *Cisco Pike* is a B-film, sitting square in the middle of the hippie-era, outsider-versus-the-system movies that would wind up becoming the psychic sustenance of my adolescence. I don't know what it is that I'm attracted to—it's all instinct. Years later I will see the consistency of aesthetic in these B-movies—that pervasive atmosphere of a world waking all disillusioned and bewildered to a mean, sour hangover after the big party-gone-wrong that was, apparently, the sixties. Not that I would know, since in the sixties I was showered and pajama'ed by 6 P.M. every night.

Something clicks for me with *Cisco Pike*, and it seems to become, however gradually, the ur-film of my imagined America. "I miss everything/I'll never be," the Smashing Pumpkins will sing years later. And I fall in love, around 1977, with a Venice Beach that B. L. Norton shot seven years earlier, which no doubt no longer exists even as I fall. Venice is the sun-drenched America of all my nostalgia, all my lost dreams.

"You know where the groove is at."

I'M HOOKED FROM THE opening scenes, as Kristofferson ambles along the dilapidated Venice canals in the late sun, past slightly gone-to-seed houses that look like the kind of shared Sydney houses where I often find myself scoring pot. They are the kind of weatherboard houses I'd been wanting to live in: no longer *House and Garden*, to be sure, no longer that surreal perfection of *Leave It to Beaver*, but still, even in *Cisco Pike*, it's their Americanness that I want. The incidental background of films remains a dominant condition of my viewing them. But now my dreams are more sophisticated. I decide to be, if not handsome and soulful and laconic, then mysterious and aloof and slightly troubled. Hippie chicks like *Cisco Pike*'s Joy Bang and just-plain-mad but sexy Viva will surely bed me in rollicking threesomes. One day I will be mysterious, and aloof, and slightly troubled. I want to live in a world where people speak like the characters in *Cisco Pike*. "What have you brought me?" asks the man in the guitar shop. "A little coke from Cuzco?" "I ain't dealin' no more, man," answers Cisco, the first of a constant refrain. "You mean you isn't dealin' no more," the guitar shop man chides. It's one of those films that takes its languid, minimalist time, and it lets whole songs play out as it rambles. "He's a poet, he's a picker, he's a prophet, he's a pusher," sings Kristofferson. "He's a pilgrim and a preacher and a problem when he's stoned." I've found a model for living.

Cisco lives with flaky girlfriend Sue (Karen Black) in a small, bright apartment across the road from the beach. When we first see her, she's meditating on a table, in the lotus position. Cisco enters, comes up from behind. "How's the ol' universe?" he says into her ear. She remains immobile. He squeezes her breasts and nuzzles her. "Ommm, ommm," he teases, before segueing into, "Ommm, ommm on the range, where the deer and the antelope play..." She giggles. Sue believes in astral projection and levitation and yogis who can "make it for twenty-four hours straight." When Dragon calls him, Cisco says, "I'm through. I quit dealing. Yeah, why don't you try Buffalo? I think he's got something. Dig you later, man." This is the territory. To this day I still have no clear idea how tongue-in-cheek it is.

"Are you sorry you quit?" asks Sue.

"No."

19

"No withdrawal pains?"

"Not on your nellie," says Cisco. "I'm gonna do this thing."

Then we're watching a police parade and funeral, and Officer Leo Holland (Gene Hackman) is among the mourners. Soon Holland steals a hundred kilos of marijuana from some Mexicans and, with threats and coercing and a promise of some help with an upcoming court case, forces Cisco back into business. Holland gives Cisco the weekend only in which to offload the hundred keys for $10,000. It seems an impossibly low price—$100 a kilo, wholesale—even for 1971. But what do I know? (Pajamas, 6 P.M.) Perhaps Holland is simply in a hurry.

Thus the L.A. travelogue begins. We're with Cisco in his rental car, a guitar case filled with bricks of compressed pot in the back, from Venice to Los Feliz, from Hollywood to the Valley. Cisco presses Officer Holland as to why he's doing this, but Holland is evasive. "You do things and, er…one day you wonder why you're doing things," he muses. Hackman is excellent and sharp in *Cisco Pike*: all bitterness and paranoia. Later, we learn the real reason for his going feral. His medical is coming up, and he knows the tachycardia he's suffering from will have him stood down with less than two years to go before he qualifies for a full pension. Fuck the police, indeed.

There are moments of ludicrous dialogue, but the film's overall effect is not entirely ludicrous. There are moments that are unintentionally funny; I forgive them utterly at fifteen years old, and still do. Doug Sahm (of the Sir Douglas Quintet) is bizarre but hilarious: "You know me though, man, you know, I'm a simple cat, man, I like that simple stuff, man, I mean, you know, you know where the groove is at, that California thing don't get it, that far-out-in-space music, man, play the real thing, man. You know, man?"

Near everything is framed in clichés like this. Sahm's manager wears a suit, says to Cisco, "I saw you guys at the Forum in, what was it, '68?" "Shrine, '67," deadpans Cisco. "Oh, yeah," says the manager. "Big grosser, that show. You haven't done much since then, huh?" Viva (of Warhol's Factory fame), playing a spaced-out pregnant groupie, asks, "Will you sell me a pound?" "Of what?" asks Cisco. "Anything you've got," she says. "I'm not choosy."

But landscape, this celluloid geography, trumps clichéd dialogue any day. I've already lived entire lives in houses glimpsed for a second in the background of The Streets of San Francisco, so not much in Cisco Pike fazes me. I imagine I might live in a city like Los Angeles, the utterly exotic and the utterly familiar yoked together, the endless ugly sprawl of strip malls and neon.

Every now and again I might need to get my head together, so I'd probably go off to New Mexico for a while. (Doug Sahm to Cisco: "I saw Moss. He said he ran into Jesse in Taos." I'd need to live in a world where phrases like that flowed freely.) I know all about New Mexico from Whole Earth Catalog and Domebook. I might build a dome one day. There's a porn mag called Gallery, and I steal from the newsagent the Gallery Girl Next Door Annual, which is basically the pre-Internet version of the "amateur" category, 200 pages of home snapshots sent in by hot, lusty, American women (or their biker boyfriends, more likely). I might one day take my flaxen-tressed, hairy-bushed, cut-off-Levi'd girlfriend and head off to New Mexico to raise kids, grow pot, and live free. I am clueless, and near divine.

"I'm lucky like that!"

"YOU BEEN USING?" CISCO asks his old friend and band member Jesse (Harry Dean Stanton), who has turned up unannounced and doesn't look so great. "A little speed for the drive down here," admits Jesse. "Then I took an upper—no, I took a downer for the up. But I'm ready now, buddy, I'm ready now." They hit the town— Jesse will accompany Cisco in his attempts to offload the bricks. Jesse has a shot of speed before they take off, and Stanton plays to a tee all the slightly-too-loud and slightly-too-fast, loopily extrapolating on the insurance money he has coming to him as a result of a car accident. "$10,000, just like that," he says. "I'm lucky like that!"

But Jesse frets about his looks. If they get the band back together, what will the crowd make of his wrinkles? "Aw, Jesse, man," says Cisco. "It ain't your goddamned body they're after, man. It's your soul." Jesse has just come from a failure-to-perform in the back seat of a car with groupie Joy Bang after meeting her at a gig at the Troubadour ("Goddamned speed, man," he says, "that's why Virginia left"). The ravages of time are weighing heavily on his mind. He will die of a heroin overdose before the movie's end. Jesse makes me sad at sixteen, perhaps because at some unconscious level I know certain ravages await me, or perhaps because the center of the film, the great art of it, is Kristofferson's immortality. Like Pacino in Dog Day Afternoon, Kristofferson attains—is granted by the gods—a moment of near-incandescent celluloid beauty. That moment is *Cisco Pike*.

Kristofferson is seventy-three now, and I am forty-eight, though very quickly this information too will be obsolete. For a long while, time stands still. In my twenties, completely beholden to heroin by this time, I watch American football on TV—you can only see one game once a week at this time in Australia, on a free-to-air station, around eleven or midnight—and I still wonder if my fantasy might ever come true, that I might be the first Australian-born quarterback to lead a team to a Super Bowl victory.

I imagine a world in which it would be possible to be a quarterback who was also a good poet.

"I'm ready now, buddy."

WHEN I FINALLY MAKE it to America, of course, at thirty-five, everything is both utterly familiar and utterly foreign. It's exciting just being in a supermarket, in the corniest way, to get to touch the packaging at last. And there's that moment of anticlimax, too: the realization that all those cereal boxes, all the shiny mass of commerce and consumerism, telling their stories of a perfect America, that these too are just stage machinery after all. After all that bother! (As when, at the end of *The Wizard of Oz*, the Wizard is unmasked.) And that you are always only wherever you are. And thus that some of Australia has been lost forever, frozen in those times when your head was in America.

In Los Angeles, the lostness of America becomes most readily apparent. The signifier is omnipresent, but what it signifies is no longer so evident. The visual detritus of pure consumerism overwhelms the senses. The sameness stretches fractally, everything repeating to scale, to boundaries that are never quite clear; eventually, suddenly, you are simply in Las Vegas, pure money with no product, nothing manufactured there but yearning.

And yet, back west, here is Los Angeles, and here is the ocean. The same ocean that was to my east is now to my west. Not just time, which Einstein told us moves in curves, connects me there to here, but this endless ocean, too. It's been forever since that time when I lived so comprehensively in two-worlds-as-one. Was there a vacuum between me and my life, in which my real life lay unused? Possibly. It was the only life I knew.

One of the movie's posters announces: "Cisco Pike is a man of the west—west L.A.!" It seems inadvertently funny now, like the tag line for a remake of *The Fresh Prince of Bel-Air*, but perhaps it meant something quite different forty years ago, when Venice was frontier as well as end of the road. In *Cisco Pike* there's nowhere farther west to go for Cisco; at the end he's heading east, out into the open space of the desert. I know that axis now: last year for two months I finally made it to New Mexico, looking after a cabin 9,000 feet up in the snows of the Sangre de Christo Mountains outside of Taos. There was no sense any more that life was awaiting me elsewhere. All that was long gone.

Not everything moves in circles, but all the ellipses and curves are uncanny. And the funny thing? There's still something dreamy and sun-drenched about Venice, something as trippy and marginal now as what you glimpse as background, as setting, as visual circumstance, in *Cisco Pike*. "Algiers," wrote Camus, and he might just as much have been talking about Venice or my beloved Bondi Beach, "opens to the sky like a mouth or a wound. In Algiers one loves the commonplace: the sea at the end of every street, a certain volume of sunlight."

I miss everything I'll never be: that is the purest form of nostalgia, the benediction and burden of the commonplace. *Cisco Pike* as a dream of light. I haven't lived in Venice yet. I live in Hollywood for now, possibly because I want to experience shallowness at depth, possibly because I want to live for a while in the last remaining nineteenth-century gold town on the planet. It will do. I can always take day trips to Venice.

FALLEN FRUIT

Jonathan Gold

VISITORS TO THE NORTON Simon Museum, the collections jimmied into the corpse of the former Pasadena Art Museum, come to admire the handsome Frank Gehry garden, the shimmering tiles by Edith Heath, and what is probably the most impressive group of Rembrandt paintings on the West Coast. There are Degas ballerinas by the bushel, Rubens by the acre, and Venetian cityscapes sufficient to decorate the parlor of any 18th-century earl. Simon, or his consultants, had a decent eye—his Cranach looks like a Cranach, and the Ingres portrait is really fine. There may not be much competition, but the Simon is probably the best small art museum in California, and as much as one personally might mourn the superb contemporary-art museum that was vaporized to accommodate the catsup millionaire's dream, as a fact on the ground the Simon is admirable.

But a casual visitor, someone there because her guidebook tells her that she should come have a peek at the Van Gogh, might be puzzled by the institution's apparent emphasis on *Still Life with Lemons, Oranges and a Rose* by Francesco de Zurbarán, a 17th-century Spanish painter who was unlikely to have come up in the Renaissance art survey course she took as an elective sophomore year. The museum's gallery map features the Zurbarán on its cover, and the gift shop is stocked with replicas of the painting in every possible size and form. It was the star of the small Norton Simon exhibition in New York's Frick last year. More to the point, the Norton Simon's galleries are laid out in a way that makes *Still Life* almost impossible to avoid, a flash of yellow in a room just off the most glamorous corridor, a magnetic yellow positioned to distract you as you rush toward the Botticelli.

When Simon bought the painting in the early '70s, it was the third-most-expensive Old Master ever sold, a stand-in for the Velázquezes that would never hit the auction block, and the $2,725,000 cost figured into the allure of what is, after all, a picture of some fruit. Zurbarán, the painting's author, was a friend of Velázquez and an admirer of Caravaggio; his work, chiefly pious religious scenes painted for his court patrons in Seville, is often compared favorably with them both. If you are an aficionado of the way a saint's loose, white robe puddles around his holy ankles, Zurbarán is the Baroque-era painter for you.

But *Still Life* is charismatic for a picture of fruit, a three-part composition of nipply lemons, oranges, and an untouched porcelain cup of water on a silver tray. An oddly specific light illuminates the composition, early morning sun perhaps, streaming through a window above and to the viewer's left, sharply focused enough to render the left face of the oranges bright and washed out, although the shadows are almost black. The wooden table on which they sit appears to receive barely enough light to do a crossword puzzle by. To the right of the oranges, the sunlight glints from the rim of the porcelain drinking cup; a white rose stained pink at its edge glows softly as if illuminated from within. On the left are four lemons: some are as defined by their sunken areoles and proud nipples as a vintage Playboy centerfold; another, in the foreground, appears to have the outline of a face with a jutting, crooked nose. If you squint, it is almost a match for the head of the leathery crone who cradles the newborn Virgin in another Zurbarán painting mounted a few feet to one side. The rough-skinned oranges, heaped in a finely woven basket, are wreathed with an arrangement of dark leaves and virginal white blossoms that seem less to grow from the fruit than to have descended from heaven.

The museum abounds in other fruit-filled still lifes of the era, and they thrum with life, the yellowing edges of leaves signifying decay, the lumps and hollows hinting at sweet temporality, even the turnips and loamy potatoes that look like tomorrow's dinner. Ants, butterflies, worms, beetles skitter along the edges of the displays, nibbling, sucking out juice.

Fruits are pure sex, the naked reproductive organs of a tree: juicy, plump with fertility, cleft with alluring, syrup-crusted fissures. When we look at Chardin's cherries or a Cézanne peach, what we see is possibility. Zurbarán's citrus may be the opposite of that— unviolated ornamental fruit meant to be admired rather than eaten. There are no crumbs. Not a bite is missing. The lemons are actually citrons, whose rind is fragrant but whose flesh is all but inedible; the oranges, like most in Seville at the time, are almost certainly bitter. These will never be eaten.

In fact, Zurburán mostly hides the naughty bits as completely as Raphael does the genitals on his half-robed saints—except for a solitary, lovingly rendered crater, the stem end of the forwardmost of the oranges, at the mathematical center of the painting and thrust out quite directly at the viewer, the pucker at the center of the world. Centered between the virginal chalice on the one hand and the voluptuous citrons on the other, the dark, bottomless pucker invites what is sometimes known as the male gaze.

The saintly glow of the fruit is indistinguishable from the one on the face of Zurbarán's St. Francis on the painting next to this, or rather to that on the skull before which the saint kneels. There are no glints of light on the oranges themselves, no shine; just brilliantly rough surface. The fruit has no physical presence—it is impossible to imagine plucking it from its basket, to smell it, to feel the heaviness of its juice in your palm— but you want to, you ache for sensation, driven by its sheer, pornographic unavailability. It is no wonder Zurbarán's oranges enraptured a millionaire.

You don't want to eat this fruit. You want to fuck it. And it's going to hurt.

TALES FROM THE TROPICANA MOTEL

Iris Berry

JUST A LIMO RIDE or drunken, one-cigarette stumble down La Cienega from the Sunset Strip, the Tropicana Motel was known worldwide during its heyday. Much like other historic addresses of bohemia, 8585 Santa Monica Boulevard was a haven and hideout for actors, artists, writers, poets, directors, sports figures, music producers, film producers, and rock stars. It was the Chelsea Hotel with poolside AstroTurf. Parties sometimes lasted for months and often ended in mayhem. There was a constant parade of groupies, photographers, and drug dealers.

Of course, the clientele also included tourists who innocently happened to share their Hollywood vacations with hookers, pimps, and junkies. Word on the street was that anything you desired—no matter how bizarre, kinky, sleazy, or unsavory—could be had at the Trop, and for an extremely low nightly rate. All just a stone's throw away from the West Hollywood sheriff's station.

In the fifties, the motel was a getaway for Hollywood's better-known character actors. But as Hollywood changed, so did the ownership. In 1963 the motel was sold to its fourth owner, soon-to-be Hall of Famer Sandy Koufax, strikeout artist of the Los Angeles Dodgers. Being a smart businessman, he immediately changed the sign to read "Sandy Koufax's Tropicana

Motel," which brought in a whole new clientele. The culture shifted, too, and the movie stars morphed into television stars and rock gods. From 1963 onward, the Trop functioned as a boho playground, pioneered by Jim Morrison of the Doors, who hung around the Palms, a low-rent (and nearly as infamous) dyke bar located directly across the street from the Tropicana. He would drink there all night before stumbling across the street to pass out. Mornings after, he'd write many of the songs that became hits for the Doors. Waves of other musicians arrived and followed the same hit-making formula. The motel was also the site of numerous photo sessions and legendary band interviews, and it served as the location for the Andy Warhol films Heat and Trash. The party kept going until 1988, when the building was razed and replaced with a Ramada Inn.

Duke's Coffee Shop, underneath the Tropicana, served copious amounts of good, inexpensive food to poor artists and musicians as well as record and film execs. The seating was family style, which meant that you could be broke enough to consider running out on your check even as you passed the ketchup to someone who could change your life in an instant. Cassettes and scripts were passed across the greasy Formica countertops; romances were kindled over hangovers.

The rooms at the Tropicana looked like Little Richard decorated them with somebody's Midwestern grandma on a lost weekend, and they were continually being trashed. The motel's plumbing was iffy at best, which meant flooded rooms were a common occurrence during all-night parties. There were a few private bungalows at the back of the property where Tom Waits and Chuck E. Weiss, among others, took up long-term residence. The kidney-bean-shaped pool was surrounded by AstroTurf and painted black. This was widely assumed to be a choice of function, not fashion: the paint hid the rust stains from the patio furniture that was regularly tossed in the water. Regulars knew better than to dive into the pool— you might have an underwater rendezvous with a chaise lounge, or, worse, a syringe or two. Under the Trop's junglelike foliage there were orgies, murders, suicides, ODs, love triangles, marriages, and drunken brawls on a daily basis. There were even a number of struggling bands living in their cars in the Trop's back parking lot (which the management was fully aware of).

It was not unlikely to see Iggy and the Stooges, Janis Joplin, Van Morrison, Bruce Springsteen, Eddie Cochran, the Beach Boys, Jim McGuinn of the Byrds, Led Zeppelin, Frank Zappa, Elvis Costello, Nick Lowe, Blondie, the Cramps, Johnny Thunders and the Heartbreakers, the Damned, the Clash, the Dead Boys, Johnny Cash, Dennis Hopper, Evel Knievel, Lydia Lunch, Sam Shepard, Levi and the Rockats, legendary photographer Leee Black Childers, Marianne Faithfull, William Burroughs, Nico, Lou Reed and the rest of the Velvet Underground, the New York Dolls, the Ramones, and locals like Rodney Bingenheimer, the Runaways, Van Halen, Guns and Roses, the Motels, the Germs, and the Red Hot Chili Peppers wandering the halls or lounging by the pool.

When the Tropicana Motel's escapades came to a grinding halt in 1988 after three decades, it marked the end of an era...or two or three. It had stood as bacchanalia central in the time before AIDS and MTV, before demographics and gentrification, and before the Reagan revolution did its damage. While it lasted, though, the Trop was ground zero for some of the best times that the underbelly of L.A. ever saw.

Anthony Kiedis
singer for the Red Hot Chili Peppers

FATHER KNOWS BEST: My first recollection of the Tropicana was when I was eleven years old, skateboarding down Santa Monica Boulevard and smelling breakfast at Duke's. I first started going to Duke's with my father. Duke's had great character. It felt very cabinlike. It was so tiny and so crowded with people, from punk rockers to ballerinas. I remember seeing Muhammad Ali there once and just being so happy to be close to him. I definitely wasn't going to talk to him or interrupt him from eating his pancakes, or even stare at him too obviously, because I loved him and I respected him, and I just wanted to glean a little bit of his essence by being near him.

I loved Duke's. It was my favorite restaurant. It was my kind of place and the waitresses were cute. It would later become a regular hangout for us: Hillel, Flea, Pete Weiss, Bob Forrest, and that whole little entourage. After a long night of debauchery, drugs, women, smoking, and dancing, we would drag ourselves up to go have coffee at Duke's. We'd scrape together our spare change for food. My favorite thing on the menu was the apple pancakes.

My most memorable and monumental experience at the Tropicana was when I was fifteen years old, which I'm pretty sure was in the spring of 1977. I lived with my father, and we had become more like best friends and partners in crime than father and son. His idea of raising a kid was to expose him to as much as possible and let him sort it out. Whether it was music, drugs, girls, nightlife, or driving the car when I couldn't even really reach the pedals. He was one of the first people I knew who was into the Sex Pistols, and he gave me Blondie's first record, which was my favorite thing ever. She was gorgeous and she talked about sex and sunshine and surfing and rifles and girls and all this fucked-up shit.

One night my dad asks me if I want to go see Blondie at the Whisky. So we go to the Whisky and I watch Blondie and my heart melts a thousand times during the course of the evening. My brain goes all funny and all I can think about is my lust and love and desire and passion to smell and taste and rub up against this heavenly creature of god's finest work, who's singing like an angel. Her voice was so clear and so strong and so girly. After the show, we all kind of mingled about and decided to go down to the Tropicana, where Blondie happened to be staying in one of the poolside rooms. This was a very common experience for my father and me, but the minute I found out we were going there, I started plotting the scheme as to how I was going to get over to Deborah Harry.

Everyone was laughing and drinking, taking Quaaludes and getting blow jobs in the bushes. I was on a mission to marry this girl I had just seen on stage. My moment came later when we were all in her room. I was in the front room and I saw her walking toward me down the hallway. The minute she got in front of me I popped the question. I asked her to marry me. With all my heart, I looked her right in the eyes and said, "Will you please marry me?" I probably only came up to her sternum at the time. She looked at me for a long time, and did not coldly reject my proposal, but kind of put her arm around me and told me how sweet that was. She pointed into the bedroom where I saw some guy sitting on the corner of the bed and she said, "You know, maybe if I wasn't already married we could talk about it, but see that guy in there? That's my husband and we're very much in love." She told me she was sure I'd find the right girl and all that kind of stuff. She let me down easy. That was my most significant night at the Tropicana.

Jerry Stahl
author of *Permanent Midnight*

S TRANGER IN A SHAG Land: The Tropicana was the first place I lived when I moved to L.A. I lived there for a couple of months in 1975. In New York I had a job as a humor editor for *Hustler* magazine. I wrote something called "Bits and Pieces." Then Larry Flynt decided to move the whole company out to L.A., and the entire *Hustler* team drove across the country together. I had a friend from high school who at the age of sixteen was already in bands; his name was Mitchell Froom, who now is a big producer. He said the Tropicana was the place to stay when you come to L.A. It was cheap and I could take the bus right down Santa Monica Boulevard to Century City, where the *Hustler* offices were at the time, and it was full of artists, filmmakers, and bands. Tom Waits and Chuck E. Weiss lived in the back bungalows. I didn't even know who these guys were, I just knew that they were infinitely cooler than I was. I mean every time I had a girl over, which wasn't often, they would make comments—they would whistle and hey, hey, hey. I wasn't sure if it was like, "You're okay," or, "You're a loser." I still don't know.

I remember this one time, for some strange reason a bunch of guys from *Hustler*—and only guys, like twenty—all convened in my room one night. I think all of us were doing acid. I'm not a group kind of guy, but anyway we were all on acid. For some reason we were all just sitting like bats in this dark room with the TV on. Legs McNeil came in. I don't remember how I knew who he was. I guess I had heard of Punk magazine. Anyway, he was there. Maybe he was doing something for *Hustler*. I don't know what the fuck he was doing, but he had this horrible little hand puppet, like a little Coco the Clown, and he kept sticking it in people's faces. I was like, "Get this asshole out of here, everyone is fucked up, get him out of here." And Legs just kept getting in people's faces, being very creepy. It was bizarre. I knew that he was a guy that I probably wanted to be around, but I couldn't talk very well at the time. And I don't think I ever saw him again until recently.

I used to buy drugs at the Tropicana—speed and pot—from somebody like four doors down. I have no idea who it was. I just remember everybody had a shag and went to the Starwood. I was the only man there without a shag. I felt really less than. It was like shag central. So one of the shags was a drug dealer. I just knew that everybody in every room was having much more sex and fun than I was. But that I was probably doing more drugs.

I remember one night I went across the street to get a massage above that lesbian bar. Loaded out of my mind, I just needed whatever, and this unhappy and possibly laziest woman in the world was woken up by the woman who runs the place and sort of read five minutes of Braille on my spine and took $70 from me.

So I sheepishly went back to my room and hated myself until it was time to go to work. Other people probably actually had sex there at the massage parlor. I was just shamed.

I never hung out at the pool at the Tropicana because I don't think I knew it was there. Was there a pool? I had a day job, which I think separated me from everybody else there. I was always working.

There were roaches, I do remember that. They were like big palmetto bugs; they were nice roaches. Not bad, a lot nicer than New York roaches. Honestly, I probably brought them with me from New York in my suitcase, now that I think about it.

The maids were cool. I remember telling the maids not to come for four days, and they'd stay out, and when they did clean they'd leave my joints in the ashtray.

I never went to parties at the Tropicana; I was never invited to anything. I was just some weirdo there. I didn't really know anybody in L.A. I had won all these literary awards in New York and I was too fucked up to know what to do about it, so I started writing porn and then I ended up at *Hustler*. I think I flew a couple women out from New York, different girls to stay with me at the time, at the Tropicana. They were all suitably unimpressed. They probably wished they were with one of the cool guys, with the shag, four doors down.

Duke's was great. I ate at Duke's every morning and pretty much every night. I saw Sam Shepard eating breakfast there once or twice. I remember I liked the way he was just sitting in the midst of a whole bunch of people, and he would be like a prairie dog coming out of a hole to look around. He seemed very above it, and I wanted to emulate that look. He had so much raw sensitivity and intelligence. He could sort of read what everybody was thinking. But with me it looked like I was just staring at their food.

Even after I moved out, I ate at Duke's all the time. Once in a while I would end up back at the Tropicana. I'd go there to write. I'd lock myself up for a couple of days at the Tropicana and get really fucked up and just write and stumble down to Duke's to eat and stumble back up to my room. It was a great place to write.

When I heard the Tropicana was torn down I felt bummed—I figured I probably still had some drugs hidden in a closet there somewhere.

Legs McNeil
author of *Please Kill Me:
The Uncensored Oral History of Punk*

TURNING PUNK: THE FIRST time I was in L.A. I stayed at the Tropicana. It was in 1977. I was on an assignment from High Times magazine. I was excited because I wanted to hang out with the Ramones. I remember a lot of parties happening in the rooms at the Tropicana, mostly in the rooms of L.A. punk bands. The guy from the Dickies kept coming around wanting to talk to me, but I didn't want any part of the L.A. punk thing—they just weren't cool. Tom Waits and Chuck E. Weiss were cool.

Chuck was living in a converted broom closet and it was a disaster. I was messy, but I was really impressed with his mess. I remember once he was looking for a piece of paper from William Morris so he could pick up a check. I said, "Why don't you clean your fuckin' room so we can find this thing, get the money, and buy some beer?" It was some small amount of money, but it seemed like a fortune to us. As he was looking around in this mess he found an old pizza that was shoved into an album cover.

It was around this time that Chuck introduced me to Tom Waits. One day Chuck was trying to teach me how to play craps and he got Tom to come into the room. They seemed really offended that I didn't know how to shoot craps. Tom told me about going to Glen Campbell's house and starting a craps game there and how Glen Campbell wouldn't get down on his knees because he didn't want to wrinkle his pants or something. That horrified Tom. I asked Tom if I could interview him and he said yes. We did the interview the next day in the lobby of the Tropicana and it was one of the best interviews I've ever done. He was so good. He talked about his father, who did Spanish voice-overs for the movies, which was great because it was a whole part of the movie industry that you never heard about. I asked him if he ever wrote a cheap paperback novel what would the title be. And he instantly said, and I always loved him for this, Love Wears Shades. At this point, a girl comes in who was obviously a junkie. She was saying, "Tom, Tom, I need to talk to you," and he's like, "Wait a minute, honey, I just gotta finish this interview and then we'll talk." She kept interrupting, and then she lifted up her skirt and on her inner thighs were huge open sores, and we both recoiled in horror. She had some weird case of the clap. Tom said in that voice, "Well, honey, you need to go to the doctor. I don't think I can help you." His voice was so deep. I kept waiting for him to clear his throat, but that was just his voice.

There was a blonde girl from Canada who would knock on my door in the middle of the night. One night I was passed out, so she came in, got in bed with me, and we started fucking. Someone started banging on the door. Turned out it was a guy she had just turned a trick with. He said he just wanted to see if she was all right. I had no idea that she was a prostitute. Then her mother called (she gave my phone number to her mother) screaming, "Where's my daughter?" After all that, I switched rooms. I thought they were gonna come and arrest me after her mother told me her daughter was only fourteen.

We didn't like L.A. punks because they seemed like they just got it and in New York we'd already been doing it for three years. The L.A. punks lived in nice houses and in New York we were broke on the Bowery. And they had cars. None of us in New York had a car, except for Debbie Harry. Debbie had a Mustang and she would park it in front of CBGB and drive everybody home every night. Now in L.A., it was about anarchy and class warfare, and for me it was about *Gilligan's Island* and the Ramones. For us, it was very fun and very joyous. After the Sex Pistols became famous you suddenly got something different.

I went up to San Francisco to go cover the Sex Pistols show and was in the bathtub with this chick when I heard that the Sex Pistols broke up. That really hit me hard. I thought it was all over. It was only about a week between the time the Pistols had became really huge and then they broke up. I went back to the Tropicana and everybody in the world was a punk now. This was 1978.

Bebe Buell
writer, painter, singer, and mother of Liv Tyler

A FINE ROMANCE…OR TWO OR THREE: My first real introduction to the Tropicana was when I met Elvis Costello, which was in June of 1978. I was with my girlfriend Pam Turboff the day before Elvis played

Hollywood High, and Pam had to drop something off at Elvis's manager's motel. That's when we went to the Tropicana. We had to walk past the pool and all the rooms. I remember thinking that it was a cool little place and Pam was telling me it's a great place if you're a rock 'n' roll band that doesn't have a lot of money. It was the poor man's Sunset Marquis. Rock 'n' roll bands either stayed at the Marquis, the Tropicana, or Le Parc. This was way past the days of the [Hyatt] "Riot House." It's interesting, the ambience and the element of romance and seediness that was entwined with the Tropicana; it just had some sort of wonderful vibe. It had a lot of magic.

I'd met Elvis briefly the night before [when Pam and I went to see the Runaways at the Whisky], but our actual romance began in the parking lot of the Tropicana. When he saw me walk by with Pam he sort of dashed out so that we would see him. I remember it was about 100 degrees outside and he was in a suit and tie and that made me laugh. Pam had this wonderful convertible and she could see he was smitten with me and wanted to hang out. He asked, "Where are you guys going?" Pam said, "I gotta go back to work, but I'll give you guys the car."

So we dropped her at work and we had the convertible for the whole day. That night we went to the Whisky to see Nick Lowe play and then all of us went back to the Tropicana. Elvis was in the Sam Cooke room and was sharing it with his drummer, Pete Thomas. I remember Elvis had the fold-out couch and I warned him that he was going to be crippled the next day because there were always those big lumps in the middle. Elvis and I had our first kiss standing there, then he dropped dead and passed out. Pam and I were laughing, and we took his shoes off and tucked him in the sofa bed. In March of '79, after Elvis and I had become a couple (we had already been living together for a few months), we stayed at the Tropicana again; it was great.

It was after Elvis and I broke up and I started to hang out with Stiv [Bators] in 1980 that I stayed there again. The Dead Boys had a show at the Whisky the night John Belushi played drums. That was a cosmic night. We were Tropicana babies; we had so much fun in that pool.

I remember one time Stiv and I were in the pool swimming and splashing everybody and George Thorogood walked by. He was wearing snakeskin boots, so Stiv called him a faggot, grabbed him by the leg and pulled him into the pool fully clothed. Now because George Thorogood thought they were scary punk rockers, he tried to act cool about it and was laughing. And me being an anal neat freak, I was more concerned about the boots than him. I'm like, "OK, let's get the boots off him." We had so much fun in that black pool. I know that the pool was the only way we could get Cheetah Chrome to take a bath. There was enough chlorine in that pool to kill Los Angeles. If you wore a black bathing suit in that pool, when you got out it would be brown.

My fondest memories were those nights when you'd have a few people come and hang out, and everybody would sit around the pool under the palm trees with their doors open and everyone running from room to room. But when I went back in the early eighties to play my own gig in L.A., my band and I stayed there, and it just wasn't the same. The Tropicana was definitely on the outs. The clientele had gone really metal. And punk

IRIS BERRY

rock and metal are just different degrees of obnoxious.
It was a whole different vibe. I knew the romantic side
of the Tropicana.

Brendan Mullen
nightclub owner, author, founder of The Masque

THE BLIND EYE: I'M originally from Scotland, but
I blundered into this town from England with
friends in about 1975 thinking there was going to be
some wild scene in L.A. But our perception when we
got here was that it was absolutely stone dead. Nothing
was happening at the Whisky and I couldn't relate to the
straight TGIF disco scene, or the action at the Odyssey
Club, since I was kind of past my fake bisexual, junkie,
rent-boy period—inspired, of course, by Lou Reed's
Transformer album. There were no local, street rock 'n'
roll bands, except for a few Kim Fowley prefab bands
with nowhere to play. Rodney's English Disco was
not long for the world, and, besides, I couldn't get the
glitter-fairy act or the silver hot pants and Spiders from
Mars platforms to work for me.

There was On the Rocks upstairs at the Roxy. But
you couldn't get in there unless you hung out with
Harry Nielson, Bernie Taupin, Alice Cooper, Richard
Perry, Jack Nicholson, or Harry Dean Stanton, and I
knew none of those people, so forget that. Next door to
the Roxy, any phony, vaguely limey accent worked like
a charm with truckloads of delightfully impressionable
wee lasses at the Rainbow Bar & Grill, another cash-
and-carry business for Lou Adler and company, where
everybody still sat around listening to Bad Company
and Led Zeppelin. So our entertainment consisted of
gawking at Keith Moon and entourage warming up for

48

the capper of the evening: the destruction of an entire suite at the Continental Hyatt, known as the Continental Riot House, on Sunset Boulevard. Maybe tonight he'd drive another Rolls Royce into the swimming pool? Who knew? Who cared? Everybody cared. Really, there was nothing else to do or talk about.

For the more intellectual boho type, there was no other option but to hang out at the Troubadour, the former folk-rock joint whose time had long, long past. There was never a soul in the place other than the bartender. The highlight of the evening was watching Tom Waits passing out at the bar and being carried back to his bungalow suite at the Tropicana Motel by Chuck E. Weiss, who could barely stand up himself.

The Troubadour was tightly tied in with the denizens of the Tropicana Motel, which at that time included Waits, Chuck E. and Ricki Lee Jones. Ricki wrote the song "Chuck E's in Love" while staying there. Those solo singer-songwriters, the old Geffen mafia, were the only thing left in town at that time. You have to understand that by this time, in 1976, the Roxy had knocked the Troubadour on its ass as the big place to gig.

Fast forward to 1979. I had a couple of clubs called The Masque. The first version was all local punk bands from Hollywood and basically L.A. County. Then I got involved in this other space on Santa Monica and Vine called The Other Masque, and at that point I booked more national acts. I flew the Cramps out from New York, the Dead Kennedys from the Bay Area, the Dead Boys from Cleveland. Then I got a call from Leee Black Childers [famed photographer of early punk and former manager of the Heartbreakers]. I got all excited, I thought I communicated with heaven or something.

He starts giving me a spiel about a rockabilly band, and he goes, "I know your club's punk but, blah blah blah blah blah, but maybe this would be different." I'm going, "Leee it's all right. You don't have to explain what it is." I guess he thought that I was a punk who thought Bowie started rock 'n' roll, you know like a lot of the Masque punks did. So, "blah blah blah, yeah it sounds good." It was wide open, anybody could play, it wasn't closed booking by any chance. So Leee says, "OK, I'm coming."

I pick up the phone at the Masque a few weeks later, and I hear, "Hellooo, it's Leee Black Childers. We're here at LAX." And I go, "Oh, you are?" He hadn't made any prior arrangements. So I scurry around and haul out there with Hal Negro, 'cause he was the rich guy and he had a car. The idea was to get them and to take them to the Tropicana.

So we tool up there, and there were these adorable guys, teenage guys with these beautiful hair cuts, quaffs from the fifties. And the threads—they were a showstopper. Usually, the first thing a manager says to me is, "So where's the venue? What time is the load in? Where's the hotel? What's our per diem? Where's the equipment?" But the only concern with Levi and the Rockats and Leee Black Childers, especially Leee Black Childers, was, "Where the fuck can we score some Crazy Color?" You know, for Leee to dye his hair blue and pink. So we tool over to Poseur, which was still on Sunset, and fixed them up before heading to the motel.

No arrangements had been made at the Tropicana, and I was thinking that Leee was going to book a whole bunch of rooms. But he goes in and books one room, hiding the band outside. He gets the keys and then they all tiptoe in. I was completely taken by surprise because there were five guys and Leee, and I said, "You're all gonna crash in the one room?" And Leee was like, "Don't worry about it." Levi and the Rockats ended up staying for a couple of months in L.A., six guys in one room at the Tropicana Motel. As it turned out, management tended to look the other way a lot and let bands crash four or five or ten to a room. That's what made the Trop what it became during the punk era—turning a blind eye.

Jimmy Zero
rhythm guitarist for the Dead Boys

Heaven and Hell: L.A. was supposed to the last stop of our American tour in the fall of '77. They checked us into the Hyatt House on Sunset and we hated it! We expected to like it because it was so notorious, and we got there and thought, "Man, this sucks, this is like a glorified Ramada Inn, except there's palm trees." So we bitched about it to Sire Records and they moved us immediately to the Tropicana, where they wisely thought we would feel more at home. We didn't even get our luggage out of our car in the parking lot before we were in complete agreement. We thought, "Now we're talking."

One afternoon I walked out of my room and Nina Hagen was out there sunbathing in a garter belt and stockings, panties and a bra, and sunglasses. I thought, that must make for interesting tan lines. We'd heard a lot about Kim Fowley and Rodney and suddenly these people were there around us in the flesh and blood. It was the coolest thing. We thought it was show biz at its finest and pure L.A. Kim Fowley came over to one of the parties at the Trop and he had his valet or whatever you call them, his "Man Friday," who never left his side.

The valet entered the room, clapped his hands and got everyone's attention. He announced "Kim Fowley," and announced all of his gold records and his platinum records, the whole rap sheet. And when he was done, Kim walked in. I'm like holy shit! You'd never see anything like that any-where else in the world. It was beautiful.

Not long after, I saw a whole bunch of chicks out in front of Cheetah [Chrome]'s room. They were waiting to get in to have sex with him. That was the first time I ever saw anyone line up outside of a motel room for sex like that. When I went in, he had this ice bucket an inch deep with Quaaludes. As I'm trying to talk to him, he picks up the ice bucket and just dumps like ten Quaaludes all over his bed and all over his face, and about two or three made it in his mouth. It was crazy. There was no talking to him.

One night, I came back to my suite and found the floor covered literally wall to wall with naked people. I'm not exaggerating. I didn't recognize one single person. It was the ugliest thing I've ever seen in my whole life. It looked like a snake pit. A slice of hell on Earth.

When Nick Lowe got married to Carlene Carter they had their reception at the Tropicana and everybody was there, Johnny Cash, everybody. The people at the Tropicana told Stiv [Bators] that there was no invitation list, but there was a list of people who weren't allowed to attend any of the ceremony, who were to be kept away. And they showed him the list and his name was at the top of it, number one. Stiv was so proud of that. He said, "I'm doing everything right!"

Henry Rollins
writer and singer for Black Flag

WAKING UP INTO THE World: In the summer of 1981 when I joined Black Flag, the police in the

South Bay, where Black Flag lived, had run us out of Torrance. So, being homeless upon returning from our tour, we crashed on the floor at that group house that they based the movie Suburbia on, the Oxford House. It wasn't too long before we wore out our welcome, so we got an office space on top of Unicorn Records, which was about fifty paces west of the Tropicana. We were extremely broke, but you could get a very good breakfast of three eggs, potatoes, and sourdough toast and coffee for about $3.50 at Duke's. We were there as many days as we could afford breakfast or dinner. If we did an interview, we would start insinuating that we were starving to the interviewer by saying things like, "Oh and you're a nice girl from UCLA and your dad's a gynecologist and you should take the whole band out to Duke's for dinner."

Because it was so close to where we were staying, we would be around the Tropicana all the time. "Hey, there's that guy Rodney who interviewed us last night, detoxing by the pool."

Whenever you heard a band on Rodney on the ROQ, chances were that about an hour after they finished the show you could go to the Tropicana and hang out with them. If you wanted to come to town and, as ZZ Top says, "be low down in the street," the Tropicana would be the place to go. Say you wanted to go meet Nick Cave and the Bad Seeds. Go hang out by the pool at the Trop.

I really liked Duke's as a feature of the Tropicana. It was a great restaurant, and if you were staying at or living in the motel it was so convenient because you go like ten drunken, chemical steps and, boom, you're in the breakfast place. It's a no-brainer if you're fucked up. I never did the drugs, but I watched a lot of people kind of sit over a cup of coffee waking up into the world.

53

Some of my memorable Tropicana experiences were waiting in the Sunday-morning line to get into Duke's. So one time we had just driven down from San Francisco playing two sets at the Mabuhay Gardens for Dirk Dirksen. You get in the van, you drive home still in your gig clothes, jeans and a T-shirt. You're aching in pain, 'cause you've slept in a fetal position. I had my face on Chuck Dukowski's back all night. We were like this intensely young, male grunge pit inside this van. So we scrape ourselves off and get out of the van and we had money from the gig. And when we had money our reward was, "We're gonna eat today at Duke's and we're gonna get omelets!" So we've basically just come from driving the Grapevine and we stagger into Duke's after waiting in that line in the blaring sun, our hair is standing up and there's this guy with a scarf around his head eating his food, staring at me. Now I'm really in a bad mood, and believe it or not I was raised to be a very polite person. I say "please" and "thank you." I don't usually look at someone and say, "What the fuck are you looking at?" But that morning I was in a really bad mood. And there's this little guy looking up at me, with his big saucer eyes tripping on me and I say to him, "What the fuck are you looking at?" And he buries his face in his food, starts eating, and gives out a sheepish "Sorry." Greg Ginn looks over at me, he's like, "Ah, that's Iggy Pop," and I'm thinking, "Oh, fuck," because how much do I worship this guy? I was so bummed. I dissed The Man!

We used to use the phones in front of Duke's with phony credit card numbers that we bought from some guy at Oki Dog. It would be me and Mugger, eyes to the street, looking out for cops because we were sure that the phone company was on to us. We'd call these record stores all over the country asking them if they had Black Flag's new album, Damaged, and if not to please order it. We'd do that for hours, and that's where I'd see the endless parade of punk-rock stars walking back and forth in and out of the Tropicana. I'd see Wendy O. a lot. She was so scary looking with her big old intense implants, and her "I've-done-a-lot-of-shit" look on her face. She was a rough woman. The last time I saw Wendy O. Williams alive was at Duke's with all the Plasmatics. They were staying there when they blew up the bus at the Sports Arena and it didn't really work.

I'm tragically attracted to femme fatales, chicks with their hair messed up, their mascara running, who look dangerous and really hot. I love women like that. I can't help it. You see these women and you know they're gonna break your heart, they're gonna tear you up, they're gonna leave you, and they're gonna laugh like Satan. Yeah, and you'll always remember them. The Tropicana was full of women like that.

The rooms were kind of sleazy. You'd walk in with the attitude, "What's so cool about this place?" Then you realized it was because you could do anything. You could die here and it would be cool. No matter what you did at the Trop, you could not get thrown out. If you ran naked up and down the hallways screaming like a maniac, they would just say, "Oh, I love that guy's record!" You could have eighty people in a room all night and no one was going to care. Me being in Black Flag didn't always get me into all the parties, plus the fact that I don't do drugs, and not only that, but in those days I was very disapproving of that behavior. Whereas nowadays I don't play judge. I just say, "Well I hope you don't die, 'cause I hate going to those funerals."

Iris Berry

Chuck E. Weiss
singer for the God Damn Liars

SIX DOLLARS A NIGHT: I met Tom Waits in Denver, Colorado. We were buddies there and wrote songs together. One day he asked me, "Why don't you move to L.A.? You can stay at my place." At the time he lived on Coronado Street, between Echo Park and Silver Lake. So I moved. Tom knew about this great place for breakfast, which was Duke's, the restaurant at the Tropicana Motel.

I'd never heard of the Tropicana before in my life, but it had been popular in the sixties because Jim Morrison would hang out there sometimes. Morrison liked to go to the Palms, the gay women's bar across the street.

[Tom and I would] drive to Duke's every day to eat, and every day I'd look at the Tropicana sign that said $6 a night. I thought, instead of driving here every day I should just move in here. And so I did. Then Tom spent so much time coming there to visit me that he decided to get a place there as well. I mean, it was $6 a night, how could you go wrong? Because of Tom's cult following, him living there put the Tropicana on the map, and the legend started. This was in 1975. I ended up living at the Tropicana for about six years, and during that time I stayed in every room they had.

The first night I moved into the Tropicana there was a gunfight between a pimp and his hooker, but I was too high to know what was going on. I was just walking down the corridor talking loud and John Drew Barrymore pushed me out of the way of a bullet. John was a real character. At first he didn't want to have much to do with me. He didn't like me because I was an obnoxious kind of a guy when I got loaded, and I

56

was always asking him to recite his piece from High School Confidential, where he talks about Christopher Columbus in a hep, Lord Buckley style. We became good friends later on, though.

The Tropicana was full of people in the middle of their big deals and projects. They were all getting ready to get famous. William Burroughs stayed there a lot. He'd stay for three to four weeks at a time. One time I saw him beat the shit out of a young woman in Duke's; he just slapped her silly, knocked all the glasses off the table, knocked her down, got up, and left.

There were train tracks that ran down the middle of Santa Monica Boulevard. The train would come at 11 at night or 3 in the morning. Waits and I used to hop the train down to the Troubadour. It was pretty weird no one noticed the train. You could come in on the train and people would say, "What, what train?" That's an L.A. thing—people here are oblivious.

When people come to a motel, they're looking for a wild time and they let all their inhibitions drop. I'd say that 90 percent of the reason I even stayed there was because of the wild exploits that I had with the opposite sex. My rent was really cheap and most of the women I got involved with at the Tropicana could supply me with dope, too. One time I was walking down the alley and this French woman was sitting on the toilet. We just started talking, and the next thing I know it's three or four days later.

Another time I was just laying by the pool and this woman comes out of nowhere, invites me in to her room, shuts the drapes and takes off all her clothes. That kind of thing would happen on a daily basis, at that motel. Everything about Hollywood that you could ever imagine happened at the Tropicana.

Iris Berry
author, poet, performance artist

W HAT THE TO-GO GIRL Saw: The first time I went
to the Tropicana Motel, at the tender age of
seventeen, it was love at first sight, and I would have
moved in if I didn't have three older brothers who
would have hunted me down and dragged me out by
my Chemin de Fers. It was 1977 and I was a bored
Valley teenager looking for punk rock and intrigued
by Hollywood after dark. One night at 2 A.M., in the
Rainbow Bar and Grill parking lot, I met punk-rock
prince Gerry Gora, who was the bass player for the
New York band Wayne County and the Electric Chairs.
We ended up partying at a radio legend's house in
Beverly Hills, straight up Coldwater Canyon and amply
supplied with Quaaludes and mountains of cocaine, not
to mention naked people hot-tub hopping and having
sex everywhere. When daylight came, Gerry took me
to Duke's Coffee Shop at the Tropicana. I knew the
minute we arrived that I'd found a home.

The line at Duke's was stretched all the way down
the block in the blazing hot sun, with people still dressed
in the previous night's attire. We fit in perfectly. Once
we made it inside, I felt as if I had been transported to
another time, in a place I had only read about in Damon
Runyon stories. With its East Coast vibe and family-style
seating (it could be hell if one were claustrophobic), it
was loud and anything but private. People talked over
the waiters yelling out food orders and the grinding of
multiple milkshake blenders, along with the clamor of
plates, the tossing of dishes into bus tubs, the trading
of ketchup and hot sauce bottles, the ringing of the
cash register and the telephone, and the comforting

sounds of the grill sizzling, crackling, and frying food that could stop a heart. Music played from a dust-and-grease-covered transistor radio perched on top of the cash register, which was plastered with band stickers, Polaroid photos, postcards, and bumper stickers. I couldn't make out what the music was, probably Art Laboe's Golden Oldies.

Sitting at the same table with us was Lita Ford from the Runaways. Gerry knew Lita, but then Gerry knew everybody.

A few years later I got a job at Duke's as the to-go girl, which meant I had a front-row seat to one of the most exciting scenes in town.

Every day at around 3 p.m., George Thorogood, who lived at the Tropicana, would arrive with his acoustic guitar and burst into song. I remember thinking, "Who is this guy? And why does he think we want to listen to him?" A few years later he was a superstar.

Chuck E. Weiss was living in the bungalows in the back, and a day didn't go by when he wouldn't come in around 4 p.m. (his breakfast time) and have his usual: a hot bran muffin. "Put it on my tab," he'd always say as he left.

Andy Kaufman came in nearly every morning, ate his breakfast, read the newspaper, went to the bathroom, and didn't return until an hour later. We all thought it was strange, but never questioned it, because, well, he was Andy Kaufman. He was quiet and shy, and very well mannered. Everyone just let him be. When he died, it was a shock to all of us. He never seemed sick.

My dad would randomly come in to check up on me, and one day he sat at the counter right next to Joe Strummer just as I was serving his coffee. I was horrified. Nothing like having your dad show up at a place where you wanted people to think you were cool. Lucky for

Dad, he knew Fred, the day manager at Duke's, so he felt like someone was always watching out for me. He also felt free to drop in at any time.

Often James Chance (the Contortions, Teenage Jesus and the Jerks) would sit at Duke's for hours reading books on Nazi Germany while eating his Duke's Hamburger, always ordered rare. The Chili Peppers were always there, too, before they were superstars and just another neighborhood band hanging out at the Tropicana coffee shop and pool.

Legendary session guitarist and keyboardist Al Kooper, who founded Blood, Sweat and Tears and became a producer and A&R icon (he discovered Lynyrd Skynyrd) was another adored regular at the counter. He and I became quite fond of each other in a platonic way, and I looked forward to our humorous banter. He later married my best friend from high school, Vivien. And I truly believe if we hadn't bonded over eggs and one-liners at Duke's that the two of them might have never married.

I also saw a lot of crazy goings-on in the rooms of the Tropicana. The motel was the well-known last stop after a long night of partying and gigs at all the local clubs. It was the perfect place to stay if you were a punk band on tour because of the management's rock 'n' roll–friendly hospitality. Although at a certain point a sign was posted that read, "No hair dyeing in the rooms!" Guests were ruining too many towels and leaving their mess on the bathroom carpets and walls.

When I heard the Tropicana was closing its doors, I wanted to stay one last night for old times' sake. I was with my boyfriend Ratsass, former singer of the notorious Sacramento punk band Tales of Terror and then singer for the band Pirates of Venus. I was in a band called the Lame Flames at the time. We were drunk and ran through the halls knocking on all the doors, screaming at the top of our lungs, "It's the end of an era!" No one seemed to respond or even bother to open their doors. It was just another night at the Tropicana.

We stayed up and watched WWF wrestling and Movies 'Til Dawn on Channel 5. When we woke up, we watched G.L.O.W.: Gorgeous Ladies of Wrestling and then went down to Duke's for the last meal. After we finished our Monte Cristo, banana pancakes, and coffee, we went to the lobby and sadly payed our tab. The bill came to $30. The management let us keep our room key as a souvenir. Later that day Ratsass complained about catching a voracious case of crabs. "Oh how nice," I thought, "another souvenir." I told Ratsass that they were probably from somebody famous. He wasn't amused.

BLOOD AND WATER

Jamie Brisick

MALIBU WAS WHERE THE world cracked open for my two older brothers and me. On the stretch of sand between First and Third points, we encountered bums, Vietnam vets, leather-clad punks, and rakish surfers. Out in the sparkling waves, West Val stoners, East Val bongheads, Hollywood vampires, Santa Monica rich kids, Venice gypsies, Topanga hippies, Colony gazillionaires, and beer-swilling Wall knuckleheads all converged, creating a magical soup that not only entertained, but provided an education no school ever could.

Take Mickey Rat, a construction worker from Woodland Hills. Mickey was a nuggety goofyfoot with long, blond hair and a thick, blond moustache. He'd trot across the beach in high-cut Sundek trunks with a yellow Kennedy single fin under arm. At the shoreline, he'd drop his board and go through a series of tai chi exercises. Then he'd take off his shorts. He'd fasten them capelike around his neck and paddle out nude.

It was horrifying to watch Mickey duckdive under a set of waves, his white ass poking skyward. It was even more horrifying to have him nearly run you over, his pumped thighs, dangling dick, soggy balls, and spearlike board streaking past like a scene from a twisted porn film. But besides being a genius at crowd control (no one dared drop in on him), Mickey was also poetic. In this odd homage to the ocean's primal, amniotic lure, a mere Clark Kent on land turned into a naked, caped Superman in the surf.

Then there was that twenty-one-year-old punk-rock hell chick from Reseda. She had hot-pink spiky hair and wore raunchy black leather skirts with torn fishnets and stiletto heels. Her boyfriend, Dog, was a surfer, so even though she seemed like she'd be more at home in a dominatrix dungeon, she was forced to endure long, sunny hours on the sand.

To help pass the time while Dog was out on the water, she'd thrill us with graphic stories of her sex life, told with such zealous hand, mouth, and hip gestures that they became soft-porn soap operas. And either because she had some latent sense of propriety or just enjoyed toying with us as a cat would a ball of yarn, she'd bring her stories right to the edge and then leave us hanging.

"That's it for today, kids," she'd say, and then sashay off toward the pier, leaving us in whatever boner-concealing positions we'd assumed.

This was in the late seventies. Kevin, Steven, and I had only recently discovered surfing, and we were awestruck and intimidated by Malibu's frenetic vibe. The lineup was packed, the surfers aggro. When sets came, six riders would be up at once and loose boards would fly over the backs of waves like corkscrew missiles.

We'd catch rides from parents, aunts, distant cousins, friends of friends' older sisters—anyone with a driver's license headed west. With butterflies in our stomachs but full of ambition, we'd pull our boards from the car, sling our backpacks over our shoulders, and cross the pearly-gate entrance to First Point. The hot sand under our feet felt like instant liberation; the water a kind of tonic in which our terrestrial problems washed away and our true selves emerged.

We came to Malibu at a turning point, both in our lives and the world around us. We came to Malibu when Mohawks and safety pins were replacing long hair and bell-bottoms, when my brother Kevin began to drift from surfing to punk.

I WAS BORN IN Hollywood in 1966, the youngest of three boys, and raised in Encino until 1973. Steven, the middle brother, is one year older than me, Kevin two. My sister, Jennifer, was born in '73. She added a dose of feminine energy to our whirl of testosterone, but she also fell victim to endless farts to the head, hurled pillows, and *Jaws*-inspired attacks in our backyard pool.

We were a golden family in the seventies. My father worked as a publisher's rep, calling on campuses throughout Greater Los Angeles. He ran five miles a day, listened religiously to Nat King Cole, and showered us in books. My mother taught preschool, cooked elaborate feasts, and knew every word to every song on Supertramp's *Crime of the Century*. On weekends she carted us to skate parks or to the beach in our green Oldsmobile Vista Cruiser. On Sunday mornings we attended Catholic Mass as a family. Every night at 8:30 P.M. we gathered around my parents' bed and said prayers.

All seemed to be going well until we moved to Westlake Village. For senior citizens, young parents, or little kids, Westlake was ideal: spacious homes in models A, B, or C, tree-lined streets with names like Three Springs Drive and Walking Horse Lane, green belts and grassy parks with jungle gyms, a man-made lake with ducks and paddle boats. It exuded order, security—a kind of Southern Californian Mister Rogers' Neighborhood.

By moving us to Westlake, my parents thought they were getting us into a better school district; we thought they were sentencing us to prison. Our spiritual allegiance was with Dogtown—a derelict stretch on the Santa Monica–Venice border—and the band of raffish skateboarders who ruled it. My brothers and I had spent enough time hopping fences and skating empty pools with our streetwise cousins from West L.A. to know to never admit we lived "over the hill."

We begged our parents to move. I contacted real estate agents in Santa Monica and Malibu. In denial, I drew Dogtown crosses on my Pee Chee folder and scrawled "Vals Go Home!" on the bottom of my Z-Flex skateboard. Skateboarding led us to surfing and surfing became a full-scale addiction during a family trip to Hawaii in '78. It wasn't just riding waves that did it, but the way the rides played back in my head as I fell asleep at night. The thrill of stroking, stroking, stroking, and then suddenly being raised up by some invisible hand; the precarious hop from prone to upright; the giddy buzz of assuming a Bruce Lee fighter stance as the wave propelled you forward—all of it returned in vivid detail. It was as if salt water had entered my veins.

After Hawaii, my brothers and I joined Bud Cravens Surf Camp, spending unforgettable days on the beach at La Conchita, a quiet, entry-level surf break a few miles north of Ventura. Though far tamer than Malibu, La Conchita gave us our first taste of the surfing life. The drill-sergeant-like Cravens insisted on ten "hop-ups" at water's edge before we could paddle out. He taught us never to grab the rails, to push from the center of the board, to stand "like a boxer."

68

Blood and Water

Between surfs we scarfed down the salami sandwiches Mom packed for us, caught sand crabs and watched them scurry up and down our gleaming surfboards. Sometimes we bushwhacked through the tunnel that ran under Highway 10. My brothers and I were practically entwined. We'd slap five as we'd surf past each other in the shore break and later fall asleep on each other's shoulders on the ride back to Westlake in Cravens's immaculately clean twelve-passenger van.

SURFING ALL BUT CONSUMED Steven and me, but after the initial rush Kevin started to lose interest. Of the three boys, he was the most intellectually curious, reading Hermann Hesse, Malcolm Lowry, Aldous Huxley, and playing Satie, Chopin, and Schubert on piano by the time he was fifteen. When my father read aloud passages from Jack London, Robert Frost, and C. S. Lewis, it was Kevin who came back with questions. When our grandpa told stories of bouncing from gig to gig as a big band musician, Kevin was all ears. And when we pulled into London at the tail end of a family trip through Europe in the summer of '79, Kevin understood that the punk rockers, with spiky hair, safety-pinned noses, and anarchy A's, were on to something more than just looking cool, that they were the beginnings of a cultural revolution.

Our lives were forever changed the night we saw Iggy and the Stooges play the Stardust Ballroom in '79. We'd been listening nonstop to Generation X, Buzzcocks, Dead Boys, and the Sex Pistols since we had gotten back from Europe, but this was our first live show.

Entering the roller-skating rink turned concert venue, I was stunned by the wall-to-wall punks and scared by how evil everyone looked. It was one thing to see this stuff on the inner sleeve of an album; it was quite another to be a thirteen-year-old pressed up against sweaty, pasty strangers in a dingy, smoky, smelly room off Sunset Boulevard with the music thumping at a deafening level. I didn't know that pogoing was such a spastic, violent dance, and though I'd heard of heroin, I had no idea you could accidentally step on nodded-out junkies in the darkness and they'd hardly budge. I remember thinking, They're dead and no one even cares!

The way Iggy darted on stage, ripped off his shirt, writhed and contorted, and then flung himself from the rafters somehow managed to evoke sex, violence, and death within the first few bars of the very first song. It became difficult for me to stay on my feet. The push and pull of slam dancing was like the surge and retreat of a powerful shore break, albeit one with elbows, spike bracelets, and the occasional steel-toe boot. A couple times I went down, but as soon as I hit the floor there were ten hands lifting me up. In the middle of the thrashing, I remember a pinch on my thigh and a punk girl reaching out to me through the strobe lights, and a green-haired kid in a ragged T-shirt with "Kill me I've never died before" scrawled on a ragged T-shirt.

Our curfews allowed us to stay for only three songs, but it was enough to create a seismic shift in our little lives. In Earth science class the following morning, I felt smug and superior, as if I'd been privy to a secret world my fellow eighth-graders knew nothing about. I couldn't stop thinking about Iggy's defiant performance and how slam dancing around a mosh pit was oddly comforting.

But for all its subversive allure, punk came at a time when Steven and I were deeply immersed in surfing, devoted to Malibu. Though we'd continue going to shows and would occasionally streak our hair green or blue, nothing was going to pull us away from the beach.

Kevin, on the other hand, was wide open. Puberty had not been kind to him. High school rewarded swagger and brawn, not intellect and sensitivity, particularly at cliquish, judgmental Agoura High. The ever-curious star son who reveled in our parents' praise of his straight-A report cards and exquisite piano recitals sunk into an apathetic torpor. The punk scene was Kevin's antidote.

So while Steven and I stayed home on Friday nights waxing our boards and psyching up for a weekend of surfing, Kevin went to places like the Starwood, the Hong Kong Café, and Godzillas. And when Steven and I awoke at 6:30 A.M. for dawn patrol, Kevin was just returning from whatever debauchery he was getting up to on the streets of Hollywood.

ADOLESCENCE CAN SOMETIMES SEEM like a constant search for a safe haven. Malibu became my refuge, the scene of my best and worst moments.

One of the best was when Larry Bertlemann, Dane Kealoha, and other members of Hawaii's flamboyant Town and Country surf team showed up at Third Point. It changed the way Steven and I thought about waves. No longer was it about posing elegantly in the trim line—now it was about slashing up and down the wave, throwing spray.

In 1980 I surfed my first contest and placed second. I was oblivious to strategy and wave selection, but the thrill was addictive. After that, I got sponsors—

McCoy Surfboards and Rip Curl Wetsuits—and started collecting trophies. I discovered a bastard desire and focus I never knew before.

Malibu was also the scene of my bittersweet victory in the Western Surf Association Invitational, something I'll never forget. I'd been on the contest circuit for a couple years, and my bedroom had become a shrine to my pro-surfing dreams. In the corner was my five-foot-six McCoy Lazor Zap with a pink-and-yellow explosion sprayed on the deck. On my walls were posters: Tom Curren blasting out of the lip, Titus Kinimaka standing tall in a tube at Inside Sunset, Gary "Kong" Elkerton in a committed backside hack. On my desk was a stack of contest entry forms and a calendar with nearly every weekend spoken for. On my dresser were roughly twenty-five trophies, many of them for first place. I did sit-ups and push-ups and stretches before bedtime. I fell asleep imagining colossal victories, champagne showers.

The WSA Invitational was an important event. Held in glassy, head-high waves at Third Point, it provided me both home-beach advantage and a chance to prove to my fellow Malibu surfers how far I'd come. To top it off, my sponsors would be there.

In the first ten minutes of the twenty-minute final heat, I racked up three high-scoring waves. The scores settled my nerves and let me get down to some serious wave riding. I outran shimmering, seemingly unmakeable sections, carved dramatic slashes out of dimpled, teal-blue walls, and whipped a dizzyingly quick 360. For the first time in competition, I tapped that dolphinlike, meld-with-the-ocean place that serious surfers aspire to. I won by a large margin. I felt euphoric.

I carried that feeling up to the parking lot, where about fifty sun-reddened surfers huddled around a yellow Vanagon for a makeshift trophy ceremony. David Lansdowne, the pioneering African American surfer, announced the results from sixth place to first. When my name was called to hoots and applause, someone patted me on the back and someone else yelled, "Yeah, Brisick!" I stepped up and received my two-foot-high trophy with a shiny, gold surfer on the top. I was buzzing.

But a few minutes later I saw Kevin, shuffling across the parking lot. He looked unmistakably high.

"You going home anytime soon, James?" he asked. "My asshole ride left me on the side of the road. I need a lift home."

"No," I told him, feeling self-conscious, worried about who was watching. "I'm going out for another surf."

He muttered something, we exchanged unceremonious goodbyes, and he went on his way. I was relieved to see him go. The illusion of sunny optimism I'd managed to project to my sponsors and fellow competitors, who knew nothing of my home life, was safe for now.

But the facade was cracking.

I think of the day Kevin announced he was trying out for the Agoura High football team. How he pumped iron, drank protein shakes, and flexed in the mirror. It was, with hindsight, a sort of last-ditch effort to feel a sense of belonging. The football team turned him down.

Soon after, he shaved his head into a Travis Bickle Mohawk and fell in with a dodgy, itchy bunch. This crowd seemed less about punk rock defiance than a kind of nihilism. Kevin withdrew from the family.

He, Steven, and I carpooled to and from school every day, but we said little to each other. Kevin's life became a mystery.

We got as good at keeping secrets from each other as we did from the outside world. We kids were shielded from how much our parents were struggling, going through what my father would later call "the ennui of twenty years of marriage." My mother remembers taking a long walk with my father on the manicured green belt behind our house, during which she tried to voice her unhappiness. She told my father that if things didn't improve, she would move out. In quintessential, Westlake Village fashion, my parents maintained the illusion of rock solidness. We kids were oblivious. We thought Mom and Dad were spending romantic time together when, in fact, they were discussing the logistics of separation.

There was also a creeping separation between Steven and me. Before surf contests entered the picture we were inseparable. We could stay up all night discussing Larry Bertlemann's iconic cutback or the balletlike hand jive of Tom Curren's bottom turn. We communicated in codified surf speak that only we understood. "Two peas in a pod," my father said. But the contests changed things. I did better, got sponsored, and made contacts with players in the surf industry. Steven resented me. It was nothing we talked about, but the rift between us was palpable.

Then there was Jennifer. Seemingly overnight she went from putting Rick Springfield posters on her bedroom wall and writing boys' names in lipstick on her dresser mirror to trying acid and getting hit on by a parade of doctors, actors, and pot dealers fifteen years her senior. She got kicked out of Agoura High and ended up at Indian Hills, a continuation school notorious for its degenerate students. She put the fear of god in Dad, Mom, Kevin, Steven, and me.

I ran for the water and didn't look back.

WE WERE BLINDSIDED. WE knew he was dabbling and I'd heard he'd been seen at a party in the Valley shooting cocaine, but we had no idea how bad it had gotten.

I'm at the house of my friend, John Fiedler, playing Pong with his sister Julie in her pink bedroom when the phone rings. It's the day after my win at the West Coast Championships, an important victory on my road to professional surfing, and I'm full of myself, contemplating greatness. The Go-Go's "We Got the Beat" is playing on the stereo and Julie smells of grape Bubblicious.

Mrs. Fiedler comes in the room. "Jamie, phone for you."

It's my mother. Her voice is shaking. She tells me Kevin has slashed his wrists; he's in the hospital. I feel my stomach clench into a fist, but I try to not betray anything to the Fiedlers.

"I have to go help my dad," I lie.

Kevin looks horrible. His face has a sickly pallor; his lips are oddly purple and chapped. He seems to have shrunk. Kevin's bandaged wrists terrify me. It's taken something like sixty stitches to sew him up, and while the worst of it is buried under layers of gauze, the spray of cuts climbing his forearms make me wince. There is awkward silence, deflected eyes. I feel as if I've stepped into a movie scene, and that whatever comes out of my mouth will sound clichéd. We imagine ourselves as emotional action figures, rising to the moment and taking charge. But it doesn't always happen like that. We lose courage among the gurneys and hospital gowns, become tongue-tied under fluorescent lights.

Back at the house, a trail of blood stretches from the driveway to the foot of the stairs, where my mother had intercepted Kevin. He'd slashed himself with a razor in a nearby alley, driven home, and apparently planned to crawl into bed and never wake up. With a sixth sense that something was wrong, my mother waited up for him.

"Kevin," she called from the top of the stairs in total darkness. "You've cut yourself."

That afternoon, I ride my skateboard to the place where it happened. It looks like a crime scene. A flurry of scarlet shoe prints surrounds a pool of blood on the pavement—was he pacing in circles? Streaks of blood stain a nearby wall—did he try to stamp out the pain in his wrists the way one grinds out a cigarette? I feel squeamish and delicate, as if the slightest graze against even the bluntest object would tear a chunk out of me.

I have a horrific time trying to fall asleep that night. I shut my eyes and see razor blades gouging flesh, blood spurting. And then, in that dreamy state just before slumber, comes a recurring image: I'm riding along in the back seat of a moving car. I open the door, hang my bare foot out, and grind my heel into the pavement. Flesh, bone, cartilage, and blood splatter in a trail of red. It's cartoonish, but so real that when I shudder awake, I reach down to check my foot.

KEVIN WENT AWAY TO UC Berkeley in the mid-eighties. He fell in love and then swiftly had his heart broken when his girlfriend left him for a woman. Soon after, he OD'd and landed in the hospital again.

The next couple of years turned into a blur of overdoses, rehabs, and parole officers. His addiction trumped everything else in his life. The pattern became all too familiar: a few days or weeks of sobriety, a telephone call to one of his insalubrious friends, then a slip out the front door with a casual, "I'm goin' out for a bit." He'd come back home a few hours later, stoned. We tried an intervention, but all we accomplished was betraying Kevin's trust. After seventy-two hours in rehab he went straight back to using. He did a stint at Ventura County Jail when he was arrested for possession of heroin. Occasionally we'd see flickers of the old Kevin, flashes of the compassion, tenderness, and insight the drugs were burying.

Our relationship was spotty, reduced to brief exchanges in the den or kitchen. Once, Kevin tried to explain to me the lure of heroin. He told me of the time he was loaded, peddling a ten-speed at night. He ran into a curb and went over the handlebars and tore himself up pretty badly. But he was so blissfully high that he felt none of it. What's more, he'd forgotten that he'd been on a bike. He walked home and crawled into bed, oblivious. As he told me this story there was a zealous sparkle in his eyes, as if he'd glimpsed another world, one devoid of pain.

But even the bubble of heroin couldn't keep some things at bay. During a surreal family dinner one night, my parents announced their divorce. My father broke into tears; my mother spoke clearly and articulately. She and Jennifer would move to a nearby condo; Dad, Kevin, Steven, and I stay put.

I joined the pro tour in '86 and traveled to Japan, South Africa, England, France, Spain, Brazil, Australia, and Hawaii. My surfing heroes were suddenly my peers, and we moved from coast to coast like some sun-kissed traveling circus.

It was insanely exciting. I surfed Jeffrey's Bay, spiraling Burleigh Heads and terrifying ten-foot Pipeline. The fraternity of surfers lifted my spirits and ensured that a good chunk of the day was full of laughs. The contests, two a month with prize money for the taking, kept us constantly on the chase. On a Sunday we'd be in Biarritz competing in the Arena Surfmasters; on a Wednesday we'd be in Rio for the first rounds of the Hang Loose Pro.

I had a mediocre first year, scraping by on my meager sponsor wages and picking up the odd $300 for placing in the top half, but the gold-rush mentality was intoxicating. Never before had I felt such a heightened sense of purpose.

I felt safe abroad, where I had no history and could make myself up as I went. I imagined I was a sort of Ivan Lendl–Iggy Pop hybrid. I read Tennis magazine to inspire me as an athlete, and Rolling Stone to feed my inner rock star. And then I'd come home and be hit with reality.

Dad retreated to his office, where he read and wrote in solitude. Compared to my loud, starry-eyed life, he seemed like a recluse. He dressed sloppily. He had no interest in dating. Instead of the festive meals we once enjoyed as a family, we ate overcooked pasta with canned sauce. The dinner table was forever half empty. The house felt sad and lonely.

Mom and Jenny's condo was just the opposite. Spotless, warm, and potpourri scented, it oozed my mother's resolve to carve out a new life for herself. She got her real estate license and was making headway as a mortgage broker. She saw a therapist and read everything she could about drug addiction. Where my mother strived to stay upbeat and maintain a social life, my father delved inward. Where my mother stopped attending Sunday Mass, my father went every day.

Kevin continued to struggle. He worked temp jobs to earn money and talked about going back to school. Because his friends were mostly drug addicts, getting sober would mean solitude, starting over. On his bookshelf was Jimi Hendrix's *'Scuse Me While I Kiss the Sky* next to *Twelve Steps and Twelve Traditions*, on the nightstand a bottle of vitamin E oil. He would rub the ointment into the scars on his wrists as if trying to rub out his past.

Steven and I remained distant. I was sure my adventures on the road would only upset him, so I kept them to myself. Meanwhile, Jennifer was fourteen and raging. When I ran into her at Margarita Night in a Malibu bar, I ratted her out to Mom and Dad.

I spent endless hours in the water, took classes in tae kwon do, and followed the strict high-carb diet promoted in *Eat to Win*. I swam laps and put in daily ten-mile bike rides, peddling so furiously my thighs felt like they would explode. I was sure that the answer to the chaos at home was success on the pro tour. Win a contest, get a massive raise from Quiksilver, buy a modest condo in Malibu, and transform into a superstar athlete, complete with a sports car and long-legged woman.

And then on July 31, 1987, the thing I'd been chasing and the thing I'd been running from collided.

MY '87 SEASON STARTED off well, with solid results in Japan and South Africa. I was in Oceanside, an expansive beach break north of San Diego, for the Stubbies Pro on the day Dad, Kevin, and Jenny returned from Europe. They had visited Germany, Austria, Yugoslavia, France,

Italy, and Switzerland. For the extent of the trip, anyway, they felt close again. Kevin had stayed clean and seemed inspired. He'd spoken of enrolling in German classes and finding a girlfriend.

The Stubbies was my chance to prove to my fellow Californians, sponsors, and the American surf media that I was a force to be reckoned with. And I finally felt like one, too.

While my dad, brother, and sister were clearing customs at LAX, I was beating Australian Bryce Ellis in the second round of heats. And while Kevin was having lunch with my mother in Westlake, a lunch at which she described seeing "the old Kevin, a Kevin full of optimism and clarity and sensitivity," I was surfing against Aussie Mark "Occy" Occhilupo, one of the most famous surfers in the world.

This was around 2 in the afternoon on a hot, cloudless Friday. The Stubbies was a major international pro event, and it seemed like half of Southern California had turned up to watch. The beach was a sea of spectators, and the concrete Oceanside Pier swayed under the weight of fans who cheered our every wave. A group of girls draped a sign over the pier: "We HEART Occy."

I'd never felt so fired up in my life. Every turn, every gesture—shoulders, arms, hands, even fingers—felt magnified. It seemed as though I was both out of my body, observing myself, and never more connected to it. I managed to fit in five off-the-tops on a wave that I'd normally barely manage three on. On another, after a late floater in which I cockily skittered my board to show who's boss, I heard my name shouted by people I did not know.

I lost to Occy, but put up a hell of a fight. It was my biggest result to date.

My mom was dropping off Kevin at my dad's house as I was exiting the water and being mobbed by autograph seekers. Kevin unpacked and made a couple phone calls. Around dinnertime he told my dad he was "goin' out for a bit," and left the house.

I went back to a friend's house where I was staying. A newspaper reporter I'd met earlier in the day called. He asked about my life as a pro surfer. Still glowing, I told him I planned to make the top thirty, then the top sixteen, then who knows? I remembered the profiles I'd read in *Tennis* and *Rolling Stone* and tried to be quotable.

Kevin met someone and scored. Sometime between 8 and 10 P.M., he went to a small lake near Chauncey's restaurant, about two miles from my father's house. Someone saw a body floating face down in shallow water and called the police.

A KNOCK ON THE door gets my father out of bed at 10:25 P.M.

"Who's there?" he calls from the upstairs window.

"Ventura County sheriffs."

My father greets the two cops in his pajamas. In the dining room, they hand Kevin's driver's license to my father.

"Is this your son?"

"Yes," my father says, staring into the photo.

"I'm sorry to inform you, sir. Your son's body was found in the Chauncey's lake."

"That's not a lake," my father responds, eyes fixed on the photo, "that's a pond."

He calls my mother. She and Jennifer race over, Steven arrives later, and the four of them gather in the living room for what will be the worst night of their lives. According to the autopsy report, Kevin had ingested a mixture of PCP and heroin. I'm asleep on a couch in Carlsbad, dreaming of imminent glory.

The following morning I catch a lift from Oceanside to Malibu, where I plan to surf till dark, then go home to catch up with the family. There is a WSA contest happening at Malibu that day and news of my exploits have already traveled north on the "coconut wireless." I'm treated like the hometown hero. I say "thanks" about fifty times. And it's in this puffed-up state that I run into Tom Maddox, my mother and sister's neighbor, a kid I hardly know.

"Have you talked to your mom?" he asks.

"No, I've been down in Oceanside."

"Well, um, you should call her. Your brother's dead."

His words cut from the inside out. My guts are shredded, but my face holds that stupid, proud smile. I actually thank him for telling me. And then I walk a few paces and think, There's got to be some mistake. This fuckin' kid doesn't know what he's talking about!

The stretch between Third Point and the payphones along PCH feels alien—I feel alien. My face is wooden, my ears ring, my legs are noodles. It takes extraordinary effort to walk. It's a blazing Saturday morning and a stream of friends and acquaintances salute me as they head out to Third Point to watch the contest.

Yeeeaaah, Brisick!

Right on, dude!

Good job!

I force smiles, nod greetings, and then put my head down and sprint for the phones.

"Mom, what happened?"

"Jamieee honeyyy," she says with that tenderness, that soothing, selfless, maternal stretch of the eees. "We've been waiting for your call."

I can hear in her voice that it's true.

"Tell me what happened."

"Where are you?" she asks.

"At Malibu. At the payphones."

"Don't move. Daddy and I are coming right now."

I hang up the phone, delicate, wobbly. I'm standing on a stretch of sidewalk where surfers gather to check the waves. The last thing I want is to run into someone I know.

Across PCH is a scrub-covered slope that overlooks the whole of Malibu. On big south swells, in-the-know photographers use this spot to shoot panoramas of the machine-like waves wrapping around the point. I climb the perch and sit on a rock, hugging my knees, trying to process the news of my brother's death, vacillating between my typical evasions and defenses, and then being bowled over by something like real emotion.

My face is heavy and I want desperately to cry, but instead my thoughts latch on to the OP Pro, which starts in three days. I wonder whether the funeral will interfere with my heat times. I envision my against-all-odds victory and the accompanying headlines: Tragedy Turns to Triumph. I hear Mr. Rhee, my former tae kwon do instructor, pushing me the way he did during sit-ups: C'mon, James, you can do it! Go, James! Go, James! I think about McEnroe and Lendl—how would they respond to something like this?

Some voice in my head chimes in and tells me that I'm not supposed to be thinking these thoughts. This is not about you, you selfish fuck! I try to picture Kevin, but I'm blocked. Then, a deluge of guilt, shame, hole-in-the-stomach, tears.

I look down at my red, patent-leather Adidas high-tops and Quiksilver-stenciled sweatpants and feel just plain disgust.

BALLAD OF THE TRUNK MONKEY BANDIT

David Schneider

2011 Best Magazine Feature, Los Angeles Press Club

THE TRUNK MONKEY COMMERCIAL was filmed on what would have been Anton Chekov's 100th birthday, January 17, 2004. I had been performing in Chekov's *The Cherry Orchard* for several months for very little money. A good friend told me not to worry about the money—that Anton's spirit always protects those who choose to take on his work.

In the commercial, for Suburban Auto Group, I play a bandit who breaks into a car only to have the intrepid Trunk Monkey hit me over the head with a Maglite and throw me off a bridge. The commercial became a sensation during YouTube's infancy. It got tens of millions of hits, played on the JumboTron at Lakers games, and appeared multiple times on America's Funniest Commercials. Its notoriety helped me build a modest career as a commercial actor and make decent money while I continued my quest for a more "serious, artistic" career.

By the beginning of 2007, despite the fact that I had two national commercials running, $15,000 in the bank, and no debt, my desire for that "serious" career was all but a cross-faded memory in a smoke-filled room. Disillusionment was the order of the day. I'd been beat. Even though I was technically a working actor, it didn't feel as though I worked or acted. My days were mostly spent getting stoned, having coffee with friends, chasing girls. My friend Tom* would drop by every month or so and leave me quarter pounds of weed, gratis. I mean, not totally gratis—he always needed something, a friend to catch up with, someplace to sleep, a secure apartment to make six-figure transactions.

Tom and I met when we were both studying film and theater at the College of Marin. The first day of class he waltzed into Advanced Production an hour late and, rather than scold him, the teacher stopped class to hear about Tom's summer travels to Africa. It's the classic tale of the guy who walks into the room and, for better or worse, gets all the attention. Tom was about five-foot-six, 125, and at first I thought he was a little prick with a Napoleon complex who just knew how to work a room. But when we were assigned to be partners on the class's first project, we instantly connected. He understood exactly who I was and, more importantly, where I was.

I'd gone to the college to play on the basketball team and figured that film class was a good way to stock up on units without having to do too much. A career as a hoops coach of some kind made lots of sense, but as Tom and I got to know each other better he insisted that I pursue acting and film and drop the sports thing, which I did. He introduced me to some kids he'd worked with in the theater, and soon we were a family. I trusted him, thought him to be untouchable, and felt untouchable in his presence.

After two years of junior college, I studied acting at Circle in the Square Theatre School in New York and then came to Los Angeles. Tom dropped out, chose a life of psychedelics and counterculture, Burning Man, ganja farms, geodesic domes, and dysfunctional love.

---

*   *Some names changed to protect the not-so-innocent*

He tried Los Angeles twice and both times vanished with little more than a voice mail. I never knew if he gave up on his dreams or if they weren't ever his dreams in the first place. As he'd often say, I was on my path and he was on his.

Tom joined forces with some folks up north and, when this story begins, is doing what they do up there: farming. Los Angeles is a good place to bring his crop. Not only do I enjoy his visits, I cherish and look forward to them. But when my girlfriend Amy, finds out he's coming to town, she decides to spend the weekend with her parents in Ojai.

"I'm sorry, I just—I totally disapprove of him," she tells me. "He's a horrible influence on you."

I nod. "Go see your folks. It's the right thing to do."

Amy is moving to New York in less than a month. We'd been neighbors for a while before we started spending more intimate time together. She was getting out of a bad relationship and I was a neighbor with a good ear and just as much free time. At first I welcomed the closeness. But closeness quickly turned into expectations, expectations into rented films, dinner with her friends, claustrophobia. As her imminent move east grew closer, I began, once again, craving insanity.

A couple hours after Amy leaves, I go to her apartment to fetch a lamp I had lent her. The place is cold and empty, full of newly familiar smells, her personal effects and annoyingly wonderful memories of the time we've spent together. Prismatic bars of winter light are broken up by Jalousie windows. The whole scene gives me an ill and normal feeling. I rip the lamp cord out of the wall, go back to my place, smoke a blunt, and call Tom to see why in the hell he's late already.

TOM ARRIVES ABOUT 10 P.M. Then, around twenty minutes later, a man called Particle—that's right, Particle—shows up in a white Volvo 240. He pops out of the car dressed in chic rags. His hair is shaved on the sides and the back, and long and wild on top. Tom and he embrace. I say hello; he notices the North Face logo on my vest and the Nike swoosh on my shoes, makes eyes at me, then at Tom.

"David and I been close friends for ten years. He's cool," Tom assures him.

"As long as he's on the conscious tip," Particle says casually. I chuckle. Tom collects these kinda guys.

They catch up a while; we all drink gynostemma tea.

"You wanted a five pack, right?" Tom finally says.

"That cool?" asks Particle.

"Of course."

They go out to Tom's car and come back, each wheeling a suitcase. They head to the bedroom, close the blinds and Tom opens one of the suitcases. Inside are fifteen vacuum-sealed, one-pound bags of Tom's homegrown, fitly manicured buds. Particle takes off his backpack, pulls out a brown paper bag of cash.

"Gracious host," Tom calls in my direction, "help me count?" My fingers are black by the time I am done: $17,500 in mostly small bills. Tom peels off five hundreds and gives 'em to me. Particle kicks me two more—location fees, standard.

After bagging on Apocalypto for an hour, Particle leaves and Tom and I smoke a spliff and cook some food. He tells me about business, that things are going really well for him. I'm thrilled.

I tell Tom about Amy leaving—that I'm sad, but not really; excited but, eh, not really. I tell him that along with Amy, I also have something with a girl who lives in New York. She's got a boyfriend and wants to move west, but I already know that she's a liar and a cheat and that she'll ruin me, which is, basically, exactly what I want. I tell him that my "Hungry Bruno" Taco Bell residuals are up more than $25,000, but despite that I feel old and lost; like it's the end of my life.

Tom listens intently, sitting in half lotus and wide awake despite being sleep deprived and completely stoned. When I'm done, he answers, all the while making circles with his thumbs.

"Bro, I see what tears at you. I know what you want and what you really want—it's good. But there is this thing, bro, your thing, and, sure, you get some pussy, your little commercials—your fix, and you're happy. You're Hungry Bruno, the cellphone guy, the fucking Trunk Monkey... You make some dough, people recognize you once in a blue moon and you're sort of ashamed, but you more than sort of love it, too. You land a film role, maybe sell a screenplay, whatever! You fuck a bunch of vampirical little whores from places like Denver and Phoenix and it all keeps a smile on your face until you realize at a certain point that the only one you're fooling is yourself. You go through a crisis, swear off nineteen-year-olds.

"Eventually, you fall in love, get married, get all caught up in that bullshit, and now you're chasing the perpetual dragon, you keep working to become something, but what the fuck are you going to become? All the things you swore you'd never become? Maybe not. What the hell do I know? And along the way, you make concessions; everyone does, it's part of fucking life and that's okay, because it means such different things to you now...'It's not selling out,' you say. 'It's knowing how to pick your battles' or some goddamn buzz phrase like that. But all the while this unrest, this thing that is tearing you up inside right this very minute, that thing grows quietly inside you, it lives off you, feeds and grows from everything you covet and desire and fucking want, want, want...to be envied and admired... You have a couple kids; your daughter wants her nose bobbed so she can look like Natasha Gregson-Wagner, then goes to Harvard or Stanford, or University of the Puget Sound, and you and your Botoxed apparition of a wife get to travel and go on wine tours in Temecula. Then one day your doctor tells you there's a tumor on your colon the size of a softball and you spend the rest of your life shitting in a bag taped to your inner thigh. It happens faster than you think, David. So nip that shit in the butt...Drink some ayahuasca, take a heroic dose of psilocybin, and check that fucking ego at the door. Figure out who you really are, what you really want."

Even though I'm not sure exactly who Tom is talking about, the warning is noted. It's always a funny thing between us, because we both know that a big part of him still wants to be an actor, and a big part of me wants to live off the grid. Our interludes fuel and fulfill both of our desires to live as two different people. We get our fix and go our separate ways.

But this visit feels different. Tom hasn't previously dealt this amount and at this frequency. Despite the fact that changes in California state laws work to his benefit, he walks a fine line, keeping details secret from everyone, including me. Tom isn't exactly paranoid, but I wonder if he's taken on more that he is comfortable with. We turn on the Criterion Collection of *Brazil* and both fall asleep in front of the screen. I never get a chance to call Amy.

Ballad of the Trunk Monkey Bandit

THE NEXT MORNING, I'M drinking coffee at Groundworks, staring out the window on Cahuenga Boulevard. Tom is outside, talking on his phone. He comes in, turns his phone off, and takes the battery out. "GPS," he explains.

He orders a mocha, comes back to me after taking his time looking at photographs on the wall. "Here's the thing," he starts in, unusually pensive. "Some people down here were supposed to buy a twenty-five pack, but things are gonna fall through. Soooo, guy in Birmingham will take it off my hands, but this kinda trip...not something I should really do alone. Only three kinda guys roll cross-country solo. The first is fucking Jack Nicholson from About Schmidt—slaves who just dropped their depleted 401(k)s on an RV, a George Foreman grill, and an economy-size bag of Lays Sour Cream and Onion. The second and third are both drug dealers. One kind is the coiffed douche bag wearing Oakleys and a Tommy Bahama shirt who just graduated from UC Irvine and is selling Lipitor and Zoloft. I'm the other kind." The caffeine has Tom on a roll. I'm excited already.

"Also, I'm supposed to meet some people in Portland next week, so I wouldn't be able to drive back anyway." He leaves an opening, giving me an out, but I just wait for his plan.

"So I was wondering if you want to come with—make a mission out of it."

I hesitate. "I'll give you a thousand dollars," he says. I agree.

We head to Burbank airport to get a car. "Find something for me with out-of-state plates."

Nevada is the best I can do. I want to get a Cadillac. We decide on a Chevy Impala. Tom has no credit card, only a debit card, and the folks at National don't accept it. So we put the car on my card and under my name.

First night we get all the way to Flagstaff. Tom says to leave the weed in the car. It's not like your car gets broken into in motel parking lots in the first place, and even though it feels like having twenty-five pounds of weed in the trunk would increase the chances of theft, it actually does not.

Flagstaff has the last organic grocery store before Birmingham, so we stock up on kombucha, green tea, apples, oranges, bananas, blueberries, avocados, olive oil, lemons, greens, and sprouted grains. We hit the road in the late morning. Tom drives the whole way.

That evening, we get into Texas and Tom is drifting. He wants to get through into Oklahoma, so I take over the wheel and he gets pissed off at me for smoking a joint while he is asleep. I realize he's right, that we can't really be so careless; can't get too arrogant. We find another motel and crash out somewhere in Oklahoma. We make our only other Oklahoman stop at an Indian casino right off the highway—a godforsaken place full of godforsaken folks. I remember it fondly.

The third day we drive all the way through. During the trip, I take loads of photographs and short videos. I'm relaxed and thoroughly enjoying talking about life, love, the war, the coming revolution, the government, the future, the heavens, the earth, the underworld, psychedelics, ancient cultures, the ocean, Woody Allen, our friends, our families, our unborn children, sex, why I keep playing this one Arcade Fire song over and over again, and basically just who we were, when we were, what we were here to do and how the fuck were we supposed to do it.

I only call Amy once or twice, and she isn't so much pissed as disappointed and worried. She decides to spend the entire week with her parents. The conversations are brief. Tom and I arrive in Birmingham at about 4 A.M., and Tom checks us into an Embassy Suites, a few blocks from the guy we're supposed to meet, a childhood acquaintance of Tom.

Next morning the exchange goes smoothly. We stuff $123,890—vacuum sealed in $5,000 increments—into the new backpack Tom suggested I get for this occasion. The three of us head out for a nice dinner and then to a strip club. It's my first time and I hate it. Tom's friend pays for me to have a lap dance with a nineteen-year-old I'd been staring at while she danced. She says her name is Angel.

After she finishes, Angel looks back at me and asks, "Aw, you didn't like that?"

"No, it was fine," I nod nervously. "Thank you."

Truth is, I just wanted to go to the movies that night and then to bed. Lack of sleep has finally caught up to me, and I'm stressed out and exhausted from the drive. Not to mention that Tom overslept that morning and failed to take me out for what he promised were the best biscuits in the South, something I'd been looking forward to the entire trip. By the time I drop him off at the airport I'm pleased to be on my own, looking forward to hitting the road, taking more photographs, checking out some towns. I plan on spending a night or two with friends in Santa Fe. Also, there's a girl there I'm thinking about looking up.

I LEAVE BIRMINGHAM AT 1 P.M. and around dinnertime in an Arkansas town I drive past the usual chain restaurants and find an elegant brick building. Folks are spilling out, talking in the street. I walk inside and discover the place is a private dinner club. Turns out

I stopped in a dry county—only "private clubs" can serve alcohol. The host tells me to wait while he checks if anyone will sponsor me. Someone does, and I'm allowed to eat.

I sit at the bar, eat fried chicken and mashed potatoes, and strike up a conversation with a guy who sells preschool playground equipment. He's forty-six, divorced, curious about what someone like me is doing here in Bum Fuck, Arkansas, eating dinner alone at the bar of a private club with a huge backpack on his lap. I tell him I'm just driving across the country, taking photographs, seeking respite from my life. I like the guy so much that I almost tell him the truth.

I drive until about 3 A.M., stop just east of the Texas border in Elk City, Oklahoma, and check in to a Comfort Inn. As I get ready for bed, it begins weighing on me that neither of my parents knows where I am or what I am doing. I haven't called Amy, nor has she called me.

I have a horrible night of sleep, wake quickly, shower, put on my clothes, light a cigarette, and look out the window. It's dark and I can barely see the cars bustling down Interstate 40 in the hazy morning. I look around the room and make sure I have everything from the car: my clothes, laptop, some food, and the backpack full of money. I share the elevator with a group of guys in Halliburton work clothes. They are all dressed in red. I have to ask.

"Pipelines," they say. "We're laying pipelines." I nod, walk out, pack the car, and start driving.

I cross into Texas around 1 P.M. and about an hour later notice a K-9 Texas state trooper vehicle parked on the right side of the road. It seems like he notices me, but I continue driving, not thinking much of it. About a mile down the road, I see his SUV weave around a car to get closer to me. A Texaco station appears at the next exit, and I decide to pull off the highway at exit 113, in a town called Groom, for gas and coffee. The trooper follows me on to the exit, flashes his lights, and pulls me over. I stay in my car. He comes to the window.

"Howdy," he says.

"Hi, how are you?" I reply.

"I pulled you over because you made an illegal lane change." He's looking in the back of the car—it's full of garbage, stray clothes, empty bottles.

"Okay," I say.

"Do you have a license, registration, and proof of insurance?"

"Well, uh, it's a rental car, so I can give you the rental agreement. We took insurance."

I hand him the rental agreement, which has my name and Tom's on it. He studies it a moment.

"Where are you coming from today?" he asks.

"Uh, well, I was, um…Last night, I stayed somewhere in Oklahoma, the Sleep Inn, I think."

"Sleep Inn, huh. Okay, how about before that?"

"Hmm, well, before that…the night before that? I was in Birmingham."

"What were you doing there?"

I don't answer.

"Where's your friend?" he asks, the brim of his cowboy hat resting on my car.

"He, uh, had to fly to Portland," I say.

"Your friend was smart," he nods, looks at my hands. "Why are you shaking?"

"I just…I don't know. I just haven't ever been asked this many questions before."

"You mind sitting in the passenger seat of my vehicle?" he asks nicely.

I get out of the Chevy Impala and take a seat in his SUV. His K-9, an elegant, black German shepard, starts barking the second I get into the car. The cop gets in, the dog calms down. I notice the name tags: the dog is Rex II, the cop, Ingle. He takes off his hat and throws it on the dash.

"You mind taking off your sunglasses," he asks. I take them off and stare off into the horizon. The sun burns my tired eyes.

"So," he looks at the rental agreement, "David, what were you and, uh, Tom…is that right? What were you guys doing in Birmingham?"

"Well, actually," and this is part true, "we're working on this documentary. Um, it's called 1977 at 30. So I was—we were taking photographs of the country and interviewing people born in 1977 and just, you know, talking to them about their lives, what they think about the world, what they are doing and such, you know, as they turn thirty."

He looks at me and I repeat, "1977 at 30…Since that's when I was born, 1977."

He looks at my driver's license. It confirms my birth year; it also still has my father's address.

"So, you live in San Francisco?" he asks.

"Well, no, I live in Los Angeles."

"Uh huh, and where does your friend live?"

"He lives in San Francisco…and Los Angeles sometimes."

"What do you do for money in Los Angeles?" he asks as he runs my license on the computer.

"I am an actor, mostly," I say.

"Uh huh, and Tom, what does he do?"

"He's an actor, too…well, actually, he's a waiter." I figure that might sound legit, since everyone knows that all actors in Los Angeles are waiters.

"Actors, sure," he says. "Been in anything I seen?"

"Well, right now I am in these two Taco Bell commercials. I play a Russian eating champion called Hungry Bruno..." Ingle isn't responding.

"I lift my arms up like this and say, I'm full! You really haven't seen those?"

He laughs. "No."

He takes his time. "Did you know you are driving on a suspended license and that there is a warrant out for your arrest for a failure to appear on a jaywalking citation issued in Santa Monica, California?"

"No...I...wait, my license is suspended?"

He looks at me closer. "You been in anything else I might have seen?"

"Well, I was in this commercial a few years ago, called the Trunk Monkey. I break into a car and then this chimpanzee hits me over the head with a flashlight and throws me off of a bridge."

The trooper rips his sunglasses off and looks at me, and a big smile grows across his face.

"You kidding me?" he says.

He squints his eyes, tilts his head to the side, trying to see if he can recognize me.

"Holy shit, is it you? You know, that might be my favorite commercial in the world. I got it sent to me on e-mail and I loved it so much I sent it to all my friends. Everyone goes crazy for that Trunk Monkey. That's not really you, is it?"

"Yeah, it is...actually, it's funny because my agent—"

"How much you make for something like that?"

"Coupla grand." It's a lie. I only made $350.

"Not bad for a day's work. How long something like that take?"

"That one took a day."

"Well, shoot, that ain't bad." He shakes his head. "I can't believe this, what luck. The Trunk Monkey. This is amazing…I just can't wait to tell all my friends, just no one is going to believe me."

I laugh and play along, hoping my casual approach to the whole ordeal will throw him off. It doesn't.

He takes a long time making notes, running backgrounds, doing whatever police officers do when you are waiting for them to be finished with you. All the while he keeps shaking his head, saying things to himself things like, "The Trunk Monkey…hot damn!"

I look out the window at the Texas panhandle. The landscape is rich with browns and light greens; there's clear, unpolluted sky as far as the eye can see. This is Texas, I think to myself. This is America.

"Okay," he finally says, "so I am going to write you a ticket for the illegal lane change and one for driving with a suspended license."

He hands me the tickets and I sign them both.

"Okay." I put my sunglasses back on. He adjusts himself in his seat.

"Oh, hey, by the way," he starts.

"Yes?"

"You don't, by chance, have any firearms in your vehicle, do you?"

"No, sir."

"What about any illegal drugs? You ain't got none of them?"

"Nooo."

"What about large sums of money?"

I contemplate giving myself up.

"Ummm…no."

"Great," he says, "So then—okay if I search your car?"

We all know the answer to this question is no. And I take a moment here to think this one out. Thing is, if I say no, I come off as suspicious. He takes the suspicion, runs with it, makes a phone call or two, gets a warrant to search the car, and finds the money anyway. My only chance is to bluff. Only an idiot would consent to a search while carrying illegal drugs or large sums of money. I gamble that he thinks I'm not an idiot.

"Yes, you can search my car."

"Okay, hand me your keys," he says.

"My keys? You want me to give you my keys?"

Suddenly, the trooper turns stern. "I told you to keep the sunglasses off of your face!"

My hands are sweating, shaking. I take off my sunglasses and try to pull the keys out of my pocket. I finally do and hand them to him. He puts them in his lap and continues doing paperwork. He opens his door.

"Okay," he begins, "now I want you to get out of the car...you are going to stand right there where I can see you." He goes right for my trunk. Before he opens it, he turns to me a final time. "Are you sure you don't have anything you want to tell me about that's in here?"

I think about it.

"If you talk to me about it now, things could be better for you."

I say nothing.

"Okay," he continues, "now, I am only going to ask you this once—if I find anything in this trunk, is it going to be yours?"

I'm fucked. I know it. He is going to find the money, no doubt about that, but I figure as long as I've gone this far, I can't just give myself away. I am actually more afraid of what might happen to Tom. I think, well, it's not my money, so how much trouble can I get into for

101

it? Tom is the one who could get in trouble, not me. Then, I think about my father, my mother, I think about Amy, I think about all the kids I grew up with who have become lawyers, doctors, teachers, husbands, fathers. I just say I am about to lose everything, which thankfully isn't much. I tell him, simply, "Sure, it'll be mine."

The trooper opens the trunk and looks around. Inside are two empty suitcases that reek of weed. Both are full of empty baggies, a vacuum sealer, rubber bands, pens, and other garbage. Then he gets to the backpack. Since Tom was paying, I'd bought a nice one that I could keep for myself once I got back to Los Angeles. It has lots of cool pockets, is made of some waterproof, meshy, Gortexy materials, even has a padded compartment in the center, perfect for a laptop.

I hear it unzip. I had covered the money with a pair of shorts—why, I'm not sure. I see the shorts go up in the air. Trooper Ingle says nothing, just reaches for his belt, pulls his handcuffs off, and walks right at me.

"Come here," he says motioning with is forefinger. "You're under arrest. You have the right to remain silent. Anything you say can and will be used against you; you have the right to an attorney." He puts the cuffs on, tight.

"Is this money yours?"

"No," I say, calm, numb.

"How come you said 'yes' before?"

I shrug my shoulders. "I don't know. I lied, I'm sorry."

He says nothing, just looks at me. I begin to panic.

"I'm so sorry, oh my God, I am so sorry for lying."

I start pacing in circles. In every direction are spectacular panoramas. The land is flat, the air so dry and clean and clear. I can't help but admire the vast and desolate beauty.

"Stop moving around!" he yells. "You stay in one place, understand?"

But I can't stop. If I stopped for even a second, it would be real and I'd have to deal with it. I'm not ready for it to sink in. I still think I can run, still think it might be a joke, still pray it's all a bad dream. He walks at me. I fall to my knees and put my forehead on the ground. The wet bleeds through my jeans. He goes back to the car. I'm not crying but cursing myself, asking God for forgiveness for everything questionable that I've ever done or even thought in my entire life. After fourteen seconds of reprise, I look up and see that the trooper has emptied the contents of my car all over exit 113. He's having a blast. I get up and walk into the open field off the freeway.

"HEY! You!" This time he comes at me fast, full of anger and fear. "Didn't I tell you to stay put?"

He grabs my arm and moves me toward the passenger door of his car. I stumble and fall on the ground. He drags me a few feet until I regain my footing.

"Just please, can you, sir…can you just please tell me what's going to happen?"

"That'll be up to the judge," he says.

"Judge, what judge? Sir, the thing is, you have to understand—"

"Okay, listen, you need to stop talking. You are doing yourself a real disservice by acting like this. Now you need to let me do my work and just sit tight in my car. You got caught. It's over. Best thing you can do right now is just relax."

He puts me into the car, my hands cuffed behind my back.

Ingle goes back to my car and continues his search. I sit in the car. Rex II is behind me, his tongue hanging out, breathing in my face, swallowing.

"Hey, boy," I try. Rex II whimpers at me. "Who's the good boy, huh? Rex II, what a good boy you are."

The dog ignores me. I need to talk to someone. I need to talk to Trooper Ingle. I try to reach the window button with my hand or elbow, but I can't, so I use my tongue. The window goes down. "Sir," I call to him out the window.

"HEY! I thought I told you not to touch ANYTHING! Now, you better listen to what I say or your problems are going to get a lot bigger than they are right now. And right now they are big already!"

"What does that mean?" I laugh.

"HEY, nothing funny is happening here!" He then reaches inside the car and takes his shotgun.

"What!? You think I'm going to touch your gun?" I ask, smiling.

"This is SERIOUS. You are in serious trouble, are you not getting that? I have no idea what someone as stupid as you is capable of considering what you've already proven to be capable of."

Just then, another cop car pulls up to the scene. A tall, lanky guy steps out of his car, looks up at the sky and yells, "Yee ha!" He really did that.

The cop and Trooper Ingle talk. The new guy keeps looking at me in the car, his mouth agape. Ingle continues to search and the other guy comes to the car. He opens the driver's side door and talks to me.

"You really the Trunk Monkey?"

"Yessir."

"I like that commercial a lot. Given me a lot of laughs. My boys, too. It's a family favorite."

"Thank you," I say. "I really appreciate that."

"You're welcome. You're a funny actor. How you get a job that like?"

"Uh, well, I have an agent."

"Do you, now? So, how's that work, he gets you jobs?"

"She, yeah. I mean she sends me on auditions and, you know, if they want to use me, they call her and she negotiates the money or whatever."

"Interesting."

Ingle comes to the car, puts Rex II on a leash and takes him on a sniffing tour of my vehicle. Both cops are now "yee hawing" and "ooh mama-ing" their way around, doing all they can to get Rex II barking and worked up. I know that there is nothing left for them to find.

Ingle finishes the search and the other guy takes off without saying goodbye.

"Sir," I begin.

"Yes?" he says, not looking at me.

Jerome Ingle, Texas state trooper, is a conventional-looking Tex-Mex of sorts. He has thick arms, a stout figure, large, brown hands, and a crew cut.

"I don't under—what did I do wrong exactly?" I play the moron card.

"You're under arrest for money laundering in the state of Texas."

"Oh, okay. So, does that mean I am going to jail?"

"Sure does."

"Okay. Uh, sir?"

"What?"

"How much time can I get for that?"

"Not less than a year, I don't think."

"A year, huh…Okay." I ponder doing time.

"How much money you reckon is in there?" he asks.

"Uh, a little over a hundred grand."

"Where'd it come from?"

"It was the inheritance of a friend's and I'm taking it back to California for him."

"That's a good one," he laughs. "You expect me to believe that?"

"I don't."

"Why didn't your friend want to take his own inheritance home with him?"

"Well, he was—he had to be somewhere. He had a commitment and asked me to drive it for him."

"You're a good friend."

"Thanks, I like to think so. People trust me."

"We are going to wait for a tow truck to come. Shouldn't be long." He stares off at the horizon. The silence is terrible.

"You from around here?" I ask.

"What?"

"I say, are you from around here?"

"Yes," he answers.

"Married?"

"Twenty-two years."

"Oh, that's great. I need to get married. I think. Yeah, I think that's what I need. Marriage…It just seems like a great thing."

"Tough, but worth it."

"Did you play sports in high school?"

"I ran track and played JV football."

"Oh yeah! What events did you run?"

"Are you kidding me, kid? Do you understand the kind of trouble you are in?"

"I know, but please, just talk to me. I'll start freaking out again if we don't talk…please."

"I ran the 400 and the 800."

"Oh, yeah? What was your best time?"

Ballad of the Trunk Monkey Bandit

WE DRIVE, MILES AND miles down a two-lane road. Trooper Ingle's phone rings.

"This is Gee-rome...Oh, hey...No, I'm good, thanks. Uh huh, uh huh...No, just some kid, hundred grand in his trunk. Oh, get this—you know the Trunk Monkey? Well, I caught the Trunk Monkey...Yeah, I know."

I look out the side window. The sun is setting. It'll be dark soon. It's kinda neat that these guys all know me from the Trunk Monkey, I guess. I wonder if I'll get out of jail before Amy moves to New York.

"Hey, kid, will you take a picture with my friend if he comes meet us later?"

I nod yes. Ingle says goodbye and hangs up. We drive in silence for a few minutes.

"Actually, you're the monkey," I say finally.

"What's that?"

"Well, in the commercial I break into the car, the monkey hits me over the head and throws me off the bridge. So the monkey is the cop and that is you. You didn't catch the monkey, you are the monkey."

We follow the tow truck into a warehouse. There is no police station, no cars parked outside, no other guys, no jail. A garage door opens when we pull up and it closes behind us. Inside, Ingle takes me out of the car and cuffs me to a pipe on the wall. I sit on the ground. A crew of cowboy-boot-wearing, nonuniformed folks begins ripping the seats out of the rental car, shaking their heads, looking at me. I do the math: five of them, $125,000, one bullet in my head.

I take a photograph with one guy, sign an autograph for another. They all love the Trunk Monkey. My thoughts of pending doom are interrupted when the cavalry, headed by Special Agent Jimmie Perez, Immigration and Customs Enforcement, arrives. Perez, along with two state DEA agents, Donald Fleming and Brian Frick, takes me into a nice, warm office.

They read me my rights again. A tape recorder is turned on and the interview begins. Frick asks the questions. He is youngish, has a wedding ring, baseball cap and an unfortunate goatee.

"Did Trooper Ingle read you your rights?"

"Yes, sir."

"Do you have any questions?"

"No, sir."

"Okay, so where were you coming from?"

"Birmingham." I keep staring at the digital recorder.

"And what were you doing there?"

"Sir, do I get a phone call? I need to talk to my father. He's a lawyer and I need to talk to a lawyer."

"Okay, look…you can talk to a lawyer. That is one of your rights, but this is your chance to help yourself. If you talk to us now, you can help yourself and we can help you. But if you talk to a lawyer, then all that's out the window. We can't do nothing for you once you talk to a lawyer, because once you talk to a lawyer all that you tell us is no good."

"Listen, I'd love to help you guys, I really would, and I still hope that you're gonna help me, but I just…I know I shouldn't be talking to you right now."

Frick ignores me and resumes the questioning.

"Now I am going to ask you about drugs and you answer truthfully."

I look at Special Agent Perez, who says nothing.

"Just…can I make a phone call maybe?"

"Have you smoked marijuana?" Frick asks.

"Yes."

"How often?"

"Every day."

"Cocaine?"

"No, not since I was young."

"Ecstasy?"

"I tried it twice."

"Heroin."

"I smoked it a few times with a friend, but honestly the taste was just, eh."

"Acid?"

"No."

"Pills?"

"No."

"Mushrooms?"

"Oh, sure."

"When was the most recent?"

"I don't know, a year ago. Why can't I make a phone call?"

"Are you involved in the cocaine trade?"

"What? No. Please, just let me call my father."

Suddenly a new voice chimes in, loud and fast. It's Special Agent Jimmie Perez. "How much weed did you and Tom bring out from California?"

"Not that much."

Special Agent Perez pulls off his glasses and looks me right in the eye.

"How much did you get paid?"

"I just did it for fun, to see the country. I got a thousand bucks, but that was just for my time. Oh, and I got some cash, you know for food and gas."

"Is this Tom's money, Tom's drug money?" Perez has the rental agreement.

"I can't say."

"This guy is not your friend, David. Now either you are going to go to prison or he is. You gonna protect someone who gave you a shit wage to take this type of a risk?"

"I told you I needed a lawyer. Why can't I talk to a lawyer?"

"Whose money is this, David?"

"I don't know. I don't know whose it is…These guys, they grow weed. It's legal, it's legal to grow. I don't know who they are or where they are, but…and…I don't know. I don't have anything to do with it."

"So, then, explain why someone would trust you with this kind of money, when you have nothing to do with it." I think for a second and answer as simply and honestly as I can.

"Because I would never take anything that didn't belong to me."

They all look at each other. They know it's true.

"Are you part of a drug cartel?"

"I'm not part of anything. I was just doing a favor. I just…I just really wanted to see the frontier." My Dances With Wolves reference goes over their heads.

"David, will you tell us who you are going to be giving the money to?"

"I need a lawyer. I need a lawyer. WHY can't I make a phone call? I know my rights."

It's somewhere around there that the tape is turned off and Perez and I are left in the room alone.

"Son, do us a favor, stop talking right now." I nod.

Frick comes back into the room.

"State of Texas is not going to press charges. We're gonna keep your money, let you deal with this on your own."

I look at Perez. Perez looks at Frick. My smile is full of tears. I'm getting out of it.

THEY TAKE ME BACK to the warehouse and cuff me to the pipe again. Special Agent Perez makes a call on his cellphone. Ingle hovers; his cuffs are still on my wrists. The special agent's call goes on a long time and only once does he look over his shoulder at me. I see him nodding and scratching his head underneath his hat, then suddenly he snaps his phone closed and walks toward me, reaching into his pocket to pull out more handcuffs. There is a hint of sadness in his voice as he says, "You're under arrest for conspiracy to launder money…You have the right to remain silent." As he reads me my rights, Ingle laughs. Frick's eyes open wide.

Ingle looks at me. "Lousy actor you are," he says, laughing.

Perez put his cuffs on me. Good ol' Gee-rome just can't help himself; as he removes his cuffs, he whispers in my ear, "Son, your life's about to change."

Ingle leaves and Special Agent Jimmie Perez takes me to a holding cell in another warehouse. There, I'm finally allowed to call my father, who at first laughs, thinking I'm joking with him. It isn't until the special agent starts talking that my Dad realizes this is for real.

"Sir, this is Special Agent Jimmie Perez. We picked up your son traveling west on I-40 with a large sum of what we believe to be the proceeds of—"

"David, listen to me. Listen to me right now! DO NOT TALK TO ANYONE! DO NOT TALK TO ANYONE ABOUT ANYTHING! DO YOU UNDERSTAND ME?"

"Yes. Dad, I'm so sorry, please…I'm so sorry." I start to cry.

"Don't worry, just promise me that no matter what you've said already, that you are not to talk to ANYONE about ANYTHING from this point forward!"

"Listen to what your father is telling you," Perez says under his breath. He takes back the phone and says, "Sir,

I need to hang up the phone now. He'll be at Randall County Jail. When I take him there, which should be in about an hour, he'll be able to call you, but only collect and you can't call cellphones."

"Okay, thank you…David, I'll be at the house in an hour. I'll wait by the phone. Just be strong. I love you."

My father comes out the next morning. It's the weekend, so I'm left to watch the Colts win the Super Bowl. The heated debate that day in jail is whether Prince, who plays the halftime show, is a fag. After spending four days at Randall, I'm released on a personal recognizance bond (no money) and I return to Los Angeles. When I get my official indictment, it reads "The United States of America vs. David Henry Schneider, aka The Trunk Monkey Bandit." A few weeks later, Amy moves to New York and I move into my father's house in San Francisco.

I take a job teaching preschool—I'm not a convicted felon yet and, besides, it's my mother's school. I go to NA meetings, get letters from teachers and rabbis, do everything I can to appeal to the judge that this experience has been enough—that I am a changed man and don't need prison to get the point. My lawyer in Texas, one Selden B. Hale, begins to think I have a chance at getting probation, but during my sentencing Judge Mary Lou Robinson, the eighty-two-year-old federal judge from the Northern District of Texas, sentences me to six months in "custody." The feds are kind enough to let me serve my time in California at the Taft Correctional Institution. On August 28, 2007, I turn thirty doing time at Taft. It's one of the most memorable birthday parties I ever have.

GOLDEN: THE EDUCATION OF A YOUNG POOTBUTT

Jervey Tervalon

WILD HAIRED, WITH AN expansive Afro, comics in my back pocket and Arthur C. Clarke's *Childhood's End* in my shoulder bag, I was on the grand adventure of my young life: freshman year at the University of California, Santa Barbara. The moment I drove up from South L.A. and set eyes on San Nicolas dorm, I knew I'd arrived in California's promised land, where State Street was paved with gold and money grew on eucalyptus trees. Or at least it seemed that way when I made my way to the end of the financial-aid line and hit the jackpot: a student worker handed me a check for $500 and told me that all of my expenses were handled—Cal Grant B paid my fees and I would receive a check for $129 a month. I asked the stoner surfer dude what I needed to do with the money from the check, thinking maybe I had to pay some other bill. But he shook his head and said, "Do whatever you want with it. Buy beer."

I put the money in the bank. For one thing, I didn't like beer much. And I couldn't believe that this land-of-plenty stuff would last. Sad to say, I was proven right thirty years later. It's hard to imagine a young pootbutt like me getting a full ride at UC Santa Barbara today.

At that moment, though, on that sun-bathed campus surrounded by cooling breezes from the Pacific Ocean and Santa Ynez Mountains, I felt safe for the very first time. Not having to fear for my life on the increasingly brutal streets of South L.A. was worth more than gold to me. I will say here that those streets might have been brutal, but they were often pretty, jacaranda-lined streets with lemon-and-rosemary-scented air, and spectacular, smog-enhanced sunsets. But my arrival in Santa Barbara wasn't some lucky break—it's how California's public university system was supposed to work.

I've long suspected that I have some kind of reptile inside of me, not a superego or id, but a lizard so lazy that it responds only to the most desirable rewards, the juiciest flies. Somehow, my inner lizard settled on UC Santa Barbara as recompense for an education in the L.A. Unified School District, especially for what I had to go through at Foshay Junior High, where every day was a Kafkaesque institutional nightmare. Now, I fear, a lot more California schools are looking like Foshay misadventures. Who knew then that if you wanted to see the future of California public education that you'd look not to UC Santa Barbara but to Foshay Junior High?

YOU WANT THE MONEY?" asked Lamont, the big kid sitting next to me in class.

I did. I wanted the money very much. Fifty cents in 1973 was a gang of change for me; I'd be able to get a cheese toast, a burrito, or one of those sugar-crusted coffee cakes at morning nutrition. But I had to pass.

"I ain't gonna ask you again, you want the money?"

"No," I said. "Thanks."

"You stupid. You could have had 50 cents for free."

Certain there was a trick, I was reluctant to take the money from Lamont because he was big and surly

116

and taking the 50 cents probably meant he got to fire on me, or the money belonged to somebody else who would knock me out to get it back. Lamont lost interest, though, and I went back to reading my modern science textbook.

For a moment it was quiet, then from the corner of my eye I saw someone outside rushing toward our classroom windows. A sweaty-faced woman with a scarf on her head and a plaid shirt came right up to the room's broad, horizontal windows (the kind that don't open all the way) and yelled at us to leave school. Lamont smiled at her as though he were telling her, Stupid lady, I ain't studying you! Everybody in the class turned to look.

"Class, get to work. Don't waste time," Mr. Robbs, our big-headed teacher, shouted. But nobody paid any attention to him—more angry people were running toward us and soon they blocked almost the entire bank of windows. Just as Mr. Robbs started to close the blinds, Lamont spotted a flying object, popped up, and with his long legs stepped over the desk. I didn't see the brick until it crashed through the window, sending shards everywhere. It landed neatly on the desk where Lamont had been sitting, right next to me. Dazed, I sat there, picking glass from my hair.

That was Foshay. We all knew why it happened: the speech a couple days before at one of those crazy-ass assemblies. I hated assemblies—hundreds of kids in an overcrowded and noisy auditorium—because you couldn't see somebody chucking an eraser in the dark. People would start throwing things and then a fight would break out and then kids would go really berserk. And I hated when kids went really berserk.

At the assembly two teachers were supposed to give us a talk about free lunch tickets and how we should use them. It seemed the new federal free-lunch program at Foshay wasn't going over too well. Nobody wanted to be seen with those tickets because they were afraid they'd get bagged on. The lunch tickets were left, unused, on homeroom desks, and the school was stuck with boxes and boxes of untouched submarine sandwiches and unopened cartons of chocolate milk.

After we were seated, Mr. Davis, a biology teacher with an Afro, and Ms. Harris, a gym teacher who always wore a dashiki, came to the microphone.

"Greetings, brothers and sisters," they both said. "Welcome to the black history assembly."

Mr. Davis stepped in front of Ms. Harris and gazed out at us with a profoundly serious look. He was a no-nonsense man who wore a leather jacket and tough-looking boots. Kids whispered he used to be a Black Panther.

"Today, we are going to see a film about the life of Martin Luther King."

Maybe Mr. Davis expected some interest, but everybody carried on, talking and laughing.

Ms. Harris stepped in front of the mike and took her shot. "We were going to see a film about the life of Martin Luther King, but now we want to discuss with you the importance of the free lunch program. We want to encourage you to use your free lunch tickets. People have worked real hard for you kids to get a good lunch. But those lunches aren't some handout. See, these lunches are owed you. It's nothing you should be embarrassed about. You're entitled."

"That's right," Mr. Davis said. "When we were freed over a hundred years ago, they promised us something for making us slaves and we never got it. You know what they promised us way back then? They promised us forty acres and a mule. Now, y'all might not be too impressed with no mule, but forty acres—that's a whole lot of something."

Now we listened intently, all 800 of us. It got a lot quieter in that huge auditorium. They said the right thing—what we were supposed to get. That's what we wanted to hear, what we were interested in.

Ms. Harris took the lead now that we were sufficiently warmed up.

"You never gonna see that forty acres. That's just one more promise they broke. And that mule, just what would you do with a mule these days? Some of you might not know why we would be entitled to such things. The president a long time ago promised us land so we can get a start in this country," she said with ever-increasing anger. "We were slaves, we didn't have a pot to pee in and they said they would give us a start. But what we got are these free lunch tickets."

"Y'all shouldn't be ashamed," Mr. Davis said.

"Eat the lunches before they take that away!" they shouted in unison.

That did it. We were hanging on their words. Usually assemblies weren't worth listening to, but this was different; the auditorium was under their total control.

"So come to school!" Ms. Harris and Mr. Davis shouted, and we roared our approval.

"And eat those lunches!"

We roared even more.

"It's your right!"

The auditorium rocked with cheers and claps. Some kids were jumping up and down like in church. A few girls near me were even crying.

The assembly ended too soon.

After Mr. Davis and Ms. Harris left the stage and the lights came on, there was Mr. Oak, the principal, telling our teachers to take us back to class. After students did their booing and cursing, the teachers managed to move us out.

At noon, we all lined up to get our forefathers' reparations: a submarine sandwich, an apple, and a four-pack of Oreos. I wanted the lunch, but I couldn't get a ticket—both my parents worked and made too much. That pissed me off because it was the same thing I was paying 50 cents for.

Then Ms. Harris and Mr. Davis were fired.

Those first-period students who had a look at the replacement teachers for Ms. Harris and Mr. Davis got the word out fast. "They got rid of them," I heard somebody say in the crowded, dimly lit hallway, "'cause of those lunches." By noon it was stale news. In my biology class, Mrs. Green, a very uptight black woman who didn't seem to know much about or have much interest in biology, brought up the firing as soon as we were seated.

"You know they fired those teachers because of what they said, because they wanted y'all not to be embarrassed about eating those free lunches."

Some kid raised his hand and said, "They fired them 'cause they black."

Mrs. Green didn't need to answer. All over the school the same opinion was being shared among the black faculty and students. At this junior high school, political action wasn't something the student body was about. We just wanted to get home without getting jacked or stomped. This situation of fearful coexistence changed overnight.

The next school day was tense, like something had to happen. Teachers kept their doors locked and shut, no matter how stuffy the classrooms got—and with all those kids not showering after gym it was especially funky. Some students, the hard-looking ones with the big Afros and the bomber jackets and shiny Levis, stiff from too much starch, and with red or black handkerchiefs dangling from their back pockets, hung outside the gates of the school ready to get into some shit. All of us pootbutt scrubs made wide, cautious detours around them. Sometimes the principal or one of those gym teachers, the true enforcers of authority with their walkie-talkies and coach shirts and shorts, would come up and try to scatter them, but it didn't work. They stayed cohesive, defying the gym teachers.

Nothing happened yet, no rocks were thrown, though soon enough the gangsters started drawing others out of class, even some of us pootbutts. Girls started ditching, too; fine ones, not just the Criplets, chicken-headed mugwug girls who remade themselves into gangster molls. Administrators attempted to gain control, but they had little effect. Finally, the police started roundups, forcing students into the school. But soon as they came in, they'd head around to the other side of the school and hop a fence. In desperation, the principal decided to chain and padlock the gates of the school so that no one could get in or out. By then, though, parents had gotten wind of the controversy at Foshay and started showing up, trying to get their kids. The locked gates confused and angered them; soon all kinds of people were coming up to the school, even some militant types, including the one who chucked the brick that landed on Lamont's desk.

We were locked in the school, maybe 800 kids and sixty or so teachers, a whole lot of people who didn't feel safe. That's when the fire marshal showed up with a crew of firemen, who spent an hour with big metal shears cutting all the chains and confiscating them.

"Listen," the fire marshal said to the principal, "if you chain these doors again I'll close this school down and have you arrested."

The principal shrank from a big man to somebody knee high, less than a pootbutt scrub. He couldn't do anything about the students ditching class and raising hell on the gym field. He had to worry about nuts and fools getting onto campus or students ditching en masse, so gym teachers were sent to man the entrances, leaving us students on our own with minimal supervision. My desire was to stay out of the way of all this craziness, but we all had to go to the lunch area to get punch and coffee cake and those nasty burritos and submarine sandwiches.

I sat at my usual bench, near where one of the deans of boys usually planted himself to watch the lunch area. He was gone today to work at the hopeless task of keeping out the invaders. Still, lunch seemed pretty calm, no fights or anything. No bunch of boys trying to pull well-developed Mary May Flowers's dress up over her head. Most kids were eating and screaming at each other as always, when suddenly somebody yelled, "Look at this shit, a bug in my sandwich!"

Kids rushed to see, and the guy, a ninth-grader with a peanut head, showed off the sandwich as though it were a war wound. He smiled broadly, exulting in the bug crushed between two pieces of bread, squashed on top of lunch meat and lettuce. Soon he had to stand on a bench so the pressing crowd could see his good luck. Then, when unknowing kids were about to eat their own sandwiches, we screamed for them not to, that those were roach burgers.

"Hey!" someone yelled after getting hit in the head with a flying roach burger. Then they all started flying; a hail of sandwiches fell on us all, thug and pootbutt alike. The food fight got crazier with only a few adults around to make half-hearted attempts to end it.

The craziness spilled away from the lunch area and out to the gym field—a big expanse of asphalt in the center of the school. The pootbutts were the first to scatter at the sight of a wave of food fighters with rock-hard burritos, cocked and ready to fling. But some weren't cowering; the hurt ones, the ugly kids who hung out among themselves on the bleachers near the fence, came pounding down the steps, serious as heart attacks. Ugly guys and girls—fat and short haired, skinny and short haired, all with bad teeth, rushed in, throwing blows at the turf invaders, dead set on defending their precious isolation. All thoughts about the fired teachers dissipated into the free-floating rage that hung over Foshay.

The bell rang, but nobody responded. They stayed out there and fought until they got sick of busted heads and knuckles. Teachers were happy to see empty classes after the tardy bell rang, and hurried to shut doors and lock students out of classrooms.

I sat out there with Roy, a kid more shell shocked than I was, wondering when the fighting would slow down or when we would truly be in danger.

The principal finally just gave up. No one was in class. Fools were trying to sneak into the school, while we were trying to flee from food fights and riots. Coach Ken appeared with a megaphone and announced the retreat.

"School is canceled. Exit on Exposition. School is canceled. Leave immediately!"

That did it. Students stopped all that fighting nonsense; burritos dropped from clenched hands and were trampled as we deserted the school.

It wasn't over. The Exposition Street exit let out into a pretty rough neighborhood, blocks away from the path I usually took home. We moved like a herd, hoping for protection in numbers, but I lived east so I broke off in that direction with some gangbangers I was on good terms with and a dozen or so other stragglers. We were about two blocks south of Western when we saw another bunch of kids running at us, or if not at us, away from something. We started running like spooked wildebeest, fleeing in all directions, racing for higher ground if it could be found. Finally I made it to Second Avenue, exhausted and bitter for having had to work so hard to travel such a short distance.

"What was all that up at Foshay?" my brother Jude asked as I came into the house. I ignored him, turned on the television, and settled onto the couch.

I was safe, at least until school tomorrow, but the school slowly became a ghost town. More and more kids stayed away until only a handful of us walked halls empty enough for tumbleweeds to roll through.

Mama heard about me sneaking off to school from Jude. She called from work to see if I was there and Jude said something like, "He ain't here. He went to school. He never does what you want him to."

"If you go back to that school, I'm gonna come up there and pull you by your hair all the way home," Mama said after she heard how dangerous Foshay had become.

And so I didn't go to school for a couple weeks. I stayed home, watched TV, and hung out in academic exile.

But soon enough I graduated to Dorsey High and continued on until I reached UCSB, where I missed the start of the rock-cocaine epidemic in my old neighborhood and how it made a difficult world impossibly more so, culminating in the 1992 riot/ uprising. Instead, I hung out with artists and scientists, dated women from affluent families, saw that I didn't need to be rich to live a rich life—unless I wanted to live really close to the beach. (And with a sufficient number of roommates, I could afford to get close enough to the beach to at least see the ocean.)

After I graduated I lingered in Santa Barbara for years, not wanting to return to Los Angeles, but eventually it seemed necessary, so I decided to teach. I was hired at Locke High School, where students lived in conditions that were far worse than what I had experienced at Foshay, where sudden, deadly violence was a constant threat. I talked to many of the students about seeing the world, about going to college, and some did. One former student studies computer science at UC Santa Barbara; another graduated from UC Berkeley and returned to teach at Locke.

TIMING CAN BE EVERYTHING, and the California I knew when I first attended UCSB many years ago was still golden. Now it doesn't even seem shiny; it's more like unrecyclable plastic. In a post-Prop. 209 world, where affirmative action is now a historic anomaly, far fewer African Americans and non-Asian minorities attend UC schools. And it's only going to get harder. Instead of rationally solving the state's budget problems, our politicians keep jacking up fees, putting us on the path to privatizing our best public universities.

Things aren't much better in the Cal State system, where I taught happily for years. The Cal States graduate most of our teachers, mechanical engineers, and nurses, but we're making those degrees ever more unaffordable at a time when we have more working-class students in need of a quality higher education. Now that California is a majority minority state, what worked to create prosperity for the majority white population in the twentieth century is now out of reach. The unfairness is a kind of educational apartheid.

Maybe it's only a coincidence that the minority coalition that opposes education funding increases in California is overwhelmingly white. It might be the first time in our history that an ethnic minority could help determine the economic fate of the majority of Californians. Tea baggers can bag all the tea they'd like, but they need to take their hands off of our education. I can't stand to think of all those kids who, because their families aren't rich or connected, won't have the experiences that I had, that meant so much to me and made my life infinitely better. It's time to start listening to the likes of Mr. Davis and Ms. Harris again. It's time to get militant about it: education through any means necessary.

FORTRESS LA

C. R. Stecyk III

WILL THE CIRCLE OF containment be unbroken? It's jokers wild until the cards run cold. Be the bullet. Your ass is already bet, because you are dwelling on the center dot of the target. Tactically consider the reality of the Angeleno situation: no matter where you live, hide, or pass through in Greater Los Angeles you are in the shadow of military facilities, major defense contractors, and innumerable support personnel. California has 42.7 million acres of federally controlled land. That comprises 43.6 percent of the state. The terror that is already here might be more ominous than any that could be coming.

Down range at Fort Hunter Liggett, a Julia Morgan hacienda once commissioned by the world's richest man is next to a Spanish mission. Over the hills from here, the National Reconnaissance Office commands advanced global investigation systems. The first use of satellites to gather intelligence was executed there. Any spot in California is just a button push away from multiple-phase interdiction.

It used to be easier to read the game board. Gun emplacements on Point Dume and Fort MacArthur, aerospace plants scattered amid think tanks like Rand and Systems Development Corporation, base camps on all the Channel Islands, armories with ceremonial cannons in every civic sector, an AF psyops film studio atop Lookout Mountain, and Nike nuclear missiles poised in Malibu, by Marineland, and on Van Nuys Boulevard. Today Los Angeles Air Force Base is still active in the heart of the megalopolis. And the Southern California Operations Area supports the largest concentration of naval forces in the world. Eyes in the sky overwatch all. And millions of contiguous acres are armored in the desert interior. Our contemporary sustainability strategy is to fire and forget.

God's cruel kingdom is a wilderness of weird populated by snake eaters, spooks, squids, high- and low-altitude jumpers, frogs, grunts, and company men. It is crowded in Indian country. These motivated individuals do not necessarily like you, but they will die for you. Their commitment is built on the understanding that their sacrifice allows you the luxury of hating what they stand for.

When it started I have no clue, but I can pinpoint the exact day I knew it was over. I never planned to take this group of photographs. They were each incidental views, which were indecipherably woven into the landscape tapestry of Los Angeles. October 14, 1997, dawn…I stood on the Edwards AFB flight line. Brigadier General Chuck Yeager pulled up in a blue Cadillac with personalized BELL X1A license plates. We talked briefly during a majestic sunrise over the dry lake bed. That occasion was announced as being Yeager's last supersonic flight. I was certain that I was witnessing the end of the dominance of the military-industrial complex. It was doomed like the dinosaurs. But Chuck did indeed go on to break more sound barriers over the years. Eventually I learned that like all good systems, covert and overt actions reproduce their own kind in perpetuity.

A line of demarcation across a dry lake bed.

At what height does this navigation marker resolve itself as a directional device?

ie wake from a surface-running submarine crosses the bow plank of an aircraft carrier.

B-2 Spirit stealth bombers have flown more than 14,000 sorties to date.

They have a range of 10,000 nautical miles on a single aerial refueling

and are capable of delivering twenty tons of nuclear ordinance.

They cost $2.1 billion apiece in 1997 dollars.

The bad news is that they are always there, everywhere.
The good news is that you need them and cannot escape their area of operations

SEMPER EN OBSCURUS

THE PIRATE OF PENANCE

Joe Donnelly

WHEN LOREY SMITH WAS 12 years old, her father loaded her and her brother into his black 1965 Mustang and drove them down the Pacific Coast Highway to this cool little shop called Mystic Arts World. The store sold arts and crafts, organic food and clothing, books about Eastern philosophy, and other things, too. Lorey's father knew some of the guys who ran Mystic Arts and he thought the outing would be a nice diversion for the kids. It was a short drive from Huntington Beach but an exotic destination, at least for the girl in the back seat.

The year was 1969, and Laguna Beach, once the sleepy refuge of surfers, artists, and bohemians of little consequence, was a center of counterculture foment after a band of outlaws and outcasts went up a mountain with LSD and came down as messengers of love, peace, and the transformational qualities of acid and hash. They called themselves the Brotherhood of Eternal Love, and Mystic Arts World was their public face, a hippie hangout where vegetarianism, Buddhism, meditation, and all sorts of Aquarian ideals spread like gospel.

Lorey says she felt like Alice in Wonderland when she crossed the threshold and entered Mystic Arts. "It was like walking into a different world," she tells me 40 years later. "Everything from what was on the walls to the way people were dressed gave off this feeling of love, and, like, freedom."

Her father bought the kids some beads to keep them busy and Lorey fashioned a necklace. She walked up to a big, handsome guy with long hair and handed it to him.

"He opened up his hands, took the beads and had this big, beaming smile," she recalls, "and I just felt like, love, and I thought, Someday I want to marry someone like that."

Into the Gran Azul

SECURITY GUARDS ARMED WITH machine guns patrol the grounds of the Gran Azul resort in Lima, Peru. It's the kind of place you have to know someone to even get close. But on an early winter day in 1975, Eddie Padilla, one of the founders of the Brotherhood of Eternal Love, has no trouble booking a room. He is a familiar face on a familiar errand.

Checking in with Padilla are Richard Brewer, a Brother from way back, and their friend James Thomason. "I chose Richard because he's a good guy," Padilla remembers. "He'll get your back. He's not going to run away. That played out in a way that I never, ever expected." Thomason is along for the ride—to party and taste some first-class Peruvian flake.

As the manager walks the men to their bungalow, he delivers a strange message. "Your friend is here," he says.

"Friend?" Padilla asks. "What friend?"

As soon as the manager says the name Fastie, Padilla curses. He's known the guy since high school where Fastie earned his nickname because he always knew the shortest distance to a quick buck. As far as

Padilla is concerned, Fastie is a flashy, loud-mouthed whoremonger—the worst kind of smuggler. Padilla told him not to come to Lima while he was there. To make matters worse, Fastie's girlfriend is with him, and she has a crush on Padilla. When they run into her, she complains that Fastie has been taking off and leaving her at the hotel.

"She knows he's been going to see whores and coking out," Padilla says. "We're like, Oh, god." Prostitutes and police are thick as thieves in places like Lima, Peru.

Still, there's no reason to be paranoid. "All I have to do is spend the night, pick up the coke, give it to a few people, and peel out in 24 hours," Padilla remembers thinking. Everything was set up ahead of time; the deal should be an in-and-out affair.

Though they had agreed to keep a low profile, Padilla, Brewer, and Thomason decide to go to the compound's bar that night. It's an upscale place and they get all dressed up. Fastie is there. Things are tense and Padilla knows better than to dance with Fastie's girlfriend. But when she asks, something won't let him say no. Maybe he just wants to rub Fastie's face in it. Maybe he's the guy who has to let everyone know he can have the girl. Whatever it is, when they get off the floor, Fastie isn't amused.

"All of a sudden, in a jealous rage, he gets up, scrapes everyone's drinks off the bar, and throws a drink on [his girlfriend]," Padilla says. "The bouncer, some Jamaican dude, kicks him out."

Fastie returns to his room and tosses his girlfriend's belongings out the window. She ends up spending the night in Padilla's bungalow.

The next morning, the girlfriend leaves to retrieve her belongings. She never comes back. Fastie isn't anywhere to be seen either.

If they'd been reading the signs, they might have waited until things settled down to pick up the coke. Instead, Padilla and Brewer stay on schedule and head to a nearby safe house for their load—25 kilos of cocaine worth nearly $200,000—and return to the bungalow without a hitch. Things seem to be back on track.

"It's so fresh, it's still damp," Padilla says. "So I've got it on these big, silver serving trays, sitting on a table. James is making a paper of coke [think to-go cup]. Bob Dylan's *Blood on the Tracks* is playing. Richard's doing something…I don't know what. And I'm writing down numbers. All of the sudden, the door opens. I look and all I see is a chrome-plated .32. Oh, shit. I just thought, wow, my life just ended."

The Making of Eddie Padilla

THIRTY-FOUR YEARS LATER, EDDIE Padilla emerges from Burbank's Bob Hope Airport into a balmy Los Angeles autumn night. He has a well-groomed goatee, a shiny, bald dome, and a nose that clearly hasn't dodged every punch. Wearing a black jacket and tidy slacks, Padilla is muscular and sturdy at 64. He walks like a slightly wounded panther and offers a knuckle-crushing handshake. "Hey, man, thanks for coming to get me," he says with a lingering SoCal-hippie-surfer accent.

We grab a coffee. Padilla speaks softly, with an economy that could be taken for either circumspection or shyness. The circumspection would be mutual. I had been approached about Padilla through his literary agents; they'd been unsuccessfully shopping his memoir. Right away, I was skeptical. Padilla's story was epic, harrowing, and hard to believe. Aggravating my suspicions was the memoir's aggrandizing tone. Plus,

I'm not a fan of hippies and their justifications for what often seems like plain irresponsibility or selfishness. Still, I have to admit, if even half of his story is true, Eddie Padilla would be the real-life Zelig of America's late 20th-century drug history. And, as is apparent from his first handshake, he has Clint Eastwood charisma to go with his tale.

I drop Padilla off at one of those high-gloss condo complexes in Woodland Hills that seem designed especially for mid-level rappers, porn stars, and athletes. His son, Eric, manages the place. Though Padilla lives a short flight away in Northern California, he has never been here before. Tonight marks the first time in nine years that he will see his son. For 20 years now, Padilla has been literally and figuratively working on reclaiming his narrative. Reuniting with his son is part of that effort. I may be too, and I'm not sure how I feel about it.

As we approach, Padilla falls silent, unsure of what to expect. Eric is waiting outside the lobby when we pull up. He looks like a younger, slightly smaller version of Padilla. They greet each other with wide smiles and nervous hugs. I leave them to it.

I pick Padilla up the next morning to go surfing. He's in good spirits. The reunion with his son went well. Plus, he hasn't been in the water for a while and surfing is one of the few passions left from his earlier days.

Out at County Line, it's a crystalline day with offshore winds and a decent swell kicking in. For Padilla, I've brought my spare board, a big, fancy log that would be cumbersome for most on a head-high day at County Line. Padilla inspects the long board like it's a foreign object.

"I don't know about this," he says. "How about if I take your board and you use this one?" Worried about the danger I'd pose to others and myself, I refuse. "Okay, then," he smiles, and we paddle out.

Padilla's reservations disappear as soon as the first set rolls in. He digs for the first wave, a fat, beautifully shaped A-frame. He deftly drops in, stays high on the shoulder, slips into the pocket, and makes his way down the line, chewing up every ounce of the wave. It's one of the best rides I see all day. But he's not done. Padilla catches wave after wave, surfing with a fluidity and grace that puts most of us out here to shame.

Exhausted after a couple hours, I get out of the water. When Padilla finally comes in, he is grinning ear to ear. "Who'd have thought I'd have to go from Santa Cruz to Los Angeles to find some good waves?" he jokes.

Buoyed by the return to his natural habitat, Padilla lets his guard down and begins to tell me about his life over lunch at an upscale chain restaurant in Santa Monica. Though Padilla is forty years her senior, the attractive waitress is definitely flirting with him. Whatever it is that makes women melt, Padilla has it. He's magnetic and likeable. As for his story, it could stand as a metaphor for the past few turbulent decades—the naïve idealism of flower power, the hedonism of the 1970s and '80s, the psychosis and cynicism of the war on drugs, and the recovery culture of more recent times. It's a story that's hard to imagine beginning anywhere but in Southern California

Edward James Padilla was born in 1944 in the same Compton house where his father, Joe Padilla, was raised. Joe, a dashing Navy guy of Hispanic, Native American, and African-American ancestry, married Helen Ruth McClesky, a Scots-Irish beauty from a rough clan of Texas ranch hands who moved to Southern California, near Turlock, during the Dust Bowl.

Both family trees have their troubled histories. Joe's mother killed herself when Joe was 12. The family broke apart after that and Joe had to fend for himself through the Depression. "He had no idea what it was even like to have a mother," Padilla says.

Helen's father turned to moonshining and bootlegging in California. Padilla recalls how his grandfather liked to show off the hole in his leg. As the story goes, Federal agents shot him during a car chase. Padilla raises his leg and imitates his grandfather's crotchety voice: "That goddamn bullet went through this leg and into that one."

When his grandfather finally ended up in prison, the family moved down to South Los Angeles where work could be found in the nearby shipyards. Padilla says his mother and father met in high school, "fell desperately in love," and got married. This didn't please the old man, who didn't want his daughter mixing with "Mexicans and niggers." Helen found both in one.

As the son of a mixed-race couple before such things were in vogue, Padilla got it from all sides. He wasn't Mexican enough for the Mexicans, white enough for the whites, or black enough for the blacks. He was also a frail kid who spent nine months with polio in a children's ward.

Padilla would get beaten up at school, and for consolation his father would make him put on boxing gloves and head out to the garage for lessons with dad, a Golden Glove boxer and light heavyweight in the Navy.

"If I turned my back, he'd kick me," Padilla says about his father, who died in 2001. "He was trying to teach me how to fight the world. My dad was a different kind of guy."

The family moved to Anaheim when Padilla was 12. There, he says, he became aware of the sort of prejudice that you can't solve with fists, the sort that keeps a kid from getting a job at Disneyland like the rest of his friends.

"That's when I started really getting ahold of the idea that, hey, I'm not being treated like everybody else. I'm sure I had a chip on my shoulder."

Padilla got into a lot of fights, got kicked out of schools and wound up in juvenile hall where he received an education in selling speed, downers, and pot. By the time he was 17, Padilla was making enough as a dealer to afford his own apartment and car. But it wasn't exactly the good life. He was doing a lot of speed, and one day he got arrested for what must have been an adolescent speed freak's idea of seduction.

"I started taking handfuls of speed and I got so crazy. I mean, I got arrested for exposing myself to older women because just do that and we'll have sex. That's how psychotic I was."

To make matters worse, he got in a fight with the arresting officer. The incident landed him 13 months at Atascadero State Hospital in San Luis Obispo. He came out feeling like he needed some stability in his life, or at least an 18-year-old's version of it.

"I need to get married and settle down and be a pot dealer. I remember clearly thinking that. So, I married my friend, Eileen."

Padilla and Eileen were 18 when they married on August 22, 1962. Marriage, though, didn't solve certain problems—like how to get a job, which was now even tougher with a stint in a psych ward added to his résumé.

"It would have been really cool if I could walk in somewhere and get a job that actually paid enough to pay rent and live, but from where I was coming from, I'd be lucky to get a job sweeping floors," he says. "I tried everything. So, it was easy to start selling pot."

He turned out to be good at it.

The Pirate of Penance

Mountain High

EDDIE PADILLA TURNED 21 in 1965. Cultural historians wouldn't declare the arrival of the Summer of Love for a couple of years, but for Padilla and a group of trailblazing friends, it was already in full swing.

He figures he was already the biggest pot dealer in Anaheim by this time. For a kid who grew up watching *The Untouchables* and dreaming of being a mobster, this might be considered an achievement. But something else was going on, too. The drugs he was selling were getting harder and his lifestyle coarser.

He started sleeping with several women from the apartment complex where he and his wife lived. He spent a lot of time in a notorious tough-guy bar called The Stables. "That's where I started being comfortable," Padilla says. "This is where I belonged. Social outcasts for sure."

Eileen eventually had enough and took off for her mother's. But it wasn't just the philandering. Padilla also had an aura of escalating violence about him.

"I had a gun. I felt like I was going down the road to shooting someone, just like hitting someone is a big step for some people. So, that's kind of insane. I was going to shoot someone just to get it over with. It doesn't matter who, either."

Then, early on the morning of his 21st birthday, one of his friends picked him up and drove him to the top of Mount Palomar. Joining them was John Griggs, a Laguna Beach pot dealer and the leader of a biker gang whose introduction to LSD had come when his gang raided a Hollywood producer's party and took the acid. On the mountain with them were several others who would soon embark on one of the 1960s' most influential and least understood counterculture experiments, the Brotherhood of Eternal Love. They climbed to the mountaintop and dropped the acid. Padilla says he was changed immediately.

"I was completely convinced that I'd died on that mountain," he remembers. "It was crystal-clear air, perfect for taking acid. I came down a different person. It was what's called an ego death. I saw the light. I can't ever explain it."

A birthday party was already set with a lot of his old friends for later that night. Back home, in the middle of the celebration Padilla says he looked around at the guests, some of the hardest-partying, toughest folks around, and realized he didn't ever want to see those people again. He took the velvet painting of the devil off his wall and threw it in the dumpster. He dumped the bowls of reds and bennies laid out like chips and salsa down the toilet. He kept his pot.

"I went up the mountain with no morals or scruples, a very dangerous and violent person," he says, "and came down with morals and scruples."

From that day on, a core group of hustlers, dealers, bikers, and surfers, who at best could be said to have lived on the margins of polite society, started convening to take acid together.

"Every time we'd go and take LSD out in nature or out in the desert or up on the mountain, it would be just this incredible, wonderful day," Padilla says. They were transformed, he claims, from tough cases, many of them doing hard drugs, to people with love in their hearts.

Things moved fast back then. The Vietnam War was raging; revolution was in the air, and the group that first started tripping on mountaintops wanted to be a part of it. Under the guidance of John Griggs, by most accounts the spiritual leader of the Brotherhood, they decided they needed to spread their acid-fueled revelations. In the foothills of the Santa Ana Mountains, they took over a Modjeska Canyon house that used to be a church and started having meetings. Soon, they were talking about co-ops and organic living; they were worshipping nature and preaching the gospel of finding peace and love through LSD.

The Brotherhood of Eternal Love incorporated as a church in October 1966, ten days after California banned LSD. The Brothers petitioned the state for the legal use of pot, acid, psilocybin and mescaline as their sacraments. They started a vegan restaurant and gave away free meals. They opened Mystic Arts World, which quickly became the unofficial headquarters for the counterculture movement crystallizing among the surfers and artists of Laguna Beach.

The Brotherhood proved both industrious and ambitious. Soon, they were developing laboratories to cook up a new, better brand of LSD and opening up unprecedented networks to smuggle tons of hash out of Afghanistan. They were also canny; they carved out the bellies of surfboards and loaded them with pot and hash. They made passport fraud an art form and became adept at clearing border weigh stations loaded down with surf gear and other disposable weight, which they'd dump on the other side so they could return with the same weight in pot stuffed into hollowed-out VW panel trucks. In their own way, they were the underground rock stars of the psychedelic revolution.

Soon, their skills and chutzpah attracted the attention of another psychedelic revolutionary. By 1967, Timothy Leary was living up in the canyons around

Laguna Beach carrying on a symbiotic, some would say parasitic, relationship with Griggs. Leary called Griggs "the holiest man in America," And more than anyone else, the Brothers implemented Leary's message to turn on, tune in, drop out.

"The Brotherhood were the folks who actually put that command into action and tried to carry it out," says Nick Schou, author of *Orange Sunshine: The Brotherhood of Eternal Love and Its Quest to Spread Peace, Love, and Acid to the World*. "Their home-grown acid, Orange Sunshine, was about three times more powerful than anything the hippies were using. They were responsible for distributing more acid than anyone in America. In the beginning, at least, they had the best of intentions."

The group, Schou says, was heavily influenced by the utopian ideals of Aldous Huxley's Island.

"There was a definite plan to move to an island," Padilla says. "We were going to grow pot on the island and we were going to import it. We need a yacht and we need to learn how to grow food and farm, and we need to learn how to deliver babies... We were just little kids from Anaheim. God, these were big thoughts, big thoughts."

The End of Eternal Love

AROUND THE TIME LEARY was setting up camp in Laguna Beach, the island ideal took on a new urgency for Padilla. No longer just a local dealer, he'd made serious connections in Mexico and was moving large quantities around the region. In one deal, Padilla drove to San Francisco in dense fog with 500 pounds of Mexican weed. But something didn't feel right. Padilla thought someone might have tipped off the cops. He was right: He was arrested the next day. It was the largest pot bust in San Francisco history to that point. In 1967, Padilla was sentenced to five to fifteen in San Quentin. With his son Eric on the way, Padilla was granted a 30-day stay of execution to get his affairs in order.

"On the thirtieth day, I just left and went to Mexico, went to work for some syndicate guys," he says. "I bailed."

Padilla's flight was also precipitated by a schism within the Brotherhood that some trace to its ultimate demise. Acting on Leary's advice, Griggs took the profits from a marijuana deal, funds that some Brothers thought should go toward the eventual island purchase, and bought a 400-acre ranch in Idyllwild near Palm Springs.

Padilla never cared much for Leary, nor for his influence over Griggs and the Brotherhood. "He was a glitter freak," Padilla says. "A guy named Richard Alpert, who became Ram Dass, told us, 'You guys got a good thing going, don't get mixed up with Leary.'"

Padilla saw the Idyllwild incident as a turning point for the Brotherhood. "This is betrayal. This is incredibly stupid. You're going to move the Brotherhood to a ranch in Idyllwild? To me, it was like becoming a target."

The Brotherhood split over it. Many of those facing federal indictments or arrest warrants took off for Hawaii. Others moved up to the ranch with Griggs and Leary. As the Brotherhood's smuggling operations grew increasingly complex and international, revolution started looking increasingly like mercenary capitalism. Any chance the Brotherhood had to retain its cohesion and its gospel probably died in 1969 with John Griggs, who overdosed on psilocybin up at the Ranch.

161

"That was John," Padilla says, smiling, "take more than anybody else."

Not long after, Mystic Arts burned down under mysterious circumstances. It seemed to signal an end, though the Brotherhood would continue to leave its mark on the era. The group masterminded Timothy Leary's escape from minimum-security Lompoc state prison following his arrest for possession of two kilos of hash and marijuana. Funded by the Brotherhood, the Weather Underground sprung Leary and spirited him and his wife off to Algeria with fake passports.

To facilitate his escape to Mexico, Padilla raised funds from various Brothers and other associates to gain entree with a Mexican pot syndicate run by a kingpin called Papa. His Mexican escapades—busting partners from jail and other adventures—could make their own movie.

One time he drove his truck to the hospital to visit his newborn son, Eric, who was sick with dysentery. On the way, he noticed a woman with a toddler by the side of the road. The kid was foaming at the mouth, the victim of a scorpion bite. Padilla says he threw the boy in the back of his truck and rushed him to the hospital. The doctors told him the kid would have died in another five minutes. They gave him an ambulance sticker for his efforts.

"I put it on my window," he tells me. "I was driving thousands of pounds of marijuana around in that panel truck. When I'd come to an intersection there would be a cop directing traffic. He'd stop everybody—I'd have a thousand pounds of weed in the back and he'd wave me through because of that ambulance sticker."

In Mexico, Padilla ran a hacienda for Papa, overseeing the processing and distribution of the pot brought in by local farmers. For more than a year, he skimmed off the best bud and seeds. Meanwhile, he kept alive his dream of sailing to an island.

The dream came true when he and a few associates from the Brotherhood bought a 70-foot yacht in St. Thomas called the Jafje. The Jafje met Padilla in the summer of 1970 in the busy port of Manzanillo. From there, it set sail for Maui.

"It was five guys who had never sailed in their lives," says Padilla. On board was a ton of the Mexican weed.

The trip should have taken less than two weeks. A month into it, one of the guys onboard, a smuggler with Brotherhood roots named Joe Angeline, noticed the stars weren't right.

"He said, 'Eddie, Orion's belt should be right over our heads.' But Orion's belt was way, way south of us. We could barely make it out."

When confronted, the captain confessed he didn't know where the hell they were but had been afraid to tell them. "There's a hoist that hoists you all the way up to the top of the main mast and we hauled him up there and made him sit there for a day," says Padilla. "That was funny."

Eventually, they flagged down a freighter and learned they were more than a 1000 miles off course, dangerously close to the Japanese current. The freighter gave them 300 gallons of fuel and put them back on track to Maui. He'd made it to his island with a load of the finest Mexican marijuana.

"The seeds of that," Padilla says, "became Maui Wowie."

Spiritual Warrior

MAUI WOWIE? THE HOLY grail of my pot-smoking youth, one of the most famous strains of marijuana in history? When Padilla tells me he played a major role in its advent, my already-strained credulity nears the breaking point. I spend months looking into Padilla's stories, tracking down survivors, digging up what corroborative evidence I can. And, well, he basically checks out. But there are his stories and there is his narrative—how an acid trip on Mount Palomar transformed a 21-year-old borderline sociopath into a man with a purpose, a messenger of peace and love. That one's harder to swallow. While sitting over coffee at the dining room table in his son's apartment, Padilla finally tells a couple stories that beg me to challenge him.

Back in the mid-'60s, he and John Griggs make a deal to purchase a few kilos of pot from a source in Pacoima. They drive out in a station wagon with 18 grand to make the buy. But the sellers burn them and take off with their money in a black Cadillac. The next day, Padilla and spiritual leader Griggs go back armed with a .38 and a .32. Padilla goes into the apartment where the deal was supposed to go down and finds one of the men sleeping on the couch. The guy wakes up and makes for a Winchester rifle sitting near the sink. Padilla runs up behind him and sticks the barrel of his gun in the guy's ear and says, "Dude, please don't make me fucking shoot you." Griggs and Padilla get their money back.

"So, that stuff went on. I've been shot at. People have tried to kill me. I've had bullets whizzing by my ear," he says. "But I've never had to shoot anybody."

Padilla tells me of similar episodes in Maui where the locals, understandably, see the influx of the hippie mafia as encroachment on their turf. They set about intimidating the haoles from Laguna, often violently. One newcomer is shot in the head while he sleeps next to his son.

At his house on the Haleakala Crater one night, Padilla opens the door to let in his barking puppy only to find "there's a guy standing there with a pillow case over his head and holes cut out and the guy behind him was taller and had a pager bag with the holes cut out."

One of the men has a handgun. Padilla manages to slam the gunman's hand in the door and chase off the invaders. "I'm going to kill both of you," he yells after them. "I'm going to find out who you are and kill you."

Padilla discovers the men work for a hood he knew back in Huntington Beach called Fast Eddie. Like a scene out of a gangster movie, Padilla and Fast Eddie have a showdown when Fast Eddie, in a car full of local muscle, tries to run Padilla and his passenger off the road. They all end up in Lahaina, where Fast Eddie's henchmen beat up Padilla pretty good before the cops break up the brawl.

"Hey, bra, you no run. Good man," Padilla recalls the Hawaiians saying to him. When Fast Eddie emerges from the chaos, Padilla points at him and tells the Hawaiians, "I want him. Let me have him.

"I worked him real good and that was that. People robbing and intimidating was over."

I tell him it doesn't seem like his life had changed very much since that day on Mount Palomar.

"You know, don't get the wrong idea," he laughs. "I'm still who I am. We're still kind of dangerous people. Just because we were hippies with long hair and preaching love and peace doesn't mean we became wusses."

"It doesn't sound like you had a spiritual awakening to me," I say.

"I was very spiritual," he replies. "I thought I was making a life for myself."

"As what?"

"A warrior. A spiritual warrior."

"What was your spiritual warring doing? What were you fighting for?"

He falls silent. "I never thought about it before... Remember, I grew up in South Central. I already had an attitude from a young age. So, by the time I got to Maui, it was like, here's your job, dealing with these people.

"The warrior part was, like, we want to live in Hawaii. We're not going to accept you guys running our lives. This is what we were trying to get away from. So, my job as a self-motivated warrior was pretty clear, but it's really difficult to explain."

"So, your job was protection?" I offer.

"I was never paid."

It occurs to me that Padilla really wanted to live beyond rules, institutions, and hierarchy, like some romaticized ideal of a pirate. "So why," I ask, "feel the need to color it with this patina of spirituality? Why not just call it what it was—living young and fast, making money, getting the girls, fucking off authority?"

"Uh, wow...I mean, you're right; it was about all that. It was living fast and really enjoying the lifestyle to the max."

"Why the need to justify it?"

"Well, it just seemed to me that was what was moving me."

"It seems that way to you now?"

"Now, yeah now. But then, I felt more, and this sounds really self-righteous, that we were the people who should be in charge, not the ones who were beating people up and taking their stuff and shooting them. So, spiritual warrior, maybe it doesn't look like that to anyone else, but it sure as hell looks like that to me now." His voice is soft and intense. "I didn't have a sign on my head that said spiritual warrior but I definitely felt that's what was going on...Nobody else was standing up to them. Nobody else would pick up a gun, but I sure as hell would."

"You have a massive ego," I suggest.

"Massive."

"And that's been your greatness and downfall all along?"

"Sure, yeah, I see that."

I ask again, amid all the chaos, how his life had improved since his supposed awakening on Mount Palomar.

"My life was incredibly better. I was surfing, sailing, living life. All this other stuff was just, you know...I'm not in San Quentin," he says. "That was the healthiest and clearest time of my life."

Then, he met Diane Pinnix.

Pinnix was a tall, beautiful girl from Beach Haven, New Jersey, who came of age when Gidget sparked a national surf-culture craze. It's not surprising that a headstrong girl from New Jersey would catch the bug, and she became one of the original East Coast surfer girls. Legend has it that when Pinnix decided she wanted to get away from New Jersey, she entered a beauty contest on a whim. First prize was a luggage set and a trip to Hawaii. Pinnix, then 18, won.

Pinnix's mother, Lois, still lives in Beach Haven. When I call her, she has a simple explanation for her daughter's flight to Hawaii and her subsequent plight. "It was the times, it was the times. She wanted to spread her wings. Drugs were a part of the thing, but I was very naïve. I was a young mother and in the dark."

Padilla first ran into Pinnix when he went with a friend looking to score some coke from a local kingpin.

Pinnix was the kingpin's girlfriend. "I looked at Diane and she looked at me and the attraction was so strong," Padilla recalls. "That was it."

He started making a point of showing up wherever Pinnix was.

"We're traveling in the same pack and we started talking and flirting," says Padilla. "It came to the point of ridiculousness...and my own friends were saying, 'Why don't you just fuck her and get it over with?' But that wasn't it, you know. I wanted her. It was an obsession. A massive ego trip, for sure, but at the same time there was an attraction unlike anything I'd ever experienced before."

By all accounts, Diane Pinnix, a stunning surfer girl/gun moll, with a nice cutback and blond hair to her ass, was the sort of woman who could make a man do things he hadn't bargained for.

"One day, we're getting ready to paddle out, waxing our boards, and I say, 'So, you want to be my old lady?' And she says, 'You have a wife and kids.' And I say, 'Okay.' I was willing to let it go right there and I start to paddle out and she says, 'But wait a minute.' And that was it. It was all over. And that's pretty much when I lost my mind."

Pinnix was a committed party girl, and Padilla started doing coke and drinking excessively to keep up. After getting iced out of a big deal by a new crew on Maui who claimed Brotherhood status, Padilla decided to go out on his own. He made connections in Colombia and was on his way to becoming a coke smuggler.

"There was no more spiritual warrior," he says. "This was a guy on his way to hell. I had gone against everything that was precious to me. I left my wife and kids. I wasn't living the spiritual life I was back when we had the church and it was the Brotherhood of Eternal Love."

"Why did you do it?" I ask.

"Money. For Diane and me. I probably knew deep inside that if I didn't have enough money and coke, that she wouldn't stay with me...whether that's true or not, I'll never know. The bottom line is I became a coke addict, plain and simple."

Paradise Lost

A FEW DAYS BEFORE he's supposed to arrive at Peru's Gran Azul with Richard Brewer and James Thomason, Eddie Padilla is thousands of miles away on a beach in Tahiti. He sits and looks out at the ocean, contemplating how far things have degenerated, both for him and for the Brotherhood. He thinks about the messages of love, the utopian ideals, and the notion that they could change the world. All that is gone. What is left are the 1970s in all their nihilistic glory. The drugs, money, women, and warring, spiritual or otherwise, are taking their toll, and damn if he isn't feeling beat already at just 30.

In Tahiti, Padilla at last finds the island paradise that eluded him in Maui. And with Pinnix set up in style on the mainland, it's a rare moment of peace in his increasingly out-of-control life. He wants more of that.

"It was incredible," he says. "The best surfing and living, the best food on the planet. While I was in Tahiti, I really got sober and all of the sudden, I was looking at what I'd been doing and I didn't want to go back."

Smuggling coke isn't about peace and love; it's about money, greed, and power. He suddenly sees his life as a betrayal of his ideals, and he wants out. Feeling something like a premonition, Padilla decides that this next trip to Peru will be his last. Decades later, he remembers the conversation he had with a friend on that Tahitian beach.

"She says to me, 'What are you doing, how did you get into coke?' And I just look at her and say, 'I don't even know, but I know right now that I don't want to go back there." He's trapped, though. Too much money has already been invested in the deal. "I'm totally responsible and there's a whole bunch of people involved. But I'll be back,' I told her. That was the plan. 'I'll be back.'" He books a return flight to Tahiti. He never makes it.

Back at the Gran Azul, just hours before Padilla and his crew are scheduled to leave the country, quasi-military police agents storm the bungalow. One slams Padilla to the floor, another kicks Brewer in the stomach, and quickly Padilla, Brewer, and Thomason are all in cuffs.

"At least 10 or 12 of them come in through the door and they all have guns drawn. I didn't have a chance," says Padilla.

A man they will come to know as Sergeant Delgado takes a hollow-point bullet from his gun, starts tapping it against Thomason's chest, and says, "Tell me everything."

In some ways, Padilla is a victim of his own success. While he's been hopping between Hawaii, Tahiti, Colombia, and Peru building his résumé as a coke-smuggling pirate, Richard Nixon has been marshaling his forces for the soon-to-be declared War on Drugs. It's the beginning of the national hysteria that will see Nixon pronounce the fugitive Timothy Leary "the most dangerous man in America," and today has more than 2.3 million Americans in prison, a vast majority of them for drug offenses.

Nixon's strategy in the drug war is announced with his Reorganization Plan No. 2. It calls for the consolidation of the government's various drug-fighting bureaucracies into the Drug Enforcement Agency. The DEA is formed, at least in part, to do something with Nixon's boner for the Brotherhood's members and associates, dubbed "the hippie mafia" in a 1972 *Rolling Stone* article. Congress holds months of hearings on the need for this new agency in the spring and summer of 1973. One is titled "Hashish Smuggling and Passport Fraud, The Brotherhood of Eternal Love."

After the DEA starts putting too much heat on his Colombian connections, Padilla sets up shop in Peru. But the DEA's budget shoots up from $75 to $141 million between 1973 and 1975, and Peru, the world's largest cocaine-producing country at the time, quickly becomes a client state in the drug war. Some of that DEA money goes to fund and train the notorious Peruvian Investigative Police, or PIP (now called the Peruvian National Police). The PIP operates with near immunity and is expected to get results in the war on drugs.

Sergeant Delgado heads the force. A mean-spirited thug with dead, black eyes, he is one of the most powerful men in Peru. An Interpol agent known as Rubio is with Delgado.

Before the DEA put Peru in its crosshairs, Padilla would have been able to buy out of the arrest. Naturally, his first reaction is to offer up the $58,000 in cash he has with him.

"Don't worry," he remembers Rubio telling him. "Don't say anything about this and when we get to the police station, we'll work something out."

The three Americans are taken to the notorious PIP headquarters, known as the Pink Panther, a pink mansion that the police confiscated (they are rumored to have executed the owners). With no tradition of case building, Peruvian detective work at the time pretty much consists of coerced confessions and snitching.

The PIP is famously brutal. During the two weeks the guys are held at Pink Panther, Padilla says they're surrounded by the sounds of women being raped and men being tortured.

The country's shaky institutions are rife with corruption, and there is little to no history in Peruvian jurisprudence of due process or jury trials. Prisoners wait for years to have their cases heard before a three-judge tribunal, only to see their fates determined in a matter of minutes. Their arrest immediately throws Padilla, Brewer, and Thomason into this Kafkaesque quagmire.

In a 1982 *Life* magazine story that details the horrors of the Peruvian prison system, and two men who tried to escape it, a survivor tells of his time in the Pink Panther.

"My god, I was in tears after they went at me," Robert B. Holland, a Special Forces Vietnam vet recounts. "I did a couple things in 'Nam I might go to hell for. But Peru was a whole new day."

When their escape attempt fails, the two primary subjects of the *Life* story commit suicide by overdosing on sleeping pills. In a final letter to his wife, one of the men, David Treacly, writes, "I have no confidence in either their concept of justice, their methods of interrogation and inconceivable brutality, or in the bumbling incompetence and indifference of our embassy...So, I'm going out tonight...John not only accepts and understands, but has decided he wants to go with me...Given the circumstances, I cannot think of anyone I'd rather go with."

In this atmosphere of brutality and corruption, Padilla and his friends strike a deal with Delgado. The deal is Delgado will keep the money and the cocaine, probably to resell, and Padilla, Brewer and Thomason will say nothing to the DEA about the drugs or cash—it's their only leverage. When they go to trial, Delgado is supposed to testify that he never saw the coke on display until he opened a black travel bag. The story will be that a jealous Fastie planted the bag as revenge for Padilla flirting with his girlfriend. With Delgado's testimony, they are assured, they will be home in six months. In the meantime, though they will have to go to San Juan de Lurigancho prison.

"'Don't worry,'" Padilla remembers being told. "'You'll be out in four to six months. And the prison is nice. There's basketball, soccer, a great pool.'"

La Casa del Diablo

THERE ARE, OF COURSE, no pools or athletic facilities at Lurigancho. There aren't even working toilets. Built in the 1960s to house 1,500 inmates, Lurigancho has more than 6,000 by the time Padilla is processed. (Today some estimates put the number of prisoners there at more than 10,000.) Going in, though, Padilla still has an outlaw's cocky sense of exemption. Besides, he's paid off his captors.

"It's just like an adventure," he remembers thinking. "I'd been in prison. I'd been in jails."

That feeling doesn't last long. Padilla says the conditions are "like a dog kennel." Food is a bowl of rice a day—with beans on the lucky days. "People starved to death."

The running water, when it runs, comes from a community pump, which the prison often shuts down to clean rats out of the pipes. The water is full of worms and bacteria. Everybody has dysentery.

"If you got the runs, you better find a plug, because everybody's going to be real pissed if you shit in a cell," he says. "I had dysentery every day."

The toilet, a hole in the ground that prisoners line up to use, seems designed to make the most of this affliction. It constantly overflows with shit and piss so the prisoners resort to relieving themselves onto an ever-growing mound of feces.

"The whole place smells like shit," says Padilla.

The American prisoners and some other expats live together in the same cellblock, a more modern facility built off the big hall, which is a real-world incarnation of Dante's Inferno, where murderers, rapists and the destitute teem together in a bazaar of daily strife. There, Padilla says, you see people starving, drowning in tuberculosis, being beaten and stabbed to death.

Padilla's description of the prison is in keeping with interviews that a former human rights activist, who is familiar with Lurigancho, has conducted for this story with past and present volunteers in Lima. All have requested anonymity.

One volunteer says the guards have surrendered the place to the prisoners. Everything from cots to a spot in a cell must be purchased. Those with no resources are left to wander the outskirts of the cellblocks, relying on handouts and picking through garbage like zombies.

Another volunteer, who worked at Lurigancho when Padilla was imprisoned there, says, "There were always ugly things…We felt very powerless against the mistreatment." She says there are constant fights between prison pavilions, wars between inmates and murders tacitly sanctioned by the guards, who are often paid off to look the other way.

The Pirate of Penance

As it becomes increasingly clear that his chances of getting out quickly are about as good as going for a swim in the pool, Padilla's days are given over to survival, often in a haze of pasta, a particularly toxic paste form of cocaine smuggled into the prison and sold by well-connected inmates. Nights are filled with the sounds of screaming and snoring, and the insane beating of drums from the big hall.

Padilla doesn't hesitate when asked to describe the worst thing he witnessed.

"Watching a whole cell block get killed," he says. "Watching a .50 caliber machine gun, at least a dozen rifles and a half dozen pistols…until no one is moving. And then, they open up the door and storm it. They shoot everybody."

The massacre comes, Padilla says, after a handful of prisoners take some guards hostage and demanded better conditions. The inmates release the guards when the prison warden agrees to their demands. The next day, the military comes in and shoots the place up. Padilla believes hundreds of inmates are killed in the attack.

On another occasion, Padilla says confused guards open fire on prisoners returning on a bus from court, killing dozens. "One of the [wounded] guys was in our cell block. He came up to the cell block just covered in blood."

The prison's atrocities mostly escape international attention until December 1983, when police shoot and kill a Chicago nun being held hostage by prisoners attempting to flee. Eight prisoners are also killed. Lurigancho gains further notoriety when, in July 1986, police kill anywhere from 124 to 280 (accounts vary) rioting members of the Sendero Luminosa, or Shining Path, Marxist guerillas incarcerated at Lurigancho.

Lurigancho's tableau of evils, both epic and banal, earn the prison the name La Casa del Diablo, the house of the devil. It remains a hellish place; the Associated Press reports that two people a day still die in Lurigancho from violence or illness.

Despite being imprisoned in the midst of this, Padilla doesn't slip into despair. Not immediately. It takes something more potent. It takes Diane Pinnix.

Femme Fatale

QUICKLY AFTER THE ARRESTS, Diane Pinnix flies down to Lima, ostensibly to aid and abet Padilla's release. Before long, though, Peru's attractions prove irresistible and she starts partying. Padilla worries she'll get in trouble, the last thing he needs. He decides he has to get out of Lurigancho fast. His chance comes with a Colombian coke dealer named Jimmy, another inmate who's been supplying pasta for Padilla, Brewer, Thomason and other cellies to smoke.

During a delivery one day, Jimmy tells the guys how he plans to escape Lurigancho. Jimmy's lawyer will bribe clerks to get him called to court, but his name will be left off the judge's docket. At the end of the day, in the chaos of transferring prisoners, Jimmy's lawyers will hand the soldiers in charge counterfeit documents saying the judge has ordered his immediate release. If the plan works, it's decided that Pinnix will give Jimmy what's left of Padilla's money to set up the same deal.

But Jimmy takes Padilla's money and never returns to Lurigancho. Nor does Pinnix. Word filters back through the prison grapevine that Diane has been seen on the streets of Lima holding hands and kissing someone who fits the description of Jimmy.

Padilla spirals into a rage. He thinks only of revenge. To exact it, he seeks out a violent man known as Pelone, the boss of a neighboring prison cell. Through Pelone, Padilla orders a hit on Jimmy, an expensive proposition for which he has no money. Padilla promises to pay up when Pelone's pistolero cousin brings back Jimmy's finger, the traditional token of a successful hit. Padilla knows that with no money, it might be his life he pays with, but he wants Jimmy dead. In the meantime, he needs pasta to numb his pain. Pelone is more than happy to supply on credit.

Months go by with no success in the hit and Padilla falls deeper into despair. In the back of his mind is an inescapable fact: the pain he is feeling is the same pain he caused his wife, Eileen, and his kids, when he walked out on them for Pinnix. His spirit breaks.

"I gave up because of Diane. Not just because of Diane, but because I was betrayed and that brought on all the betrayal I gave Eileen, my kids. My dedication to God, you know it was just gone. I turned my back and betrayed all of it. Betrayed my soul."

Padilla rarely leaves his bunk. He interrupts his sleep and sobbing only to smoke pasta. When the pasta runs out, he turns to pills. In his bunk, he dreams of surfing, and of Tahiti and Maui. He gives up his battle with dysentery.

"That's how I got. I became absolutely disgusting. I stunk. I reeked," Padilla says. "Richard and James are pretty sure I'm going to die."

His death seems assured one night when Padilla turns over in his bunk and sees Pelone wearing a leather jacket zipped to the top. Padilla's cellmates aren't around and Pelone has seized the opportunity to come calling for his debts. Pelone pulls a long shank from under his jacket and comes at Padilla. Using his boxing skills, Padilla manages to dodge the first couple of stabs, but Pelone is skilled with a blade, and Padilla soon finds himself staring defenselessly at a shank aimed for his midsection. Just as Pelone is about to thrust, one of Padilla's cellies miraculously appears and grabs Pelone's shoulder before he can stab. The opening gives Padilla enough time to throw a left cross into Pelone's nose, breaking it, he says. They tumble to the floor and by then a group of Padilla's cellmates storm in and disarm Pelone. The guy who has saved Padilla pays off the $400 debt to Pelone—a prison fortune—on the condition that Padilla gets his shit together.

In order to survive, Padilla realizes he needs to get back to some idea of God, to find a way to live beyond his fear. He quits doing drugs and starts meditating. He trains in boxing again. But his biggest challenge is still beyond him: the big hall. If he can master that, he thinks, he can master his fear. But he's not ready. He needs something more than God to hold onto. For Padilla, that could only be a woman.

One day during visitation, a young, indigenous woman named Zoila catches Padilla's eye. Padilla sees something in her that he hasn't seen in what seems like forever.

"She was the purest, most wonderful thing that could happen to me," he says. "She was like a gift from God."

The note Padilla throws down to Zoila from his cellblock feels like a life preserver. When someone hands her the note and points to Padilla, she smiles and waves. After that, she becomes Padilla's regular visitor and something like a love affair unfolds.

"She helped me heal so much in the prison. That was grace. I crack when I think about that experience." And he actually does crack when he tells this story, reinforcing my suspicion that beneath the surface of every tough guy is a heartbroken mama's boy.

With his dignity on the mend, Padilla knows there's something he must still do to be worthy of Zoila. After jumping rope one day, he decides it's time. He asks a prison guard to open the door protecting his cellblock from the big hall. The guard smiles contemptuously and opens the door.

Padilla walks through the maze. He sees men lifting a dead body out of the way. Blood from tuberculosis stains the floors like abstract art. His journey through the hall is quick, but he survives. Before long, he goes back again, this time under the guidance of a man named Chivo, a leader in this strange netherworld of Lurigancho. After a while, Padilla is allowed to pass the big hall with immunity. Something has changed.

Escape

MORE THAN THREE YEARS after they were taken to Lurigancho, Padilla, Brewer, and Thomason finally have their day before the tribunal. As a matter of course, the Peruvian Supreme Court reviews cases after the tribunal renders its verdict—but guilty verdicts are rarely overturned. The tribunal will be the trio's biggest test. They have a couple of things working for them. First is Zoila, who packs the courtroom with family and friends. They also manage to secure the services of a sympathetic translator, without which they wouldn't stand a chance.

On the stand, all three stick to the story: Fastie planted the coke in their room and nobody saw it until

Delgado opened the black travel bag. Thomason is just a friend who happened to be there. The key witness will be Delgado. Nobody knows whether he'll keep his bargain to back up the tale.

When Delgado walks into the courtroom, eyes as black and dead as ever, a visceral terror shoots through Padilla's body. But Delgado takes the stand and, to Padilla's surprise, gives a brief statement corroborating their account of the arrest. The tribunal has little choice but to render absuelto in all three cases—absolved. It's the first good news in years.

That evening, Padilla and Brewer are taken to a hotel while Thomason is held back at a holding pen in the Lima neighborhood of Pueblo Libre. He has draft-dodging issues. Jimmy Carter had pardoned all draft dodgers while the men were in prison, but that means little to the Peruvian authorities. There's no telling how long or how much money it will take to sort this out. The longer it takes, the more likely it is that Padilla's decade-old San Francisco conviction will turn up like an albatross around his neck.

There are other complications. Padilla and Brewer have recently been implicated in the arrest of a former associate who Jimmy and Pinnix tricked into doing a coke deal with them by saying the proceeds would go to help spring the guys. If that case makes it to court before they're free, they are done for sure. Padilla and Brewer have to decide whether to make a break for it or wait for Thomason. They stay.

When Padilla and Brewer return to Pueblo Libre the next day, bad news awaits. The Supreme Court will be reviewing the case. Their lawyer mentions Padilla's "FBI problems." Freedom is near, they're told, but it'll take money. Padilla, Brewer and Thomason are put in a cell at the Pueblo Libre jail to await the Supreme Court's review.

Facing more than 20 years each should their verdicts be overturned, Padilla and Brewer know a return to Lurigancho is certain death. They start working on an escape plan. Thomason, facing just three years, wants no part of it.

Months go by in Pueblo Libre while Padilla and Brewer prepare for a moment that might never come. They ask an Episcopalian reverend, an Englishman who has started visiting them in Lurigancho, to bring them towels, maps of the city and the Amazon wilderness beyond it. He also brings them money. They scope out the jail and determine they can get over a wall on the roof if given a chance. They make an effort to befriend their jailers, to show they pose no threat. Brewer swipes a serving spoon and hides it in his shoe.

In June of 1978, soccer-mad Peru makes an unlikely run through the first round of the World Cup being held in neighboring Argentina. During Peru's match against Scotland to advance to the second round, the atmosphere in Lima is ecstatic, even in the jail. The guards bring in beer and booze and good food, which they share with the Americans. They leave the jail cell open believing the only way out is past them since the steel door leading to the roof is spring-locked.

The partying gets more intense as the game plays. The guards are rapt. Brewer wakes up Padilla, who is sleeping off some whiskey. It's time to go, he says. Padilla says he's ready if Brewer can spring the lock to the steel door. They are worried about the loud noise the lock makes when it releases. Then, something incredible happens just as Richards jams the spoon into the lock and springs the steel door open: Peru scores! It's pandemonium in the jail. Nobody hears the door, or them as they scurry up the stairs and onto the roof.

On the roof, Padilla and Brewer scale the wall and look up at the barbed-wire-topped chain link fence. They throw towels over the barbs and hoist themselves up and over onto the freedom side of the two-story wall. They'll have to jump down onto another rooftop, scramble to the jail's outside wall and scale that to get to the street. Their plan is to split up and reconvene at the reverend's church in Miraflores.

At the outside wall, Brewer urges Padilla to jump. Padilla hesitates and in a flash, Brewer is hurtling down into a patch of light, landing hard on the ground below. Brewer grabs a ladder propped against a shack and hauls it over to the outer wall. Padilla finally jumps into the dark and lands with a thud on a pile of lumber. Pain immediately shoots through his body. He tries to stand but crumples. His ankle swells up immediately. His heel is broken. Padilla crawls and hops to the ladder and pulls himself up, the lower half of his body dead weight. He makes it to the top of the second wall and lets himself fall to the ground.

Out in the street, Brewer tries desperately to hail a cab. Padilla calls to him. Seconds go by like hours. Finally, Brewer sees him and comes racing back, asking what the fuck happened; how did he get so dirty? Padilla tells him he can't walk. Brewer races back and hoists Padilla over his shoulder, carrying him across the street into the shelter of an alley. He flags down a car and they make their way to the reverend's church in Miraflores.

Thirty-one years later, the same reverend answers a call at his home in the English countryside. Retired for 20 years, he asks that his name not be disclosed while he recalls for me the night the two men he'd been visiting in prison for months showed up at his door.

"It was unexpected. One of them had broken a bone in his heel and was having a tough time getting around. I think there was a lot of adrenaline going," the reverend says with typical English understatement. "We gave them some food and clothing and moved them onto a contact they had…The police came around to find out what part I had in their escape and held my passport for awhile."

Padilla and Brewer next enlist the cousin of an inmate Padilla befriended in Lurigancho. He is a travel guide with the Peruvian tourism industry with access to an underground network of friends and relatives. The guide's family, like many others, has suffered at the hands of Delgado and the PIP as the war on drugs has conflated with political persecution and the other abuses you'd expect in a police state.

A domestic flight, arranged through a sympathetic airline worker, takes Padilla and Brewer to the Amazon River city of Iquitos. They stay for weeks at the lodge of a man who used be a PIP agent, but quit over the agency's brutal practices. There, the natural beauty of the Amazon and their first taste of real freedom bring Padilla and Brewer to tears. The hum of jungle birds and the roar of big cats at night almost drown out the sounds of snoring, screaming and drumming at Lurigancho, still echoing in their heads. Padilla thinks of Zoila. He feels she's out there in her village somewhere in the Amazon wilderness. It breaks his heart that he'll never be able to thank her enough.

After a close call with PIP agents in Iquitos, Padilla and Brewer acquire forged documents identifying the two as Peruvians going to visit family in Colombia.

They fly to the Colombian border town of Leticia and reach a hotel owned by an expat. Padilla calls his ex-wife Eileen and she sends money on the next flight in. They pay off the Colombian equivalent of the PIP to write a temporary visa that gives them 72 hours to get out of the country or be arrested.

During their brief stay at the hotel, Padilla and Brewer befriend a group of college kids. One of them is a Colombian girl who rooms with Caroline Kennedy at Radcliffe. The friendship pays off in Bogota, the girl's hometown, when Padilla and Brewer can't get a hotel room there because they have no passports. They're terrified they've come all this way only to get picked up for being indigent. Then, Padilla remembers he has the girl's phone number. Their last night in South America is spent at the penthouse home of Caroline Kennedy's college roommate. The next day they get a flight to Mexico City and then it's on to LAX.

Home.

As they exit the airport through a stream of people, Padilla puts his hand on Brewer's shoulder and they stop for a minute. Padilla looks uncertainly at Brewer and his look is returned. Until now, they've known what they were running to. Now that they're here, they both realize the hardest part comes next.

Epilogue

TWELVE YEARS AFTER SHE entered Mystic Arts World, Lorey Smith has grown into a woman already disappointed by marriage. She is cautious and jaded. To help get her out of her funk, Smith's sister suggests she come down to Corona del Mar for a party. A friend of her uncle's is going to be there and he can show her a good time. She hesitates, but when her sister tells her that the guy used to be in the Brotherhood, she softens.

"I had this thought, okay, he's not anybody's who's going to harm me," Smith says. "I felt safe. So, I said, 'I'll come down.'"

The party is in full howl when Smith arrives. Every time she turns around, she bumps into her uncle's friend. His name is Eddie.

"He was following me all over the house. I thought, 'What is up with this guy?' My sister would say, 'Oh, he's fine. He's fine.' I didn't know everybody had been partying for the last three weeks. She left that part out."

Little by little, Smith settles in. She and Eddie start talking. They dance, despite Eddie's obvious limp. Two days turn into four. Smith is compelled by this guy, but unsure. He seems haunted, hunted even.

"I didn't know he was blasted on coke and had drank who knows how much by the time I got there—I just knew something was wrong. But once we actually started talking, and it did take a couple of days, then, I was like, 'Wow, what's his story? All this pain.'"

At some point during the partying, Smith loses track of Eddie. "All of a sudden, I heard this noise, like moaning, like pain and moaning. And I opened the front door and he's out on the lawn, by this bush...just in this really, really bad place.

"I tried to get him to talk a little bit about it, and he did, and he shared enough with me sitting on the grass that one particular night that I was just...fascinated that he was even sitting there having been through what he'd been through."

Over time Eddie tells Smith more and more about what he's been through, about Lurigancho, a prison in Peru known as La Casa del Diablo. About how he escaped with his life, but wasn't sure about his soul.

185

"I was like, 'Whoa, you're kidding, you should write a book.'"

Smith tells this story at a small kitchen table in her small condo in Santa Rosa, California. It's the middle of December and a relentless, cold rain has been pounding for days. Smith serves up some sandwiches as she talks. The oven is on for heat.

Padilla comes in from the living room when he hears us talking about how he and Lorey met in Corona del Mar. "I wasn't fit for polite company," he jokes. Lucky for him, Smith wasn't too polite and they kept seeing each other. It didn't take them long to figure out they'd met before, when a wide-eyed 12-year-old handed a handsome man a handmade necklace and that man accepted it with a smile.

Eddie Padilla and Lorey Smith have been together since 1981. It's one of the few happy endings in this story.

Jimmy the dealer and Diane Pinnix stayed together until Jimmy beat her up badly, putting her in the hospital. Jimmy briefly went to to jail before he bailed out and fled to Colombia. He was eventually gunned down in the street.

Diane Pinnix died a junkie's death seven years ago in Jamaica. "The unfortunate thing is she died alone," says her mother. "She was beautiful when she was younger."

Drugs and alcohol continued to dictate the life of James Thomason, the man Padilla says did his time with more courage and grace than anyone else. I visit Thomason at the Rescue Mission in Tustin. His shoulder bears a tattoo that reads Lurigancho 75-78. His hard life has punched in his face.

When I ask about his time in prison, he says. "I don't know what hell is, but Lurigancho is as close as I can think of."

Thomason tells me of the dysentery, the filth, the flies, people getting stabbed, and Padilla's descent into despair after Pinnix betrayed him with Jimmy.

"That's when he really lost it," says James. "He was a lowly person in that Peruvian prison and nobody cared. He wasn't Eddie Padilla anymore. He was a prisoner."

When I ask about the massacre, Thomason's eyes go distant and his galloping speech slows to a near-halt. "They came in with rifles and the machine gun," he says.

These days Thomason dreams of being able to afford an apartment by the beach, watch TV, drink a few beers, and live out his days. Though he seems a poster boy for Post-Traumatic Stress Disorder, he admits to no lasting ill effects from his time in Lurigancho. It occurs to me that surviving Lurigancho is both the worst thing that ever happened to him and his greatest accomplishment.

Richard Brewer died a little more than two years ago. Upon his return from Peru, he quickly went back to his old ways. But he never lost his outlaw's code of honor. At Brewer's memorial, friends gathered to paddle his ashes out to sea. Afterward, they had a bonfire on the beach. Everybody had stories to tell, but Padilla had the story.

"I said, 'You guys know the story...but what you guys probably don't know is, he came back for me. We had agreed to go our different ways. He knew I wasn't going to be able to walk, and he came back for me."

We had just finished watching a documentary on Lurigancho and sifting through a kaleidoscope of memories—some better than others—when Padilla relates this. It's late in a long day and he starts sobbing.

"All those guys called themselves the Brotherhood for so long, but you know what? Richard was a real brother. He came back for me. He carried me...I always thought that if anybody came back for anybody, it would be me coming back for them."

As Padilla says this, embarrassed by his tears, it feels like a fresh revelation. In some ways, I think the simple fact that he wasn't the rescuer but the one who was rescued may have turned out to be the god Eddie Padilla was looking for his entire life—the ego break that neither acid, the Brotherhood or his misguided idea of freedom could provide. Perhaps this newfound humility allowed him to admit, where others didn't, that Lurigancho broke him. Maybe it gave him the strength to ask for help and to claw his way back after descending into a deadly alcoholism and drug addiction, fueled by his crippled leg and fractured psyche.

At death's door, and living on the streets, Padilla finally made it into rehab and set about on the long road back to recovery. He went to AA meetings and therapy for years. He managed to earn a degree in drug and alcohol counseling, and has made a career of working with juveniles and cons. He hopes his memoir will be useful in his work, both as a cautionary tale and a story of redemption. In the end, he just might have earned the narrative he seeks.

"You know when they first started telling me about the Brotherhood, that seems like what it was all about—it was people helping people," says Padilla's brother Dennis, who was instrumental in helping Padilla stay sober in those first crucial years of recovery. "It wasn't about money and things and I think that's where he's at today."

Sergeant Delgado was killed in a shootout when a friend of one of the doomed guys in the *Life* article tried to bust them out. According to the report, it took 11 rounds to bring him down.

BABY KILLER

Richard Lange

2011 Best American Mystery Stories

Pᴜᴘᴘᴇᴛ sʜᴏᴏᴛɪɴɢ ᴛʜᴀᴛ ʙᴀʙʏ comes into my head again, like a match flaring in the dark, this time while I'm wiping down the steam tables after the breakfast rush at the hospital.

Julio steps up behind me with a vat of scrambled eggs, and I flinch like he's some kind of monster.

"Que pasa?" he asks as he squeezes by me to drop the vat into its slot.

"Nothing, guapo. You startled me is all."

I was coming back from the park and saw it all. Someone yelled something stupid from a passing car, Puppet pulled a gun and fired. The bullet missed the car and hit little Antonio instead, two years old, playing on the steps of the apartment building where he lived with his parents. Puppet tossed the gun to one of his homies, Cheeks, and took off running. He shot that baby, and now he's going to get away with it, you watch.

Dr. Wu slides her tray over and asks for pancakes. She looks at me funny through her thick glasses. These days everybody can tell what I'm thinking. My heart is pounding, and my hand is cold when I raise it to my forehead.

"How's your family, Blanca?" Dr. Wu asks.

"Fine, Doctor, fine," I say. I straighten up and wipe my face with a towel, give her a big smile. "Angela graduated from Northridge in June and is working at an insurance company, Manuel is still selling cars, and Lorena is staying with me for a while, her and her daughter, Brianna. We're all doing great."

"You're lucky to have your children close by," Dr. Wu says.

"I sure am," I reply.

I walk back into the kitchen. It's so hot in there, you start sweating as soon as the doors swing shut behind you. Josefina is flirting with the cooks again. That girl spends half her shift back here when she should be up front, working the line. She's fresh from Guatemala, barely speaks English, but still she reminds me of myself when I was young, more than my daughters ever did. It's the old-fashioned jokes she tells, the way she blushes when the doctors or security guards talk to her.

"Josefina," I say. "Maple was looking for you. Andale if you don't want to get in trouble."

"Gracias, señora," she replies. She grabs a tray of hash browns and pushes through the doors into the cafeteria.

"Que buena percha," says one of the cooks, watching her go.

"Hey, payaso," I say, "is that how you talk about ladies?"

"Lo siento, Mamá."

Lots of the boys who work here call me Mamá. Many of them are far from home, and I do my best to teach them a little about how it goes in this country, to show them some kindness.

AT 12 I CLOCK out and walk to the bus stop with Irma, a Filipina I've known forever. Me and Manuel Senior went to Vegas with her and her husband once, and when Manuel died she stayed with me for a few days, cooking and cleaning up after the visitors. Now her own Ray isn't doing too good. Diabetes.

"What's this heat?" she says, fanning herself with a newspaper.

"It's supposed to last another week."

"It makes me so lazy."

Irma and I share the shade from her umbrella. There's a bench under the bus shelter, but a crazy man dressed in rags is sprawled on it, spitting nonsense.

"They're talking about taking off Ray's leg," Irma says.

"Oh, honey," I say.

"Next month, looks like."

"I'll pray for you."

I like Ray. Lots of men won't dance, but he will. Every year at the hospital Christmas party he asks me at least once. "Ready to rock 'n' roll?" he says.

My eyes sting from all the crap in the air. A frazzled pigeon lands and pecks at a smear in the gutter. Another swoops down to join it, then three or four smaller birds. The bus almost hits them when it pulls up. Irma and I get a seat in front. The driver has a fan that blows right on us.

"I heard about the baby that got killed near you yesterday," Irma says.

I'm staring up at a commercial for a new type of mop on the bus's TV, thinking about how to reply. I want to tell Irma what I saw, share the fear and sorrow that have been dogging me, but I can't. I've got to keep it to myself.

"Wasn't that awful?" I say.

"And they haven't caught who did it yet?" Irma asks.

I shake my head. No.

I'm not the only one who knows it was Puppet, but everybody's scared to say because Puppet's in Temple Street, and if you piss off Temple Street, your house gets

193

burned down or your car gets stolen or you get jumped walking to the store. When it comes to the gangs, you take care of yours and let others take care of theirs.

There's no forgiveness for that, for none of us coming forward, but I hope—I think we all hope—that if God really does watch everything, he'll understand and have mercy on us.

Walking home from my stop, I pass where little Antonio was shot. The news is there filming the candles and flowers and stuffed animals laid out on the steps of the building, and there's a poster of the baby, too, with "RIP Our Little Angel" written on it. The pretty girl holding the microphone says something about grief-stricken parents as I go by, but she doesn't look like she's been sad a day in her life.

THIS WAS A PRETTY nice block when we first moved onto it. Half apartments, half houses, families mostly. A plumber lived across the street, a fireman, a couple of teachers. The gangs were here, too, but they were just little punks back then, and nobody was too afraid of them. One stole Manuel Junior's bike once, and his parents made him bring it back and mow our lawn all summer.

But then the good people started buying newer, bigger houses in the suburbs, and the bad people took over. Dopers and gangsters and thieves. We heard gunshots at night, and police helicopters hovered overhead with their searchlights on. There was graffiti everywhere, even on the tree trunks.

Manuel was thinking about us going somewhere quieter right before he died, and now Manuel Junior is always trying to get me to move out to Lancaster, where he and Trina and the kids live. He worries about me being alone. But I'm not going to leave.

This is my little place. Three bedrooms, two bathrooms, a nice, big backyard. It's plain to look at, but all my memories are here. We added the dining room and patio ourselves, we laid the tile, we planted the fruit trees and watched them grow. I stand in the kitchen sometimes, and twenty-five years will fall away like nothing as I think of my babies' kisses, my husband's touch. No, I'm not going to go. "Just bury me out back when I keel over," I tell Manuel Junior.

Brianna is on the couch watching TV when I come in, two fans going and all the windows open. This is how she spends her days now that school's out. She's wearing hardly anything. Hoochie-mama shorts and a tank top I can see her titties through. She's fourteen, and everything Grandma says makes her roll her eyes or giggle into her hand. All of a sudden I'm stupid to her.

"You have to get air conditioning," she whines. "I'm dying."

"It's not that bad," I say. "I'll make some lemonade."

I head into the kitchen.

"Where's your mom?" I ask.

"Shopping," Brianna says without looking away from the TV. Some music and dancing show.

"Oh, yeah? How's she shopping with no money?"

"Why don't you ask her?" Brianna snaps.

The two of them have been staying with me ever since Lorena's husband, Charlie, walked out on her a few months ago. Lorena is supposed to be saving money and looking for a job, but all she's doing is partying with old high school friends—most of them divorced now, too—and playing around on her computer, sending notes to men she's never met.

I drop my purse on the kitchen table and get a Diet Coke from the refrigerator. The back door is wide open.

This gets my attention because I always keep it locked since we got robbed last time.

"Why's the door like this?" I call into the living room.

There's a short pause, then Brianna says, "Because it's hot in here."

I notice a cigarette smoldering on the back step. And what's that on the grass? A Budweiser can, enough beer to slosh still in it. Somebody's been up to something.

I carry the cigarette and beer can into the living room. Lorena doesn't want me hollering at Brianna anymore, so I keep my cool when I say, "Your boyfriend left something behind."

Brianna makes a face like I'm crazy. "What are you talking about?"

I shake the beer can at her. "Nobody's supposed to be over here unless me or your mom are around."

"Nobody was."

"So this garbage is yours then? You're smoking? Drinking?"

Brianna doesn't answer.

"He barely got away, right?" I say. "You guys heard me coming, and off he went."

"Leave me alone," Brianna says. She buries her face in a pillow.

"I don't care how old you are, I'm calling a babysitter tomorrow," I say. I can't have her disrespecting my house. Disrespecting me.

"Please," Brianna yells. "Just shut up."

I yell back. I can't help it. "Get in your room," I say. "And I don't want to see you again until you can talk right to me."

Brianna runs to the bedroom that she and her mom have been sharing. She slams the door. The house is suddenly quiet, even with the TV on, even with the windows open. The cigarette is still burning, so I stub it in the kitchen sink. The truth is, I'm more afraid for Brianna than mad at her. These young girls fall so deeply in love, they sometimes drown in it.

I CHANGE OUT OF my work clothes into a housedress, put on my flip-flops. Out back, I water the garden, then get the sprinkler going on the grass. Rudolfo, my neighbor, is working in the shop behind his house. The screech of his saw rips into the stillness of the afternoon, and I smile when I think of his rough hands and emerald eyes. There's nothing wrong with that. Manuel has been gone for three years.

I make myself a tuna sandwich and one for Brianna, plus the lemonade I promised. She's asleep when I take the snack to the bedroom. Probably faking it, but I'm done fighting for today. I eat in front of the TV, put on one of my cooking shows.

A knock at the front door startles me. I go over and press my eye to the peephole. There on the porch is a fat white man with a sweaty, bald head and a walrus mustache. When I ask who he is, he backs up, looks right at the hole and says, "Detective Rayburn, LAPD." I should have known, that coat and tie in this heat.

I get a little nervous. No cop ever brought good news. The detective smiles when I open the door.

"Good afternoon," he says. "I'm sorry to bother you, but I'm here about the boy who was killed Sunday, down at 1238?"

His eyes meet mine, and he tries to read me. I keep my face blank. At least I hope I keep it blank.

"Can you believe that?" I say.

"Breaks your heart."

"It sure does."

The detective tugs his mustache and says, "Well, what I'm doing is going door to door and asking if anybody saw something that might help us catch whoever did it. Were you at home when the shooting occurred?"

"I was here," I say, "but I didn't see anything."

"Nothing?" He knows I'm lying. "All that commotion?"

"I heard the sirens afterward, and that's when I came out. Someone told me what happened, and I went right back inside. I don't need to be around that kind of stuff."

The detective nods thoughtfully, but he's looking past me into the house.

"Maybe someone else then," he says. "Someone in your family?"

"Nobody saw anything."

"You're sure?"

Like I'm stupid. Like all he has to do is ask twice.

"I'm sure," I say.

He's disgusted with me, and, to tell the truth, I'm disgusted with myself. But I can't get involved, especially not with Lorena and Brianna staying here. A motorcycle drives by with those exhaust pipes that rattle your bones. The detective turns to watch it pass, then reaches into his pocket and hands me a business card with his name and number on it.

"If you hear something, I'd appreciate it if you give me a call," he says. "You can do it confidentially. You don't even have to leave your name."

"I hope you catch him," I say.

"That's up to your neighborhood here. The only way that baby is going to get any justice is if a witness comes forward. Broad daylight, Sunday afternoon. Someone saw something, and they're just as bad as the killer if they don't step up."

Tough talk, but he doesn't live here. No cops do.

He pulls out a handkerchief and mops the sweat off his head as he walks away, turns up the street toward Rudolfo's place.

MY HEART IS RACING. I lie on the couch and let the fans blow on me. The ice cream truck drives by, playing its little song, and I close my eyes for a minute. Just for a minute.

A noise. Someone coming in the front door. I sit up lost, then scared. The TV remote is clutched in my fist like I'm going to throw it. I put it down before Lorena sees me. I must have dozed off.

"What's wrong?" she says.

"Where have you been?" I reply, going from startled to irritated in a hot second.

"Out," she says.

Best to leave it there, I can tell from her look. She's my oldest, thirty-five now, and we've been butting heads since she was twelve. If you ask her, I don't know anything about anything. She's raising Brianna differently than I raised her. They're more like friends than mother and daughter. They giggle over boys together, wear each other's clothes. I don't think it's right, but we didn't call each other for six months when I made a crack about it once, so now I bite my tongue.

I have to tell her what happened with Brianna though. I keep my voice calm so she can't accuse me of being hysterical; I stick to the facts, A, B, C, D. The questions she asks, however, and the way she asks them, make it clear that she's looking for a way to get mad at me instead of at her daughter.

"What do you mean the back door was open?"

"She acted guilty? How?"

"Did you actually see a boy?"

It's like talking to a lawyer. I'm all worn out by the time I finish the story and she goes back to the bedroom. Maybe starting dinner will make me feel better. We're having spaghetti. I brown some hamburger, some onions and garlic, add a can of tomato sauce, and set it to simmer so it cooks down nice and slow.

Lorena and Brianna come into the kitchen while I'm chopping lettuce for a salad. They look like they've just stopped laughing about something. I feel myself getting angry. What's there to joke about?

"I'm sorry, Grandma," Brianna says.

She wraps her arms around me, and I give her a quick hug back, not even bothering to put down the knife in my hand.

"That's okay, mija."

"From now on, if she wants to have friends over, she'll ask first," Lorena says.

"And no beer or smoking," I say.

"She knows," Lorena says.

No, she doesn't. She's fourteen years old. She doesn't know a goddamn thing.

Brianna sniffs the sauce bubbling on the stove and wrinkles her nose. "Are there onions in here?" she asks.

"You can pick them out," I say.

She does this walk sometimes, stiff arms swinging, legs straight, toes pointed. Something she learned in ballet. That's how she leaves the kitchen. A second later I hear the TV come on in the living room, too loud.

"So who was he?" I whisper to Lorena.

"A boy from school. He rode the bus all the way over here to see her."

She says this like it's something sweet. I wipe down the counter so I don't have to look at her.

"She's that age," I say. "You've got to keep an eye on her."

"I know," Lorena says. "I was that age once too."

"So was I."

"Yeah, but girls today are smarter than we were."

I move over to the stove, wipe that too. Here we go again.

"Still, you have to set boundaries," I say.

"Like you did with me?"

"That's right."

"And like Grandma did with you?" Lorena says. "'Cause that worked out real good."

We end up here every time. There's no sense even responding.

Lorena got pregnant when she was sixteen and had an abortion. Somehow that makes me a bad mother, but I haven't figured out yet how she means to hurt me when she brings it up. Was I too strict, or not strict enough?

As for myself, the boys went kind of nuts for me when I turned fourteen. I wasn't a tease or anything; they just decided that I was the one to get with. That happens sometimes. I was the oldest girl in my family, the first one to put my parents through all that. My dad would sit on the porch and glare at the guys who drove past hoping to catch me outside, and my mom walked me to school every day. I got a little leeway after my quinceañera, but not much.

Manuel was five years older than me. I met him at a party at my cousin's when I was fifteen. He'd only been in the U.S. for a few years, and his idea of dressing up was still boots and a cowboy hat. Not my type at all. I

201

was into lowriders, pendejos with hot cars. But Manuel was so sweet to me, and polite in a way the East L.A. boys weren't. He bought me flowers, called twice a day. And after my parents met him, forget it. He went to Mass, he could rebuild the engine in any car, and he was already working at the brewery, making real money: they practically handed me over to him right there.

Our plan was that we'd marry when I graduated, but I ended up pregnant at the end of my junior year. Everything got moved up then, and I never went back to school. My parents were upset, but they couldn't say much because the same thing had happened to them. It all worked out fine though. Manuel was a good husband, our kids were healthy, and we had a nice life together. Sometimes you get lucky.

I DO THE DISHES after dinner, then join the girls in the living room. The TV is going, but nobody's paying attention. Lorena is on her laptop and Brianna is texting on her phone. They don't look up from punching buttons when I sit in my recliner. I watch a woman try to win a million dollars. The audience groans when she gives the wrong answer.

I can't sit still. My brain won't slow down, thinking about Antonio and Puppet, thinking about Lorena and Brianna, so I decide to make my rounds a little early. I can't get to sleep if I haven't checked the lock on the garage door, latched the gate, and watered my flowers. Manuel called it "walking the perimeter."

"Sarge is walking the perimeter," he'd say.

The heat has broken when I step out into the front yard. The sun is low in the sky, and little birds chase each other from palm tree to palm tree, twittering excitedly. Usually you can't hear them over the kids playing, but since the shooting, everybody is keeping their children inside.

I drag the hose over to the roses growing next to the chain-link fence that separates the yard from the sidewalk. They're blooming like mad in this heat. The white ones, the yellow, the red. I lay the hose at the base of the bushes and turn the water on low, so the roots get a good soaking.

Rudolfo is still at work in his shop. His saw whines, and then comes the BANG BANG BANG of a hammer. I haven't been over to see him in a while. Maybe I'll take him some spaghetti.

I wash my face and put on a little makeup. Lipstick, eyeliner, nothing fancy. Perfume. I change out of my housedress into jeans and a nice top. My stomach does a flip as I'm dressing. I guess you could say I've got a thing for Rudolfo, but I think he likes me, too, the way he smiles. And for my birthday last year he gave me a jewelry box that he made. Back in the kitchen I dig out some good Tupperware to carry the spaghetti in.

Rudolfo's dog, Oso, a big shaggy mutt, barks as I come down the driveway.

"Cállate, hombre," Rudolfo says.

I walk to the door of the shop and stand there silently, watching Rudolfo sand a rough board smooth. He makes furniture—simple, sturdy tables, chairs, and wardrobes—and sells it to rich people from Pasadena and Beverly Hills. The furniture is nice, but awfully plain. I'd think a rich woman would want something fancier than a table that looks like it belongs in a farmhouse.

"Knock, knock," I finally say.

Rudolfo grins when he looks up and sees me standing there.

"Hola, Blanca."

I move into the doorway but still don't step through. Some men are funny. You're intruding if you're not invited.

"Come in, come in," Rudolfo says. He takes off his glasses and cleans them with a red bandanna. He's from El Salvador, and so handsome with that Indian nose and his silver hair combed straight back. "Sorry for sawing so late, but I'm finishing an order," he says. "That was the last little piece."

"I just came by to bring you some spaghetti," I say. "I made too much again."

"Oh, hey, gracias. Pasale."

He motions for me to enter and wipes the sawdust off a stool with his bandanna. I sit and look around the shop. It's so organized, the lumber stacked neatly by size, the tools in their special places. This used to crack Manuel up. He called Rudolfo "the Librarian." The two of them got along fine but were never really friends. Too busy, I guess, both working all the time.

Rudolfo takes the spaghetti from me and says, "Did that cop stop by your house today?"

"The bald one? Yeah," I reply.

"He told me he's sure someone saw who killed that baby."

Someone who's just as bad as the killer. I know. I run my finger over the blade of a saw sitting on the workbench. If this is what he wants to talk about, I'm going to leave.

"Are things getting crazier?" Rudolfo continues. "Or does it just seem that way?"

"I ask myself that all the time," I reply.

"I'm starting to think more like mi abuelo every day," he says. "You know what he'd say about what

happened to that baby? 'Bring me the rope, and I'll
hang the bastard who did it myself.'"

I stand and brush off my pants.

"Enjoy your spaghetti," I say. "I've got to get back."

"So soon?"

"I wake up at 2:30 to be at the hospital by 4."

"Let me walk you out."

I wave away the offer. "No, no, finish what you were
doing."

Puppet and his homies are hanging on the corner
when I get out to the street. Puppet is leaning on a car
that's blasting music, that BOOM BOOM FUCK FUCK
crap. He is wearing a white T-shirt, baggy black shorts
that hang past his knees, white socks pulled all the way
up and a pair of corduroy house shoes. The same stuff
vatos have been wearing since I was a kid. His head is
shaved, and there's a tattoo on the side of it, Temple
Street.

I knew his mom before she went to prison; I even
babysat him a couple times when he was young. He
went bad at ten or eleven, though, stopped listening to
the grandma who was raising him and started running
with thugs. The boys around here slip away like that
again and again. He stares at me now, like, "What do
you have to say?" Like he's reminding me to be scared
of him.

"Baby killer," I should shout back. "You ain't shit." I
should have shut the door in that detective's face, too.
I've got to be smarter from now on.

I HAVEN'T BEEN SLEEPING very well. It's the heat, sure,
but I've also been dreaming of little Antonio. He comes
tonight as an angel, floating above my bed, up near the
ceiling. He makes his own light, a golden glow that

205

shows everything for what it is. But I don't want to see. I swat at him once, twice, knock him to the floor. His light flickers, and the darkness comes rushing back.

My pillow is soaked with sweat when I wake up. It's guilt that gives you dreams like that. Prisoners go crazy, rattle the doors of their cells and scream out confessions. Anything, anything to get some peace. I look at the clock, and it's past midnight. The sound of a train whistle drifts over from the tracks downtown. I have to be up in two hours.

I pull on my robe to go into the kitchen for a glass of milk. Lorena is snoring quietly, and I close her door as I pass by. Then there's another sound. Whispers. Coming from the living room. The girls left something unlocked, and now we're being robbed. That's my first thought, and it stops the blood in my veins. But then there's a familiar giggle, and I peek around the corner to see Brianna standing in front of a window, her arms reaching through the bars to touch someone—it's too dark to say who—out in the yard.

I step into the room and snap on the light. Brianna turns, startled, and the shadow outside disappears. I hurry to the front door, open it, but there's no one out there now except a bum pushing a grocery cart filled with cans and newspapers down the middle of the street. Brianna is in tears when I go back inside, and I'm shaking all over, I'm so angry.

"So that talk today was for nothing?" I say.

My yelling wakes Lorena, and she finds me standing over Brianna, who is cowering on the couch.

"Let her up," Lorena says.

She won't listen as I try to explain what happened, how frightened I was when I heard those voices in the dark. She just grabs Brianna and drags her back to their room.

I wind up drinking coffee at the kitchen table until it is time to get ready for work. Lorena comes out as I'm about to leave for the bus. She said that the boy from Brianna's school came to see her again, and she was right in the middle of telling him to go away when I came in. She says we're going to forget the whole incident, let it lie.

"That's the best way to handle it," she says. "I want to show that I trust her."

"Okay," I say.

"Just treat her like normal."

"I will."

"She's a good girl, Mom."

"I know."

They've beaten the fire out of me. If all they want is a cook and a cleaning lady, fine.

MY STOMACH HURTS DURING the ride to work the next morning, and I feel feverish, too. Resting my forehead against the cool glass of the window, I take deep breaths and tell myself it's nothing, just too much coffee. It's still dark outside, the streets empty, the stores locked tight. Like everyone gave up and ran away and I'm the last to know. I smell smoke when I get off at the hospital. Sirens shriek in the distance.

Irma is fixing her hair in the locker room.

"You don't look so good," she says.

"Maybe it's something I ate," I reply.

She gives me a Pepto Bismol tablet from her purse, and we tie our aprons and walk to the kitchen. One of the boys has cornered a mouse in there, back by the pantry, and pinned it to the floor with a broom. Everybody moves in close, chattering excitedly.

"Step on it," somebody says.

"Drown it," someone else suggests.

"¡No! ¡No mate el pobrecito!" Josefina wails, trembling fingers raised to her lips. Don't kill the poor little thing! She's about to burst into tears.

The boy with the broom glances at her, then tells one of the dishwashers to bring a bucket. He and the dishwasher turn the bucket upside down and manage to trap the mouse beneath it. They slide a scrap of cardboard across the opening and flip the bucket over. The mouse cowers in the bottom, shitting all over itself. The boys free it on the construction site next door, and we get to work.

I do okay until about 8, until the room starts spinning and I almost pass out in the middle of serving Dr. Alvarez his oatmeal. My stomach cramps, my mouth fills with spit, and I whisper to Irma to take my place on the line before I run to the bathroom and throw up.

Maple, our supervisor, is waiting when I return to the cafeteria. She's a twitchy black lady with a bad temper.

"Go home," she says.

"I'm okay," I reply. "I feel better."

"You hang around, you're just going to infect everybody else. Go home."

It's frustrating. I've only called in sick three times in my twenty-seven years here. Maple won't budge though. I take off my gloves and apron, get my purse from my locker.

My stomach bucks again at the bus stop, and I vomit into the gutter. A bunch of kids driving by honk their horn and laugh at me. The ride home takes forever. The traffic signals are messed up for blocks, blinking red, and the skyscrapers shimmer in the heat like I'm dreaming them.

Baby Killer

I stop at the store for bread and milk when I get off the bus. Not the Smart & Final, but the little tienda on the corner. The Sanchezes owned it forever, but now it's Koreans. They're nice enough. The old lady at the register always smiles and says gracias when she gives me my change. Her son is out front painting over fresh graffiti. Temple Street tags the place every night, and he cleans it up every day.

A girl carrying a baby blocks my path. She holds out her hand and asks me in Spanish for money, her voice a raspy whisper. The baby is sick, she says, needs medicine. She's not much older than Brianna and won't look me in the eye.

"Whatever you can spare," she says. Please."

"Where do you live?" I ask.

She glances nervously over her shoulder. A boy a little older than her pokes his head out from behind a tree, watching us. Maria, from two blocks over, told me the other day how a girl with a baby came to her door, asking for money. The girl said she was going to faint, so Maria let her inside to rest on the couch while she went to the bathroom to get some Huggies her daughter had left behind. When she came back, the girl was gone, and so was Maria's purse.

My chest feels like a bird is loose inside it.

"I don't have anything, I say. I'm sorry."

"My baby is going to die," the girl says. "Please, a dollar. Two."

I push past her and hurry away. When I reach the corner, I look back and see her and the boy staring at me with hard faces.

The sidewalk on my street has buckled from all the tree roots pushing up underneath it. The slabs tilt at odd angles, and I go over them faster than I should while carrying groceries. If I'm not careful, I'm going to fall and break my neck. I'm going to get exactly what I deserve.

Brianna's eyes open wide when I step through the door. A boy is lying on top of her on the couch. Puppet.

"Get away from her," I yell, and I mean it to be a roar, but it comes out like an old woman's dying gasp.

Standing quickly, he pulls up his pants and grabs his shirt off the floor. Brianna yanks a blanket over her naked body. As he walks out, Puppet sneers at me. He's so close I can feel heat coming off him. I slam the door and twist the deadbolt.

IT WAS ONE MONTH after my fifteenth birthday, and all everybody was talking about was a party some kid was throwing at his house while his parents were in Mexico for a funeral. Carmen and Cindy said, "You've got to go. We'll sneak out together." Stupid stuff, teenagers being teenagers. "You tell your mom that you're staying at my house, and I'll tell mine I'm staying at yours." We were actually shocked that it worked, to find ourselves out on the streets on a Saturday night.

The crowd at the party was a little older than we were, a little rougher. Lots of gangbangers and their girlfriends, kids who didn't go to our school. Carmen and Cindy were meeting boys there and soon disappeared, leaving me standing by myself in the kitchen.

One of the vatos came up and started talking to me. He said his name was Smiley and that he was in White Fence, the gang in that neighborhood. Boys were always claiming to be down with this clique or that, and most of them were full of it. Smiley seemed like he was full of it. He was so tiny and so cute.

Things move fast when you're that age, when you're drinking rum and you've never drunk rum before, when you're smoking weed and you've never smoked weed before. Pretty soon we were kissing right there in front of everybody, me sitting on the counter, Smiley standing between my legs. I was so high I got his tongue mixed up with mine. Someone laughed, and it bounced around inside my head like a rubber ball.

Following Smiley into the bedroom was my mistake. I should have said no. Lying down on the mattress, letting him peel off my T-shirt, letting him put his hand inside my pants—I take the blame for all that, too. But everything else is on him and the others. Forever, like a brand. I was barely fifteen years old, for God's sake. I was drunk. I was stupid.

"Stop," I hissed, but Smiley kept going.

I tried to sit up, and he forced me back down. He put his hand on my throat and squeezed.

"Just fucking relax," he said.

I let myself go limp. I gave in because I thought he'd kill me if I didn't. He seemed that crazy, choking me, pulling my hair. Two of his homies came in while he was going at it. I hoped for half a second that they were there to save me. Instead, when Smiley was finished, they did their thing, too, took turns grinding away on a scared little girl, murdering some part of her that she mourns to this day.

Afterward they made me wash my face and get dressed. I wasn't even crying anymore. I was numb, in shock.

"White Fence," Smiley said right before he walked back out into the party, into the music and laughter. "Don't you forget." A warning pure and simple. An ugly threat.

I never told my friends what happened, never told my family, never told my husband. What could they possibly have said or done that would've helped? Nothing. Not a goddamn thing. The sooner you learn it, the better: some loads you carry on your own.

THEY MAKE A BIG show of it when they come for Puppet. Must be six cop cars, a helicopter, TV cameras. That detective wasn't lying: all it took was an anonymous phone call. "I saw who killed the baby."

One minute Puppet is preening on the corner with his homies, acting like he owns the street, the next he's facedown on the hot asphalt, hands cuffed tight behind his back.

I run outside as soon as I hear the commotion. I want to see. Lorena and Brianna come, too, whispering, "Oh my God, what's happening?"

"It's the bastard who shot little Antonio," says an old man carrying a bottle in a bag.

We stand at the fence and watch with the rest of the neighborhood as they lift Puppet off the ground and slam him against a police car. Then, suddenly, Brianna is crying. "No," she moans and opens the gate like she's going to run to him. "No." Lorena grabs her arm and yanks her back into the yard.

"José," Brianna yells. His real name.

He can't hear her, though, not with all the shouting and sirens and the CHOP CHOP CHOP of the helicopter circling overhead. And I'm glad. He doesn't deserve her tears, her reckless love. Instead, I hope the last thing he sees before they drive him off is my satisfied smile and the hatred in my eyes, and I hope it burns him like fire, night and day, for as long as he fouls this earth.

IT'S FRIDAY EVENING, AND what a week. The freezer at work broke down, Maple changed the rules on vacation time, and one of the boys cut his finger to the bone, chopping onions. There was some good news, too: looks like Puppet isn't going to be back. As soon as they picked him up, his boy Cheeks flipped on him and told the cops everything. A few punks still hang out on the corner and stare the neighborhood down, but none of them know that it's me who took out their homie.

I fall asleep on the couch when I get home and don't wake up until a few hours later, but that's okay, because I'm off tomorrow, so I can go to bed whenever I want tonight and sleep in. I couldn't do that when Lorena and Brianna were here. They'd be banging around in the kitchen or blasting the TV every time I tried to rest. Or I'd be cooking for them or doing their laundry.

I love them, but I wasn't sad to see them go when they moved out last week. They're in Alhambra now, living with a fireman Lorena met on the computer. He's really great, she says, with a big house, a swimming pool, and an RV. And so good with Brianna. I was thinking she should ask him about his ex-wife, find out why she's not around anymore, but I kept it to myself.

When I get up, I finish watering the garden and pick a bunch of tomatoes. The sun has just set, leaving the sky a pretty blue, but it's going to be one of those nights when it doesn't cool down until past midnight. The kids used to sleep out in the yard when it was like this. Manuel would cut up a watermelon he'd kept on ice all day, and the juice would run down their faces and drip onto the grass.

I sit on the back porch and watch the stars come out. There's a little moon up there, too, a little silver smile in the sky. Oso barks next door, and another dog answers. Music floats over from Rudolfo's shop, old ranchero stuff, and I think, You know, I'll never eat all these tomatoes myself.

213

Rudolfo looks up from the newspaper he's reading as I come down the driveway, trailed by Oso.

"Blanca," he says. "Buenas noches."

He reaches out and turns down the radio down a bit. He's drinking a beer, and a cigar smolders in an ashtray on the workbench. Picking up the ashtray, he moves to carry it outside.

"Go ahead and smoke," I say.

"You're sure?"

"No problem."

He lived next door for years before I found out that he had a wife and son back in El Salvador. He got in trouble with the government there and had to leave. The plan was that he'd go to the U.S. and get settled, then his family would join him. But a few years later, when it was time, his wife decided that she was happy where she was and refused to move north. I remember he told this like it had happened to another person, but I could see in his eyes how it hurt him.

"I brought you some tomatoes," I say, setting the bag on the workbench. "I've got them coming out of my ears."

"You want a beer?" he asks.

"Sure," I say and lower myself onto a stool.

He reaches into a cooler and lifts out a Tecate, uses his bandanna to wipe the can dry.

"I'm sorry I don't have any lime," he says as he passes it to me.

"It's good like this," I reply.

He lifts his can and says, "Salud."

I take a sip, and, boy, does it go down easy. Oso presses his cold nose against my leg and makes me jump. I'm wearing a new skirt. A new blouse, too.

"Another wild Friday night, huh?" I say.

Rudolfo laughs. He runs his fingers slowly through his hair and shakes his head. "I might have a few more in me," he says. "But I'm saving them up for when I really need them."

He asks about Lorena and Brianna, how they're doing at the new place, and wonders if I'm lonely now that they're gone. I admit that I'm not.

"You get used to being by yourself," I say.

"Yeah, but that's not the same as enjoying it," he replies, something sad in his voice.

I like the way we talk to each other. It feels honest. Things were different with Manuel. One of us always had to win. Husbands and wives do that, worry more about being right than being truthful. What goes on between Rudolfo and me is what I always imagined flirting would be like. It's kind of a game. We hint at what's inside us, each hoping the other picks up on the clues.

I didn't learn to flirt when I was young. I didn't have time. One year after that party I was engaged to Manuel, and the last thing I wanted him to know were my secrets.

A moth flutters against the bare light bulb suspended above us, its wings tapping urgent messages on the thin glass. Rudolfo tells me about something funny that happened to him at Home Depot, how this guy swiped his shopping cart. It's his story I'm laughing at when he finishes, but I'm also just happy to be here with this handsome man, drinking this beer, listening to this music. It feels like there are bubbles in my blood.

A song my mom used to play comes on the radio.

"Hey," I say. "Let's dance."

"I don't know, it's been years," Rudolfo replies.

"Come on." I stand and wiggle my hips, reach out for him.

He puts down his beer and wraps his arms around me. I pull him close and whisper the lyrics to the song in his ear as we sway so smoothly together. You forget what that feels like. It seems impossible, but you do.

"Blanca," he says.

"Mmmmmm?" I reply.

"I'm seeing a lady in Pacoima."

"Shhh," I say.

"I've been seeing her for years."

"Shhh."

I lay my head on his chest, listen to his heart. Sawdust and smoke swirl around us. Que bonita amor, goes the song, que bonita cielo, que bonita luna, que bonita sol. God wants to see me cry. He must have his reasons. But for now, Lord, please, give me just one more minute. One more minute of this.

ARTICH͚KE

Erica Zora Wrightson

Best American Essays, Notable

THERE IS THE LIGHT coming through the bone-white blinds in the morning. There are the hot baths, Constant Comment tea, Laura Nyro songs, and chocolate-dipped honeycomb. After the radiation, when you can no longer walk, your appetite narrows—a sudden decrescendo as the body accelerates toward an end.

It is no surprise. In the final year of your cancer, the limbs slow, but the mind does not. Thin bouquets of hair stay behind on your pillowcase. The body nudges the skeleton into the foreground, becoming more subject, less frame.

In the side yard, plums ripen and sparrows place bets on the crop. You have never had this much time in your house; you were always working. You try to cook, navigating the square corners of your kitchen in your wheelchair. On your lap, you rest a small wooden cutting board, and with a paring knife slice plum tomatoes from your garden, the translucent juice running onto numb legs. Friends bring food to fill the house with the scent of comfort: meatloaf, quiche, minestrone soup. These are not unlike meals you made once every day, but they are not yours. There is less to prepare, but you would rather think about lasagna than death. You would love to make summer salads and in the mornings bake scones for the kids; you would love to walk to the stove on strong legs and boil a pot of water for tea.

In illness, the appetite hovers. It is the ghost of hunger, desire transposed into need. It is impractical. A slice of coffeecake that was once the center of your perfect breakfast is grainy and brown; it is a wedge of sand and sugar. Toward the end, there are artichokes. Like you, they are time's material—a rationing of leaves. Artichokes make sense when you move through days in a body, just fifty-three years old, that has aged decades in a year. Busy dishes are difficult to digest. An artichoke is reliable symmetry, edible geometry. You find comfort in its layered chamber of leaves and the final pleasure of its heart.

On Saturday mornings your daughter goes to the farmers market alone; it is too difficult for her to maneuver you in your chair through the crowd now, and the uneven pavement makes your back sore for days. The spring artichokes are huge. You watch your child trim the pointy tips. Her technique is uneven, but you will not correct her. You are learning to let go.

You sit with her on the porch, eating with your hands. The men are out. It is Friday night and the sun takes its time to set. It is hot, but you like the fresh air and prefer to witness the sunlight deepen on the large oaks of Mar Vista Avenue. You watch the squirrels bicker over acorns in the street; young couples push their children in strollers. You sit beside your daughter, plucking dark green leaves, dipping them in a mixture of plain yogurt and mayonnaise, dragging them between your teeth. One artichoke is all you eat. You undress the thistle, anticipating the heart. Your daughter gives you the larger half, scooping out the lavender center.

In a few months, on a Sunday afternoon, the street will be crowded with everyone you know. The neighbors will climb ladders to hang paper lanterns from the oaks and the camphors. Your son will write a song that he and your daughter will play with a jazz quartet right there on the lawn. Your friends will pot succulents in your memory; a Jewish chaplain and a Unitarian priest will say words. The man you have loved since you were fifteen will read the Ferlinghetti poem that you quoted on your wedding invitation, the one from *Pictures of the Gone World* that starts, "Fortune has its cookies to give out…"

A week later, there will be traces. A crow will catch its leg on a forgotten lantern cord still draped over an oak branch. The meals will continue to arrive. Your family will not gather the plums, and the sparrows will peck at the windfall. Artichokes will enter and exit seasons, obeying the map of their own private harvests.

FREEWAY

Dana Goodyear

Sensitives can feel it in their headaches
and their bones, this afternoon
the color of coyotes on the loose:

the city's set to burn.
Mothers grab their two-year-olds
—they are the shape of prey—get

in their cars and drive away.
The wind comes on like a dry drunk,
out of the desert junkyards

with one thought. This is how it starts,
child with a love letter, man with an itch,
a patch of inexplicably hot earth.

On the freeway, a tumbleweed of hair
and teeth; uterine pink insulation;
a mound of fur you could put your hand

inside for warmth; and the roadkill
palm fronds shiny as cicada
shells—the world's agglutinative

slough, its shuck and mud and food,
effluvia and fuel.

MEXICAN GRINGO

Daniel Hernandez

IN MEXICO CITY, NOISE, like smog, means people, commerce, signs of life. There is safety in noise as there is safety in numbers. This is not an easy concept to embrace. On the block of my new apartment in the Centro, ambulantes, street vendors, blast music through stage-grade speakers from their enclosed market, from 11 in the morning to about 9 at night. Every day. The speakers are on the concrete sidewalk, facing the open air.

Early on, I debate whether I should go down to the guys who sell Shania Twain and Beyoncé, cumbias and reggaeton, Vicente Fernández and an audio English-learning program, and tell them, "Yo, guys, can you turn it down a little?"

This is one option. My other option, I think, is to complain to my borough government, a very American gentrifier thing to do. But then, at the delegación they'd probably ask for my name, my address, and who knows what they might do with that information. I picture it somehow getting back to the mafias that run the street vendors—the D.F. government negotiated to get them into their new indoor spaces, off the sidewalks—and then somehow, in a not-so-nice way, it getting back to me.

My third option, the most winsome of all, would be to write them a clear, direct, handwritten note calmly asking if they would please not play their music at full blast all the time, maybe just downscale it a bit. I would sign the letter and slip it under the grates of their market in the middle of the night and wait for something to happen. It's like something I would do if I were thirteen years old, but I'm desperate.

Shortly after I move in, I go next door to meet my neighbor, Osvaldo, an architect. With a simple hello he walks past me and heads to my apartment, just to check it out. It is empty except for my bed and desk.

"How do you deal with the noise?" I ask Osvaldo. "From the ambulantes?"

Osvaldo looks at me flatly. He says he read a book and took a course on how to disconnect himself from it.

I'm having a hard time disconnecting. The noise comes in every day as I settle in, invasive, unapologetic, mocking me. I ask the landlord, the licenciado, what he thinks about the noise when I go downstairs to pay my first full month of rent.

Well, he tells me, he tried to go over there to tell the guys there's a lady in the building who is sick, and they don't care. They just say they have to play it loud or else they don't sell anything.

"It's just the way it is," Osvaldo says.

My friend Uriel concurs. "It would be like talking to a window." It's noisy, he admits, but at least it's good noise. At least it's decent music most of the time. I mean, music that when it comes on, you don't 100 percent mind having to listen to it. Even "Feel Like a Woman." At least it's not nineties high-energy Mexican techno on loop or "Dance with the Devil," or something awful like that.

Uriel is right. I have to learn to live with the noise. I have to realize that something about the racket is nourishing.

Mexican Gringo

After smog, noise is the most prevalent pollutant in Mexico City's air. Both have their obvious drawbacks but both also have their magic. When I lived in Los Angeles, the toxic coastal smog created some of the most spectacular and psychedelic sunsets I have ever seen. Here, in the high, landlocked capital, the smog sits on you but it also makes for dazzling skyspaces. Neon orange, electric gray, brilliant purples, and slanting pinks. I begin to consider the noise as a security blanket.

Silence is not to be trusted, because in Mexico City silence is insincere. The city never wants to be quiet. There is peace to be made with the noise. I now try to picture my square, little apartment as a magical, urban tree house hidden above a really exciting river of people and energy. There is magic on the streets, I tell myself. The hustle! The raw kernel of big-city life! Listening to Beyoncé or Wisin y Yandel blast through my bathroom window every day reminds me, of all things, that I live in Mexico City. That means a place in the world with too many people, too much pollution, and too much noise. It is a place, like so many others in the world, that runs on illegal street commerce, on pirated content, on pirates, like my fantasies of cities in Africa and India and the Middle East, and the borderless barrios that those places share with neighborhoods in London and New York and Chicago.

It is a truly cosmopolitan place because here, in the orbit of Tepito, every kind of film, concert video, or album, no matter how obscure, is within grasp, expanding our boundaries and influences.

More than extravagant parties or roaming mariachis, life in Mexico City means an English lesson on fruits and vegetables booming in my ears, supersize and out of my control, during my morning shower.

"Loco, you like Sublime, loco?"

I am in a living room above a busy lateral avenue in Mexico City's Colonia del Valle, listening to Mexican and U.S. MCs on a two-turntable sound system that belongs to a graffiti writer with a few central interests: tagging, dogs, hip-hop, and maintaining anonymity. The graffiti writer is suspicious of any phone call and prefers that his name—even his tag—not be disclosed. His insistence makes him a bona fide graffiti fundamentalist, one who sees tagging as vandalism and vandalism as a form of anarchic resistance, one who moves about the city like a phantom, furtively leaving his markings in the night. When his friends drop in, they flip through magazines—about dogs, about weed, pornography catalogs—and discuss music, skating, and the North. A potbellied Rottweiler lies about, inhaling a cloud of sweet marijuana smoke.

Andrew, the graffiti writer's friend who has just asked about my musical tastes (yes, I admit, I like Sublime), lived in Southern California for six months. He went north to skate and made money working at a Japanese restaurant and other odd jobs around Orange County. "The skating over there!" he exclaims.

But even though Andrew wears a 2005 Dodgers opening-day T-shirt (bought at a tianguis in Mexico City), he says he's glad to be back in Mexico.

"It's crazy over there, vato!"

Andrew addresses me with cholo diminutives—vato, loco—terms of endearment and respect among the urban warriors of California's barrios. I am not a cholo, but I am a Mexican American. My heritage is something people can almost smell on me here. It is a skin I cannot shed.

After three years in Mexico City, strangers on the street still call me güero—white boy. To capitalinos who know enough about what a U.S. upbringing produces— our manner of walking, for one, quick and exasperated, and our tentative Spanish, that pocho accent—I am a gringo regardless of how dark my skin might be. I am a Mexican gringo.

Güeros are regarded with some level of suspicion in Mexico City. Native capitalinos see us as cultural bastards. In the city of swindlers, people might also presume pochos pose an easy opportunity for some extra pesos. And if a Mexican gringo wears the uniform of a cholo, he has it even harder.

There's a guy I run into a lot in the Centro, for example, who used to live in Compton. Let's call him Joe. He has a single teardrop tattoo below his right eye, a symbol in some barrios that he has killed someone in his days banging. He says he was in the L.A. gang Florencia 13 and spent six years locked up in prison at Chino. He lost his girl and his kids and now lives here "in la Guerrero."

Everywhere Joe goes looking for work he is turned away. He walks into businesses in the Centro, asking to speak with the owner or manager, and workers respond with fear upon their faces. "What do you want?" they ask.

Joe, who wears a long, gray sweatshirt with a fat, blue L.A. on his chest, says he doesn't want to "fuck it up again." He has a new lady and tells me he doesn't want to be like those "fools" who get deported, as he did, after serving time in California, and just get right back into it—banging in Mexico, becoming transnational gangsters.

For a few months I see Joe work the entrance at a cantina, the only place that will hire him. He holds the doors open for people entering and leaving, making sure no one takes off without paying. He breaks up fights when necessary.

Outside the door of the cantina, I tell him that I used to live in L.A., and that I know his area, Compton, Inglewood, Long Beach.

"Cool, cool," Joe says, and then gives me the handshake. The barrio instinct. Two hands clap, knuckles lock, one arm grabs the opposite elbow, opposite shoulders meet in a friendly bump.

I run into guys like Joe all the time. Booted from their homes in the U.S. to Mexico—a place where they might have been born but which has become foreign to them—they wear close-fade haircuts, baggy jeans, and L.A. caps and sweatshirts. Prison tattoos are often visible. Sometimes they end up selling candy on the metro.

Their presence in the D.F. is not exactly new, but their numbers have grown as deportations from U.S. prisons have risen sharply in recent years. And the cholo look predated the present wave of deportations.

Beginning in the 1980s, young guys in the outskirts of the city were drawn to the styles and cultures represented in popular U.S. movies about pachucos, gangsters, and life in the barrio: Zoot Suit, Colors, American Me, Mi Vida Loca, Blood In Blood Out. The cholo subculture then flourished in nearby Ciudad Nezahualcóyotl in the 1990s, when migrants began returning home after time spent in California, bringing their influence unfiltered by Hollywood directly to the streets of Mexico City. They formed Mexican copycat versions of some of the most fearsome pandillas from the North: Barrio Logan, the Mara Salvatrucha, Sur 13, the Latin Kings, and Florencia 13.

"These guys are responding to the binationality we are living in Mexico," photographer Federico Gama tells me one day. "The border is no longer Chihuahua, Tijuana, Reynosa. The border is now all of Mexico. The border [came] to Mexico City, the heart of the country, and now there is a strong relationship with Los Angeles, with New York, with Chicago."

In *Cholos a la Neza: Another Identity of Migration*, a photography and essay book by Gama and Pablo Hernández Sánchez, Gama's images show a self-contained world populated by guys who look exactly like guys in California barrios—gang tattoos, Dickies slacks, tough poses, gang signs—in settings that appear completely transplanted from north of the border: Chicano murals, lowriders, tricked-out bikes.

"For them the American dream is not the same as you guys understand the American dream to be," Gama says. "The American dream is coming back with Nikes, Dickies pants, jerseys, with caps, with tattoos. When they see someone like that, they go, 'Orale, that's a real gringo.'"

For those of us who are back and forth in our cultural stance and worldview, we can feel each other when our paths cross on the streets of D.F. No words are necessary. We move about Neza, Iztapalapa, Tepito. We sense and spot each other on the street, on the metro. We share a quick nod, a mutual regard, less amicable than respectful, vaguely competitive. Anywhere in Mexico, I know another barrio guy from the U.S. Southwest when I see one, even from behind. This is how Mexico City is making me more instinctively aware of my Californianess.

"What part of the U.S. are you from?" a girl asks me plaintively one night.

She is making a deep and accurate assumption; until now, not a word has been shared. I am with my friend Susana at our downtown bar in the alley near the mound of garbage. I tell the girl where I am from, and she just starts crying on me, there in the middle of the cantina, by the jukebox. She cries about how she misses her man on the other side. She holds on to me tight, clutching my shoulders, feeling for my California skin.

"There, there," I say, holding her. For a moment, I am her transmitter, connecting her to her migrant husband, the man who left her behind.

It takes a tall Scandinavian woman with lanky features and a rough tenor of a voice to break down to me, finally, what it means for me to live in Mexico City.

It is early 2008. I'm wandering the desolate, gloomy streets of Colonia Roma, hoping to fight the wave of depression that comes with the dusk of Sunday, every Sunday, without fail, no matter what city I'm in. I meet up with Josh, a twenty-one-year-old student from Louisiana, and we talk about home, about graffiti, and our parents. We sit down for tacos on Álvaro Obregón, then find our way to his friend's apartment, to sit around on leather couches and watch the TV show *Dexter* with subtitles on, except for the parts where the Cuban police officer throws Spanish into the dialogue.

We sip tequila and have popcorn and packaged chicarrón chips doused in lime and chile. When dusk has passed and I can walk home without too much Sunday gloom, I thank the hosts and get up to leave.

"And what's with the English?" the tall Scandinavian woman, Josh's friend, asks suddenly.

"The English?"

"It's very good," she says.

"Oh," I respond. "I'm from California."

"You're not Mexican?"

She is genuinely confused.

"No, no, I'm Mexican American."

"Ah! Well, you've come home," she concludes happily.

"Well, no one in my family has been here," I reply. "I'm the only one who's made it here."

Made it here. The words roll together and fly away. The girl smiles big, and when our cheeks meet in the customary good-bye kiss, she tells me, "Welcome home."

Back I go to the sidewalks, toward metro Hospital General. The night is chilly, crisp, and still for January. I listen to the streets and walk steadily. I had been trying to communicate to Josh's friend that I am not "home" because my family is not native to central Mexico, but to her it doesn't matter. To her I am in my epicenter, the belly button of my ancestral homeland. She is proud for me.

I stroll down busy Cuauhtémoc, past the door at number 226, where I lived for a few weeks in summer 2002, three stories above the roaring boulevard, with two Scots and a Mexican from Torreón. I peer in. It looks the same, the heavy glass-and-metal door, the tiled art deco passageway, the box elevator and narrow staircase. I'd go up every night and sit on the porch and watch the river of traffic below and wonder what exactly I was doing here. Tonight everything is the same. The Scotiabank branch downstairs, the Sanborns café down the block, the stark hotel across the street, the Benidorm, still somehow in operation. The city has miles and miles of "passing-through" hotels. For lonely businessmen, hapless tourists, lunchtime trysts between married men and their mistresses, married men and their male lovers, drug deals, dying.

Walking to the metro station, I feel the flash of familiarity. The torta and taco stands, the homeless people begging for small coins, the reeking steam rising from vents leading to a subterranean nowhere.

This is home, the impossible megacity. Some find it in New York, some in Los Angeles, for some it is in Europe or East Asia. For some it is Mexico City. Walking here, I could be anywhere. Streets and people and sounds and bad smells. Sidewalk obstacles and sex shops. A new jetliner cruising down to earth on the established pathway overhead.

Megacities do not pretend to be pretty or picturesque, do not pretend to deny that ours is now a planet overrun by humans, and that humans are filthy and destructive creatures but are also prone to romancing one another. The megacity is the perfect place for romance. Romance between two people, between strangers exchanging quick looks on a platform. Romance for the entire tenuous proposal that is a global society.

On the platform at metro Hospital General, two teenage couples ravenously make out. On the train, an African man in hip-hop gear who must have teleported onto Mexico City's Line 3 from the subway in New York or Paris nods in my direction. Easy listening plays softly from a few strategic speakers in the transfer corridors of metro Centro Médico. Then, in the Tacubaya station's main transfer passage, three deaf people, one man and two women, happily chat to one another in Mexican sign language. They have found each other.

It is Sunday, so more love, more couples making out on the escalators up. Back on the surface, a costumed clown, in full makeup, heads home after a long day's work. Clowns work parties, then drum up extra earnings performing wacky skits on the trains. The clown and I nod to one another when our paths cross. Everyone leaving the metro tonight is going along to the humid little boxes that we call our bedrooms, home, aware that in the modern megacity the walls that separate our homes are membranes that only temporarily keep apart the millions and millions of people who must, at all times, breathe the same city air, eat the same city food, share the same treacherous city sidewalks, and greet the same city clowns heading home on Sundays in red plastic noses and long floppy shoes.

RETURN TO SENDER

Cindy Carcamo

2012 French-American Foundation Immigration Journalism Award, Winner; 2011 Livingston Awards for Young Journalists, Finalist; Best News Feature, 2012 Orange County Press Club, Second Place; 2012 PEN Center USA Literary Award in Journalism, Finalist

A DUST-COVERED BUS EMERGED from the jungle and stopped in a dark and quiet Guatemalan village. The driver opened the door, letting out an earful of thumping reggaeton as a single passenger stepped off. Across the highway, a boy stood waiting.

"Chello!" the boy called out.

The man brushed off his jeans, tossed a camouflage backpack over his shoulder, and looked toward the silhouette of his ten-year-old nephew, barely visible in the glow of fireflies and brake lights as the bus roared into the night.

"Erick!" called back the man, nicknamed Chello. The boy kicked his foot in the dirt as the man approached, and then gave his favorite uncle a hasty embrace. Behind them, in a flat, open-air house that doubles as a roadside diner, the lights flickered on one by one. Melvin Eliceo Súchite Hernandez was home. Maybe this time for good.

Faces exhausted, eyes emptied of emotion, and shoulders slouched, the 117 airline passengers barely whispered as their plane lifted off the desert tarmac and headed for the lush, volcano-dotted country some thought they'd never see again.

It was a Friday morning, October 8, 2010, many hours before Súchite's Guatemala homecoming, as his chartered flight left Phoenix-Mesa Gateway Airport.

Just as you'd see on any friendly, no-frills airline, the flight attendants wore khaki pants and blue polo shirts. But on this ride, they gave their announcements from the front of the plane, not venturing past a phalanx of security agents who stood from their seats as soon as the jet was airborne and stationed themselves along the plane's aisle, resembling statues as they towered over their charges. Thirteen of the passengers wore shackles.

Most of the travelers to Guatemala City had been wearing the same grimy clothes for days. Some had never been inside a jetliner, and their eyes darted about the cabin with curiosity. Others stared outside the windows, already lost in the clouds and endless sky. A few anxiously rubbed their arms, as if trying to console themselves. The air was thick with the smell of humanity.

The crew—the pilots and flight attendants, the onboard nurse and security agents—were contract hires. Normally, a single officer from U.S. Immigration and Customs Enforcement (ICE) would be aboard to supervise, but for this flight, with two reporters, a TV cameraperson, and a newspaper photographer along for the ride, two extra ICE agents came to assist.

Behind their stoic masks, many of the plane's passengers were coming to terms with what they considered a failure. Some lamented the thousands of dollars still owed to the smugglers who helped them cross into the United States. But at least one of the travelers viewed the flight as something of a process— and a blessing, certainly not the worst result in a game where risks are high and death is possible.

"Who knows?" Súchite said as he shrugged his shoulders and settled in to enjoy the ride. "Perhaps a rattlesnake waited for me in the desert." This was his third time on a U.S. deportation flight.

THE FIRST TIME SÚCHITE tried to emigrate to the United States, in 2006, he went to a smuggler and paid the Guatemalan equivalent of $5,000 for a three-try package deal. On his first try, he didn't even get to the U.S. border. He was caught in Mexico and deported. On Súchite's second try, he managed to get through the dangerous Mexican traverse and made it into Arizona, but was quickly apprehended after crossing over.

On his third attempt, success. After four nights and three days walking through the Arizona desert, he evaded ICE agents and made it to a coyote-hired truck at a designated meeting spot. The driver hauled Súchite and several others to Los Angeles and then to Las Vegas, where he met up with his brother, Benjamin Jr., now thirty-two (Súchite, twenty-five, is the youngest brother of thirteen siblings). The pair hugged, gorged themselves at a $20 casino buffet, and traveled to Wyoming, where Súchite worked for a year and a half before getting caught without documents and sent home.

Paying another $5,000 for a new three-try deal was out of the question for his most recent trip north. So when Súchite decided to reclaim his job working on gas lines in the Wyoming desert, he knew he'd have only himself to rely on.

In late September, following the scraggly notes he'd written during his last coyote-led trip, Súchite set out from Buena Vista, his eastern Guatemalan hometown, which is inland from the Caribbean port town of Livingston, along the road to Peten in the department of Izabal. With Gatorade, water, and cans of corn and tuna in his backpack to sustain him, he hopped aboard a series of rickety buses and trucks that snaked their way into Mexico, past the U.S. border, and up into the Arizona desert.

At first, after trekking safely across the U.S. border, it looked as if he'd have no trouble reaching Wyoming. But nearly three and a half hours into the Sonoran Desert, on September 28, 2010, a U.S. Border Patrol agent nabbed Súchite in Ajo, Arizona. ICE records showed that Súchite had been caught previously at the border and had signed a voluntary deportation order. Súchite was arrested and taken to a cell at the Arizona Removal Operations Coordination Center, the deportation hub at the Phoenix-Mesa Gateway Airport that ICE opened in March 2010 to send Central Americans, most of them Guatemalan, back to their home countries on regularly scheduled flights.

As of September 18 in fiscal year 2010, ICE centers around the country deported 158,964 people on flights to destinations worldwide on what some call ICE Air. Nearly 18 percent of those people—28,204—were sent to Guatemala City, most of them on flights from Mesa-Phoenix Gateway. After Mexicans, according to ICE data, Guatemalans make up the second-highest number of deportees from the United States. Deportations from Mesa took a sharp rise during the Bush administration, as the Arizona Republic reported, from about 6,150 in fiscal year 2003 to nearly 16,000 in 2006. The numbers have continued to grow under the Obama administration. And the flights aren't cheap—for each one-way trip to Latin America, the federal government spends an average of $560 per deportee, according to 2010 ICE data. Little of this cost goes to passenger amenities. The in-flight meal on Súchite's plane was a sack lunch that contained a cheese sandwich and a juice box.

Juan Sebastian Chavez, a few rows up from Súchite, was a first-time flier from Mesa-Phoenix Gateway. A forty-two-year-old from a community inhabited by a handful of mostly indigenous families, Chavez resembled most of the plane's passengers—high cheekbones, ashen complexion, small frame. And like many of the deportees, he was worried about money.

Chavez left his wife and children in Colcoquitz, an isolated village near Mexico in western Guatemala, where the people speak Mam, one of the country's twenty-three recognized Amerindian languages. There are no roads in or out of Colcoquitz—it's a three-hour mountain trek to Ixchiguan, the nearest town. In 2005, Hurricane Stan shattered the hamlet and carried away the village's topsoil, making it impossible for residents to grow corn, a Guatemalan staple.

"There are no fields to work," Chavez explained in Spanish.

Desperate to feed his family, Chavez borrowed the equivalent of about $1,250 in quetzales at 15 percent interest to fund a trip to visit his friend in the U.S. who promised to help him get a job in Minnesota. Chavez was caught on his way north, and is now deep in debt. He doesn't know whether he'll try the trip again.

Immigrant-rights activists paint those who cross the border illegally as the poorest, most vulnerable in society—the exploited backbone of the American economy. Anti-illegal immigration activists describe them as job stealers, invaders, and leeches who are contributing to the eventual downfall of an overly generous United States.

Súchite doesn't consider himself part of either group. Unlike Chavez and many of the others on the plane, his reasons for venturing north have little to do with surviving. It's about thriving, he explained.

"Sometimes you have to take risks," he said, "or else you'll never achieve anything."

Most Guatemalan men are married with children by the time they are in their early twenties. But Súchite, who is Ladino, a mix of Spanish and indigenous blood, had none of the usual attachments when he decided to set out on his own.

"In Guatemala you have two alternatives to make something of a good life," he said, holding up two fingers. "You join the narcos or you leave for the United States."

In his stylish, well-fitting jeans and Puma-like shoes, Súchite stood out on the planeful of men, who mostly wore dusty work boots and oversize pants and shirts. Savvier and more educated than the typical deportee, he showed off his ruby-encrusted gold ring from his 2004 high school graduation—an achievement in a country with a 30 percent illiteracy rate.

Three brown beaded bracelets Súchite bought on his way through Mexico decorated his arm. But he had hopes for a better souvenir from his trip, an iPhone 4.

Súchite said the temptation of joining the narcotics trade is a lure for young men like him, who carry ambition and want more in a country where social class follows a family for generations. But many who join the narco trade end up dead. Migrating north, he said, is a less-dangerous alternative.

"Over there you can make a pretty good life and you can save something," he said. "Over there you can treat yourself to nice things."

During the four-and-a-half-hour flight, many of Súchite's fellow passengers slept, awakened only by the announcements of two escorted bathroom breaks and lunch. As the plane neared Guatemala City, a few pulled yellowed family photos from their pockets while everyone buckled their seat belts and braced themselves for what U.S. Immigration and Customs Enforcement considered the end of the journey. For the deportees, though, the real journey was just beginning.

The welcome center created for the thousands of Guatemalan migrants who return home every year is a drab concrete building that blends into the rest of the Guatemala City airport, a scar on the green tropical range enclosing it. Some of the new arrivals from Arizona sighed with relief as they filed inside. Others smiled uneasily, scratching their heads. A few hastily covered their faces with their hands and T-shirts, hiding from the local press, who were there to report their arrival.

A half-dozen Guatemalan immigration officers in white polo shirts handed out sack lunches, jotted down the repatriated men's information, inked their thumbs, and directed them to sit in a waiting area.

Above them, a sign written in Spanish and Quiché read: "Ya estás en tu país y con tu gente. It ko chupan ri a tinamit ki kin ri ka winiäg." Translation: "You are now in your country and with your people."

One of the Guatemalan immigration officials stood before his captive audience and greeted the group with his best line: "Welcome back to your country, young men. Because there are people who leave and never return."

The men inhaled their meals as the Guatemalan official spoke, but it wasn't until the ICE officers left the building that their sober faces thawed. Whispers became yells and teasing among friends. Noisy conversations erupted as long lines formed behind a bank of telephones—each of the men was entitled to a free, three-minute call.

"I'm leaving for home right now," Súchite said into the receiver when he reached his mother and told her that he was okay.

He hung up and then made one more stop to recover his backpack, which got through transit with all of his money and personal items intact. It's part of protocol for U.S. officials to return all belongings found on deportees at the time of capture, and Súchite said that during his three times in U.S. custody he's never had anything taken.

It's different in Mexico, Súchite said. He heard stories of police theft, brutality, and worse against Central Americans when he was caught there and thrown into jail next to inmates convicted of robbery and homicide. "Mexico is dangerous for us."

But so is Guatemala City for a freshly arrived deportee. The capital has a reputation for theft, kidnappings, even killings, and the returnees, some with wads of dollars in their pockets, are easy marks.

At a makeshift money-exchange counter at the airport terminal, Súchite received 1,200 quetzales for $150 he was carrying, and then entered the noisy and congested mess that is Guatemala City. Cars honked. Sirens wailed. Trucks burped fumes. Pedestrians breathed in plumes of exhaust.

Three unmarked white buses idled, waiting to take the deportees to terminals across the city. After that, they'd be responsible for paying their own way home.

While Súchite had plenty of money to get back to his small tropical town, many others did not. Súchite handed one man he befriended 60 quetzales—about $7.50—and split about 110 quetzales among six others running toward the buses.

"Poor guys," he said. "They didn't even have enough for their bus fare back home."

As the government-provided buses began to fill, Súchite hung back. A seasoned deportee, he knew it would be smarter to find his own transportation right from the start. The government vehicles, he claimed, were moving targets for potential thieves.

"Besides, they're too slow," he said. "I want to get home as soon as possible."

Súchite then jumped into a taxi with a couple of other deportees he was helping out. The older of the two talked about how he had to find a way north again, to the wife and children he left behind in the United States. He was on the hunt for a coyote.

Ervin Lopez, a fifty-two-year-old who has chauffeured deportees for the past three years, ricocheted his white Toyota-turned-taxi past dented vehicles and pedestrians in a ride that resembled a game of Frogger.

"This was today's second flight of deportees," he said. Snarled in traffic, he cranked down his window. His brow beaded with sweat, Lopez began his daily lecture. "The truth is that I think what they do, traveling up there, is not correct," he said of the deportees. His waving finger punctuated his lesson. Súchite and his friends pretended not to listen.

"One can make it here if one is astute enough," the driver said. "Really, if you can't make it here, how are you going to make it on the other side—lost among Americans?"

Some of his passengers, Lopez said, have cried in his taxi. He spoke of the naturales—the indigenous folks who barely speak Spanish, indebted up to $6,000.

"They should invest that money here instead," he said.

Later, Súchite dismissed the taxi driver's opinion as "ignorant," but at the bus terminal he thanked the driver and paid him 60 quetzales. He and the other two men exchanged numbers and hugs before separating. A moment later, Súchite realized that he'd missed the 3:30 P.M. bus, and the next one wouldn't get him all the way home. A quick ride on a second taxi and another 60 quetzales took him to a separate terminal ten minutes away.

Súchite grabbed a ticket and collapsed into seat forty-three—the last seat sold. This bus wasn't as nice or as fast as the one at the first terminal, but it would have to do.

Súchite surrendered to six and a half more hours of travel. No air conditioning. Windows rolled down. Dust caked around the torn cushions. Some of the passengers stood, gripping the luggage compartments above.

"I hate how they allow people to stand," Súchite said. "There's no order here, compared to the U.S."

A second later, the bus growled its way through the city's oldest neighborhoods, squeezing through narrow colonial streets originally built for travelers on horseback.

The heat radiating from the diesel engine cooked Súchite's feet. Motorcycles zoomed past the bus. Big rigs hauling weighed-down trailers sped by on a two-lane highway, passing the bus rolling north through the country's green interior.

"PEANUTS. QUESADILLAS," YELLED A woman as she climbed aboard the bus, carefully balancing her wares. The sales pitch woke Súchite, who had been sleeping for the past couple hours.

He beckoned the woman and paid 20 quetzales for two corn tortillas topped with tomato-doused chicken.

"Organic," he said. "Not like that stuff Americans call chicken. Not the same taste."

About an hour later, the bus screeched its way into Morales—essentially a town with a cafeteria and gas station, serving truck drivers and travelers.

Súchite bumped fists with Ever Aldana, a twenty-three-year-old who supervises the station. They are old high school classmates.

"I thought you were in the United States," Suchite said. Aldana replied that he's never had the desire to go.

Soon enough, Súchite was back on the bus, only about an hour south from home. The highway, which heads north en route to El Petén and eventually Mexico, is the same route Súchite has taken many times—north to Naranjo on the border of Guatemala and Mexico.

With about a half hour to go before his stop, the bus lurched to a halt, near the Cruce de Ruidosa. Two Guatemalan transit officials climbed aboard. Súchite was about to undergo an immigration check in his own country. The officers were looking for foreigners—specifically other Central Americans making their way to the United States.

"They do this all the time," Súchite said, throwing up his hands in exasperation.

The uniformed men worked their way down the bus aisle, demanding identification from each passenger.

"Documents?" they barked.

One of the officials stopped before a husky man sipping on a water bottle.

"You have none?" the official said. "Out," he commanded, and pointed to the door.

Then the official stopped before Súchite. "Documents," he ordered.

Súchite got out his identification card. "Son of a bitch," he murmured under his breath when the official turned his back. Súchite pointed out that Central Americans are allowed to move and work freely within the region without a visa. "Still they hassle them," he complained. "All for money. They're just transit police. This isn't even their area. They'll probably take 50 to 100 quetzales from each of them. It's wrong what they do to these people."

At least ten men were forced from the bus. Salvadorans, Nicaraguans, Hondurans—all lined up, inspected up and down by an official pointing a flashlight at them.

Soon after, the bus engine revved and the men who'd been kicked off ran toward the door, hopping on just before it shifted into gear. Back at their seats, the murmurs and questioning began as a love song by Ana Gabriel blasted from the chauffer's cab.

The husky man seated in front of Súchite, a Salvadoran, introduced himself as Jose. He wouldn't give his last name. Jose said he was heading to Miami. It was his third trip north. He wouldn't say whether the officials took any cash from them, and didn't seem bothered by the inspection. The hardest part of the journey, Jose pointed out, awaited them in Mexico. Neither the authorities there nor the drug runners show mercy toward migrants. They rob and accost people at will. He rubbed the sweat off his brow and took a sip from his water bottle.

"You know," Súchite whispered, "Jose is the coyote. He told the guy next to him to have the money ready for the police."

The bus accelerated. The driver, looking to make up lost time, zoomed past Rio Dulce, a town overrun by American and European expats and tourists. Their white yachts glistened in the river, dwarfing the one-engine fishing boats belonging to locals. Merengue music flowed out of a popular nightclub called Disco Bahia. It was a Friday night after all, Súchite pointed out. He was only twenty minutes from home.

A FEW HUGS. A pat on the back. No tears. Unlike a telenovela, Súchite's family reunion was drama free. After the roadside greeting from his nephew, Súchite stepped inside his childhood home, where his parents invited him to take a seat at the head of the dining table.

Above them was a tin roof; below, a concrete floor. Rebar poked out of cinder blocks where a door should have been, and much of the dining room was open to the outside. Two hammocks swayed across the de facto concrete porch, which becomes a nightly domain for several geckos.

The home is undergoing a remodel, Súchite explained. There's not much money to finish the job.

Súchite's older sister Suceli, thirty-five, emerged from the kitchen with a plateful of refried black beans and a couple of stiff corn tortillas topped with two anemic pork rinds.

A carpenter by trade, Súchite left a wooden railing around the open-air room half finished before heading north.

"Now that he's back he'll have to fix it for me," said his mother, Edith Consuelo Hernandez de Súchite. She laughed. "We're going to put him to work."

The first time Súchite left for the United States, in 2006, Edith was overcome with sadness. While she still worries, this time around things felt more routine.

"Thank God he's here and he's okay," she said. "I never wanted him to go because it's a great risk. One has fear for one's children. There are so many stories of disaster."

"Here life is hard," said Súchite's father, Benjamin Súchite Cordón, who is considered something of a philosopher in the family. "That's why there are so many over there."

The seventy-year-old with a jack-o'-lantern smile wore a blue-and-white sports band on his head to keep what's left of his wild hair in place. He flipped through a book covered in cartoonlike wrapping paper and transparent tape. He studies the Bible and the dictionary every day.

Neither Edith nor Benjamin have ever wanted to visit or move to the United States. "I'd rather visit Israel," Edith said, adjusting a white cotton cloth covering her head. "We're evangelical."

Edith's kitchen serves passing travelers willing to pay for refried black beans, coffee, sugar-laced plantains, and whatever else she can coax up that day. There's a plastic sign outside advertising the diner—called Comedor Glendy, after her twenty-two-year-old daughter—but the restaurant is not much more than the family dining table.

"Business is still bad," she said, "but at least we have something coming in, enough to buy beans to eat."

Even though the diner is right along the main highway, a prized spot, business slowed after September 11, 2001.

"That's when things really got bad," Edith says. The crackdown on the U.S.-Mexico border after the terrorist attacks in the United States has meant fewer travelers heading north on the Guatemalan highway.

At first, Súchite says, the town experienced a tidal wave of locals returning to Buena Vista, some after decades in the U.S. But with fewer dollars funneling into town, the returning migrants had less money to spend at local businesses, including Edith's diner. Competing diners opened by deportees trying to start their lives anew dealt a second blow to Comedor Glendy.

Edith used to serve fifteen to twenty traditional meals on a given day. Now she's lucky to see five customers trickle in. Suceli and her young daughter, Noemi, pitch in by selling clothing and shoes from the diner. But the family mostly survives on whatever money Benjamin makes on side deals as an ad-hoc real estate broker. And on this day Benjamin had promising news. A Brazilian visitor may have some buyers interested in a 1,613-acre piece of land that Benjamin has been brokering on the outskirts of town. On the other hand, this parcel has been in play for five years. Edith rolled her eyes at the mention of the deal.

Still, if the land were to sell, Benjamin would stand to earn a 5 percent cut. The land is priced at 12 million quetzales, or about $1.5 million. That would be $75,000 for Benjamin. The money would go to finish the remodel, attend to Edith's diabetes, and other needs that have been put off for years.

With the money he earned in the U.S., Súchite managed to buy a few of his own plots of land, bordering his father's holdings. But he has yet to develop or cultivate the property. And so, for now, Súchite would crash at his parents' home.

He's not the only one. Suceli returned home with Noemi after the girl's father abandoned them for the capital. They rarely hear from him and he never sends money, Edith said in a hushed voice when Noemi looked away.

Another of Súchite's sisters left her son, Erick, in Buena Vista with her parents when she emigrated to Honduras and started another family with a new husband and new children.

Glendy, the youngest of the thirteen, will likely never live on her own. Edith called her a slow learner, and Súchite later explained that his sister may have slight mental retardation, but she's never been diagnosed.

"We had them out of respect for God," Edith said to explain her large family. "He said to grow and multiply, so we accept what God gives us."

"You see the years I have and I'm still working," said Benjamin, pointing to liver spots on his hands.

Súchite excused himself from the table to get ready for bed and Noemi followed. Then Erick, Glendy, and Benjamin rose from the table and blocked the dining room's entrance with plastic chairs—a nightly ritual.

"It's very safe here," Edith said. "The chairs are to keep dogs and other animals away from the kitchen." She grabbed the plates and shuffled her way to a concrete basin that serves as the kitchen sink.

"He's the most level-headed and centered of our children," Edith said of Súchite, as if revealing a secret. "He's the only one who graduated from high school out of the thirteen. He really liked school…he's also one of the few who looks out for us."

Súchite plopped into a sun-bleached hammock, stepped away from the back garden, and soon fell into a deep sleep.

ROCK SPRINGS, WYOMING, IS a kind of Mecca for job seekers. In the midst of the economic downturn, the city's official website still advertised its low unemployment rate to prospective residents. It was a promising place for Súchite to follow Benjamin Jr. and work alongside him at a plant creating, sandblasting, and painting gas pipes.

"They didn't ask for a Social Security card or papers," Súchite said. "They provided training in English and Spanish. I made $1,300 a week. Not in a month, in a week." Sometimes with overtime, he was paid up to $1,800 for a week's work.

He quickly warmed to American culture, developing a taste for country music.

"I like that Strait guy," he said, referring to country music legend George Strait.

Every month, he'd join the locals at the civic park to listen to country music. Other times he'd attend rodeos. It reminded him of his bull-riding days as a youth, when he earned the nickname "Matador."

"It was like out of a Western movie," he said.

Mostly, Súchite's American life revolved around work and hoarding pennies. Once in a while, he'd join his brother on road trips to Las Vegas, Oregon, or Los Angeles—places he found more interesting but less lucrative than Wyoming. "Too many immigrants and low-paying jobs," he said. In Rock Springs, he added, "there were...maybe twenty-five to thirty homes in town."

He regularly sent money home to his parents. On occasion he'd send packages full of talking dolls, stuffed animals, and other knickknacks for Erick and Noemi, who quickly became their uncle's biggest fans.

"If you are well behaved and finish your work, you won't get into trouble," said Súchite, who added that he never felt discriminated against. "I have no complaints."

And yet, even though he lived with his brother and other fellow Guatemalans, Súchite started to feel isolated in Wyoming and thought about returning home.

The first time he left Wyoming, however, it was against his will. Local authorities knocked on his door looking for a roommate who had abandoned his vehicle after drunkenly plowing into a kiosk. Instead of the roommate getting into trouble, clean-and-sober Súchite ended up in confinement when he was the one who answered the door and couldn't show that he was in the country legally. A few weeks after his April 2008 deportation, Súchite crossed back over the border and was quickly back at his old job.

But his glimpse of home stirred a longing for the family, friends, and slow-paced way of life he'd left behind in Buena Vista. After a few months back in Wyoming, he was still homesick. And so, in 2009, he returned to Guatemala, this time without the help of U.S. immigration authorities.

At first, he was thrilled to be home again. But after several months without finding a job that paid even close to what he was earning in the U.S., he realized he'd have to go north again to make a better life. And he was starting to miss Wyoming.

"I missed the work," he said, "the dollars, the country concerts and rodeos."

THE SOUND OF EDITH's weathered hands thumbing corn kernels off their cobs and into a plastic container on her lap was the first sound Súchite heard when he awoke.

"The hens are hungry," she said as she mixed their breakfast.

Erick and Noemi helped Suceli sort through blue, fuchsia, and mustard-yellow sandals and flip though racks of clothing in the next room, taking inventory of the items and hoping they might make a sale today. Most of the clothing was tagged with stickers that read "Made in China." Months earlier Suceli bought the lot at a discounted price from another lady who bought it wholesale abroad.

A teenager selling the local paper Nuestro Diario rode by on a rust-speckled bicycle, and Erick ran toward the boy to stop him. He paid 2.50 quetzales for the paper, which had a photo of a bloodied body on the front page.

"Many people call the paper Matan Diario [The Daily Kill]," Edith said, thumbing through the pages.

"Here in Guatemala," said Benjamin, "we're subject to a lot of natural disasters and then drugs and killings. Central American justice is justice at its lowest."

He took a sip of instant coffee and lowered his voice. "I like to speak truth," he said. "But the truth can be shocking. That's why lies are so popular here."

Just as in Colombia, Benjamin explained, local drug lords have started building schools, medical clinics, and roads, essentially filling the void of an inept government that is too corrupt to care. "The narcos. These people help the town, the poor," Benjamin said, shaking his head in disapproval. "But they control the people." He gazed at a neatly trimmed house in the neighborhood, which dwarfs the Súchite home.

In this town of banana trees and make-shift businesses, Súchite said, the trinity of providers have been the church, the drug runners, and the United States.

LINES OF LAUNDRY BAKED under the sun in the front yards of a mostly residential street as Súchite took a walk through town. He waved to friends driving by. They responded with honks and waves, as if he'd never left. Others he bumped into on foot urged him to come by later. His return to Buena Vista was nothing new. The novelty wore off years ago.

Of his five brothers, one half-brother, and six sisters, only Benjamin Jr. remains in the United States. Still, Súchite said, it's rare to run into young men between twenty and thirty-five years old in Buena Vista.

"They're in Georgia," said Súchite, pointing to a home on the left as he walked along the highway that cuts through town. "And they're in New Jersey..." He gestured toward another home, and then another. "That's New York, I think...Utah...Denver...

"They're all up there," he explained. "Most never return. They've been gone for eight, fifteen years."

This is a community inextricably linked with the United States. The town is marked by large, cinder-block homes paid for with dollars from the north and large trucks decorated with Virginia, Wyoming, and Utah license plates. "In almost every house," Súchite said, "there is someone on the other side without documents."

A local but now-retired coyote lives in a mustard-and-ketchup-colored home. Súchite waved at the man, who was sporting a cowboy hat and taking refuge from the sun underneath a covered porch.

"He used to take people up through Tijuana," Súchite said. "There, they were met by an American rancher who would take them to Los Angeles."

That was in the early eighties, though, when crossing was much easier.

"Here if you see a nice house it's because they have family on the other side," Súchite said, "or they're narcos."

The homes tell the story of each migrant's success or lack of it in the United States. Súchite gestured to a cinderblock one-story house with a Spanish-tiled roof. A locked gate fortified the property.

"They're now U.S. citizens and only visit every few years," Súchite said. "They ask friends or relatives to keep it looking good, and at the end of the month they send them money from the U.S."

Others lose their homes outright, giving up their land titles as partial collateral for safe passage across the border.

Up the road, weeds conspired to invade a half-built, white-washed home; its rusted door barely hung on its hinges.

"You see that house?" he said. "They've been away for years and have not done any improvements. They say that the couple still rents over in the U.S. After nine years, they still haven't bought a house there. Supposedly they drive around in big SUVs and live it up, drinking. They have nothing to show for their troubles."

Súchite, who cringes at the sight of anyone who litters, said he kept clear of drugs, alcohol, and other mischief during his two years in Wyoming.

"I was there to work and to save money," he said. "Imagine...risking your life and throwing it all away on vice."

Súchite thinks that Latino immigrants who drive around the United States in souped-up trucks after having a few beers give others a bad name.

"They really don't deserve to be in the United States," he said. "They just earn money to blow it and don't think about anything else but partying."

Still, he understands that money brings all sorts of temptations.

"Let's say you make $300 a week and you can buy a twenty-four-pack of beer for $30," he said. "Here you are paid 300 quetzales a week and a twenty-four-pack will cost you 240 quetzales, so you really can't afford to drink.

"You see all the money and everything so cheap there. People just get crazy," Súchite said. "Wrongly, they think they'll never get in trouble. They think, Once I cross, I'm free of trouble or danger."

SÚCHITE HELD NOEMI'S TINY hand as they meandered past palm trees under the blue tropical sky. He was checking out his three plots of land, tributes to his quick but successful stint in the United States.

"I hope to build a home here someday," he said.

He trudged onto the fertile land, overgrown and flourishing under the year-round sun. Unlike Rock Springs, where minus-twenty-five is typical winter weather, Buena Vista reaches sweltering temperatures in the thick of summer, forcing residents to sleep in hammocks because a bed is simply too hot to lie on.

As Súchite prepared to climb into his brother's mud-caked truck, Noemi clung to her uncle's leg, begging him to take her into Rio Dulce. He reluctantly put her down.

"Some other time," he promised. This trip to Rio Dulce, a twenty-minute drive away, was all business.

Once in town, he slowed to a putter, swerving past backpackers and other tourists, as he backed his truck into an official parking space.

His first stop was to remind a friend of money owed, but the friend wasn't home. At an Internet café, he checked up on his fifty-four Facebook friends, scrolled through e-mail, and picked up a cellphone.

Shopping for dinner was next on his list. A scrawny boy standing on a boat tied to the port threw some mojarra into a black plastic bag. The fish flopped about as Súchite steered his truck down a bumpy mud path toward a field on the outskirts of town where his thirty-five-year-old brother Edvin grows okra.

"Maybe I should grow okra," Súchite pondered out loud.

The cottonlike plant grows well in Guatemala and, spurred by demand in the United States and Europe, the country has become a major exporter of the vegetable in frozen form. Súchite would hardly get rich growing okra, but his brother makes an okay living at it.

"This way I can have some income for some sort of study." Súchite was thinking about going to law school.

"My family, my land," he said, "it's all here."

BACK IN BUENA VISTA, Súchite's father laid on his hammock, holding his wife's hand. He had bad news. The land buyers didn't come through. The Brazilian made excuses and tried to delay the sale.

"I think he was lying to you all along," Edith said.

The situation is just another example of what sparked Súchite's most recent attempt to return to the United States. Now that he's back, he's not sure what he will do. Stay and grow okra and try to earn money for law school or try his luck in the north once again? While it's become increasingly difficult to cross into the U.S., Súchite thinks that if one is smart and careful, it's not as dangerous as most make it out to be.

"Three times I've tried crossing and I've never seen a dead person," he said. "The ones who die are those who allow drugs to be stuffed into their packs so they don't have to pay. Or they allow themselves to be put into the back of trailers. Those are the people who die. I'd rather walk the whole way."

Martita Aguilar, his twelve-year-old niece, listened closely as Súchite talked. She said she wants to try her luck up north, too. But she doesn't want to do it her uncle's way—illegally.

"I want to go earn dollars," said the fair-skinned girl with an innocent smile. "Actually, I really want to go study over there. I just wish we could all go."

She's a good student, Súchite said of his niece. He wants to get her a scholarship, perhaps some sort of exchange through a local Rotary Club. But he'd hate for her to cross into the U.S. the way he did.

While he would never deny anyone else's right to make the journey north—he'd even be okay with a future son trying his luck—he said it's different for women. He's heard about and seen smugglers take advantage of the young, pretty girls, and he thinks the coyotes would likely have their way with Martita.

Then it was Erick's turn to speak up. He'd like to make the trip, too.

"It would be an adventure," Erick said. "I want to work for dollars."

He admired one of the Mexican bracelets his uncle gave him after an earlier trip. His fingers grazed the leather strap around his arm as he looked out to the highway and watched the buses zip by the front porch. Most of them were headed north.

RUNNING WITH THE DEVIL:
A LIFETIME OF VAN HALEN

John Albert

THE FIRST TIME I hear Van Halen I am fourteen years old, riding in a car through the foothills of the San Gabriel Mountains. My friend Steve Darrow is riding shotgun while his dad steers the dusty old Volvo station wagon. Chris Darrow is in his forties and has long hair and a slightly drooping cowboy mustache. In the sixties and early seventies, as a member of the Nitty Gritty Dirt Band and an obscure but influential group called the Kaleidoscope, he, along with Gram Parsons, Linda Ronstadt, and others, forged what became the classic California sound. His long-haired, Black Sabbath-loving son, Steve, would go on to play in an early version of Guns N' Roses. But on this particular night, Chris is driving us and another friend named Peter home from a party thrown by a local ceramics artist. While the aging hippies and college professors sipped wine and purchased meticulously decorated casserole plates, my friends and I hiked into a nearby orange grove to smoke pot in the moonlight. And as the car heads home along Baseline Boulevard, passing the silhouettes of orange groves and vineyards, the three of us are still incredibly stoned and no one is talking much.

Someone turns on the radio. It's tuned to KROQ, a small, independent station that has little in common with the corporate behemoth it would become. In 1978, the station broadcasts a strange mix of surreal sketch comedy and new music across the Southland. A show called The Hollywood Night Shift riffs on "barbecue bat burgers" and "downhill screen-door races." Meanwhile, the station's present-day last man standing, Rodney Bingenheimer, who morning goons Kevin and Bean use as a prop for their moronic shtick, introduces punk music to kids across Southern California. By this time, my friends and I have already fallen under the sway of the raw, new sounds emerging from a ripped, torn, and safety-pin-adorned England.

As we cruise along Baseline, I have no idea what's on the radio. I stare out the window into a passing darkness with hazy, Mexican-weed-induced tunnel vision. Then, suddenly, this extraordinary sound from the car's stereo snaps me back. Steve reaches over and turns up the volume. It's guitar playing, but not like anything we have heard before. Until this very moment, the reigning guitar heroes have been English, amateur warlocks, such as Jimmy Page and Ritchie Blackmore, playing sped-up, bastardized versions of American blues. But this is faster and weirder. Toward the one-minute mark, the playing veers into completely uncharted territory, and the final forty-two seconds sound like Gypsy jazz legend Django Reinhardt on CIA acid.

It is a style of playing that will so dramatically alter the musical landscape that thirty years later it will sound normal, even rote. But in 1978, this burst of unabashed virtuosity and noise, something we'll later learn is appropriately called "Eruption," earns unexpected respect from three punk rock children and one middle-aged country rock musician. As the whole thing reaches a frenzied crescendo of undulating distortion, the four of us start to laugh.

Until, that is, the distortion immediately segues to a revamped version of the Kinks' classic "You Really Got

Me," rumbling through the car's little speakers. This is not hard rock as we know it—no high-pitched, operatic wailing about sorcery or Viking lore. With no visual reference to go on, it seems to have as much in common with early punk as with bands such as Led Zeppelin and Rush—except, of course, for the crazy, outer-space guitar solo. In retrospect, this makes perfect sense. Before it became one of the biggest bands in the world, Van Halen routinely played on bills with prepunk bands like the Runaways, the Mumps, and the Dogs.

When the song ends, Steve's dad, who may or may not be stoned as well, just nods his head and says, "Far out."

IT IS THE SOUNDTRACK to a world that doesn't exist anymore. I know because that world is where I come from.

Van Halen had been playing the suburbs east of Los Angeles for several years before we heard them on the radio that night. In fact, the previous year, Peter's diminutive, science-teacher mom, who when speaking tended to coo pleasantly like a pigeon, unwittingly supplied Van Halen with several bottles of bourbon and tequila. The occasion was the band's appearance at a show on the local college radio station hosted by Peter's older, but still underage, brother and some of his friends. Following seventies rock etiquette, they felt it only proper to provide the band with alcohol and other recreational substances.

I remember this because my friends and I had been coerced into distributing fliers announcing the band's appearance on the show. Most of our peers glanced at the crudely rendered image of a young David Lee Roth flaunting his soon-to-be-legendary chest pelt and bulging package and simply tossed the fliers away. A lot of those same kids would, several years later, pay large sums of money to see the band headline the massive Forum in Inglewood.

In the years leading up to their record deal and worldwide fame, the Internet was still science fiction and the only video game widely available, Pong, mimicked ping-pong only without the riveting excitement and health benefits. As a result, kids were primarily focused on two things, rock music and getting wasted. Days were spent under the sun and smog, getting high, playing sports, skateboarding in empty swimming pools and on downhill streets. Weekend nights were devoted almost entirely to massive backyard parties. And Van Halen ruled the backyard party scene in and around the San Gabriel Valley.

Unsuspecting parents would leave town and hundreds of kids would descend on a designated home like tanned, stoned locusts. Down the block from my parents' house was a large, ramshackle manor known as the Resort. Sunburned British drunks lived there, and their kids were a wild and eccentric brood bearing names such as Yo-Yo, Kiddy, Sissy, Lad, and Mims.

Parties at the Resort were notorious. I remember watching a formally attired adult couple slow their car in front of the Resort as a party raged inside. Some long-haired kids staggered into the street, walked onto the hood of the couple's car and then its roof, howling like wolves. My preteen friends and I finally mustered the courage to venture inside one of the parties. There, we discovered a maze of hedonistic delights: the dining-room table lined with cocaine, a cracked door revealing a nubile high school girl having sex, people jumping from second-story windows into the pool, fights and noisy drag races in the street out front. Throughout

272

the beautifully raucous affair, a young rock 'n' roll band named China White stood precariously close to the swimming pool playing with all the swagger of the Rolling Stones at Madison Square Garden.

While Van Halen played the huge outdoor parties and lucrative high school dances, China White was the band of choice in my immediate neighborhood. The group was composed of young heroin addicts who wore cowboy hats and played Southern rock. Somehow, it was a style that made perfect sense in the slowed-down, drugged-out seventies suburbs. Besides a few performances at the Resort, the band's highest-profile gigs were at the palatial hillside estate of a local ice cream fortune heir. The band's leader, John Dooley, now lives in Bangkok, where he teaches music and plays in a rhythm and blues revue.

"Those were some epic fucking parties," Dooley says when I reach him by phone in Bangkok. "We had a big stage on the tennis courts and the pool house was our backstage area. We invited 500 fellow students, charged a cover, and then got all my older brother's biker buddies to bounce and run screen for the cops. There would be close to a thousand kids there and we would be getting high and fucking chicks in the pool house between sets. I remember we left with our guitar cases stuffed with cash."

But it was with his next band, Mac Pinch, that Dooley's path began to cross regularly with Van Halen's as the two bands shared bills both locally and in Hollywood. "I was always really impressed by Eddie Van Halen and their bass player [Michael Anthony]. They definitely stood out musically, especially Eddie," Dooley says. "Their singer, Roth, was like the guy we had—by no means a great singer, but really loud and worked the crowd well. They used to have a party van with the Van Halen logo painted on the sides, and Roth was always out there in that van. He was kind of obnoxious, but he had a real knack with the ladies. He would bring them out to that van one after another. I had more than my share, but Roth did better than his band and ours combined. We used to play this biker bar in Downey with them called the Downey Outhouse, where they served popcorn in bedpans and beer in urinals.

"It got pretty competitive between the bands, and one time our roadie unplugged Van Halen during a show at the Pasadena Civic."

During these years, roughly 1974 to 1976, Van Halen surpassed all rivals, including San Fernando Valley stars Quiet Riot, to emerge as the premier hard-rock act in Los Angeles. Besides a willingness to play nearly anywhere at any time—the band once played an early-morning breakfast concert at my high school a few years before I attended—the band's rise seemed due, largely, to two distinct qualities. One was the playing of Eddie Van Halen, who had perfected the innovative method of using the fingers of his picking hand to pound the guitar's fret board, creating a lightning-fast, quasiclassical style that quickly became the talk of Southland musicians. Van Halen reportedly became so guarded about this technique that he began to play solos with his back to the audience.

And while the teenage boys came to marvel at Eddie's technical virtuosity, the girls flocked to see the band's flamboyant lead singer. David Lee Roth would take the stage shirtless, wearing skin-tight spandex pants or fur-lined assless chaps, none of which dampened his enthusiasm for jumping into the air and doing karate kicks and splits. Visually, Roth resembled a stoner superhero with his wild, long blond hair, muscular physique and exaggerated party bravado. But what set him apart from so many aspiring front men of the time, was that, unbeknownst to his mostly blond-haired, blue-eyed audience, Roth was Jewish. And though his father was a wealthy ophthalmologist, young Roth went to public schools and ended up attending primarily black John Muir High in Pasadena. As a result, he was able to merge an over-the-top, borscht-belt-like showmanship with the booty-shaking sex appeal of his Funkadelicized classmates. It was a combination that made Roth a near perfect rock star for those hedonistic times.

While Van Halen's star rose, my friend Dooley and Mac Pinch were on a different trajectory. Instead of showcasing alongside their one-time rivals at Hollywood clubs such as the Starwood and the Whisky, the drug-addled young cowboys started booking USO tours and playing military bases to support their various nonmusical habits. When Van Halen finally had its big breakthrough and signed to Warner Bros. Records, Mac Pinch was off playing to halls of drunken Marines.

"Those were serious smack days for me," Dooley reflects. "Eventually it all caught up to me and I had to come back home and do some jail time, and that was the end of the band." (We don't discuss how Dooley stole my parents' television set.) I ask him if he has regrets after seeing his former rivals go on to such massive success.

"Do I think we should have tried harder? That maybe it could have been us?" he offers. "Sure. But we had a lot of fun playing those parties. I have some great memories. It was a pretty awesome time to be young and playing in a rock 'n' roll band."

TWO YEARS AFTER FIRST hearing Van Halen on the car radio, the world around me seems a dramatically different place. My once-long hair is now short and jagged and I'm wearing studded wristbands with a spider-shaped earring punched through an infected hole in my ear. In suburbs across Southern California, punk rockers have swelled from a besieged minority to an increasingly aggressive subculture. There are pervasive hostilities between the heavy-metal-loving "stoners" and the new punks. Both sides instigate violence. By now, I have been expelled from the local high school for truancy and am enrolled in something called Claremont Collegiate Academy. Despite its snooty name, the place is filled with kids who have failed at the local high schools. My classmates are mainly long-haired drug users, agitated Iranian immigrants, and kids with assorted behavioral disorders. The principal will eventually be arrested on child porn charges.

During one lunch break, I stroll out into the school parking lot and am greeted by the pounding, tribal drums of Van Halen's latest single, "Everybody Wants Some," blasting from the open doors of a huge four-wheel-drive truck. Two very attractive teenage girls stand on the truck's roof, dancing to the music. Both are outfitted in tight, shimmering spandex pants, halter tops, and moon boots. They bump their perfectly shaped asses together and sing along with David Lee Roth: "Everybody wants some/I want some too/Everybody wants some, baby, how 'bout you?" As I walk by, a girl with feathered blonde hair points at me and sneers, seductively, singing, "Everybody wants some, baby, how 'bout you?"

I do.

A week later, I end up ditching school with the monster truck's down-jacket-wearing owner and the two dancing girls. We drive into the nearby mountains to sip Southern Comfort and smoke pot. The girls tell me that Van Halen singer David Lee Roth is a "super fox" and they both desperately want to fuck him. On the drive home, I'm in the truck's back seat making out with the blond girl. Her lip gloss tastes like raspberry candy. I caress her nipples through her shirt and eventually slip a finger between her legs, which seems like a monumental achievement. I stop when I realize she has fallen asleep in my arms. A few days later, she pulls me into an unoccupied darkroom between classes and we fondle one another for a few seconds. After several more brief flirtations, the pull of our opposing camps is just too much and we eventually stop talking. A year later, I run into her at a local hamburger stand, where she works behind the counter. She hands me my food and waves me off before I can pay.

I'M AN EIGHTEEN-YEAR-OLD IN the basement of a Hollywood nightclub called the Cathay De Grande. Slumped in an empty booth, my eyes are closed and my head rests on the table. Fifteen minutes earlier, I injected heroin inside the cramped restroom with the sound man. It is a Monday night and a local blues outfit called Top Jimmy and the Rhythm Pigs are on the small stage. They are fronted by a white-trash blues legend, Top Jimmy, and play the club every Monday night. The place is nearly empty. The Rhythm Pigs are cool, but like most in attendance, I am really here to score drugs. This accomplished, I nod off, lost in some distant dream world as the band plays their hearts out just a few feet away.

When I eventually drift back to reality, something odd catches my ear. Instead of Top Jimmy's throaty voice, someone lets loose with an exaggerated, arena-rock scream. Perplexed, I lift my head and focus on the small stage. There, sandwiched between the band's rotund bass player and slovenly guitar player, Carlos Guitarlos, is none other than David Lee Roth, holding the microphone and striking a majestic rock pose. It's surreal seeing one of the most successful singers in the world standing in this dilapidated basement club alongside a bunch of musicians teetering on the brink of homelessness and liver failure.

"Whoa-bop-ditty-doobie-do-bop, oh yeah, baby!" Roth yells out, putting his arm around an inebriated Top Jimmy. As bleary-eyed Jimmy leans in and begins to sing, Roth watches him with a beaming smile, clapping his hands and laughing in exaggerated-but-sincere appreciation. "Top-motherfucking Jimmy!" he yells out, as if addressing a sold-out arena instead of several stunned junkies and alcoholics. The reaction from the sparse crowd is indifference bordering on hostility. There is nothing less cool in the Hollywood underground than a seemingly happy millionaire rock star. But Top Jimmy is smiling with his arm around Roth. And a few years later, when Van Halen releases its multiplatinum-selling record 1984, the album features a track called "Top Jimmy."

"Top Jimmy cooks, Top Jimmy swings, Top Jimmy—he's the king," Roth sings in tribute to his friend, who would eventually die of liver failure.

THE NEXT TWO DECADES are a creative dark age for Van Halen. After years of ego-fueled turmoil from all sides, David Lee Roth leaves the band to pursue a doomed solo career. An entirely unremarkable singer named Sammy Hagar replaces him and Van Halen becomes one of the most boring bands in existence. Roth recedes from the limelight, studying martial arts and making an ill-fated stab as a radio deejay. Eddie's excessive drinking begins to take a toll. One night in 1993, at the height of the grunge years, a drunken Eddie appears backstage for a Nirvana concert at the Forum. He reportedly begs Kurt Cobain to let him join the band on stage, explaining, "I'm all washed up; you are what's happening now." He also, for unexplained reasons, supposedly sniffs Cobain's deodorant before calling Nirvana's half-black rhythm guitarist Pat Smear a "Mexican" and a "Raji." Needless to say, he is not allowed on stage.

In the following years, news of Van Halen is sporadic, largely unsubstantiated, and generally not positive. One story has Eddie sitting in with guitarless rap-rock buttheads Limp Bizkit. When they are slow to return his prized equipment, Eddie supposedly goes back with automatic weapons. An acquaintance of mine who sells rare guitars does some business with Eddie and subsequently receives lonely, rambling, late-night phone calls from him. An old friend who is now a teacher hosts a day for his students to bring in their grandparents. One student inexplicably brings in Eddie Van Halen. He stays for hours, politely talking to the kids about his Dutch heritage and childhood music studies.

During this time, Roth is arrested in a New York City park for purchasing weed. And when a meth-addled man attempts a wee-hours break-in at the singer's Pasadena mansion, the intruder is surprised to find "Diamond Dave" wide awake and at the ready. Some accounts have Roth training a gun on the intruder while others have the lifelong martial-arts enthusiast, resplendent in silk pajamas, subduing the man with a lightening-fast nunchuck demonstration.

But as the years pass, "important" bands like Nirvana feel increasingly dated while the celebratory party anthems of Roth-era Van Halen continue to dominate the airwaves. Their songs are played repeatedly every day on multiple stations throughout the civilized world. And after several well-publicized misfires including an aborted reunion and a stint with a much-maligned singer named Gary Cherone, Eddie Van Halen and David Lee Roth finally find their way back to each other in 2007. The group announces it will be hitting the road, though original bassist Michael Anthony is to be replaced by Eddie's sixteen-year-old son, Wolfgang, who reportedly suggested the tour and persuaded his dad to reconcile with Roth. What ensues is the band's highest-grossing tour to date.

I catch Van Halen's show at the gleaming new Staples Center in downtown L.A., anticipating a heartfelt homecoming. Instead, I get a slick and entertaining professional rock show. There are no missteps, but little if anything seems spontaneous. Then, leading into the song "Ice Cream Man," Roth stops and delivers a monologue. I later learn from watching videos online that it's pretty much the same speech in every city. Still, it has particular significance in Los Angeles, mere miles from where it all started. "The suburbs, I come from the suburbs," Roth says to the cheering crowd. "You know, where they tear out the trees and name streets after them. I live on Orange Grove—there's no orange grove there; it's just me. In fact, most of us in the band come from the suburbs and we used to play the backyard parties there…I remember it like it was yesterday."

NOT LONG AGO, I'M at my parents' house in those very suburbs, visiting with my dad, who is slowly dying, his body wasting away. After leaving his house, I stop for gas. As I stand at the pump, a tall, disheveled man approaches me. He begins to ask for spare change, then stops and stares at me. After a moment, he says my name. I look back blankly and he awkwardly introduces himself. It turns out that we grew up together. The once-handsome and talented athlete has been drinking hard and using cocaine, and his life has unraveled in dramatic fashion. The last I'd heard, he was living behind a local bar in an abandoned camper shell but was asked to leave for having too many guests and making too much noise. I ask how he is and he just shakes his head. I take out my wallet and offer a twenty, which he refuses. I insist, and he eventually palms the bill and slides it into a pocket. After some strained small talk, he asks for a ride to a friend's apartment. I reluctantly agree.

The two of us drive through the streets of our shared childhood in awkward silence. The orange groves have long since turned into a sprawl of tract housing and circuitous dead ends, both literal and figurative. I turn on the radio, scan stations, and eventually stop on Van Halen's 1977 classic "Ain't Talkin' 'Bout Love." I turn up the volume. After a few seconds, the propulsive guitar riff fades down and David Lee Roth begins to talk.

"I been to the edge, an' there I stood an' looked down/You know I lost a lot of friends there, baby, I got no time to mess around."

The music builds in intensity before exploding into a powerful, defiant chorus: "Ain't talkin' 'bout love, my love is rotten to the core/Ain't talkin' 'bout love, just like I told you before, before, before/Hey hey hey!" By this time, my old friend is singing along and pumping his fist in the air. His eyes are moist from either alcohol, sadness, or both. The song finishes just as we pull in front of a dilapidated apartment complex, and he climbs out. He hesitates and looks in at me.

"Hey man, remember those crazy parties back in the day?" I nod and force a smile. "Those were some good fucking times," he says, reaching in and slapping my shoulder affectionately before disappearing into the darkness.

MUSHR<u>oo</u>MS T<u>o</u> MECCA

Matthew Fleischer

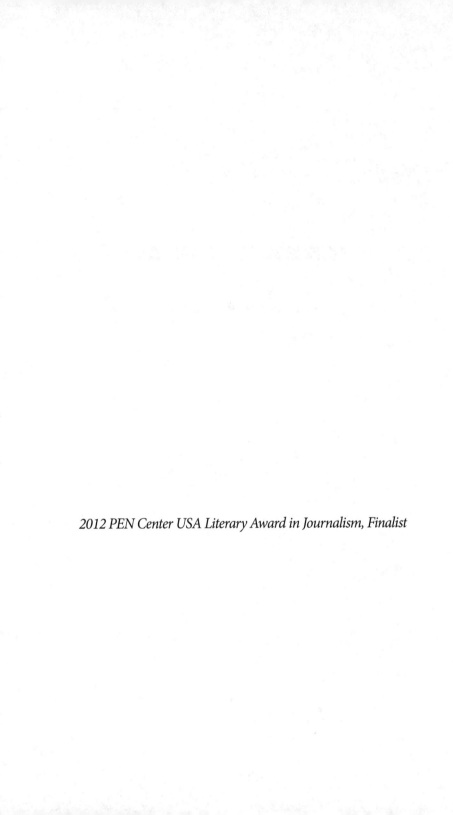

2012 PEN Center USA Literary Award in Journalism, Finalist

MY TEST OF MANHOOD begins at 4 in the morning in Glendale, California, on the first day of the hajj. The pigeons are still sleeping. In some countries they call pigeons squab and eat them as a delicacy. In America, we tend to let them feed on our scraps and then get pissed when they shit on our cars—a resource turned into a filthy, disease-ridden nuisance. You can learn a lot about a place by its birds.

By the time I get to Highland Park the roosters are waking up in hidden coops. Two hours and six miles later in South Pasadena the sun is up and the bourgeois parrots are squawking like mad on telephone wires. That's another thing we're good at in America: kidnapping exotic animals from their natural habitats, importing them in cages, and then setting them free.

The only people awake at this hour are Latino— Mexican, mostly. Prep cooks, bakers, and doughnut makers in Highland Park, landscapers in Pasadena. Except for the odd jogger, white people in these parts don't surface until around 8. Latinos, especially Mexicans, are the glue that holds this city together. Anyone who lives in Los Angeles knows this to be true, at least on a semiconscious level. But walk through the city three hours before you usually wake up and you'll experience it in a way you could never appreciate otherwise.

I'm twenty-nine and hovering near poverty when this journey begins—the scent of failure and emasculated rage wafting off me like a rat decomposing in your cupboard. I've just been laid off from what should have been my dream job, staff writer for the L.A. Weekly. When I was in high school, I imagined such work would entail lots of drugs and sex and long nights cultivating elegant prose. Instead I found myself working for a company that treated writing like my ex-girlfriend treated sex—a never-ending, soul-sapping negotiation. My dissatisfaction became more readable than many of my stories. Like a true child of the eighties, I was downsized faster than you can say Reaganomics. To the pliant goes the health insurance.

Unemployment has a way of inspiring introspection, and the conclusions I arrive at are not good. My thoughts drift to the last woman generous enough to sleep with me before my sacking. She nicknamed me "Tender Hands"—sadly, not for any extraordinary sensual prowess, but for my smooth, womanly, work-free hands. It's a cute-enough moniker when you're a staff writer for a well-known publication, but beyond pathetic when you're unemployed.

Tender hands…

When the apocalypse comes, when our crumbling economic order finally collapses for good, I'm fucked. Can't hunt, can't fish, can't raise crops, can't find water, can't fight, can't kill. I'll die a horrible, painful, embarrassing death—on my knees begging, or maybe alone and broken like a dog. Maybe I'll get lucky enough to catch a head shot from some wacko in a three-bedroom modular defending his lawn gnomes and aspirational furniture into eternity. But odds are, I'm going to drink untreated water from a drainage ditch or a scum-coated pond and contract diarrhea. I'll shit myself to death—which is how most people on Earth meet their untimely ends.

Imagine shitting yourself to death.

Something else soon dawns on me: I am going to be poor the rest of my life.

This would be fine if I had grown up that way. If I had learned to scrap. But I grew up in the suburbs, predestined for higher education. I'd spent my entire existence reading and cultivating ideas and masturbating plaintively out of boredom. I'd never done a day of real work in my life. Writing was the only thing I was remotely good at. And I even got lazy with that.

Now I'm unemployed and tethered to a collapsing industry, poor and useless—the most humiliating combination imaginable.

In theory, I have options. There's always public relations. But whether it took a few weeks, a month, or even a year, it would be only a matter of time before that gutless profession drove me to gun up an office. Most of my other mental career explorations also end with me gunning up some imaginary office.

So I decide I need to flee, to get out of Los Angeles for my safety and the safety of those around me. I may be done for, but there is no way I'm going to take my lot like a slob, stewing in my own filth, watching TV in sweatpants until my unemployment checks run out. No, I need the dignity of flight—to leave all my shit behind like a goose and see if I can find a new watering hole thousands of miles away.

Afghanistan looks promising. Maybe losing a limb to a roadside bomb or a landmine would absolve my class guilt. A PR gig could look pretty good to someone with a stump. But long, aimless rambles are one of the few human joys I have in this life. I can't bring myself to risk it.

Then it hits me like Ike Turner: how about a walk? A really long, punishing walk. I've always been capable of dainty, Thoreau-like strolls. How about a feat of strength?

I check the map. Punishing snow-capped mountains to the north, with the revolting Central Valley beyond. Ocean to the west. Orange County to the south. Ugh.

That leaves east to the desert. But where in the desert? I'm no survivalist. I can't just wander out into the middle of the Mojave. Then I see it—a small town just miles from the Salton Sea: Mecca, California.

It just so happens that December is fast approaching and so is the hajj—the time when Muslims make a sacred pilgrimage to their Mecca. Perfect.

Except the hajj lasts just four days and my Mecca is 160 miles away...

Fuck it, I say, I'll walk it in four days. Can't blow a perfectly good metaphor just because I'm soft.

Be clear, this isn't one of those gimmicks writers do to get book deals. You know: my year of working at Walmart; my year of living with Mexicans; my year of drinking breast milk. No, this is about salvaging a shred of manhood: 160 miles in four days with no training and no real gear—other than a few days' food and water. This will be my attempt to satisfy the delusion that I'm an actual human being—capable of noncommercial acts of creative insanity.

IT IS A COLD December morning, even after the sun comes up. My breath—heavier than normal thanks to the weight of my pack and two years of fitness-free living—spews uncontrollably from my mouth in cloudy white streams. But it feels good to be moving, to have some actual direction.

I have about forty pounds of provisions with me—water mostly, but also food, clothes, and a sleeping bag. The extra weight is fine on my legs, but not so much on my feet. I'm wearing a pair of hefty boots I used for mountain climbing and long-distance hiking trips before I became sedentary. But walking on pavement is different from walking on a dirt trail, and even though it feels good to be on the road, trouble is boiling underneath my socks.

You may ask why I feel the need to carry forty pounds of supplies walking through one of the densest, most populous counties in the country. It's because Los Angeles isn't built for humans. It's built for cars. Walking through South Pasadena can be a quiet, lovely experience. But as nice as it is to gaze at other people's conspicuous wealth, you can walk four or five miles before you encounter a store—and that's an awful lot of ground to cover when you're dehydrated.

Preparedness is a step toward manliness, or so I reason, anyway.

In keeping with that sentiment, I planned a route. A roving wander would be more fun, and probably more liberating. But if you set out to cover 160 miles in four days, you'd better know where you're going. My plan for the day is to walk thirty-two miles, mostly along the Arrow Highway, to the Puddingstone Reservoir in San Dimas, sleep for eight hours, wake up before dawn, and then walk forty miles to a hotel in San Bernardino. There, I will assess my physical and mental well being before continuing on my long journey to Mecca.

Things begin well enough. The cool morning air in South Pasadena gives way to unseasonably warm noon temperatures in Temple City. For the first fifteen miles of my walk, life is good.

This part of the San Gabriel Valley is stocked full of pleasant, one-story little boxes—occupied mostly by Chinese families. Mushrooms sprout from their otherwise perfect green lawns.

I once learned from a mycologist that mushrooms only grow naturally in Southern California under a canopy of fallen oak leaves. The weather is simply too dry for them to survive in the sun without constant watering. If you see mushrooms out in the open in Los Angeles, it's a sign of unapologetic waste. They simply can't exist without excess. A brief and disheartening sensation of kinship with the mushrooms unexpectedly overwhelms me.

I walk up Longden Avenue, mile after mile, house after house, no bathrooms, no shops, no public buildings—an uninterrupted parody of the suburban dream. In one ten-mile stretch I pass only one park—it doesn't have a bathroom. These neighborhoods are wealthy and well groomed, but have sacrificed all shared space and any sense of community to become impenetrable and fortresslike to outsiders. A true green desert.

And so I rest in the shade of electrical boxes on the sidewalk and pee in the bushes of houses I find particularly gaudy or ecologically offensive.

Finally, after eighteen miles of walking, the lush, shaded, wealthy L.A. suburbs open up into something I'm not expecting—hell. Otherwise known as Irwindale. I have arrived at the Arrow Highway, a six-lane surface street with no sidewalks, no trees, and not a shred of humanity. The surrounding landscape is hollowed out, empty except for the scars of industry. Almost worse is the Irwindale Speedway and its massive parking lot. Light and reflected heat pulse in all directions. Hundreds of freight trucks blaze past at unsafe speeds. With no sidewalk and no breakdown lane, I'm forced to walk in the right-hand lane. An unceasing volley of horn blasts and waves of hot air dog me as the trucks pass inches to my left.

Thankfully I make it one mile to a stoplight, where I make eye contact with a Latino guy in a pickup truck. "Mind giving me a ride to a safe spot?" I ask. "Sure, hop in," he replies, mercifully. Two miles later, on the other side of the 605, a sidewalk reemerges and the man pulls over to let me out—into the Covina ghetto. "Thanks," I tell him. Hood rats cruise the streets in beat-up, barely functional hoopties. Teenage Latinas and Asian girls line the main drag, hands on their hips, bored out of their minds, waiting to get pregnant. Many of them already are. The fertility in the air hovers as dense as smog. As I move deeper into Covina, Irwindale suddenly makes perfect sense. It's an urban-planning stopgap. A poisonous, industrial Gandalf screaming to the proletariat hordes, "You shall not pass!"

I want to impregnate every girl I see and lead my illegitimate progeny on a mission to conquer the western 'burbs, marching to the sea like Sherman, burning every green lawn in sight—especially the ones with mushrooms. Instead I meet Carlos, a tiny, clearly gay community college student, who, with his hair parted evenly down the middle, bangs folded around his ears, somewhat resembles Pedro from Napoleon Dynamite. Carlos sees me from the window of his city bus and is curious enough to get out and ask me what I'm doing. I tell him I've been laid off from my job, and with the absence of anything else to do, I'm walking to Mecca.

"Cool," he replies.

For the next mile or so, Carlos tags along with me—promising to show me a spot to buy Gatorade. In the meantime we talk about life in Covina. How he hates it. How he wants to get out and move to Los Angeles one day.

"I'm working at Sizzler right now," he says. "Maybe I can get a transfer to a different franchise when I graduate."

Carlos is a nice kid, and I appreciate his company after nearly seven hours of walking in isolation. He has a plan, even if it isn't a big one, and I admire him for it.

After twenty minutes of chatting, we reach the store as promised. Inside, two cholos sporting Raiders paraphernalia eye us dismissively as we purchase our Gatorade.

"Faggots," they yell at our backs as we leave.

Carlos flinches knowingly, as if expecting some kind of projectile to follow the words. When none does, a wave of relief crosses his face.

As I start to say goodbye, Carlos invites me back to his apartment. A part of me wants to join him. This kid deserves some sympathetic company. I almost feel bad enough to toss a pity hand job his way. But I'm not the charitable type. And I have to keep moving.

A few months later, two teens are arrested for plotting to gun up their Covina high school. The news doesn't surprise me in the least.

FOURTEEN HOURS AFTER SETTING out, I make it thirty-two miles as planned to the Puddingstone Reservoir. I spend the first night of my hajj in a row of scruffy, tall bushes. Rats crawl in the branches above me as I try to sleep. I wake up to them trying to break into the food stores in my pack and shoo them away.

Aside from the rats, it's the perfect place to camp for the night—an urban oasis isolated from street noise and foot traffic. But the walk has taken its toll. My feet are, as feared, ground chuck. These blisters seem to defy draining—pop them and moments later they are fluid-filled again. I hope a night's sleep will ease the pain, but my feet are just as disastrous when I awake two hours before sunrise. I tape them up and continue on the best I can.

At first, all feels good. Puddingstone stretches for several miles, bracketed by dirt trails running from San Dimas all the way to La Verne. In the predawn hours, with the stars out in the thousands, plus the natural adrenaline that comes with walking through the woods at night—too many horror movies as a kid, I guess—the idea of actually making it to Mecca in four days seems possible. Anything seems possible.

But a few miles later it's back to unforgiving pavement, and my pus-filled feet, calmed by the gentle dirt trails, are screaming again. A familiar feeling of failure slithers through my bile duct.

Still I soldier on, through the relatively rural La Verne before veering south into Montclair—where a stray, scarred pit bull greets me upon arrival and follows me for several blocks. Other than the stray, the neighborhood is practically empty. Here is the heart of the American housing crisis—a faux, middle-class suburban paradise, constructed on the cheap and marketed to a working underclass unable to really afford it. For-sale signs mark half the neighborhood, and foreclosure notices fill the spaces in between.

As the sun comes up, moving trucks begin to arrive. Families by the dozen, mostly Latino, pour out of these tiny, boxed homes to load up—off to destinations unknown: presumably a more affordable real estate scam like Victorville or Hesperia.

The hours roll by and Montclair gives way to Ontario. I am now firmly into big-box country. Fast food and you-name-it marts everywhere. Homeless people loiter in the streets in front of the malls. They don't even bother asking for change.

If you're ever feeling too good about life, go to any Inland Empire city's website. It will read something like this:

"City of X was founded in 1895 by intrepid miners/ farmers from back East. They grew citrus until wealthy industrialist Y built a factory here in the wake of World War II. Wealthy developer Z then tore down the citrus groves and built thousands of homes. But then the plant folded/moved to Mexico/moved to China/exploded due to shoddy construction and nonexistent safety procedures, and the tax base eroded. Schools started closing and the city descended into poverty. So we built a mall. And, brother, all was right again! Until it wasn't. So we built a newer mall! And some more shoddily constructed houses to boot. And all was right again."

Except it isn't. It definitely isn't. Not with the Inland Empire, not with me, either. I have walked about twenty miles and my boots are filled with a fluid I'm pretty sure isn't sweat. I push as hard as I can, but marching on becomes impossible. Pavement is an unforgiving bitch.

I want to experience Fontana, Mike Davis's hometown, which he famously dissects in City of Quartz. But there is no shade in big-box country and no place to rest—other than the fast food joints. It isn't going to happen. I get some eggs and pancakes at a shitty IHOP and take a series of buses to San Bernardino.

"HEY, WHITE BOY. METH, junk, crack cocaine?"

Thirty seconds off the bus in San Bernardino and I'm already being offered drugs—a personal record. I do look rather crackish, I suppose—all my worldly possessions seemingly on my back, hobbling like a leper and reeking of body odor.

I've never been to San Bernardino before, though I've heard it's become a repository of sorts for black families pushed out of South L.A. by redevelopment schemes, rising home prices, and upwardly mobile immigrants. It clearly attracts other elements, too. The place is postapocalyptic—dilapidated rows of housing, empty lots, drug addicts, and scavengers everywhere. Street signs for a giant mall up ahead are plastered on every intersection.

I politely refuse the offers for crack and scuffle a few blocks to the nearest hotel in sight—a surprisingly nice national chain, given the environs. My arrival is greeted with skepticism at the front desk, but money talks and my credit card is accepted, security deposit and all. I retire to my room to pop my blisters and soak my feet in soapy, warm water. They burn for the next three hours.

Almost as soon as the pain subsides, I fall asleep. Sixteen hours later I wake up at sunrise. It's about seventy miles from my hotel to Mecca. The odds of making it the entire way on foot in the next two days are basically nil—but I need to at least give it a final go.

My route for the day is one I'd been looking forward to the entire trip—a shortcut through San Timoteo Canyon, a narrow, one-road corridor sandwiched between the San Bernardino National Forest and the Moreno Valley. Looking at the map, I guessed this would have to be where the SoCal sprawl ends. You can't stick thousands of tract homes and a bunch of megamarts in a narrow, isolated canyon. Can you?

Not yet, thankfully. As the sun rises higher, the detrital streets of San Bernardino open up into San Timoteo Canyon Road, and for the first time in my nearly eighty-mile trek, I see an orange grove. It's a rare sight. Sure, I'm breathing rancid diesel fumes from the freight trucks that pass by, and, sure, the groves are covered in pesticides and I'm presumably breathing that in, too—but there is still something pure about the scene. And so I walk in relative satisfaction, miles and miles of oranges to my left and to my right.

Around noon, I come across my first fellow human being in San Timoteo Canyon, a Mexican fruit salesman with a chile, lime, and mango cart. I buy a bag for five bucks and try to strike up a conversation. But I'm beyond squirrelly after barely speaking to anyone for three days. My Spanish fails me. So I sit near him in silence and eat, just happy for the company. A few minutes later, a county health-code inspector comes by and asks the vendor for his permits. When the man can't produce the documents, the inspector takes out his pen, writes a hundred-dollar ticket, and says, "Estás fin por la día."

The fruit salesman shakes his head knowingly and closes up shop. Easy pickings. This appears to be a semiregular routine for the pair. I finish my fruit and move on.

The canyon is mostly orange groves, but every once in a while something else breaks up the monotony: a palm tree farm, some natural scrub. At one point I catch sight of a zebra and antelope grazing behind a tall fence. I can only assume it's some kind of wild-game reserve. Either that or the pain from my feet is causing me to hallucinate.

At some point, San Timoteo Canyon Road forks in two, with the trucks heading south into the mountains. I take the road less traveled.

Rolling hills, covered in grass as far as the eye can see. Cottonwood trees and blue and live oaks sprouting from a creek bed that runs through the center of the canyon. Not a single plot of land developed, other than the occasional farmhouse. Nirvana.

But something this beautiful can't last long in Southern California. Turns out this is all private land, fenced in and on tap to be developed—according to signs, a massive mixed-use real estate/commercial project is in the works. More pavement. More failure.

The sun is beginning to set when my feet finally give out. I've walked about twenty-five miles today. Walked is a generous term, actually. I've shuffled the last ten miles in pain.

It's cold and starting to rain. It's getting dark. Not a single car passes by to catch a ride from. And the pristine land around me is barbwired off and plastered with signs threatening trespassers. I have walked nearly eighty miles in three days, escaped L.A.'s phony economy and real estate scams, and discovered an undeveloped grassland paradise. Were I fleeing an urban apocalypse, here is where I would meet my end—a helpless, hamburger-footed wretch, ripe for the picking.

Tender hands aren't meant for feats of strength.

Have I salvaged some dignity? To this day I'm still not sure—but even if I have, it's largely about to dissipate. I take my cellphone out of my pack and make a call. Two hours later, with the sun setting, my unapologetically, aspirationally bourgeois roommate arrives in her Mini Cooper to rescue me from my adventures in manhood— her Chihuahua riding shotgun, wearing a sweater.

I AWAKE ON THE morning of the fourth day of my hajj at a shitty hotel in Palm Springs—feet so swollen I need to crawl to the bathroom. Rather than drive home, I decided to put up the roommate and her little dog here for the night.

I love Palm Springs. I have no idea why. I couldn't explain my affection if I tried. The city is an abnormality, a freak show—a siphon for Angeleno excess. It can't exist without Los Angeles—a giant mushroom on L.A.'s front lawn, its sycophantic star walk begging for Hollywood's leftovers. But it works.

Most people don't know it, but half of the city is an Indian reservation owned by the Agua Caliente tribe. They don't pay property taxes. They don't have to work very hard. They just bilk a bunch of rich people into paying them to stay in a 120-degree desert. It's brilliant.

If I ever become a billionaire, I'm going to build a giant phallic tower on top of the highest bluff overlooking the city, so that everyone who passes through will have to look at my conspicuously aroused wealth. I'll import an army of Guatemalan servant boys and Chinese slave girls, brought from their motherland in crates. I'll bind their feet and keep them chained in the basement and only let them out to slave away at the elaborate parties I'll throw. My rich friends and I will laugh as we make the boys snort meth (no sense wasting good coke on the help) off the girls and then beat each other in a drug-addled frenzy. Then, the whole party will have sex in a giant pile of money.

Unbeknownst to everyone, my phallic house will actually be a fully functional North Korean missile, bought at a Tijuana flea market. When Caligulan thrills no longer sate me, I'll blow every last dime I have on coke, invite all the celebrities and fellow billionaires I can think of, and shortly after a live performance by Christina Aguilera, I'll launch my house west to Brentwood and blow that fucking place apart.

Mushrooms to Mecca

As I said, I have a special place in my heart for Palm Springs. But it's the final day of the hajj, and even if I can't walk there, I'm going to see Mecca. Shortly after noon, we drive the Mini Cooper southeast on Highway 111.

Thinking back to my walk, I realize that heading east out of Los Angeles is like heading back in time. You can analyze it like geological strata—postgentrified urban suburbanization in Glendale; postindustrial abandoned ethnic gangland in the early stages of recolonization by white people in Highland Park; wealthy Pasadena suburbs, followed by their easterly upwardly mobile neighbors; post-Reagan ethnic gangland; failed retail-oriented ghetto 'burbs; failing retail-oriented ghetto 'burbs; post-industrial 'burbs trying to avoid ghettoization by going retail; industrial wasteland; orange groves; and, finally, undeveloped land, lying in wait for raping. A circular comedy of real estate scams and shamelessly greedy, mindless urban planning.

In the Coachella Valley these levels play out quickly: city, country club, gated community, middle-class modular housing, box-retail mega-mile, trailer park, light industry, and finally date farms. The history of Southern California told in twenty miles.

When we arrive at Mecca, however, it immediately appears that we have finally escaped the paradigm. Only a mile from the shore of the Salton Sea—perhaps the archetypal Southern California planning catastrophe—the tiny town's dirt streets and tin-roofed houses closely resemble a Mexican farming village. Loose dogs (plenty of Chihuahuas, not of the boutique variety) roam the neighborhood, free to bark and nip at whomever they choose. A giant white revival tent occupies the center of town, with miles upon miles of fields beyond: grapes, red and green peppers, spinach, and tomatoes.

I get out of the car to have a look. The harvest, when the town's population swells from 5,000 to up to 30,000, is a few months off. Virtually everyone is Mexican, and, it being the slow season, the sight of a hobbling gringo draws some intrigue.

Everyone is friendly.

My Spanish again fails me, but I learn that, until recently, there was no police station in town. People just kind of fended for themselves. Things were starting to change in Mecca, though. I decide to head to the eastern outskirts of town to have a look.

And there I see it, a newly built mini-mall—shitty faux-adobe style, stucco facade and all. The retail space is occupied by a chain pizza shop and a Verizon store. Signs proudly boast of a new Mecca, courtesy of the Riverside County Redevelopment Agency.

The comedic circle wrought anew.

Depressed and aching, I track down my roommate and head back to Los Angeles. Southern California is doomed—a hopelessly devolved place, incapable of change or consequential planning.

A failure.

We're made for one another.

BAYOULAND

Hank Cherry

No one really remembers who died first, or when the wave started. Doug Stephens of the Alcoholic Sluts overdosed. That one hit home hard. I knew Doug pretty well and remember raising our glasses to shared woes one night, the both of us having lost the women in our lives to an ambition neither of us seemed to possess. Kelly Keller owned the Circle Bar over on St. Charles Avenue, and when she overdosed a pall set in. Jason Swesnick, Swez, my old next-door neighbor, a fellow chef, overdosed somewhere in there, too. My friend and fellow New Orleans refugee Matjames called me for that one. We sat on the phone for a few minutes, sharing memories of Swez, until they overwhelmed us and we hung up. When news came that Bucky James hanged himself, having sensed nothing more than doom in his future, I realized I could no longer count the number of dead friends with two hands. Bucky embodied the town's carefree spirit. Get drunk with him, you'd end up singing in the streets as you struggled to find a taxi willing to take you the few blocks you couldn't walk to your house. If he was gone, what's left?

Friends were dying with a regularity usually seen in wartime, and the inundation of all that death ruined the perspective of time. "If time would stand still while I'm thinking of you," Irma Thomas sang, "it could be for a minute, for an hour, or from now on."

If only time would hurry back to where it was before all this bad shit started happening.

Visitors usually talk about the music's greasy rhythms, the food's richness, the hand-over-fist booze fests. But for a group of transient excon, poet, burlesque-dancing-wannabe jazzbos looking for a reprieve from the hardcore conservative blear of the eighties, New Orleans was the magic spot. It had cheap rents, bars that never closed, and a fast-developing DIY music and art scene. New York had Danceteria, the Mudd Club, and CBGB. New Orleans had the French Quarter and the Ninth Ward. I knew a handful of people who went by assumed names—out of pretension or to keep from going to jail, or both—names like Soup Chain, Strawberry, Myrna Loy, Stacy Rickshaw. And we melted together in a place somewhat foreign to the rest of the country. It was a Bayouland theme park all our own.

The city seduced me the way a muse might, and it seems fitting to me that all nine of those muses have streets here named in their honor. Our houses leaned to one side, the floorboards had holes big enough to peek at the foundations, but they sang a song that shot right past music, landing smack dab in the membrane of an emotional jackpot. The town is not for everyone. But for a decade, man, that place was mine.

When I left New Orleans on the cusp of 2000, the chips weren't down; they were missing. I was living in a squat with people I didn't recognize. And when a former debutante drove me off into the sunset in the back of a used Japanese sedan, I remember seeing a sign announce we were leaving Greater New Orleans. I shivered in anxious sweats, battling not just my addiction, but the overwhelming grief you experience when separated from someone you love.

Bayouland

By the time Katrina came and went, I'd made it to Hollywood, scrubbed clean and trying to make a dent in the screenwriter trade. Over the years, I thought a lot about the city I loved, my first chosen home, really. I thought about going back many times.

Then, on January 4, 2007, Helen Hill, artist, activist and award-winning filmmaker, wife and mother, dedicated rebuilder of New Orleans, friend to me and my friends, died from a gunshot wound to the neck. Her death was a brutal casualty of Katrina a year and a half after the levees failed. For the low-down and the dark-hour denizens among us, Hill sent out a beacon of hope, and helped vindicate the reason many of us had moved to New Orleans in the first place. There you could make your own art and survive off it. I felt a tinge of hopelessness splinter in me when the news of her murder eventually made it to Los Angeles and her New Orleans expat friends, Matjames and then me.

In the days before and after Helen's slaying, New Orleans exploded in a murderous supernova, trapping not just Hill, but also Hot 8 Brass Band founding member Dinerral Shavers, who caught a bullet meant for someone else in the back of his head on December 28. His assailant was a fifteen-year-old boy fostering a beef with Shavers's stepson.

The day Hill died there were six other murders, a total of twelve that week. *The Times-Picayune* called it "a wave of bloodshed severe even by New Orleans standards." The violent turn of events overwhelmed the small victories New Orleans had achieved after Katrina—the end of the rolling blackouts and curfews, the influx of new professionals who relocated to the region to rebuild an honorable version of the city. Only the frontierlike killing spree and the "march against violence" on City Hall in its wake made national news.

After Hill's murder I became convinced that going back was folly. By all reports, the town had turned into a swamp of violent dysfunction, something it teetered on when I lived there. At the end of this past April, though, I turned forty just as BP's oil rig exploded, sending the region into disaster mode once again. I knew I had to get back there before they sold the last of the oyster po' boys. It was only half a joke.

When I told Matjames that I was heading back, his voice creaked with the kind of excitement particular to conversations we have about our former home. "For good?" he asked.

Maybe, I thought.

THE LADY DRIVING THE rental car shuttle van jerks a flabby arm toward the windshield, her feeble passenger overwhelmed by the humidity. "You bet your ass it's hot—all of this was marshland," she bellows over the shuttle's rumbling air conditioner. We're in Kenner, pulling out of Louis Armstrong Airport. "They built this whole place on top of a swamp." I fan my face with the plane ticket. The driver might as well be speaking French. My body is shut down. But having lived in this swelter before, I know what she's talking about.

My own New Orleans experience blossomed out of a decidedly middle-class background back East. And while I took to tennis and lacrosse, I'd always felt like a misfit among the preppy set—with whatever set I got involved with, really, because somewhere I had that misfit circuitry wired into my head. For the most part, New Orleans shorted out those circuits. But as my chemical intake ramped up, I found myself reigniting those crossed wires.

As my liver failed, my lies got worse, and it got to be time to leave. I did not go back after I got clean, but slowly started making contact with the people who had mattered to me while I was there. To go back, though, that was a two-headed dog I could not face until now.

When I make it to town and dump my bags upstairs at a friend's apartment and step out into the mucouslike humidity, I realize it was all in my head. Looking across the street at Gentle Dental, where my first wisdom tooth bit the dust, I'm suddenly transported back fourteen years, standing on the corner waiting for a cab to bring me back to Port Street. Any fear I've entertained about returning evaporates. I'm home.

That night I go out to Frenchmen Street, and it is bustling with music. I see for myself that New Orleans is alive. You always hear rumors about how slow things move in New Orleans, but on this trip things happen one lightning round after another. A walk through the Quarter turns up a long-lost friend. A dog walk in the Ninth Ward turns up another. Each time I cross the railroad tracks I spot another old friend, usually traveling by bicycle, former members of the black-and-white brigade—the food-service workers. These momentary encounters rekindle the city's flame inside me. I know how things play out here. It's coded into my system.

At night, I get on the computer to do some research. I make friends on Facebook with New Orleans impresario and artist Bunny Matthews. Bunny is a New Orleans institution. His cartoon characters Vic and Nat'ly have graced the pages of *Offbeat*, *Gambit Weekly*, and *The Times-Picayune*. The duo is based on Ninth Ward stalwarts, slight caricatures of the kind of people who lived in the neighborhood long before international media began reporting on it like it were another dark continent. Every truck in the Leidenheimer bakery fleet has Vic and Nat'ly painted on its side. Everyone in New Orleans knows someone who talks like them, or looks like them, or both.

Bunny and I arrange to meet the next day at what was once the original Rue De La Course coffee shop. It's called something else now, but it's got the old tin ceilings and feels the same. I've got Ed Ainsworth in tow. Ainsworth is a writer who lives in Mississippi. He followed a trajectory similar to my own throughout the nineties. We tool round New Orleans, spotting scenes from our demise. Ed checks out the Lower Garden District while Matthews and I talk.

Bunny knows something about the Ninth Ward. He spent the days after British Petroleum's destruction painting Nint'Wardica, an ode to Picasso's Guernica and to the region he's called home since birth. Pelicans and crabs are doused in oil. An oil platform spews flames and plumes of smoke. A woman cradles a dead snapper in her arms. On one side lies an automatic weapon, on the other a martini glass. That nails it.

"You remember May 1995, the cars floated down the street?" Bunny asks me as we sit down for a coffee. It's not a memory you soon forget. You could push on the hood of a car and off it floated into a telephone pole, or a house. I remember the pumping stations kicking into overdrive, seeing the water disappear.

Bunny usually weaves optimism into even the bleakest of his post-Katrina stories. He doesn't deny the impact of BP's disaster, or the failure of the levees, nor does he blindly refuse to see the place for what it is. But he's offering an honest appraisal of such a bountiful cradle. He raised his family here, as his parents raised

_860

him. Of all the people I talk to, Bunny best encapsulates the ability to use the grief of recent times and develop from it something full of sustenance for himself and for others.

As the rest of the country felt the abrasive assault of the housing and banking crises, New Orleans was able to fend off the crash with a buffer of federal grants. It enabled the new professionals of New Orleans to continue the reconstruction. That is not to say that the rent increases that occurred right after the storm had abated, but new industry did appear. When the A&P didn't return to its long-held spot at the corner of Royal and St. Peter in the Quarter, Rouses Market, a Louisiana-owned-and-operated grocer, proudly took its place. Good things were happening.

Though the rebuilding of New Orleans made for less visceral storylines than the city-gone-wild, post-Katrina murder-spree narrative, the victories of reconstruction made an important difference to those who hadn't left, and to those who had returned to aid in the rebirth. St. Claude Avenue in the Ninth Ward, in the past mostly mentioned only in conjunction with crime statistics, became an impromptu arts corridor when a number of artists from New Orleans and around the country banded together and opened a series of new galleries. In an instant, a burgeoning alternative to the established arts scene on Julia Street in the central business district came to life. The Ninth Ward needed it. The national press ignored it.

After a while, Ainsworth returns with a book of his poetry, which prompts Bunny to read from Lafcadio Hearn, a sometime New Orleanian in the late 1800s. "The wealth of a world is here, unworked gold in the ore, one might say. The paradise of the South is here, deserted and half in ruins. I never beheld anything so beautiful and so sad. It was like young death. A dead bride crowned with orange flowers, a dead face that asked for a kiss."

A block west of where I'm staying, a car has plowed into a stop light, crumpling it like a paper flower. For the duration of my trip, the dismembered stop light lies broken and possibly forgotten in the neutral ground. Is this the kiss Hearn spoke of? Or is it something else, something like that heart-stopping pull of the city that lures you back time and again?

The media images of post-Katrina recovery—sounds of glasses clinking, Bourbon Street beads-for-boobs revelry that then fade into caustic images of the flooded city—are not what New Orleans was to me and the Ninth Warders I knew. New Orleans was more than our home; it was paradise.

Like most paradises, though, New Orleans operated in semidelusion. More often than not, the brightly painted houses we lived in sat beside blighted ramshackle heaps. I knew people who bought houses for less money than it cost to buy a busted-up car. But that was in the nineties. With the good came bad. So when the murder rate spiked and New Orleans was branded Murder Capital USA, my parents called to try and convince me to move out of town. They feared I'd become just another murder statistic.

But a lot of us felt a sense of false poetry in the crime rate, as if it were somehow romantic to live in its shadow. We all floated past it. Real violence, blood-for-blood violence, mostly happened in other places, such as the Desire projects. Or, in the days after Katrina, on the Danziger Bridge, east of where the Desire projects once stood. A bizarre shooting by a group of

NOPD officers on a group of locals took place on the Danziger on September 4, 2005, leaving dead Ronald Madison, a forty-year-old, mentally disabled man, and James Brissette, a nineteen-year-old on his way to the Winn-Dixie. Four others were wounded. The federal indictments of six police officers trumps news of the Deepwater Horizon spill in the Gulf the first day I'm back in town. It's five years later. Things do move slowly here.

The surrounding neighborhood is barren now. Decimation moves weed by weed into empty cement lots. Lack of commerce practically shouts at you to keep moving. The Danziger offers little hope. Painted the dull gray of naval ships and splotchy with oxidation, it gives off a debilitated, sickly feel, the bridge that care forgot.

IT WAS MARCH SOMETHING, 1991, when I first arrived in New Orleans, almost St. Patrick's Day. I parked, quickly found a pay phone, and called my host for directions to her crib. Out of nowhere, a head of cabbage smacked me in the face. The St. Patrick's Day Parade drunkenly pushed past me, off kilter, teeming with fire trucks for floats and men in tuxedos and green bow ties. A stranger dressed in a shiny green kimono with shamrocks painted on her cheeks planted a cup of green beer in my hand, a kiss on my cheek. Why would you ever leave a town like that?

For those of us who chose to live there, life was absolute reinvention. The Ninth offered that in spades. It also offered plenty of affordable housing with lots of space, and close proximity to the French Quarter, where service-industry jobs awaited the throng of postgraduate twenty-somethings. I rode in that army of black-and-white-clothed bicyclists who passed through the Bywater to the Marigny to the Quarter and back every day. Back then, all you had to do was bluff your way through an interview and fudge a résumé, and gainful employment was yours. Everyone was hiring, all the time.

For most of my time in New Orleans, I lived on Port Street. One of the great pleasures of that life came from sitting out on the stoop, listening as the train whistle swept into the sound of the calliope drifting over from the Natchez steamboat a few hundred yards out on the Mississippi. Some days, you could collect whole songs in the wind.

The Ninth Ward was good to me and my friends. And we were good to it. One night, after the floods of '95 had abated, I drove a borrowed rental car with three shapely bartenders onboard down to Poland Street, lost in a haze of mushroom tea and bourbon. Somehow the car got stuck on the train tracks leading into the naval base. The MPs laughed at us and saved our asses, rustling up some mammoth Marine recruits who picked the car off the tracks and moved it back to the street. "Drive safely," a tree-size Marine called after us.

Port Street broke open to impromptu parties, not a hail of bullets. Carpy lived across the street; Swez a door down from him. We fixed batches of homemade absinthe and drank until the ghosts appeared. We fed each other homemade gumbos, swapped gifts for holidays. New Orleans even functioned on a different legal basis than English Common Law—the Napoleonic Code. Time always ran slower there. It's why we stayed. Everyone we knew lived a bike ride away. If they didn't, maybe they weren't worth knowing.

Ain't no joy like a Ninth Ward boy, the saying went, ain't nothing in the world like a Ninth Ward girl. And, man, it was true.

I met Robert Starnes a week after deciding to make New Orleans my home. Robert was the one who took my addictions seriously, not personally, and did his best to help me, warning the local bartenders not to serve me when my liver began failing. He remains a trusted friend and confidant. Now, Robert greets me outside his place on Poland Street, the last street before the St. Claude Avenue Bridge takes you into the Lower Ninth, where much of the worst flooding took place.

He smiles at the sight of me surrounded by a bevy of police cruisers with sirens quelled but lights flashing. "Henry," he says, nodding to the cars mischievously.

I explain that they appeared out of nowhere, and he just laughs. Robert's hair is graying, but the light in his eyes is as bright as ever. Living through a catastrophe can have that effect. Inside his apartment, the talk quickly turns to Hill's murder.

In the aftermath of Katrina, death rippled into the streets, swayed in the branches of the live oaks like beads from a moribund parade. The city's murder rate rose to the highest in the country, just ahead of Compton. You couldn't help but think if the levees had not failed, none of this would have happened. And yet Hill's murder seemed out of place, even in all of this.

"This wasn't your typical beef murder, okay?" says Robert. "The first murder after Katrina involved two guys who grew up not liking each other, in the same hood. They joined gangs. They had minor scraps along the way, two guys running a long feud. So after Katrina they see each other somewhere, and one of them shoots the other, and there you have New Orleans murder 101. One guy zipped up in a body bag, the other on the way to the state prison in Angola. Beef."

He continues, "Helen's murder was a home invasion. That's not a New Orleans kind of crime."

But New Orleans has never been your everyday American city. It just feels different. It sits below sea level, as much as ten feet in some places. The pump stations of New Orleans are its beating heart. I remember the one on Broad Street the best. Huge metal pipes run out of the staid brick building. The pipes' turquoise color serving as a kind of ameliorative to the reality of what they represent.

When multiple pump stations failed during Katrina, the city went into a kind of cardiac arrest. The deluge that followed continues to affect the city and the Gulf Coast. The aortic valves are pumping the city clear of water again, postflood repairs having addressed their failures, but the ventricles have clogged up with angry dysfunction and proved unable to pull the town clear of its murderous climate. As the city repopulated after the storm waters receded, suicides and overdoses occurred at an alarming rate. Ancillary deaths upsetting the grief-filled waters in the wake of Helen Hill's murder.

THE TALLEST BUILDINGS IN the Ninth Ward are the churches. Most of them have been decommissioned, de-Jesus-i-fied. Still, the neighborhood teems with spirituality, a musical faith. But that faith has been waning since Katrina. Most Ninth Ward schools, where the music spread, closed. Five years later, only three Ninth Ward schools have come back to life, and the rest remain circled by barbed-wire fences, the Charles J. Colton School among them.

Colton took a battering from wind and rain and post-Katrina neglect. Mold sprouted. So much else was wrong with the city that no one tended to the building's needs until it was much too late. Colton was shut down.

In 2009, some Ninth Warders calling themselves the Creative Alliance of New Orleans stepped in, hatching a plan to refurbish the building if they could use it for studio space, which they in turn would use to provide after-school programs for the neighborhood kids. The project was approved, the poisonous black mold removed from the interiors, and the Studios at Colton were born. The after-school program blossomed. The city took notice and reclaimed the space, planning to open the school again...someday. The fences went back up.

A few blocks away from Colton comes another crushing blow. The baseball field at Stallings Center is overgrown and unused. In the dark, Stallings is the place you want to avoid. A waterlogged sign with chipping paint pronouncing the Stallings recovery project a success buckles toward the earth. It might have been a success for a week or a month or even a year. But now Stallings Field is a blemish in a neighborhood of storied blemishes.

Taken without perspective, Stallings might stand as a banner over the entrance to New Orleans, announcing, Abandon hope all ye who enter here. If you did, you'd miss the new cop shop and the new galleries sprouting up and down St. Claude, urging you to look closer at the Ninth, to divorce yourself from the Uptown comfort zone of Magazine and Prytania streets. These corridors fared well during the storm, and even better afterward. The aisle of denial, locals call it. Helen Hill would have chuckled.

HILL AND I MET a few times in passing, in 1992. Her New Orleans offered tranquility and hope; mine summoned the dark hours, the bleary-eyed and worn-down clichés. But New Orleans being essentially several small villages linked together, we sometimes passed each other on our bikes and made small talk. I lived around the corner from where Jim Jarmusch shot part of Down by Law, his absurdist wet kiss to the Bayou. Hill pointed that out to me, like a kind wind.

New Orleans lured Hill to town once, twice, and that third fatal time almost a year to the day after the storm. Hill and Paul Gailiunas, friends when they graduated Harvard in '92, moved to New Orleans that summer, drawn by the city's culture, arts, and laissez faire social clime. They were artistic, outgoing, and nice. Nice went a long way in New Orleans, where elbowy tourists overran you in search of zydeco CDs, plastic Mardi Gras beads, and hurricanes—a blistering concoction of sugar and grainy high-octane booze.

Soon they fell in love with the city and each other and got married in Hill's home state of South Carolina. She graduated from CalArts in '95 and then followed Gailiunas to Halifax, Novia Scotia, while he completed medical school.

They returned to New Orleans in 2001. Gailiunas opened the Little Doctors Clinic in the Treme, serving the poor and uninsured. He also founded a local chapter of Food Not Bombs and performed in a band called the Troublemakers that played songs advocating universal health care. Hill made animated films and taught at the New Orleans Film Collective, which she helped found, and at the New Orleans Video Access Center.

Three years later they had a baby boy, Francis. When Katrina lurked off shore, they evacuated to Alabama for about a week. When they realized they weren't going to get back to New Orleans right away, Gailiunas, Hill, and Francis headed back to Hill's childhood hometown in South Carolina.

"We stayed in Columbia for a year," Gailiunas tells me. "She worked on her film, *The Florestine Collection*. I went back sixteen days after the storm and had to wade through two blocks of water up to my waist to get to my house. Helen and I went back a month later, around Halloween, and cleaned out our house, got all her film stuff."

But Hill couldn't let New Orleans go. Gailiunis was wary—Katrina destroyed the clinic he started, and the threat of violence, natural or man made, worried him. Hill enlisted their tight-knit group of friends to send postcards to Gailiunis, recruit him to return. Many said, simply, "We need you."

The couple returned on Katrina's one-year anniversary. The mood during the anniversary parade was relatively optimistic. A sense that something good might come out of all this, that grass-roots activism and public funding might make a better New Orleans, prevailed.

Four months later, Hill was killed in a home-invasion robbery. Gailiunis was shot three times while shielding Francis. He and Francis survived.

In a heartbreaking letter to *The Times-Picayune* shortly after Hill's murder, Gailiunas wrote, "I lived in fear of the violence and unpredictability that has become a daily fact of life, but Helen loved New Orleans with a great passion. She was content only when she was in New Orleans, walking among the old shotgun houses, admiring the morning glories and magnolia trees and Spanish moss, listening to WWOZ, straining to catch a Zulu coconut…bringing visitors to the Mother-in-Law Lounge, and cooking vegetarian versions of famous Creole dishes…No one is going to fix New Orleans for you. You need to do it yourselves…and for my poor, sweet wife. I know this is what she would want."

Three years later, I reach Gailiunas in Los Angeles, where he too now lives. He's not going back to New Orleans, but he still cares about it. He also doesn't blame Helen for New Orleans's fatal kiss.

"She was a much less fearful person than I was. The reason I bring that up: the last couple months before she died—I'd never seen this in her—she definitely started to be aware of our safety. When the hurricane happened a little part of me was thinking, this just gives me another reason never to come back."

Gailiunas pauses before continuing.

"I really respected Helen, and she had this spirit of let's be part of rebuilding New Orleans…But you know, I was ready. I got a job with Daughters of Charity. They run medical clinics that take care of uninsured people and that's what I like to do. We made the decision together. She was pretty excited about it, she was really, really excited."

I WAS IN LAS Vegas in January 2010 when the Saints stole the NFC championship out from under the Minnesota Vikings. A stranger in a black Saints jersey hugged me after noticing the Saints hat on my head. Laissez les bon temps rouler, she said with a wink. A couple of weeks later the New Orleans Saints won the fucking Super Bowl. They called it Lombardi Gras. The biggest news before the Super Bowl victory was about HBO shooting a series produced by David Simon (*The Wire*) set in post-Katrina New Orleans, called *Treme*.

Mardi Gras came almost right after the game. The town was coming back to life. Population numbers were up. Though rain was predicted, the jazz festival prepared for crowds close to what they'd been before the levee failure. Then, on April 20, eleven men burned to death in the Deepwater Horizon oil-rig explosion that eventually spewed an estimated 185 million barrels of oil into the Gulf of Mexico.

Ralph Brennan of the famed New Orleans restaurant family was summoned to testify before a House subcommittee about the oil spill's impact on local industry. Brennan painted an honest portrait of the fear, anger, and injury that has plagued his industry and that of Gulf Coast tourism since Katrina.

"The oil looming offshore is an economic disaster of epic proportions," he testified. "After Katrina roared ashore…water came in, water went out. We rebuilt and moved on. That is not the case today. The ripple of damage…will have undeniable long-term consequences, dwarfing the impact of Katrina."

Mark Schexnayder is a coastal adviser with the Louisiana Sea Grant, a federally funded coastal advocate, and an expert on the Gulf Coast's wetlands. He talks to me by phone for more than an hour while he drives from the Biloxi marshes back to Louisiana. The wetlands Schexnayder is charged with repairing took a brutal beating from Katrina's storm surge. With the influx of crude sheen from the spill, all the recovery work has been retarded.

Directly in the sights of the spill are the Chandeleur Islands, barrier islands that form a critical habitat for fish and birds in the region. The islands have been steadily eroding, besieged by natural and man-made disasters.

"Ninety percent of all waterfowl in the region, from Texas to Florida, nest on Chandeleur," Shexnayder tells me. Not to mention the brown shrimp, oysters, and snapper that spawn in their tidal basin. The oil has reached the islands' precious wetlands and fisheries. And they are ailing.

The closest port to the Chandeleurs is Venice, a little more than hour south of New Orleans, in Plaquemines Parish, a slightly altered South compared to New Orleans. Yet the same stoicism many of my friends exhibited in the wake of Katrina is on display here, despite the fact that the oil spill is not just a catastrophe: it's the catastrophe.

I speak to Captain Darryl Eymard by phone. Eymard fishes out of Cypress Cove marina, in Venice. After BP discovered Eymard was taking photographers out to the controlled burns near the Chandeleur Islands, the company complained to the feds, which banned all photography near the spills. Tensions ran high. When word got out that BP drastically undersold the size of the leak, Cypress Cove went bananas.

"Worse thing BP did was use the dispersant," Captain Darryl tells me. "They didn't factor in the wind or the tides. Those big balls are gonna be here for years and years." This is borne out when, in early October, Venice fishermen bring photographers out to a huge swath of unskimmed and weathered oil heading for landfall. It is a mile wide in places.

I pass a marina on the way out of town. Parked in the lot is an ominous black trailer emblazoned with gold letters on the side: Plaquimines Parish Jail on Demand. I wonder what the fuck that is, and swing the rental in for a closer look. When I settle my camera on the squat black Jail on Demand trailer, a Crown Vic with tinted windows slowly spins in my direction.

I hit the accelerator and push for New Orleans.

A FEW NIGHTS BEFORE leaving New Orleans, I meet up with Angele at Cosimo's. Angele is a graphic designer I've known since my dive-bar days. We haven't seen each other in years, but we get past any awkwardness right off. She motions for me to follow her to the backroom. Though I'd been to Cosimo's many times before, I had no clue it had either a pool table or a back room. Of course, all my time in barrooms was spent drinking and getting down, not playing pool. Everyone beats me at pool. One of Angele's friends suggests the R Bar. I agree, eager to move on.

At the R Bar, the crowd is similar to what you'd find in any New York, San Francisco, or Los Angeles club. Except the jams are different. The deejay segues from Desmond Dekker to Augustus Pablo to Charlie Daniels into Cissy Strut. The room shifts into low gear as the Meters play, bodies moving as one, swaying side to side, back to front. But, to be honest, I'm doused in nostalgia and can't be sure if that's what's really happening. As my mother used to say when we were kids, don't quote me on that, I might be making it up.

We spend the evening sitting on the curb across the street from the bar, watching as people parade from the R Bar back to their cars or onto their bikes, continuing the endless sway of New Orleans nightlife. One girl tells outlandish, drunken stories to strangers walking by, while a couple and I exchange names of the lost friends we share. Those names have carved such a valley through us they no longer hurt to be spoken aloud.

When the skies open up for a brief but powerful blast of rain, I am relieved. Rain is a way of life here, unlike in Southern California. The R Bar has a roof over the sidewalk, and we all collide underneath it. For the first time in my life, I find myself a tourist here, happily watching the night unfold in the hands of the locals.

Angele invites me out again the next night to a family friend's Lower Garden District condo. The place has the most incredible view of the city skyline, like the developers erected a platform here and sketched out their plans for the city, then went to work. The buildings shoot up over the tree line and dazzle me in a way the Central Business District has never done before.

When a load of Popeye's chicken arrives, I dig in. There's a Popeye's down the street from our place in Los Angeles. I sometimes frequent it when I need to pretend I'm back in Louisiana. Wanting to be back. Aching to be.

Angele's sister Andrea and their friend Diane, the hostess, are vibrant, preternaturally Southern women. They talk and gesture and bring you into everything they comment on. Angele is quieter; her charm is more subtle but every bit as devastating. Conversation that night skips from topic to topic. We talk about music, we talk about drugs, we talk about the Army Corps of Engineers. And while I know but one person in the room, my opinion is solicited much as anyone else's. The evening swallows me up. These are the people who are rebuilding New Orleans, these are the people who marched on City Hall after Hill and Shavers were murdered. These are the people who refused to accept that brutal winter's lesser version of the city.

When Angele texts me later that night, the four-word message—"They all loved you"—means everything, because I am of a like mind. When I was younger, when Matjames and I plowed from bar stool to stage to bed, we saw the city like a Bayouland theme park of our own creation. But sometimes the theme park has to shut down for repairs.

Helen Hill may be at rest. But her voice is swelling. In 2009, her film *Scratch and Crow*, made while she was at CalArts, was accepted into the National Film Registry. Beyond the psychic tides of New Orleans's storm waters lies Hill's myth. Do not abandon hope, it says. Do not forget care.

THE WARLORDS OF LITTLE TOKYO

Joseph Mattson

2012 Best American Nonrequired Reading, Notable

Three old men governed the Bar That Cannot Be Named. Three old Japanese men, wise and drunk, with chests full of tar and decades upon decades of trouble. These men I called the Warlords of Little Tokyo. They called me James Dean Sad Eyes because I was young and I was white and they were fascinated with postwar fifties Americana. Mostly, they called me James Dean Sad Eyes because I had nothing to lose.

"Oh, nobody smile, Doctor Dean is in."

"Ahso, the whiskey priest has come 'gain nighttime to roost."

"Ah, Dean, so young and so sad his woman is gone."

In Los Angeles in the year 2000, there was a trapezoid of space just east of where Little Tokyo intersects with the downtown Arts District, a trapezoid of space slammed against the concrete cliffs of the railroad trenches and ominous banks of the pathetic Los Angeles River in an exacting loneliness. A space deserted, a vortex of slowed time, a wasteland mostly leveled to rubble running east to west from Vignes to Alameda and south to north from East Third to East First, a geometry of isolation suited to cavernous exiles noosing themselves from the rest of the city. Nobody bothered you, everyone was a potential ghost—the First Street Bridge, the arched leviathan, a wanting hanging tree, where since its construction in 1929 the disenchanted have made pilgrimage to take the long walk. A good-enough place to ride out the consideration of slow suicide or fast recklessness without having to worry about cops or even friends.

Standing atop the First Street Bridge, facing west, one could see over all four city blocks to where Little Tokyo glowed in a slice of expat mysticism so wrung with nightly intrigue that the less-than-one-square-mile neighborhood's moons were the foggiest in all the city for those of us with the right eyes for it, fog eclipsing the twenty miles farther west to the Pacific Ocean where it all rolls in, the wetting whistle of our otherwise dry cunt City of Angels. And it is only here, now on this page, that I finally consider an association of the word Pacific to the word pacify and the larger embodiment of hush. In that Anno Domini 2000, I spent the cruelest and most exquisite year in this liminal trap.

The trapezoid of land still stands in 2011, but it is of course filled with development, condominiums, and fabricated lofts spread like STDs—ugly but real and unavoidable—and a new public railway line. I do not know if the area has a name, if it had a name before the transition, but a decade ago I called it the Golden Trapezoid. Roaming bums and eccentric, acid-damaged fine artists exchanged nods and plotted their murders quietly among the vacant lots, the few warehouses and factories either abandoned or clandestinely in use, and the shrugging, graffiti-soaked, out-of-service rail depots. Anyone could live or die in the Golden Trap. Red stains and no questions asked. Where packs of wild dogs dragged the rotting, skinned heads of pig and steer carcasses from back-alley cut shops as far away as the Grand Central Market and Chinatown for a safe haven to gnaw, and where, too, other wolves of esoteric passion found safe haven to shoot up in broad daylight.

I lived in a warehouse at the corner of Vignes and First, and down in my hollow you could still buy the company of a Mexican T-girl at Little Pedro's, one of the only businesses in the GT, for $40. The Little Pedro's building still stands, but its guts have long since departed. I am mentioning all of this because if I stepped out—I took what little food I ate and much of my grog in Little Tokyo—all the decrepit solitude and fragmented suffering of the Golden Trap went with me, every footstep to pavement, glass to lips, mist to mouth. The dim, explicit, and inescapable hollow bore deep in my sad, beautiful green eyes. I broke hearts with a single glance.

These eyes of mine, this hollow, these were things the Warlords of Little Tokyo understood. I wound up living in the GT and in bottomless despair because I had lost a woman of major influence and was unable to look positively on any subsequent days without her. Simply but impenetrably put, those days and this story are the result of not being able to be with the person I loved most and the long road out from the pain. So let us raise a glass even tonight to the potency of simplicity, for anguish is simple in its exactness, love the lone god of it all.

When I lived in the GT, I drank. I drank at Saloon Cosmos on First Street in the heart of Little Tokyo, and I drank even more in its unnamed sister bar a few doors down—yes, gone now, Bar That Cannot Be Named— little more than a cave in the wall beneath an old thirties hotel turned rooming house. Old fashioneds were the standard, and the karaoke was taken—was sung— with the seriousness of a seppuku ritual, an emotional disembowelment that oft ended in heaps of tears for those men who surrendered their hearts to horrible love and their howling lungs to the night. Stoic, dead-eyed Japanese businessmen so alive with unimpeachable despair, here. Though I never sang karaoke—mine was a mostly silent alcoholic misery—and though we never spoke a word to each other, I counted the singers among my countrymen in a land ruled by love lost. Bar That Cannot Be Named was small, a five-stool wood with one corner table and two couches in the back for the balladry. The place was lit with electric tea lights. The Warlords held court. Sometimes they called me "doctor."

"Oh, hide your cigarettes. Here come the doctor, Doctor Dean."

"Ahso, whiskey priest on the perch."

"Ah, James Dean Sad Eyes, he'll meet his woman up in heaven, so he hopes."

I sat in that bar with the Warlords of Little Tokyo in reckless abandon and drank my savings away in such a manner that courted minor legend so far as subheroic liver and kidneys are concerned. I was a tragic protagonist of the highest comedic order to these Warlords of this Bar That Cannot Be Named, which was not called by anybody but me Bar That Cannot Be Named (contemporarily samurai-cum-noir enough— let us create our legends accordingly), and they jovially warmed to me as an oracle to the weary antihero, as archangels to the damned. They, for all the world was worth, had seen it all, and I was their little rat, running through the maze anew.

The barkeep at Cannot Be Named was a boss Japanese gangster cowboy who wore elaborately embroidered Nudie knockoffs unbuttoned down to his navel with an obligatory bandanna tied loose around his neck and a gold dope spoon dangling from a gold chain necklace that rattled against the loose snaps of his shirt as he hustled the bar. His name was Ken. He wore starched Levi's double cuffed over metal-tipped rattlesnake kuso kickers. Ken had a five-finger pompadour and chain smoked so consistently that flecks of ash were a regular cocktail garnish.

"Old fashioned, Ken, and hold everything but the whiskey," I'd say. I'd drink a dozen straight whiskeys and then finish it all off with an old fashioned replete before wandering back to my wormhole in the GT.

All of the men smoked. I smoked, too, sometimes. The old men smoked Lucky Strikes. I was rolling my own, which fascinated and repulsed them to no end. You could cut the air with a sushi knife. Usually, there was at least enough respect for absurdity still left in my emotional landscape to crack wise with the old Japanese crags, and their nightly homilies were among the only beacons of light I can recall from that time, their buoyant ball-busting holy among days of blood and breath negated and all sorts of self-medicating.

I'd first wandered into the clandestine speakeasy looking for a place to piss one graceless night—the joint had no markers whatsoever, no signs, no windows, it was merely behind a white door that looked like it led to an apartment complex's foyer. Instantly sobered by the surprise, I stomached my guts, sat down, and ordered one as if I'd known the place had been there all along. Ken ignored me for a good forty minutes that first night, but I stuck it out. I called for a whiskey about a dozen times—"Whiskey, sir," deadpan—and finally he gave me a Kirin, a drift I was supposed to catch, maybe, or a test of wills. I came back every night for six straight days, and on each of these nights I was not served. On the seventh day Ken and the Warlords acknowledged my presence, and I was for all spiritual intents allowed to stay. I was given my drink.

The Warlords were old enough to have lived through American internment camps during World War II, and without so much as a single word about it, I somehow knew each was a walking historical artifact. They'd all given themselves—or were appointed—American names: Bobby, Johnny, and Willy. Ken was Ken, never Kenny, and I heard one of the patrons call him Kenji. While Kenji, or Ken, remained a rock 'n' roll animal, the Y men wore black suits with pressed, white shirts, three-quarter sleeved, cuffs-up, and Sperry Top-Siders. Willy wore an eye patch over his left socket, Johnny had a cataractous eye gone to blue in his right, and Bobby employed a hearing aid he'd turn down during the karaoke—not because it annoyed him, rather it touched him too deeply. The communicable heartache of the balladeers seemed to remind him too much of a tantamount love of his own forever lost. These compromises of the senses were the only thing that really made the men distinguishable, although Willy had the air of a self-appointed ringleader.

Because my soul was old, because I was ruination incarnate—or perhaps by default—I became the patron whiskey saint of the Bar That Cannot Be Named. The Warlords of Little Tokyo took a shine to me and appointed me their tyro. And, like true masters on their apprentice, the old men put me to task when I finally hit bottom.

IT WAS THE NIGHT I walked into the bar, sat down, acknowledged nobody, ordered nothing, and stared into the abyss of my folded hands. I have no clear memory of the day in its earlier hours, but if my sadness had not been so ethereal and my consciousness perhaps more focused, the slow suicide of alcoholism might have jumped the wire to a swifter snuff. My beautiful green eyes gone to a bad shade of red. I felt ended, complete in a wrong way for how young I was. I finally ordered my requisite whiskey. My black leather jacket lay across my lap. When I pulled out my wallet, a syringe, still sealed in its sterile plastic packaging, tumbled out of the jacket and onto the floor.

The three old men stared at the rig, then back at me with four old eyes buzzing with disgust and understanding. Ken simply huffed, brought me my whiskey, and strode to the space between the bar wood and the two couches and fumbled with a radio, trying to find a Dodgers game. I looked down at the syringe and felt smaller than a wilted cherry blossom. If I could be any sadder, grandiosely or even infinitesimally, I then was in that moment. It was truly a heartbreaking thing for me to see.

"Uh," I stuttered. "Not mine."

"Shuh, right. You only whiskey," Willy said, nodding toward my glass. I brought it to my lips and drank.

"You think you are spared in the war?" Bobby said.

"Apparently not," I said.

"Two wars," Willy said, "inside and out." The old Warlords often talked of war, but abstractly; it wasn't exactly WWII—though they alluded to it, at times—but more the eternal struggle of the pain of being a man.

"There is one, then there is the other," Johnny said. "The wars." Then they each very gently ran their hands through all of my pockets. The four of my pants, the breast pocket of my shirt, the pockets of my black leather jacket. Johnny reached down and patted my ankles. They did not find what they were looking for.

Willy called for the bar's old rotary phone. Bobby called for a round. Johnny picked the syringe off the floor and put it in his pocket. Mouths of Japanese blur. Nobody else in the bar but Ken, Willy, Johnny, Bobby, and the sack o' me. The men stepped outside. They locked me inside the bar for fifteen minutes. I didn't move, for I was a dead man. When they came back in, rounds were poured, paid for, and swallowed in accepting silence.

Then, Ken removed his black neck kerchief and handed it to Bobby. Johnny put his hands on my shoulder, Ken poured me another shot—On the house, knock—and Bobby tied the bandanna around my head, covering my eyes, three folds of tightly woven cotton. I couldn't see a thing. Willy summoned the rotary once more and called a cab. The boys, the elders, gave me one more shot, and Bobby and Johnny on either side of me—Willy at the front—arm in arm we walked out onto the street. In the back of the cab, it was Bobby on the driver's side, Johnny on the outside, and me in the middle. Willy sat in the front passenger seat.

The cab driver did not question what three silver-haired Japanese ancients were doing with a blindfolded twenty-five-year-old Anglo 'round midnight in Little Tokyo. When the cabbie asked where we were going, I could hear Willy scribbling something on a piece of paper with a pencil. We roared off into the fog. The driver made five turns (three rights and two lefts), but I couldn't for the life of me gauge the distance because the driver was hot for punching the gas. When he dropped us off, the fare was $6.35. We stood in silence as the cabbie drove away. The Warlords withdrew their cigarettes and lit 'em up. I started to question them, but thought better of it, leaving the O-ring of uncertainty voiceless and dry on my lips.

After a long five minutes—Bobby gave me drags of a Lucky Strike, and these men were not prone to fronting cigarettes—another driver picked us up. The car was not a taxicab. A four-door sports sedan with deep leather seats, it felt clean. It was June, night of fog and cool enough to bring the jacket out of hibernation, but humid enough for sweat to pool through the back of my shirt. My black leather jacket lay across my lap as useless as an emptied shotgun. Willy spoke to the driver in Japanese and Bobby scolded him for it even though I'd remained honest with them about my ignorance of the tongue. Willy and the driver got out of the car to continue their discourse.

When the two men got back in, the driver punched it faster than the cabbie. We took five lefts and six rights before the drop. Despite the whiskey, I was at least sober enough from the intrigue to count, but it was useless other than the above footnote: I hadn't any inclination of where we'd traveled, senses of time and space destroyed by the blindfold. From the second drop-off, we walked. Maybe a block. Willy went ahead of us, and when we reached our destination Bobby and Johnny each held their hands over my ears as we entered one door and then another, then walked up a long flight of stairs, slowly; even with the escorts the disorientation of blindness was laborious. We walked down a long hallway and through another door. We were in Chinatown. I could tell by the smell. At the last door we passed a man. No words were exchanged, but I felt him there, guardian to the gate.

THE ROOM WAS FILLED with sweet, metallic smoke. Johnny removed the bandanna and it took a minute for my eyes to adjust from the darkness of blindness to the darkness of shadow. The room couldn't have been more than fifteen feet by fifteen feet. It was charcoal dark—the dim luminescence in the room was of a color split between dying ash and half-burned mesquite, a graying orange of underglow—some candles lit in each corner were the only light other than the flicking tongues of sulfuric flame on an opium pistol.

There were three bunks built into the walls, two to the left, one to the right, making six tight coffinlike beds lined with thin mats and ratty ornamental pillows. An old Chinese man lay in one of the bunks, the lower bed of the bunk to the right. An aging but beautiful Chinese woman was holding his pipe, while her daughter—their daughter?—I supposed it was at least her daughter, for they were the stunning replicas of each other split only by a generation—lit the glory-ball stuck on a pin. The smell in the room, masked somewhat by equally exotic incense, was of smoking opium, and the punk for the fire in the daughter's delicious right hand was a tool to light opium. The old Chinese man puffed in seeming disregard of our presence.

The three Warlords of Little Tokyo took off their shoes and hung their suit jackets on hooks near the door and nodded for me to do the same. I spied Johnny sliding the packaged rig back into my jacket pocket. I was the only one who caught the gesture, and Johnny didn't see me watching. Willy nodded me over and laid me down on the lower bunk of one of the slats on the left.

The old Chinese man surrendered his pipe to a serving tray and finally got up to take measure. A knowing grunt was exchanged between the four elders—the Warlords and the opium man. The opium man did not have a long white beard or wear a cloak, nothing of what I would expect from a proprietor of an opium den if ever I found myself in one. He wore traditional work clothes, the thin cotton Chinese version of Dickies, and on his feet were old split-toe kung fu shoes worn down to ragged sandals at best. Nobody questioned my presence, and it is only now, ten years later, that I further understand trust and the price one pays to gamble with it: I somehow both did and did not belong in this place, and it was all on the Warlords' hands.

The women, now—oh, the women! They were dressed in elaborate silk cheongsams embroidered with phoenixes and blooming flowers. Horned capes skied off their delicate shoulders. The mother's dress was jade green, the daughter's rain blue. Their faces were porcelain, but in the darkness I could not tell if it was makeup or their natural skin. Both were unspeakably beautiful and catered exquisitely to the Western canon of Oriental fever dreams—and I can say with a clear conscience that they were unspeakably beautiful solely as women, period, Asian or otherwise.

Even before lying down, I felt exceptional in that I knew in my gut that this was a room where few white men were allowed to tread. I kept my mouth shut and followed the Warlords' lead. Willy, Johnny, and Bobby grunted knowingly back to the opium man, and all three spread out on their small slats. Willy got on the bunk above me. Bobby and Johnny took the bunk next to us. Functionally, the bunks seemed more like stockroom shelves than beds, and it rapidly occurred to me that the room was indeed some kind of storeroom by day—that was the cover. There were tapestries and straw mats on the wall that looked a disguise, tread upon and worn in footpaths. If necessary, the room could be quickly converted by simply tossing the rugs and mats on the floor, ditching the pillows, and restocking the shelves. In the purpose of the opium bed, the short length of the shelves forced the reclining pipe smoker to turn on his side and bring his legs up into a near-fetal position, which remains one traditional posture for taking the medicine.

The women split up, the younger attending to Bobby and Johnny, the elder attending to Willy and me. They adjusted our pillows and offered us thin paper blankets without saying a word. They did not smile, but they did not seem melancholy, either; theirs was a duty, and they carried it out with a habit of purpose tainted by neither pride nor contempt. As we had our pillows adjusted, Willy handed the opium man a small leather satchel. It was payment of some sort, money, but maybe something more. The old man took it, nodded, grunted once more, and disappeared out of the room. I guessed the relief of opium rescinded old biases, at least as I perceived them, the grunts a knowing resignation toward the body—that is, to more immediate amnesty—rather than histories of contention. I never saw the opium man again.

Our pillows and our heads ready, the women brought out the opium pistols, one of bamboo, the other ivory. The daughter brought the bamboo pipe to Bobby and Johnny, pin in the pea of the golden dragon. With the torch she lit it, and I watched them smoke. The mother waited between our bunks, facing her daughter, but she turned when Johnny took his pipe, and she caught me gazing at the ritual. I turned my eyes away. Mysteriously ashamed, I stared up at the bottom of Willy's bunk and found that he too looked on me, his head cocked over the edge of the top shelf like a merciless panther upon a jungle branch. He closed his one eye as my eyes met it, and I turned my head away from Willy and stared across the room to the empty bunk where we first found the old Chinese man. I could not shake feeling consequential.

Bobby and Johnny took about ten pipes before the mother brought the bamboo pistol to Willy and me. Lamp and pin at the ready, she handed Willy the instrument first. I kept my eyes on the empty bunk across the room until the daughter sashayed over, kneeled, holding the length of her dress behind her and off the floor, then whispered ever quietly in my ear, "Okay, you watch." They were the only words spoken by anybody the entire time we were in the den. The girl returned to the space between the bunks and prepared the pin, torch, and opium for the ivory pipe. I craned my neck out of my shelf and watched Willy take his smoke, the discomfort now being the urge to gaze upon the younger of the two women in the hope of recording and looping in my mind her mellifluous voice and fluid, dancinglike movement. Instead, I saw smoke exit through Willy's eye patch.

The mother brought the pipe down to me. I held it like an unfocused rifle as the woman held the pin of opium over the lamp and nodded when it was time for me to take the golden brown pea into the pipe. She held the lamp under the bowl like an incestuous but well-meaning mother leading her pubescent son's hand to her breast. I took the milk—the smoke—into my mouth in a hard draw, for the pipe was traditionally long, and I choked a little on the toke. It tasted of the scent of a flower I could not place, saccharine as overripe fruit, but faintly too of a mustard weed. My underarms stunk to no end, pooled with sweat—mixed with smoke of the opium pistol, the smell was raw and luscious. My sinuses filled with the sweet, metallic odor, and my body lifted. I smoked again. My skin and my bones and my organs melted into the bed, but my mass levitated, floating just above my shell, for opium is the answer to gravity. I smoked five bowls.

By the time the bamboo pistol was passed back up to Willy, he had taken three pipes of the ivory, which had already been passed back and forth between Bobby and Johnny until they had their fill. When the ivory pistol pressed into my lips and I again drew in the smoke, the room shed its charcoal cloak for an aura of blue, a soft arc light like a fluorescent left on at night in an enigmatic and luring room full of adult things that a child so much desires to step into but can only witness, for now, from afar.

Though a little nauseated, my head swam listlessly and my body was like a buoy gently commanded by the ripple. My mind was not on my heartache, as it so ceaselessly had been—and when my thoughts did return to the chasm, the perspective was skewed; it was as if a stranger were explaining to me a pain I'd just begun to inquire about, rather than the authoritative expert of it I had so wretchedly become. Smoking the opium was a salve. The old men and I, we were biting at clouds. I glanced up at Willy. He looked down on me and lifted his eye patch. The scarred hole in his head, a nasty suckling sphincter in reverse, shone in that moment like a Grecian pearl, a soft enchantment encased in a dried wash of cracked mud.

We spent about one hour in the den when Willy initiated the exodus. Gliding like water dragons, we reunited with our shoes, our jackets. Only nods were exchanged with the women, knowing nods with the old Japanese Warlords, and slightly bashful but serious nods toward me. Bobby tied Ken's kerchief around my head once more before we descended through the hallways, down the stairs, out the doors. On the street again, the same leathery sedan picked us up and made a similar haphazard series of turns before dropping us off at a corner unknown to me. Willy—suddenly using someone's cellphone; none of the Warlords of Little Tokyo ever had one before—called a cab.

THIS TIME, THE CABBIE talked. He only had questions about the blindfold, but they all centered on me getting married or a bachelor party—and I suppose, in its own mythically fraternal way, smoking with these men forty years my senior was indeed some kind of rite of passage—but the silver-haired and ancient Warlords ignored him, mumbling in Japanese.

Willy commanded the cabbie in English, "right, left, right, right, left," and nothing more. We were dropped off, the fare, $6.15 this time, was paid, and back in Little Tokyo, Johnny removed the bandanna. The entire borough glowed with the same opium-infused hue as the den, highlighted by the high, full moon, and the refracting fog that gives all of Los Angeles at night an old black-and-white television glow. We'd been let out in front of Saloon Cosmos, a few doors west of Bar That Cannot Be Named.

I did not know what to say, but without thought or restraint, "Thank you" came to my lips.

"So long, James Dean Sad Eyes," Bobby said.

Johnny withdrew a comb and ran it through what was left of his silver crown.

Willy said, "Now, we go."

I felt the rig in the pocket of my black leather jacket. Mary Jean—the love I'd lost—was diabetic, and I don't know how long that syringe had been there. I hadn't worn the thing since winter, when the woman and I were still together.

"It wasn't mine," I said, "the needle."

"That's not what I'm talking about," Willy said. If that wasn't cryptic enough, Johnny patted his own jacket pocket relative to where the syringe rested in my own.

The three old men turned for Bar That Cannot Be Named. I moved to follow—I lived in the direction—but they stopped, looked at me with those ancient eyes, and nodded toward Saloon Cosmos. I just stood there as they kept walking. Then I slid Mary Jean's syringe out. I looked at it with new eyes. The heartache returned with an unholy vengeance—though I felt no physical pain, my marrow was light.

With scholarship I understood the mouthpiece of addiction, the agency of need, whether it be woman, whether it be poppy. I'd been a journeyman of love unrequited. These men had just taught me the genuine erudition of the opiate. These codgers, these Warlords of Little Tokyo and their silver hair and liver spots and cocksureness and quiet harbors of vast sorrow, they sacrificed our friendship for it. At their tenth step they paused to check on me. We exchanged one knowing, execrating nod. It was exactly then that I opened the door to Cosmos, still in the sultry teeth of the dragon. The Warlords turned once more, but they did not make it to Bar That Cannot Be Named. Out of the corner of my eye I could see that they were turning to dust, swirling up into little tornadoes of white powdered silk, summoned by the mercy of the fog. Then they were gone.

SURVIVORS GUILD

Matjames Metson

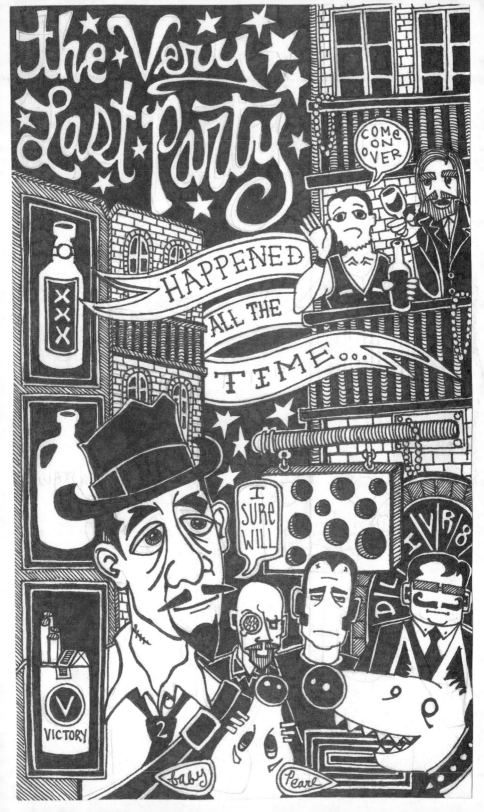

PEOPLE ALWAYS ASK ...

WHY DIDNT I LEAVE FOR THE STORM

NEW ORLEANS MY HOME xxxxxx

WHERE

ELSE

THE FIRST PLACE I EVER CALLED

home

DECEMBER 10 1990

THAT WAS A LONG TIME AGO.

WHY DIDNT I LEAVE ?

WHERE ELSE ?

IT ISNT LIKE WE DIDNT KNOW ...

GET OUT

NOT THAT WE DIDNT CARE

IF I HAD HAD A $ CHOICE

I

I WOULD HAVE STAYED xxx

AUGUST 29

ITS CRAZY BUT... IF EVERY ONE LEFT

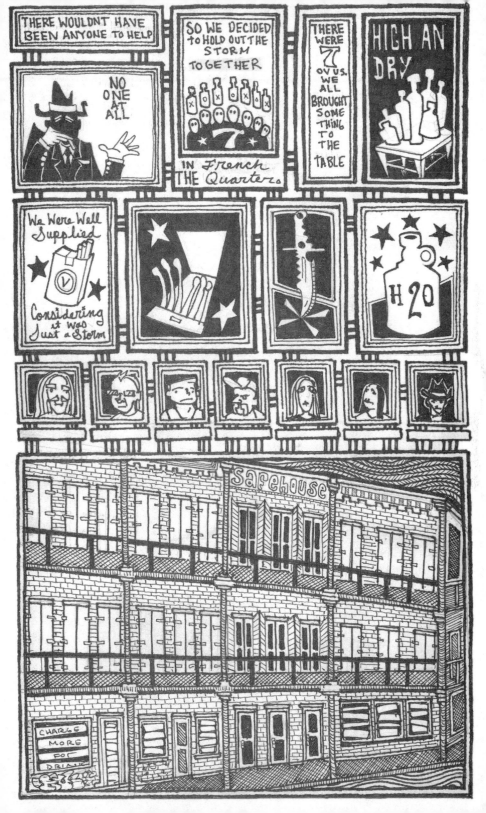

FROM THE SAFE HOUSE WE WATCHED THE STORM

and we have a lot to drunk and we had fun because its still just...

still just a storm...

Just Another Storm

it happens all the time

all the time

We didn't know yet

that the storm wasn't going to be the scarey part

MATT SAID IT AT FIRST

IT TOOK A WHILE

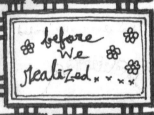
before we realized

THAT WE WERE IN A WORLD OV OV SHIT!

ITS BAD xxx

AND IT JUST STARTED xxx

WE STOOD IN AN ARCH WAY.

WE PEERED THREW THE SLATS

WATCHING WIND

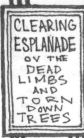 CLEARING ESPLANADE OV THE DEAD LIMBS AND TORN DOWN TREES

WE BELIVED THAT WE COULD CONVINCE A TREND
BUT THE OTHERS DECIDED TO FOLLOW A DIFFERENT END

 A TASK ANSWERED

 BY A BAND OV NEW MEN WHOM WERE JUST BOYS DRUNK WITH NERVOUS ENERGY

 to us the storm was over so we cleared the streets.

 DECATUR TO RAMPART

 GOOD SCOUTS

1 2 3 4 5 6 7

 THE STORM WAS OVER So We Wanted to Set a good example and Start Cleaning up,

 IN RETROSPECT. EMBARRASSING NAIVE FOOLISH JUST PLAIN STUPID

 Nervous X X Energy

 WE THOUGHT THAT IT WAS OVER...

 WE WERE WRONG DEADWRONG...

feeling Safe....

 WE LEFT THE SAFE HOUSE

 ...SO ...WE ..HEADED ...HOME...

BEFORE THE WINDS HAD DIED, WE WERE OUT ON ESPLANADE
THE FALLEN OAKS WERE SCREAMING
BRANCHES STILL FALLING
IN THE FLOODED AVENUE WE SET TO WORK
NOOOOO

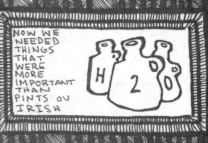

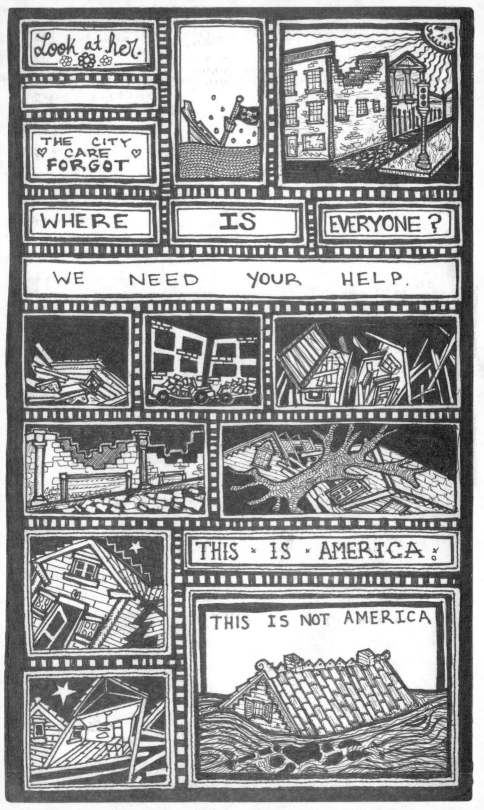

 SO.... to Live in LA

if an when I leave my little apartment

it seems NICE

 Nice enough i geuss.

it seems nice.

THE BEER STORE IS CLOSE BY. thats real nice...

 SO WE WALK THERE SEVERAL TIMES EVERY DAY...

 HOME SWEET HOME

 Sleep -N- drink.

 and dream NEW ORLEANS

 its not any ov that cutesy Louis Armstrong crap.

 N.O.

DREAM HELL

 every fucking night.

 I may live here in Los Angeles (NOW) BUT every night I AM STILL STUCK THERE IN NEW ORLEANS.

IT SEEMS TO AFFECT DAILY OPERATION

AND EVERY THING ELSE...

  it is hurting me.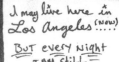

MAYBE WORSE

I DONT KNOW. (yet)

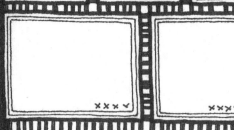

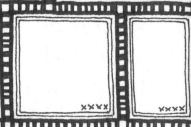

FIFTY MINUTES

Joe Donnelly and Harry Shannon

2012 Best American Mystery Stories

THE CLIENT IS A balding, sunburned man with soft, forgettable features. Running late, he enters the office at 7:02 P.M. and nearly knocks a small Buddha statue from its wooden base. He closes the waiting room door behind him and pauses, unsure of the protocol. From behind his desk, Dr. Bell watches intently. Experience has taught him that a new client will give you 90 percent of what you need just walking through the door. Dr. Bell sees that Mr. Potter is mildly agitated—perspiration rings the armpits of his Hawaiian-print shirt and his breathing is rapid. Not unusual for a first-timer, Dr. Bell thinks. The psychotherapist smiles wryly and motions for Potter to sit on the green couch. Mr. Potter collapses into the cushions and sets his leather shoulder bag in front of him. His khaki slacks are a size behind the times.

"How long does this last?" Mr. Potter asks. "An hour?"

"Fifty minutes," Dr. Bell says pleasantly.

The new client stares at Dr. Bell for a moment, takes a deep breath, and pulls a small-caliber pistol from under his shirt.

"Fine," Mr. Potter says, waving the gun at Dr. Bell. "Then you have fifty minutes to live."

An aluminum taste floods Dr. Bell's mouth. Trauma patients have told him this is what true fear tastes like, but until now he'd never taken them literally. Sure, every shrink has stories about unhinged patients. A client in the middle of a manic episode once threatened to scratch out Dr. Bell's eyes with her car keys if he didn't introduce her to her soul mate, Johnny Depp, but nothing has prepared him for this.

Coherent thoughts vanish in the vacuum of fear. Struggling to find a way back, Dr. Bell takes a quick inventory. The landline is across the room on an end table, and, besides, what would he do with it? Propped against the wall, also out of reach, is his souvenir baseball bat, a gift from a professional ball player Dr. Bell helped get back on track after he washed out on coke and hookers. Should I yell, scream, lunge for the gun? Or can this guy be reasoned with? Dr. Bell wonders. Despite the beads of sweat on Mr. Potter's upper lip, he appears relatively stable. His eyes aren't darting and he's not pumping his legs. His resolve appears to be genuine, possibly deadly. Dr. Bell tries to remain calm and go with what he knows. Talking.

"Clearly, you're quite upset. I'm sorry."

"You are?"

"I don't like to see anyone in pain."

"Really, Dr. Bell? Is that so?"

Dr. Bell looks into Mr. Potter's eyes, trying to project empathy.

"Yes. I believe that's why I chose this profession, Mr. Potter, and why, I suppose, I'm so highly regarded in my field." Dr. Bell thinks he sees Mr. Potter relax just a bit. He presses on. "May I call you by your first name?"

"No, you may not," Mr. Potter says firmly. "I know what you're trying to do. It won't work. I hated seeing her in pain, too, Dr. Bell."

"Who, Mr. Potter?"

"You know."

"Forgive me, I don't believe I do. And, needless to say, for the purposes of this discussion, that places me at a serious disadvantage. Please, tell me who you are talking about?"

Mr. Potter crosses his legs and his pants ride up too high, revealing short, black socks. Dr. Bell can see that his new client's shin is badly bruised and a bandage covers a fresh wound. Dr. Bell takes a long look at the man's shoulder bag. A slot on the front flap has a laminated name tag of the sort frequent fliers fill out. Mr. Potter glances at his watch, purses his lips as if about to give the time, but says nothing. Dr. Bell tells himself to stay in control of the situation.

"Okay, Mr. Potter," he says, as evenly as possible. "Let me try a different question. Why do you want to kill me?"

"Oh, I think you know."

"I really don't, and I must confess I have little experience with this. No one has ever threatened to kill me before. At least not seriously."

"There's always a first time, yes?"

"Mr. Potter, did you make this appointment in order to kill me?"

Mr. Potter does not answer.

He's giving me a blank screen, no expression, no emotion, Dr. Bell thinks. Perhaps he's imitating a trained therapist, maybe a therapist who has something to do with why he's here? A bit of a reach, but…

"May I ask who referred you to me, Mr. Potter, another professional?"

"I'm not the type who feels the need to talk incessantly about his feelings, Dr. Bell. You're the last therapist I expect to see in my life. And the clock, as they say, is ticking."

It suddenly comes to Dr. Bell that Mr. Potter must have booked this appointment, the last available on a Friday, at least a week ago. He's planned this well. A joke about needing to better screen first-time clients sweeps through Dr. Bell's brain like a tumbleweed. He thinks better of sharing it. He has to crack Mr. Potter's shell delicately, if it is in fact a shell. Fifty minutes isn't a lot of time to do it. But Dr. Bell is starting to realize his life depends on it.

The second hand on the grandfather clock ticks away and Mr. Potter seems to grow larger, more intimidating. Despite the urgency of the situation, Dr. Bell knows it is imperative to not let the clock rule him. He wants more than to just kill me or he'd have done that already. Let him have his theatrics for now. The need to speak will build. He'll tell you why he's here eventually. He'll have to, or what's the point?

Dr. Bell flashes back to his student days, when a gifted supervisor used father transference to reduce him to a whimpering puddle. Dr. Bell crosses his legs, struggling to appear above it all, but his knees feel weak and his fingers tremble slightly.

"Forty-six minutes," Mr. Potter announces, "and seven seconds."

Dr. Bell takes a deep breath and releases the air quietly, allows himself a thin smile. His stomach settles. He holds the smile as best he can and tries to affect something just shy of disdain. "Okay, then. This is your time, as we say. What do you want to talk about?"

"I don't want to talk about anything. I want you to do all the talking."

"What is it that you want me to talk about?"

"You know, Dr. Bell."

"No, I don't, Mr. Potter, and I fear that our time will go by in silence if it's left up to me to guess why you came here, other than to threaten to kill me. But maybe that's the best place to start. Why don't you tell me why you believe you want to kill me?"

"Because you're a fraud, Dr. Bell."

"Why do you think so, Mr. Potter?"

"I think you know."

"I really don't, and we're in danger of getting stuck in this circular dialogue, but let me try something else. Let's presume that I am a fraud, which we all are to some degree. What does that mean to you?"

"It means that I'm going to kill you."

"Do you kill all frauds, Mr. Potter, or is it just me for whom you reserve that honor?"

"Maybe I'm starting with you."

"So what comes next? Politicians, CEOs, clergymen… Jodie Foster? Is someone speaking to you, Mr. Potter, telling you that you've been chosen to do these things?"

"No, Dr. Bell, I'm not schizophrenic, paranoid or otherwise. I haven't lost my job, my home, my standing in society. I'm not mad at the world. I'm an average man, Dr. Bell. But sometimes, average men have to do extraordinary things."

Mr. Potter raises the gun. The barrel is a deep, dark well. Dr. Bell's bowels suddenly stir. He notices Mr. Potter's hand is not trembling.

"One shot through the front of your skull and you're done, Dr. Bell. I understand you fancy yourself a Buddhist. What do you imagine occurs next? Will it be a joyful reconnection with the one consciousness? Or perhaps just zip, nada, nothing? Tell me, I'm curious. You see, this is not really my fifty minutes, it is yours."

Dr. Bell tries to process quickly. "I understand" you fancy yourself a Buddhist. Not "I see" you fancy yourself one. He's either done his research or heard about me through someone else. He mentioned a woman earlier, having seen her in pain. His wife? His girlfriend? His mother? Dr. Bell struggles to think of a female patient with the same last name. Too many faces, too many names. Someone terminal, perhaps? Someone from the cancer ward? He draws a blank. The years of practice are callusing me. The faces and names and problems and patterns are all running together.

If he's realized anything over the years, it's that each and every one of his patients is sure that he or she occupies a new and entirely unique spot at the center of the universe and Dr. Bell has become all too aware of how crowded it is at that spot. Did he believe anything was different from one week, month, year, or life to the next with his patients? Did he even care anymore? Every week they pay their hundred and fifty dollars a session to say and hear the same things, and every week they leave satiated like crack addicts only to come back with that hungry, desperate look in their eyes realizing they need another fix.

Mr. Potter lowers the weapon. "Where did you go just now?" he asks, leaning forward, but not in a threatening manner. "When I did that with the gun, what did you see? Feel? I'd really like to know."

Dr. Bell swallows. "Mr. Potter, you just mentioned putting a bullet through my skull. You're pointing a gun at me. So, naturally, I felt afraid. Buddhist or not, I'm not looking forward to dying here, today, and in this way. Understandable, yes?"

"Yes, quite understandable. But we don't always have a say in what happens to us, do we, Dr. Bell?"

"You're speaking of karma?"

Mr. Potter shrugs.

Dr. Bell tells himself to keep Mr. Potter talking. Get him to give you his first name. Make yourself a human being. It's easy to hurt an object or a symbol, but not so easy to hurt another human being.

"Of course the world is often a random place. That fact does not prove or disprove the idea of karma," says Dr. Bell. "But that's a moot point right now, for this isn't at all random. You came here with a purpose. I'm trying to figure out what brought you to this place. What drove you to come here and terrorize me in this way?"

Mr. Potter scratches his nose with the barrel of the gun.

"Tell me your first name," Dr. Bell says. "I'd like to be less formal, especially under the circumstances."

Mr. Potter stands up and shakes his head. "Just keep talking," he says, pacing in front of the green couch.

"Okay, I'm thinking that if you came here just to kill me, you would have done it by now. So why don't you tell me what else it is that you're looking for? You said I'm a Buddhist. Who told you that? And does this person have something to do with why else you're here?"

"You know who that person is, Dr. Bell, and you now have forty-one minutes and thirty-two seconds to tell me why you did it."

Dr. Bell feels his forced calm giving way to a tempest of frustration, his anxiety flaring into anger. He shakes inside with as much outrage as fear. Dr. Bell has to fight his urge to charge the man with the gun, to do violence to Mr. Potter for the way he is being violated. But he knows that could be a fatal mistake. Mr. Potter seems to register this wave passing through Dr. Bell. He takes half a step back and levels the gun. He finds the edge of the couch with one hand and sits down. Smiles.

Dr. Bell takes a deep breath and reminds himself not to telegraph his feelings. "So, we know someone in common. Or, you think we do. Is that correct?"

"Yes, Dr. Bell. It is. Continue..." Mr. Potter takes another theatrical look at his watch. "Time, after all, isn't on your side."

"Was this someone a patient of mine?"

"She was. Her name was Katherine Cook."

"Katherine Cook. I don't recall seeing anyone named Katherine Cook."

"Try harder. She sometimes went by Katie."

"CAN YOU DESCRIBE HER to me?"

"She was beautiful...beautiful, and full of life. Until she met you."

"So you say. A young woman named Katie Cook. How long did she see me, for how many sessions?"

"Long enough to be destroyed."

"By me, I assume, in your worldview, which I'm beginning to think of as increasingly aberrant. Tell, me, Mr. Potter, what happened to your leg?" Dr. Bell scowls, framing the question just shy of an accusation.

The sudden change of topic confuses Mr. Potter. He glances down at his bruised leg and the small bandage, clearly startled. His gun hand goes lax and Dr. Bell thinks it's now or never if he's going to go for the weapon. But before he can make his move, Mr. Potter pushes down his pants leg, his face flush, and regains himself.

Something is there, thinks Dr. Bell.

"I want you to tell me precisely what happened," Dr. Bell says. "Did you hurt someone?"

Mr. Potter purses his lips like a goldfish at the edge of the bowl. He struggles for breath. His face reddens, tics associated with shame and anxiety, clearly a regressive response. Dr. Bell knows it's time to play his highest card.

"What have you done, Martin?"

The sudden use of the man's first name peels back another layer of defense. Mr. Potter's composure melts, his face is that of a scared child. Dr. Bell reminds himself that he's walking a fine line. Children are easy to break down, but they also act impulsively and without thought of consequence. And this one is carrying a gun. Dr. Bell eases up a little.

"It's there on your name tag," Dr. Bell says evenly. "Martin Potter, 3712 Moorpark Street, Apartment 11, North Hollywood…I can't quite make out the ZIP code."

Dr. Bell hopes this traditional disarming move, using Mr. Potter's first name, placing him at his address, identifying him as a person with a life outside this office, will blunt his aggressiveness, give Dr. Bell the room he needs to exploit Mr. Potter's insecurities. Clearly, Mr. Potter exhibits signs of regret. But where has this taken him? Is he suffering from a character disorder, severe perhaps? Is he projecting his own guilt onto Dr. Bell— reaction formation? Dr. Bell softens, leans forward, and lowers his voice.

"I'm sorry if I snapped at you, Martin," he says. "I'm deeply worried, and not just about my own safety. About you as well. Have you perhaps already hurt someone else?"

Mr. Potter stares back dully, traumatized. His fingers loosen a bit and the gun sags in his hands as if it's suddenly a great weight. Dr. Bell again considers going for it, but he's making progress breaking Mr. Potter's resolve. Best to stick with it.

Mr. Potter falls back into the couch, which nearly consumes him. "I haven't hurt anybody, Dr. Bell. In fact, I'm pretty sure you'll be the first. And you can call me

Mr. Potter, if you don't mind. We're not ever going to be on a first-name basis."

"Fair enough, Mr. Potter. Why don't you tell me about what happened to your leg then?"

Mr. Potter pauses, takes a deep breath. He regains some of his composure. "Very well, Dr. Bell, I will, since it does concern you and not indirectly."

"It does?"

"Yes. You see, Dr. Bell, I hurt my leg when I walked into Ms. Cook's apartment last Tuesday and found her…"

Mr. Potter's voice trails off, his eyes close.

Dr. Bell tries to wait him out, a game of chicken played in tense silence. He is surprised to find his own nerve fails first. "You found her?"

Mr. Potter's eyes snap open like a man tied to train tracks who hears a loud whistle. "I didn't do anything. I didn't hurt her. It was you, I know it was you."

"Ms. Cook. Tell me what happened to Ms. Cook," Dr. Bell presses.

Mr. Potter grows more agitated. He waves the weapon like a dowsing rod and Dr. Bell flinches involuntarily.

"I found her that way. Hanging there. From one of those pull-up bars you put in a doorway? She'd tied the sash of her robe around her neck and…or so it appeared…Maybe someone arranged it to look that way." Mr. Potter lowers his head.

"Go on, Mr. Potter," Dr. Bell says, voice thickening. "How did you happen to be at Ms. Cook's apartment, were the two of you…friends?"

"I didn't know her. But I loved her." Mr. Potter's eyes cloud and he looks close to crying. "It was an awful thing to see."

Dr. Bell says nothing, waits for more. Mr. Potter wipes his eyes and nose on his right sleeve. He looks up, angry now, and points the gun once more in Dr. Bell's direction. Dr. Bell recoils.

"I know what you're thinking, but it wasn't like that," Mr. Potter says. "I really did love her. From afar, yes, but it was pure and true."

Bell takes a shot. "You've been following her?"

Mr. Potter reddens again. "Yes, yes. I followed her. I saw her in that supermarket at Burbank and Laurel Canyon, buying vegetables. She looked familiar, and then I realized I'd seen her in a commercial, the one for cat food."

He waits for Dr. Bell to register a sign of recognition.

"I'm sorry, Mr. Potter. I haven't seen it. I don't watch much television and when I do it tends to be CNN or MSNBC. I don't recall seeing this cat food commercial."

"Ms. Cook was wearing a long-sleeved sweater," Mr. Potter continues, as if Dr. Bell had said nothing, wasn't even there. "It was beige, almost the color of her hair, and a pair of worn jeans. Those big blue eyes…I wanted to say something right away, but I was too shy. So I followed her to her car and watched her load the groceries. I knew it wasn't right, but what was the harm so long as I didn't harass her? Lots of men look at someone like that, all day long I'm sure."

Dr. Bell just stares back, regaining some leverage.

Mr. Potter looks away again, flustered. "Well, I went back to the grocery store the next day at the same time, and there she was again," he continues, looking beyond Dr. Bell into some darkened corner. "At first I just followed her around the store, watching her and wondering what it would be like to be with her…you know, shopping with her. Going through a day with her."

379

Dr. Bell sees an opening. "But that's not where it stopped, is it, Mr. Potter?"

"No, it's not," Mr. Potter says, mostly to himself. "I looked her up on the Internet, found her on IMDB, familiarized myself with her background. She grew up in Ohio. Went to NYU, where she studied theater. Came out here to follow her dreams, like a lot of us do, right Dr. Bell?"

"Would you say this was a healthy fixation, Mr. Potter?"

"Is love a fixation, Dr. Bell? I suppose it might be. But I did hope to talk to her one day, so why wouldn't I be prepared? I went back to the supermarket every day at the same time and saw her there. She only ever picked up a few things. Sometimes it seemed like she just did it for the routine. Routines can be comforting, Dr. Bell."

"They can be, Mr. Potter, but some are more appropriate than others. Did you ever speak to Ms. Cook?"

"I was too shy to approach her in the grocery store. I didn't want to seem like, well, I didn't want to intrude. Finally, I did follow her to her apartment building—"

"You followed her home?" Dr. Bell cuts in, accusingly.

"Yes, I did, but only because I was so enchanted. I watched her unload the bag of groceries. I sat in my car, telling myself to leave, that this was silly, but then she came right back out again and got in her car."

Mr. Potter stops, raises his head again and stares directly at Dr. Bell. "She drove here, to your office, Dr. Bell."

"So you say, Mr. Potter," Dr. Bell says, turning in his chair, putting his back to Mr. Potter, "but why should I believe any of this? I don't know you. I don't know this woman you speak of. You're obviously going through something and I'd like to help you—

"Please face me, Dr. Bell. I can shoot you just as well through that chair and I'll be inclined to do it sooner than later if you don't turn around so I can see you."

Dr. Bell takes a deep breath and turns back around to face Mr. Potter.

"Okay, Mr. Potter. You say this woman, Ms. Cook, came here?"

"Yes, here. I followed her here."

"What day was that, Mr. Potter?"

"Tuesday…of last week. She was here for nearly two hours," Mr. Potter says, fondling the gun. "Yet, these appointments last fifty minutes, yes?"

"But I don't have a client named Katie Cook. There was no Katie Cook here last Tuesday. I'm positive, but if it makes a difference, I'll check my appointment ledger."

Dr. Bell flips backward through his calendar to the date in question and runs his index finder down the page. "No, no Katie Cook, or Katherine Cook, Mr. Potter. I'm sorry to disappoint you."

"But you have an appointment booked with someone named Katherine, don't you, Dr. Bell? Didn't you? God damn it, didn't you!"

Dr. Bell tells himself to stay calm, show nothing.

"Yes, Mr. Potter. I did book a double appointment, with a woman named Katherine Friedman, a relatively new client. I was just getting to know her. She double booked because she was going to miss the following week, going to Hawaii or something. Patients do that all the time, book double appointments. You understand, right?"

"I understand that you're telling your story, Dr. Bell. I also understand that Katie Cook was Katherine Friedman's stage name, but I'm sure you know that, don't you?"

"No, Mr. Potter, I don't know that. I don't know anything you're talking about. All I know is that someone whom I suspect is delusional is pointing a gun at me and talking in riddles."

"What about that night, Dr. Bell? What happened later that night?"

"I don't know," Dr. Bell replies, feeling an icy ripple up his spine, "but I'm afraid you do."

"I waited outside in my car," says Mr. Potter, pointing his gun toward the window facing the street, "for two hours, Dr. Bell, while she was in here with you. Then I followed her home. I parked outside her apartment. I tried to get the courage to walk up and introduce myself, but just couldn't do it, you know? I just couldn't. I'm shy around pretty girls. Lots of men are."

Dr. Bell could see Mr. Potter getting more excited, his pupils dilating now, his hands wavering, one foot tapping steadily. He's coming down from some kind of meds, Dr. Bell thinks. He may already be having some auditory or visual hallucinations.

"May I change the subject for just a moment, Mr. Potter? If you don't mind my asking, are you, or have you been on, psychotropic medication? Are you taking anything for stress, anxiety, PTSD?"

Mr. Potter sneers and grips the gun tightly. "You shrinks are all alike. Don't try to twist things around. That's not going to work with me."

"I'm sorry I interrupted," Dr. Bell says, soothingly. "Please continue. You were parked on the street outside when Ms. Friedman, or shall we say Ms. Cook, came to see me?"

The door to the waiting room opens, a buzzer sounds. Dr. Bell stiffens in his chair. Mr. Potter raises the gun.

"Wait," Dr. Bell says. "I haven't scheduled anyone else."

"Send whoever it is away or I'll kill you," Mr. Potter says under his breath, leaning forward but not standing.

"If you kill me there will apparently be a witness."

"You are the murderer," Mr. Potter hisses. "You killed a patient. How could anyone blame me for killing you?"

"I've killed no one," Dr. Bell replies with as much even-voiced authority as he can muster. "I'm so sorry, but whatever you're going through here, it has nothing to do with me other than the fact that I happened to treat Ms. Friedman the day you followed her home. They call that stalking, Mr. Potter. Let me help you. Perhaps I can prescribe something that will give you some rest."

"No more pills!" Mr. Potter yells, almost infantile in his fury. "I'm tired of the damn pills. You guys have a pill for everything. I saw you." Mr. Potter's lips curl and quiver. "I saw you go into that girl's apartment. I saw you run out a few minutes later and drive away. Something about the way you left made me fear for her safety. So I went to Ms. Cook's apartment and found her. You tried to make it look like a suicide, but I know the truth, I know you killed her. What happened, did she threaten to take you to the professional board, cost you your license, tell your wife?"

Dr. Bell rises from his chair, puts his hand on his desk and speaks slowly. "I honestly don't know what you're talking about, Mr. Potter. Mr. Martin Potter, of 3712 Moorpark Street, Apartment 11. But I do know you're very upset right now, and that things feel like they have gone…out of focus. Please don't do anything rash when an event such as this is taking place. You're not stable. During these…these breaks, things that seem certain to you are not at all what you think. The subconscious is out on parade in full daylight and the normal consciousness, reality, as it were, is in the shadows. Do you understand, Mr. Potter? Do you realize you're just passing through something that won't be here when you come back?"

"No, no. It's not like that. It's not how you say. I have proof. I'm not crazy, Dr. Bell."

Mr. Potter reaches inside his pants pocket. Dr. Bell clenches and retreats to his chair.

"Proof? Proof of a manic episode?" protests Dr. Bell.

"You were there," Mr. Potter says. "See?"

Mr. Potter holds up his cellphone, which is playing a short clip of video. Dr. Bell squints. "That simply isn't me," he says. "You have a blurred image of someone my general size and weight, Martin." He pauses for a moment. "Wait, and how did you think you knew what I looked like in the first place?"

"You walked her to the outside door, Dr. Bell. I saw you say goodbye to Katie Cook," Potter says, triumphantly. "You hugged her."

"I often hug my patients, Mr. Potter. It's not something the board necessarily approves of, but it is a natural human response to a developing connection and not out of the ordinary with relatively new clients. Empathy, nothing more. And I resent the implication I'd get romantically involved with someone such as poor Ms. Friedman, or Cook as you know her."

"Sure. Protest all you want. I know."

Dr. Bell leans forward. "Mr. Potter, what I know is that you are off your meds, you've been stalking a beautiful young woman, and that you're at minimum hiding valuable information from the police. Perhaps this was a suicide. If not, you may even be implicated in a murder. And I still want to know what happened to your leg."

"Never mind my leg. Dr. Bell, why don't you tell the truth? Your fifty minutes are just about up."

"I've told you the truth, Martin. I can't tell you anymore. I had a new client who fits your description. She booked a double appointment last week before she was to go away on business. And now you say this woman is dead and you are the only person who we know was at the scene of the death and you've admitted to me that you've been stalking her. I'm sure if I wanted to, I could go to the board and find a record of your psychiatric treatment."

"Wait, wait, you're turning this around on me." Mr. Potter looks drained, his composure gone. "You, you're the one. I know it." Mr. Potter raises the gun with trembling hands. It wavers in front of him for what seems like an eternity. Something in Dr. Bell tells him this is it. He ducks behind his desk. A shot rings out and the bullet thumps into the wall above his head. The sound is dull, lifeless, like a staple gun shooting into a piece of wood. It's not at all what he would have expected. Dr. Bell stays down and waits. But there is nothing more, only the sound of Mr. Potter running out the door.

Dr. Bell holds still for a minute. Silence. He thinks about what to do next. Gingerly he opens the door to the waiting room and finds a kid there cowering on his couch, looking like he'd seen a ghost.

"Who are you?" Dr. Bell asks.

"Look...I'm, I'm just here to sell magazine subscriptions. What...what just happened?"

"Wait here," Dr. Bell says, locking the front door. "I'm calling the police. Did you get a good look at the guy? Could you describe him? He may be a murderer."

"Yeah...yes. I think I so. Yes," the kid stutters.

Dr. Bell goes back into his office and picks up his phone to call the authorities. But first he erases the message from Katherine Friedman, the actress who goes by the stage name Katie Cook, the one who'd left yet another rage-filled outburst on his office voicemail in which she said that they must speak about what was going on with them, how she'd had enough of his empty promises, how she was going to Hawaii for a couple weeks and how she expected him to have told his wife by the time she got back or she didn't know what she would do, maybe she'd tell his wife, or maybe she'd kill herself; there was also something else about how the board might be interested in his methods...Dr. Bell hadn't listened all the way through. He was familiar enough with these rants by now, familiar enough to know these were no longer idle threats.

All that was left to do now was call the police. Then he could, for the first time in fifty minutes, thank god, or whatever you want to call it, for Mr. Martin Potter.

GROUPIE

Lauren Weedman

MY BOYFRIEND, DAVID, IS organizing his sock drawer when I say to him, "You know, it just hit me, if we end up staying together, you will go down in history as the love of my life."

I lean back and position myself on the bed—fan out my skirt and fluff my hair so that when he turns around and says it back to me I'll look worthy. But he doesn't follow the script.

Instead, he says, "Aww," like he just saw a little baby with hearing aids.

We've been together four years. It shouldn't feel like I just took a gigantic risk and told him that I had a crush on him. We are at the point in the relationship where we are supposed to say either, "You are the love of my life," or, "You are not the love of my life but you have helped me figure out that I don't like bossy women as much as I'd always thought."

I sit up in the bed and smoosh down my hair. Lately David's been bizarrely excited about how his senses are starting to fail. He likes to demonstrate this as if it's a magic trick. "Do you see this lemon? Okay...I'm bringing it to my nose...and [sniff, sniff] nothing! I SMELL NOTHING!"

I wonder if his ears are going as well and maybe didn't hear me properly.

"That kind of blows my mind to think that you are the love of my life," I try.

I'm fairly certain he hears me because his hands stop balling up his socks and he looks like he's just staring at the wall. Oh my god. All I wanted was for him to simply cup my face in his hands and sob, "You are the love of my life." I thought it would be a nice midday perk.

True, I'm probably fishing for a little reassurance since this evening we're going to dinner with Jessica, an old friend of David's who I find completely petrifying. Not only because she's a yoga/healer person with whom David always makes time for long walks when we visit her hometown of Seattle, but because she did massage on Hannah, David's wife, before Hannah died of cancer nine years ago.

I've never met Jessica before, but I did get a sense of the intimate nature of their relationship when I once overheard her on the phone telling David, "I miss her hair, don't you?" For half a second I thought, "She's never even seen my hair." Then I realized what they were talking about and I knew I'd never be invited on one of their walks.

Jessica is in town for an acupuncture conference and we are going out for Indian food. Now that I've thrown the you're-the-love-of-my-life ball to the kid with no arms and watched it bounce off his head, I'm not so hungry.

The naan has barely hit the table before Jessica reaches over and gives David a little massage-y squeeze. "Oh, hey," she says. "Thank you for visiting me in my dream the other night! It was a really fun place to see you. The only tough part was waking up."

A piece of curried cauliflower pops out of my mouth. Did she miss the bit where David introduced me as his girlfriend? Am I so far from the type of woman that she imagined David being with—so polar opposite of his wife—that she's making a move on him right in front of me? I'm sure David must be as irritated by her New Age hooker talk as—

"Wow! That's so cool," he jumps right in. "I wonder if your dream happened while I was meditating, because I can go to some pretty deep places. Wouldn't that be wild?"

Ech. Here we go.

David is the most stressed-out meditator I've ever seen. The very first time I saw him "meditating" I thought he had a migraine and was rocking back and forth to help the nausea pass. If he's in the middle of his daily twenty minutes of "getting right with the universe" and hears me in the kitchen, he'll call out, "Are you making popcorn?" But he keeps his eyes closed and yells in a whisper voice, so it still counts as meditation.

Plus, David always seems tenser after meditating. Like meditation is just uninterrupted time to go over whom he's angry with. His eyes pop open when he's done and he'll be in the middle of a fight he started in his head—"Yes I did tell you that I was selling that bookcase on eBay—I know I did!"

"Go back in," I always tell him. "I don't think it took."

But at the mere mention of "meditation," Jessica scoots her chair closer to him and asks, "How are you, David? I mean, how are you?"

Usually when I ask David how he is, he acts like it's a trick question and panics: "I…I don't know—what do you mean?"

But when Jessica asks, his response is immediate and graphic.

"Well, I had a little blood in the stool," he practically yells while I'm trying to enjoy my chicken tikka masala.

Blood in the stool is like a mating call for yoga people. Jessica practically humps the table leg when she hears this. "Oh, David! David! The rectum is a warehouse for unresolved emotions…like grief."

I have to break this up before she just jams her hands down his pants.

"You know, he's fine. He got scraped by an angry peanut or something," I say, and it's true. "He's really fine."

But for some reason, David has forgotten this when she starts discussing how she'd love to do some "work" on him. "It would be pretty intense but if you trust me…" she says.

When we get home I can't shut up about it. "So when do you get your taint massage?"

But David is having none of it. In fact, he asks me to "bring it down a notch" and explains that Jessica may have come off as a little loopy but she is a wonderful person who was very important to him during the most intense period of his life. Not to mention the fact that she helped Hannah manage a lot of her pain. Jessica is a mock-free zone.

Not being able to make jokes clears space in my head, which is unfortunate because I get hit by a huge realization that I don't want to have: David can't tell me I'm the love of his life because I'm not the love of his life.

Of course I'm not—how stupid of me to even ask. Hannah, his wife for thirteen years and mother of his only child, is the love of his life. In fact, if the two of them ever discussed David "moving on" after she died I would hope he told her: "I will try to be happy for my sake and for our son Jack's sake. But you will always be the love of my life. No matter what."

He probably assumed he'd be safe in his next relationship if he chose a partner who'd be fine with not being somebody's ultimate. But since he couldn't get his first choice, an illegal immigrant, he settled for a self-hating actress/writer.

TWO WEEKS LATER WE'RE on the bluff overlooking the ocean by our Santa Monica apartment. Tomorrow I leave to do a play in Pittsburgh for six weeks and I'm in a horrible mood. I go on tour a lot—this past year I've been to New Jersey, Idaho, and Virginia—all the hot spots.

Normally, I enjoy missing David when I'm away, but this time I decide that I'm going to break up with him as soon as I get to Pittsburgh, or right before I come back. My therapist is right—for someone with huge fucked-up family issues, I've put myself in the worst possible situation. I will never be a "wife" or a "mother" with David because those titles have already been taken. I get it. But I need more. So I'm going to go do a show in a new town—be a big hit—feel like a big star and ride that confidence into the breakup. Plus, I'll use the money I earn to move out.

"Jesus, the ocean bugs me. It's so endless," I say, trying to provoke David, who is distant and doesn't seem to be making any effort to have a romantic last day together.

I shove some salami in my mouth and try to say something positive so he doesn't suspect what I'm planning. "I guess there's one good thing about living here—that homeless guy keeps taking a shit right by our cactus and now it's started to bloom."

David's eyes are closed and he says nothing...to me anyway. But in his head I'm fairly sure he's saying, "Don't worry, Hannah, she's almost gone."

IT'S THE FIRST NIGHT in Pittsburgh, and I'm listening to a girl sobbing in her car. The only words I can make out

393

are nooooo and whyyyyy? It's been going on for so long, I've started to sing along with her the way you do with a car alarm that won't stop. Nooooo…whyyyyy? There is also the occasional sound of throwing up and beer bottles being thrown. By the time it starts to get light out I'm lying in bed thinking: Forget this love-of-my-life shit. I just want a warm body next to me.

I want to stay in bed and eat smooshed PowerBars, but I think about how if David were here, he would get us up and out the door looking for a little Pittsburgh joint to have breakfast. So I set out in his honor, but I forget the most important rule of exploring a new neighborhood—stay away from the streets that are littered with beer cans, crusty throw-up, condoms, and dead baby birds.

Well, I see two dead baby birds, which seems like one too many. It's the morning after on Carson Street, the city's biggest party stop. The only joint that is open is Schultz's Market. When I walk in, I miss the dead birds and dried throw-up. The market is what my friend Allison would call "an ice cream and porno store." I don't see any porno—but I feel it. Bad porno, with the women who are missing a few fake nails and are slightly bruised on their cellulite—where it's easy to bruise. Later, the people at the theater tell me, "Oh, don't buy anything from Shultz's. They make their own meat."

I have an early interview with the local newspaper to help promote the show. I'm excited because this means the press and the fame and good vibes are gonna start now. But I can tell the reporter hates me immediately. Everything I say and do somehow screams Los Angeles to her. When I tell her I'm from Indiana, she says, "Everybody in L.A. is from somewhere else."

By the end of the interview she has me so pegged as "typical L.A." that I should just start Roller Blading in my string bikini and ask for a Red Bull, a cigarette, and some chopped celery "so I can have the illusion of eating."

I'VE BEEN IN PITTSBURGH almost five weeks now and David and I talk on the phone daily, but we're drifting further apart. I haven't broken up with him yet because being in this city has turned out to be tougher than I'd imagined. Performing eight times a week for audiences that are shuttled in from their convalescent homes hasn't quite been the diva-making machine that I'd hoped. During my curtain calls, I start mouthing I'm sorry as I bow to a room full of confused-looking old people. If we were to break up right now, I'd be taking the shortcut from deeply depressed to morbidly depressed.

My only friend is a guy I pass three or four times a day on my way to the theater. I say "friend," but I've never spoken to him and he never acknowledges me. Still, he's been there for me.

He's a large, older white gentleman who sits in front of his house blocking the sidewalk—sort of the Gatekeeper of the South Side. He never has his shirt on and he watches an old TV that rests on his lap. The trucker cap he wears has a message written on it in black marker. I've never gotten close enough to read the entire message, but I can usually make out the first and last word because they're in caps: WOMEN and LICKIN'. He's never alone. In the lawn chair next to him is a large, stuffed Wile E. Coyote. Today Wile E. Coyote is wearing a white, silky, brand-new bra. I'm guessing C cup.

When I try to use the Gatekeeper as an icebreaker with the theater people, they act like it's the craziest thing they've ever heard and say, "Only somebody from L.A. would notice a person like him." I'm like, have you guys visited your own city? At least the guy who runs the lights, who's said all of one sentence to me for the entire run of the show, doesn't just brush me off when I mention the Gatekeeper. "He's fucking Wile E. Coyote, for sure," he says, and then goes outside to smoke.

I decide to break up with David on closing night. The show is sold out—most of the tickets were bought by one woman bringing a large group. I'm hoping she's one of the wealthy Pittsburgh patrons of the arts I've been hearing so much about. Perhaps she's looking to produce a show in New York to impress all her friends. You never know. Plus, the theater is having a closing-night shindig for me, so people will at least pretend to love me for the sake of a good farewell party.

The patron of the arts turns out to be a twenty-four-year-old who brings twelve of her closest drinking buddies for a bachelorette party. Apparently she thought the show, BUST, would be a madcap comedy about boobs. It's actually about my experience volunteering with women at the Los Angeles County Jail. The bachelorettes have clearly been out drinking on Carson Street since 11 A.M.

They sit in the middle of the theater and spin their lit-up whips and yell whoo-hoo whenever they think the show has gotten remotely sexual. Like when a woman who's been arrested for prostitution reveals that she'd been molested—whoo-hoos and twirling whips light up the audience. When the prostitute character gets released from jail, I hear one of them drunkenly whisper, "This isn't like ha-ha funny...I have to pee." They all click their way out on high heels and take a group of men from the front row with them.

In the dressing room after the show, the house manager apologizes for letting the drunk women in.

"You know, when I saw that one girl sucking on that penis straw, I thought, uh-oh."

My phone rings. It's David.

"Oh my god, Lauren. I'm not even sure how I'm supposed to tell you this."

He sounds hysterical. Is he going to beat me to the breakup punch? Now that he's going to do it, it suddenly seems like the worst idea ever.

"Jack crashed your car," he blurts out. "He stole it and he totaled it. Oh my god, I can't handle this. I honestly can't handle this…"

The words "crash" and "Jack" stun me. He's only fifteen. He had absolutely no business trying to drive a car! I should know because I've seen him do it. In an attempt to do familylike things (or "group activities" as I call them because I'm afraid to use the word "family"), I've been teaching Jack how to drive. I decided I needed to stop spending all of my time trying to convince Jack how HILARIOUS! I was and to join David in helping prepare him for "manhood." I thought I could be a good influence on Jack, and then David and I would feel this shared purpose with him and I'd stop looking for sublets on Craigslist. Why didn't I just buy him some condoms or something?

Please let this be happening in one of Jessica's dreams. They can even be having sex while it's happening as far as I'm concerned.

No such luck.

David frantically recounts how Jack packed a few friends in my car and backed out of our driveway. Within a block, the police noticed the kids and pulled up behind them with lights flashing. Apparently, I'd forgotten to teach Jack an important driving lesson—when the police turn on the lights, the jig is up. Instead,

Jack tried to outrun them. On the first corner, he lost control and crashed into a fence at a Jewish day-care center. So now it's a hate crime, too.

I walk out of the theater and collapse on a stoop next to a drunken girl who looks like she's going to be sick. I start to assess the situation: I'd only gotten the minimum-liability insurance because the car had cost me just $6,000. Which is $4,000 more than I have in my bank account. In my depressed state, I've been spending money like, well, a depressed person. I'd hoped the Pittsburgh gig would provide just enough money to get me into my first month of a sublet. I want to ask David if he's going to pay for my wrecked car, but some latent maternal instinct takes over.

"Oh my god, is Jack…"

David interrupts.

"I'm not done. So he crashes the car, and, Lauren, it's wrecked. It's totaled. And then he jumps out of the window and runs from the cops. He runs from them! And then they form a perimeter around the area to catch him. And then…"

"No, please, no more," I plead, but he has to keep going.

"My god, it's a nightmare—then he tries to escape the perimeter by telling a cop that he's Jack Lighting and that he lives on Castle Street. They arrested him and now he's in juvie. I'm so sorry, Lauren. I am so sorry."

I hang up and my hands are shaking. I'm in such a state of shock that I feel like I'll never be able to sleep again, so I better have a few drinks. I walk into Dees Café, which is sort of a punk rock/steelworker bar. Everyone looks like they've just been told that their boyfriend's son almost died and nearly took fifteen innocent Jewish children with him.

Groupie

When I walk up to the bar I don't see the bartender until I look down. She's sitting on a lawn chair behind the bar. I assume that she's hidden away to secretly read a trashy novel or eat her dinner in peace, but she's just sitting in her chair and staring straight ahead. The sight is so bizarre that I need a drink before my drink. When she pours me a giant pint glass of vodka and adds a few melting ice cubes, I ask her if she has any olives. She looks at me like I just asked her to hand me the glass with her right hand while looking in the opposite direction. Which is exactly what she does.

"That will be two dollars," she says, still not looking.

Jittery and manic, I blurt out, "Two dollars! Why, that's outrageous!"

"Fine," she says and turns around and sits back down in her lawn chair.

I lean over the bar and tell her that I was kidding. "Sorry, I'm from L.A., and that's just so cheap compared to what I'm used to."

An old guy in a Steelers jersey overhears me and mumbles, "I knew it. Shove your olive up your ass and get over yourself. I ought to kick your ass."

WHEN I GET BACK to Los Angeles, we have to go to the police station to get my car released. It's late at night and nobody is around. The officer on duty smiles when we give her the case number. "Oh yeah...Jack. I was a part of the perimeter." She then tells us about Jack leaping from the car—dodging traffic and giving a false name.

"It's hard to run in all this gear," she says, tapping her bulletproof vest. I say, "I bet." So does David, but the policewoman can't hear him because he's squatting on the floor with his head in his hands waiting for his dizzy spell to pass.

The next day, we're squished side by side on a tiny love seat in our new lawyer's waiting room. Jack is still in juvie. Waiting for the court date to get him out has been horrible. The only perk for me is so clearly being the victim. It's a great role and I get excited about the lines I'll get to say, such as, "Oh no, I don't want to press charges. I think he's learned his lesson," and, "I'm just grateful that he's okay. I don't care about the car—it's just a thing."

On the day we meet with the lawyer, I'm rehearsing these lines when I remember the phone conversation I had with the detective assigned to the case. The detective had pretty much pinned the blame on David for not being stricter and for not being home in the evenings to supervise Jack. I haven't told David about this conversation and now I'm worried the lawyer is going to pile on and David won't be able to handle it. I take comfort in knowing that in my new role as the merciful victim I'll just reach out, pat his knee, and comfort him when he breaks down. Which he will do.

The lawyer opens the door to his office and motions for us to come in. At least I thought he meant us, but when we both stand up, he asks if it's okay to speak with me alone for a moment.

"As Nick's stepmother, is there anything about this incident you'd like to let me know about before I speak with you and David together?"

The lawyer thumbs through papers in his file and seems to be half listening and half thinking about lunch.

"Well, I'm not his stepmother and his name is Jack and no, I don't think so. I just know that this whole thing is going to be tough on David. I mean, he's been scared to set boundaries with Jack because of Jack losing his mother. I've been begging David to bring Jack to therapy but he just won't do it and now...well, here we are."

I nod toward the door, knowing that David is seated on the other side having a minor nervous breakdown.

"I just feel bad for him, but I also think this whole thing was inevitable. Poor David."

The lawyer looks up from the file and asks me, "So you're a performer?"

I'm about to tell the lawyer that yes, I am a performer but maybe this isn't the best time to talk about my career, but if he wants more info he can look me up on IMBD later. Before I get to all that, though, he takes out a piece of legal paper from the file and starts reading it aloud.

"His dad's girlfriend had made a joke in a newspaper article about wanting to move a photo of his mother, who is dead, during sex and when his dad confronted the girlfriend, Lauren, about making jokes like that in interviews, she brushed him off." The lawyer stops reading and looks directly at me with his eyebrows raised. I want to speak but my throat is constricting. What is happening?

He continues. "According to Jack's girlfriend, who we spoke with to get some background, you were also interviewed by a newspaper for a theater show in New Jersey and Jack read it online and saw that you made a joke about Jack's deceased mother and when Jack told you how upset he was about it, you ignored him? Does that sound right?"

Dammit! It's fucking New Jersey's fault. I thought the Pittsburgh reporter would be the one to do me in, but now I remember how the lady from the Trenton paper chided me for not providing better "newspaper-friendly quotes" about the play. To win her over, I started telling her my life story, including the joke about how when I was first dating David, I had to ask him while we were having sex to move the photos of Hannah that were right by his bed. And she printed everything I said. Jack read the article and came into my room one night when David was gone and told me that he didn't want me writing or talking about his mother.

"Why were you talking about us at all?" he asked.

"Because…you're my…group," I tried to explain.

And now Jack is in juvie being ordered by gang members to hand over his pudding or else they'd rape him…because of me!

I open my mouth to say, "Excuse me," to the lawyer but no sound comes out. So I just mouth the words and run from the office. I run past David and out into the street and start sobbing.

David leads me to into his car and tries to calm me down.

"This is going to sound horrible," I tell him, "but I just really thought it was going to be your fault!"

David sits in the car with me until I've calmed down and then puts his arm around me and walks back into the office, where David defends me to the lawyer and insists that the reason Jack took my car was because my car keys were the only ones he could find.

Jack's day in court is endless. Waiting for the trial to begin is almost as traumatic as the trial itself because we're stuck doing nothing but sitting and worrying that the judge will send him to a work camp. When I go to the bathroom to pull my hair back into a nice Mormon bun, I overhear a woman in the restroom screaming about her constipation: "It feels like I'm trying to have a baby out my ass!"

At the beginning of the trial the judge asks for the family of Jack Thane to please stand. David stands up and I stand up next to him. It's the first time that anyone has officially called us a family.

Eventually, Jack is released and we all walk out together into the blinding Los Angeles sun. Jack hugs his father and then, unable to look at me directly, tells the concrete sidewalk, "I'm sorry."

I can't look at him either, so I tell the sidewalk to tell him, "It's okay, Jack. It's really okay. Let's eat."

We find a Jamaican restaurant a block away from the jail, and naturally it's delicious. David and I wait until Jack's hands and eyeballs stop shaking before asking him what we've been dying to ask him. Why did he do it?

"Okay, first of all, Lauren always leaves her keys right out on the table so I just grabbed them—that's why I took her car." David kicks me under the table. "And I know I'm gonna get in trouble for saying this, but in the movies and stuff, nobody just pulls over. Everybody runs. Everybody."

Three months later, David and I are engaged. Every few weeks, I still find a reason to scream DISENGAGED! But somehow David—and Jack—both know I'm not going anywhere. We even survive Jack destroying the paint job on my brand-new car by washing it with the Brillo side of the sponge.

When David asks me to marry him, he gives a very long speech about hope and love and fear and dreams and health insurance. His proposal goes on for so long, I start to forget his point. But I am grateful that he knows he doesn't have to tell me that I'm the one and only love of his life. If he had, I would have run. Even if the police were chasing me.

TOMMY CROW

Sam Slovick

M Y KNEES ARE NOT what they used to be. I climb carefully down the loft's steep stairs and a drop of sweat trickles down my back. It's just a few hours after sunup and the heat is already oppressive. In my palm, I cradle the spider I found on my pillowcase as I elbow the screen door open and set her down in the dirt.

Bertram, whose knocking woke me before I was ready to face the day, steps back to give the spider room and then launches into one of his rants. "Ah, the symbolic meaning of spiders…Female, cunning…the cyclical nature of things—death and rebirth, protection and fate. You can guess where this is all going…"

I can't, and I'm afraid about how long it'll take to get there. Bertram's fat spills over the waistband of his khaki shorts, which pull too tightly against his crotch. The festival of gin blossoms on his nose and unruly hairs sprouting from his nostrils make me angry. It's too early for this. I just want him to leave the mail and go away.

"Eight legs, eight eyes…some of them, but not all. The number eight, a symbol of infinity or lemniscate," he continues with a practiced authority, as if that would make anyone listen to him. "An eight turned on its side. Eight symbolizes cycles, the passage of time, evolution."

I take in a breath and nearly gag. Bertram smells like decaying self-esteem covered in sports body spray. I want to be back in my bed, dreaming.

Bertram makes a great show of handing me a package, a special, two-day delivery, before retreating into his little truck. He disappears down a canyon road so near but still a million miles away from Los Angeles proper.

The package, meticulously bound in plain, brown paper, each corner tightly creased, seems unlikely to contain a welcome surprise. A single, long, coarse, black hair is pressed under the clear packing tape. I've seen hair like this before. Touched it and smelled it. Trapped on this package, it feels more like a warning than an accident.

I shake the box for clues, but nothing shifts. I sniff it. It smells like earth. God only knows what's inside. I can't bring myself to open it. Not today, anyway. This is a private party. The guest of honor, a strand of memories stalking me for three decades all converging here on this day. Tommy Crow's birthday.

ON THE SECOND DAY of ninth grade, Vice Principal Crombie declares the end of my formal education at Webster Stanley Middle School. With a finger raised to the heavens, orating like a dinner-theater Mark Twain, he says, "Boy, that is the last time you'll set foot in here."

When Crombie nabbed me, I was drunk on tequila after an early-morning debauch in the cemetery with the fallen cheerleader Kimmie Sablusky. I knew I had a locker and some classes somewhere, but couldn't seem to get a fix on exactly where they might be. No matter now; school's out forever and I have the whole day ahead of me.

Free at last in the summer of 1974, I almost skip the first few blocks before I notice someone following me. I stop to light a cigarette and turn my head to get a look. Straight, black hair, long and thick; bare chest, white T-shirt tucked into the back of his waistband. His skin is tanned with the deep, reddish-brown glow of someone who spends days in the Midwestern sun. He's wearing Levi flares and black Converse All-Stars. I slow just enough so that Tommy Crow can catch up, but not enough to let him know I'm waiting. We walk the first few blocks in silent shoe gazing.

I've seen him around school before, the kid from the rez. I've seen him in the park. I've seen him drunk and wilder than I'd ever seen anybody, but I've never seen him this close.

"Hey, you all right?" he asks. His voice is deeper than I thought it would be. Not the kind of manufactured man-voice you practice when you're fifteen and trying to assert your male independence. His is naturally deep, with an unexpected sweetness.

"I'm cool," I tell him, my heart banging so hard it could split my ribs. The bad boy from the rez is standing so close I can almost smell him and it makes the flesh of my balls contract.

He slides a finger in the place where the straps of my overalls form a V, timing his steps to match mine. We walk a few blocks before he speaks again.

"Probably can't go back now," he says. His words halt, as if he's saying them to himself before speaking out loud. The corners of his lips form a slight grin.

"Yeah...probably not. That's cool," I say with practiced detachment.

I sneak a look at his face. He smiles. His two front teeth are chipped. A small river of sweat streams from his hairline down his cheek, jaw, and neck. He looks away and I take another look, this time across the tight skin of his stomach, and then I follow the fine line of sun-bleached hairs down from his belly button to where it disappears into his pants. When I look up again he's looking back at me. I'm not thinking about being expelled from school or facing my mother...or my father, if he ever decides to come around, which is unlikely. I'm with Tommy Crow now. There isn't room for anything else.

We walk a few more blocks. He stops and kicks off his sneakers, stuffs them in his back pocket and walks bare foot. His toes are long and thin, his feet brown and dirty. The dark circles under his eyes don't make him look old for his age, just that he's absorbed a lot of pain.

I stop at the corner by the liquor store and count the change in my pocket. Tommy Crow leans into me. He smells like sweat and tobacco and the remnants of masturbation, like all those things that are a constant part of my olfactory experience, but also like nothing I've ever smelled before. He steps even closer; we're face to face, just a few inches between our noses. I breathe in as he breathes out. He doesn't flinch. His slightly crossed, copper-brown eyes lead me someplace I haven't been before but need to go.

"You got a bike?" he asks. "We could go to the quarry. There's nobody there on school days."

Tommy Crow looks me over from feet to waist. "We can go swimming...skinny dipping." I feel like I'm going to shit, piss, and cum all at once.

"Yeah, I got a bike. Let's go. Let's go swimming."

I wheel my ten-speed out of the garage while my mother labors over an ironing board just inside the den window. Her hair is tied up in a blue bandanna, and a soap opera barks from the Zenith in the background. I appreciate the convenience of her inattention.

Tommy Crow stands up and pedals, me on the seat gently gripping his waist. We ride past the Standard gas station on Bowen Street, past Woolworth's on Main, past the post office and the library, then onto the shaded side streets. We stay off the main thoroughfares that might attract unwanted attention to two boys in the middle of a school day. Over the railroad bridge, past the cemetery, and out to the new frontage road. We are now five miles into the ten-mile ride. It feels like hours and seconds at the same time.

Tommy leans into me, resting his ass on the tip of the seat. The sweat from his armpits streams onto my fingers. We switch places. I stand and pedal up the hill, through the trees, onto the dirt path that leads into the woods before the quarry. I sit back on the seat just enough to brush lightly against his dick. We stop at the mouth of the quarry. The old mine, now overgrown with vegetation, forms a natural amphitheater in red granite framed by willow and blackberry trees ripe with summer fruit.

With his back to me, Tommy Crow spits into the deep, green, mineral-rich water fed by underground streams. Bluegills rush to the surface to gobble the phlegm. He turns and smiles.

"Let's go in," he says, unbuttoning his jeans and letting them slide down his legs. He stands naked and faces me, waiting for me to do the same. When I do, he takes a long look and smiles again.

"C'mon," he says.

We climb to the rim of the quarry and jump from a twenty-foot cliff, screaming as we smack the surface, plunging into the depths. We swim for a while, diving down as deep into the murky water as we can, then climb onto a ledge above the water and dry off in the sun.

Tommy Crow, on his side, his head supported by the palm of his hand, looks me up and down as I sprawl on my back. The sun has dried me in minutes and I'm already sweating when he puts his hand on my stomach and kisses my chest.

"Snow white," he says and rolls on top of me.

It's dark by the time we head back. We stop at the Dairy Queen on the edge of town and ride away without paying for the hot fudge sundae. We sit on the railroad tracks and feed each other from the same plastic spoon, touching toes as the steady stream of late-model American cars pass unnoticed. We're in an alternate universe. We sit for a long time just looking at each other and not talking.

Later, after my mother goes to bed, Tommy climbs in the small basement window. We spend the night in a teenage love-lock on the orange-and-cream carpet tiles in the wood-paneled cocoon I've made into my bedroom.

EVERY NIGHT AT 10 o'clock Tommy crawls in the basement window. We ride my bike to the football field at the high school and take off our clothes and find each other in the moonlight till 4 in the morning. He rides me back to my house and disappears into the dark.

Every morning I get up and pretend to go to school. I meet Tommy Crow under the little silver bridge on the lake near the statue of the Indian chief in Menomonee Park. We smoke Raleighs, drink Boone's Farm or Mad Dog 20/20, ingest whatever substances we manage to forage, and set out to where the day takes us. We arrive at a vacant room, the far-away woods, or some other temporary sanctuary where we linger naked for hours. The cemetery, the carp pond, the sand pits, the granite quarry, an empty house or car, it doesn't matter as long as we're alone. Isolated from the world, we carry on for months, never seeing anyone except the occasional mailman on his rounds or housewife on her way to a doctor's appointment. Our movements are covert, timed for avoidance. Neither of us has any friends, so we are never missed.

ONE NIGHT A FEW months into the dream, Tommy Crow says he has to tell me something important and asks me to meet him at a special place, an old, three-quarter-size reproduction of a Mississippi paddle-wheel boat docked on the east side of the lake. Like everything else in town, the boat is named for a dead Indian chief. It's after midnight when we break the glass on the door of the main cabin and let ourselves in.

We light a candle and huddle in the corner where the particleboard walls meet the floor, the tightly compressed wood fibers under many layers of glossy paint masquerade as something better than they are.

Tommy pulls a crumpled paper bag from his pocket. Inside are twelve small, green cactus pods. He meticulously scrapes the white powder from the center of each button with his pocketknife and cuts them into small sections. Six for him and six for me. It goes down easy enough and I wait for something to happen. Nothing does for an hour. Then, I vomit over the side of the boat. Relieved, I lie on my back and close my eyes. Suddenly, I hear a tornado-force wind scream through my head and bolt upright to my feet.

"Don't be scared," he tells me. But I'm not scared. I'm elated. I'm tripping balls with Tommy Crow and loving every second of it.

He makes a small cut on his hand with his pocketknife and presses it into the skin of my chest over my heart. "We're connected forever. I love you," he says, but as soon as the words pass his lips, something shifts that I can't put my finger on. I'm seeing things about him that I don't want to see. Nothing I can identify... but still something I know to be true. Betraying my instincts, I lean into him, but for the first time it doesn't feel nice to be with him. We seem ridiculous. A secret better kept. A spell to break at all costs. It's strange and aberrant what we've been doing, not that aberrance or deviance is something I've avoided. In fact it's what I sought, or at least that's what I thought.

The medicine kicks in hard and fast, and my eyes focus on the energy grid now fully visible everywhere I look—multicolored strands articulating the vibration of everything alive. My face is about to come out of its skin. His words are almost unrecognizable; his pitch bends and twists, loses all form and shape, but somehow remains audible as he tells me he has another lover. That she is his soul mate and they've conceived a baby. It doesn't feel like terrible news. It feels like something from beyond the realm of feelings.

"It has nothing to do with us," he says. "I've known her forever. We meet every lifetime...again and again. It's always that way. We always bear a child. It never ends good. We always know it will happen." The waves slap the side of the boat, echoing in rhythm to the movement of his lips, licking the inside of my ears with their cold tongues. I know it's a trick, but I hang on every word, struggling to understand.

"She's gotten herself in trouble," he says. "I can't help her."

I start sinking fast, struggling not to cave in or burst into hysterical laughter, but I'm in over my head. Tommy Crow has become the center of everything; now I wish he'd never been born. I wish his mother had smothered him in his crib. I wish he'd disappear in front of my eyes. His face begins melting from the top of his head, and drips of flaming molten plastic fall from his chin. Somewhere inside I hear myself praying, making deals with God and wishing I were like other kids who did their homework and loved their parents…and liked girls instead of boys. Who didn't feel like they were getting swallowed up and spit out of a flaming, Day-Glo kaleidoscope by Tommy Crow.

I close my eyes to slow it down. When I open them, the yellow paint on the cabin walls bubbles and gurgles, melting into milky goo, streaming to the floor, forming a sinister puddle at my feet.

"Kill me," I think. "Just cut my fucking throat this very second or I'll bash my own brains out on the floor right now…just make it stop!"

But it isn't going to stop anytime soon.

"This time it's bad," he says. "She's in jail. She's in jail because she told them everything." He's watching me, waiting for the exact moment I betray him for my own good. But I can't…even in the middle of all this. Then he drops the bomb.

"She's my mother."

I feign confusion, but it isn't confusing. The shock of it brings me a few seconds of relief from my nightmare, but just a few. I reason the pieces together and consider vaulting over the edge of the boat and running to the emergency room at Mercy Hospital a few blocks away and begging them to inject me with morphine to anchor this hideous trip. Then, unexpectedly, a nurturing voice inside my head tells me that the only way to escape this wickedness is to take off my clothes and baptize myself in the lake.

I climb back onboard, shivering wet, enveloped in a golden swirling bliss. Now purified, I understand the risk of exposing my soul to someone infected with so much darkness. But it doesn't matter. I'm with Tommy Crow and it eclipses reason.

"Yes," I say, without realizing I'm speaking.

"Yes…what?" he asks.

"Yes everything," I say.

He takes off his shirt and wraps it around me, pulls me on top of him. He starts to cry and it goes on for hours. I prop myself up against the side of the cabin and pull his thin frame into me, wrapping my arms and legs around him tightly. He is shaking and convulsing; his snot and saliva collect on my chest and stomach. I accept that he won't be able to watch out for me. He's too fractured. I figure that the story about his mother is a lie. Some kind of test or something. But it doesn't matter. Not yet.

THE NEXT MORNING AS I pretend to prepare to leave for school, I scan the cover of The Daily Northwestern over my mother's shoulder as she takes a long pull off a Benson & Hedges and washes down a couple mood elevators with her coffee: Pregnant woman hangs self in jail. All the facts laid out in sequence in black and white.

Tommy Crow confessed to Detective Busby that he, now a fugitive from Child Services, was the father of his mother's unborn child. He walked out the front door of the police station shortly after the detective went to question his mother, Theresa Crow.

Busby made some assumptions based on his own ideas about refugees from the rez and Theresa's well-documented history of psychiatric problems and promptly arrested her.

Theresa Crow gave birth to her daughter hours after she was booked on child-endangerment charges at the women's county jail. A day later, she hanged herself from the door of her cell with a bed sheet.

She is survived by one son, Thomas T. W. Crow, fifteen, and two daughters, Angela Elizabeth Crow, eighteen, and another yet-unnamed girl now two days old. Theresa Crow's estranged husband is presumed to be somewhere in Canada.

"So sad," my mother sighs before breaking some news of her own: "We're moving back to Chicago in two weeks...with your father." She'd already given the landlord notice and bought the packing boxes. "It's not like you're in school here anyway," she says, just to let me know that she was well aware of my charade. She says she's sorry I have to leave my friends, knowing full well that I don't have friends. Only the orphaned, juvenile fugitive, my lover...Tommy Crow.

TOMMY IS WAITING UNDER the silver bridge like always.

"The world is trying to hurt me," he says. "Trying to kill me or make me kill myself, but it won't work. I won't do it."

There's nothing for me to say. I don't tell him I'm moving. I don't tell him I'm trying to figure a way to bring him with me. Now that his mother is dead it seems like a real possibility.

Midnight on July Fourth, we push my mother's Volkswagen bug down the driveway and into the street and down the block before we pop the clutch and start it up. We drive to the carp pond outside of town. All I hear is my own breath and the crickets in the pitch black when we turn off the car light. The moon lights up the night and the smell of gunpowder lingers from the fireworks in the park a few miles away.

We sit in silence in the back seat for an hour before he spits in my hand, rubs it on my dick and slides it in his ass. It's different now. It's desperate and in a way better. His face twists as he pulls me in harder. His eyes are wide open when I turn him over, bending him in half. Forcing his knees toward his shoulders, I kiss him. He wants me to hurt him, so I do.

In silence, we cut our fingers and press our fluids into each other's veins. I'm now bound for eternity in a bloody marriage with Tommy Crow. We drive home and fall asleep on the floor in the basement. When I wake up he is gone.

CHICAGO IS A NEW universe with a black hole at its center. I'm two grades behind in school and refuse to discuss going back. I write Tommy Crow ten letters in ten days with no response.

It's a cold and rainy autumn morning when my mother gets the news from a police detective, who calls to say I have to come in for questioning.

Sixteen days after our Volkswagen passed the city limits heading south on Highway 41 toward our new home, Tommy Crow climbed the water tower behind my grandmother's old house and jumped...fell 250 feet to the ground, where he died instantly of massive internal injuries. It was his sixteenth birthday.

THE THREE-HOUR DRIVE FROM Chicago back to the scene of the crime was a blur, and now I'm sitting in Detective Busby's office. He motions for my mother to wait outside and I watch her disappear, leaving me to fend for myself.

The detective whose clutches I've been narrowly avoiding since he was just a beat cop finally has me in his cross hairs. The pat-downs in the park, the jaywalking tickets and constant but subtle harassment never fully satisfied him. For me, they were all just line items in a long list of petty affronts that a boy like me is forced to endure from people like him.

The wood paneling at the police station is the same as the basement bedroom where I fell in love for the first time. But it feels different. It's not in agreement with the gray-speckled linoleum floor. The greasy dust cemented in the crevasses where the tiles meet is an eternal fact. Too much time has gone by since a broom or mop has passed this way. Everything here is wrong and the green glare of the florescent lights just exacerbates the situation.

My mother reappears through the window behind Busby, chain smoking in the parking lot half full of cars, a whirlpool of leaves swirling around her.

"The deceased was presumably intoxicated. He left a suicide note," Busby says in the perfunctory, accusatory cop tone…as if I am somehow responsible for Tommy Crow's death, which of course I am, the extent to which he could never know or understand.

"The sister took possession of the deceased's belongings," Busby says with what seems like pleasure, as if to say, See what happens to people like you? But there is nothing in his bag of tricks that can touch me. He is a bee buzzing around my head that I would just as soon squash before it can sting me.

"Is there something you want to tell me about you and Mr. Crow? About the nature of your relationship?"

My eyes focus on his nose, an owl's beak with thin, blotchy flesh pulled tightly across. His belly, his tits, the sparrow's nest of black hair sprouting from his ears, I look anywhere except his eyes.

"Tommy's sister tells me you had a, uh, friendship with Tommy. Correct? You seem like a nice young man.

I can see you care. Would you mind looking at some pictures?" he says, interrupting my internal rant.

Care? I don't care! I couldn't care less. I'd just as soon jump across this desk and rip a piece of your bloated face off with my bare teeth. I'd just as soon stab you in the throat with your fucking badge and watch you bleed out on the floor. That's what I care about. But I say nothing because I want every last drop of Tommy Crow I can get from him. I sit quietly, nodding my head in agreement.

Busby plops a legal-size manila folder on the desk. Three Polaroids spill out: Tommy Crow. Dead. Legs splayed, arms akimbo, his body broken in too many places to count. Neck twisted almost backward, a Jackson Pollack splatter of crimson oozing from his nose, mouth, and ears.

Busby waits for me to recoil, but I don't flinch. I look closer in defiance. Tommy's face is a clown's mask of pulp and cartilage. This could be anyone's face now...but it isn't anyone. It's Tommy Crow. Eyes wide open in a stew of plasma and tissue, like he's watching me, still waiting for me to abandon him and betray him. Like he's thanking me for showing up for him in this sad little police station at 2 P.M. on the loneliest Friday afternoon ever.

Other snapshots of the evidence are neatly assembled and tagged: a pair of black Converse sneakers, a white T-shirt, Levi's, a library card. I confirm that they belonged to Tommy Crow. It's enough to satisfy the cops. After all, he's just another dead Indian.

I push the pictures back in the folder and look into Busby's worn-out eyes. "Where is he buried?" I asked politely.

"With his relations," Busby says, and I know he has no idea about the truth of his words.

What remains of Tommy Crow's body is buried on the Indian reservation where he grew up, a place force-fed government cheese and transgenerational shame. He's buried without a headstone next to his mother and his grandmother and her grandmother, and that's that.

Tommy Crow has been returned to the earth, eternally been reunited with all his relations in the spirit world.

I'M STILL STANDING IN the middle of the room when I see Bertram walking back to my door with a little green slip of paper.

"Hey, friend," he says, but he knows I know he doesn't have any friends.

"What's up, Bertram?" I ask through the screen door.

"Forgot to have you sign the certified mail receipt. My bad."

I open the door and he hands me the slip and a pen.

"What's that?" he asks of the small black feather in my hand.

"This? This is...come in and I'll tell you what this is."

He is delighted that anyone would engage him about anything other than official post office business. He smiles, and in that moment I see Bertram for the first time beyond his face and body. I open the door and let him in and sit him down in the big chair by the window. I bring him a glass of water with a lemon slice and ask if he needs to use the bathroom. Then, I gently hand him his feather.

"It's a crow feather," I say. "Someone gave it to me when I was a kid. I've had it for years."

Bertram considers the feather carefully. He holds it to the light, and the pain of being Bertram comes into sharp focus—the isolation and the emancipation of being so hideous. I see the hours hunched over a computer in a pornographic, masturbatory spasm, and then endlessly uploading facts and information to his overdeveloped brain in an effort to finally control the meaning of things. I see his lonely life laid out in front of me, his absolute surrender, and finally...I see myself in the reflected glare of his suffering.

"A present from our friend the crow," he says.

"I wonder what the meaning of that is?" I ask and brace myself for a long ride.

"For the Celts, the crow is a sacred bird," he says, clearing his throat. "They thought crows escorted the sun during his nocturnal path, that is to say, in Hell. A symbol of evil, contrary to swans, which, of course, symbolize purity. In the Bible, the crow is sent by Noah to search the Earth after the flood. But the crow neglected to tell Noah that the flood was finished. Hence he is considered selfish. To the Tlingit Indians of the Pacific Northwest, the crow is the main divine character. He organizes the world, gives civilization and culture, creates and frees the sun..."

When Bertram finishes, I ask if he wants an orange and he accepts it before leaving, wedging it in his pocket. Bertram pauses and turns just before he gets back in the little truck. "For the Haida Indians of Canada, the crow will steal the sun from the sky's master to give it to the Earth's people."

"Thank you, Bertram. Thank you." I smile.

The return address on the package is a post office box in rural Wisconsin. I peel the tape and unfold the paper as carefully as it had been packed. Inside is something wrapped in a torn piece of muslin that I recognize as Tommy Crow's favorite Spanish wedding shirt. He wore it every Friday night and once on a Thursday on my birthday.

Folded in the cloth is his long black ponytail tied in a knot. It is not as shiny as the one I remember. He'd cut it off before he jumped. Some basket-weaving materials that I recognize as the elements of a ritual he told me about from when he was twelve years old. A ceremony where he was acknowledged as a child with equal parts masculine and feminine. Also a small white envelope now yellow with the years, my name carefully written on its face. I open it and take out a single piece of neatly folded, wide-lined, off-white paper. The kind of paper used in grade school when learning penmanship. A few words in thoughtfully rendered block letters that struggle not to stray from the lines: Not what you think.

I don't know what I think. For thirty years thinking about Tommy Crow left me with a feeling as hollow as the day he died and as wide as the expanse of first love. Like a scorpion that's been cast in amber resin, its sting fossilized forever, it's never shifted, not even slightly.

A few days later, I sit at my desk reading an e-mail forwarded from my editor at the newspaper I write for. It's from Tommy Crow's little sister. Then my cellphone rings.

"Did you get the package?" she asks and continues without waiting for my response. "My sister had it in her things. Angie. She's dead now. She didn't like you. She died a few months back. Tommy gave it to her to send to you but she never did. She had her reasons, I'm sure. I'm calling you as a favor to my brother. I'm Tommy's sister…I'm his cousin, too. I want to make sure that you have the package he tried to send to you back then."

"I'm sorry she didn't like me," I say stupidly. A bird caught in a net, my heart banging in my chest so hard it could crack my ribs, I stammer, "Thank you…Um, you're Tommy's little sister? The one who was born in the jail? What's your name?"

"Yes, that's me. My name is Tamara Crow. Tommy's in Canada," she says. The blood drains from my head and neck. I sit and then lie down on the floor in the middle of the room. "His phone number is on a piece of paper in the box," she says and my brain goes numb. She's already hung up when I come back into my body.

THE AMTRAK TO MONTREAL crawls like a snail as I replay the conversation with Tamara Crow in my head a million times before I make any sense of it.

"He wanted you to know the truth," she said. "My mother was assaulted…raped. Beat and left for dead by a drunk asshole…my father…Tommy's cousin. My cousin. She never had sex with Tommy. He made the whole thing up. My brother never had sex with a woman in his life, but you already know that. Our mother found out he stopped going to school and she threw him out of the house. He was sleeping outside. He was mad. When the social worker came around he made up the story to punish her. He said they were lovers, or something like that. They took him to the cops. The cops locked her up the same day. She was due with me. She told them she was raped, but they didn't believe her. To them, she was just some crazy Indian and they wanted to believe the worst, so they did.

"The body the cops found was what was left of my father after my uncles finally caught up with him. Him and Tommy were almost the same age. They said he was possessed by a demon, I don't know. He might just have been drunk. Tommy threw the body off the water tower with the note so he could get out after all the trouble

424

he caused. After she killed herself, he knew he couldn't come back. That's it. That's what happened. My brother's in Canada. He's been here the whole time. He's lives on a rez where his father is. He wants to meet. He wants you to call him."

"Are you coming?" Tommy asks when I call. He sounds exactly the same as I remember. Like a moment ago we were sitting on the railroad tracks…three decades earlier.

"Yeah, I'm coming. It's all I'm doing, I'm doing nothing else besides," I say, and he laughs, but I can tell he isn't really laughing. I can feel him at the same exact place we left off and he can feel me feeling him there.

Every cell frozen in time is now thawing, and the clock is ticking backward. As the train pulls into the station in Winnipeg, I'm still fifteen years old in Tommy Crow years.

I can't feel anything until I see him standing on the platform. Blue jeans, white T-shirt, black hair to his shoulders. We say nothing as we walk the platform, Tommy close behind me, matching my steps. His breath on my neck, smelling like earth and tobacco.

Tommy Crow, now aged to perfection, smiles his chipped-tooth smile. "It's not what you thought," he says as we pull up to his little house in the middle of nowhere and climb out of the truck.

His finger circles the top button of his Levi's before we're even inside the door; as if he knew I'd spent thirty years staving off the temptation to abandon his memory, languishing until we inevitably plunged back into the depths.

WRONG SIDE OF THE TRACK

Elizabeth Banicki

2012 Best American Essays, Notable;
2012 Best American Sports Writing, Notable

L OU SITS THERE ON his stool when I pull up to the
guard shack at Gate Five. I wave and he smiles a
big, sweet, toothless smile. Stale cigarette smoke wafts
through my car window. The few strands of hair left on
Lou's shiny, speckled head are combed over and greased
down. I ask how he is and he says he's looking forward
to seeing his new grandson. Lou rushes his answer as if
he thinks I'll get bored talking to him. He's learned that
people rarely listen and that often the best conversation
an old man can have is with himself.

Lou used to gallop horses in the seventies, but gave
it up after one flipped over and landed on him. His
pelvis nearly cracked in half and he was never able to
ride again. After that, he settled for a job at the entrance
to the backside of Santa Anita Park. The backside, where
the horses are kept, is the stage behind the curtains, the
place most fans never see. Lou came to the track when
he was about fifteen, the way most lifers do, and now he
sits in a guard shack waiting for a heart attack. The way
most lifers do.

At Santa Anita, a once-prestigious sport still survives,
barely, on its past glory. The track here works the same as
any chicken-wire, bush-league track in West Virginia or
South Texas. Everyone has a purpose and plays a role and,
with luck, eats at the end of the day. I drive up to the stables
and the sweet smell of horse shit replaces Lou's cigarette

stench. I sip my coffee and climb out of my groggy morning haze. It's not yet light out, but it's time to ride.

Santa Anita is nestled at the base of the San Gabriel Mountains' foothills, and the rising sun on this October morning lights them up just enough to see their massive silhouettes. My chaps, boots, helmet, and flak jacket wait in the back of my car. My morning ritual is to park and tie a bandanna around my head before putting on my helmet, and then wish I could stay in my car, where it's safe and warm, while I watch horses flying by under the huge spotlight at the quarter pole.

Rudy, the groom for my first horse, is studying the set list when I walk into the barn. The same jeans he's been wearing for four days are tucked into his rubber boots and covered in bits of hay, dirt, and poultice. Rudy's Tecate belly spills over a stressed-out waistband.

"Güera, you ready?"

His hands are on his hips and he stares at me, his baseball cap pushed up above his forehead and his dusty, black hair sticking out underneath. He's been in the barn since 4 A.M. and has already fed and cleaned the stalls of the five horses he oversees.

"Cual caballo?" he asks.

"Ah, whatever," I say. "Just bring 'em out."

I look down the shed row, which is the barn's aisleway. Huge wheelbarrows, bales of straw, chickens, bunnies, and bouncing horses clutter the small dirt passage. Pigeons flap their wings and make small dust storms as they carry bits of straw up to the pipes that line the barn's low ceiling. I grab a whip from inside the tack-room door and walk out to the tow ring where Rudy, with miraculous efficiency, has already made three turns warming my filly.

"¡Ándale, güera!"

He legs me up and we move slowly to the exercise track. I'm exercising the filly for Bob Baffert, the three-time Kentucky Derby-winning, Hall of Fame trainer. I see Laura, a girl who also exercises horses for Baffert. She's running barefoot across the dark parking lot, wearing a tight, short, sparkly dress. Her blond hair looks a mess and dangly earrings bounce around on the sides of her head. She's even later for work than I am, and from the looks of it she's had about eight hours less sleep. Laura and I met in New Orleans right after September 11. I was living in New York when the World Trade Center towers went down and needed to escape the chaos. So I found a job working for a Kentucky-based trainer taking a string of horses south for the winter meet at the Fair Grounds in New Orleans.

Laura and I were both nineteen and wild as hell, running roughshod through the French Quarter. She came out to California a few years after I did and got a job working for Baffert. Between the two of us and a few others, we were probably the most sought-after exercise riders around. We exercised horses into making millions in purses for Baffert.

"She gives it away like government cheese," says Larry from his horse, which is quickly approaching mine from behind. Larry, who has been at the track for at least forty years, catches up and rides next to me, smiling and shaking his head.

"Oh, whatever," I tell him. "You'd go for it given the chance."

Larry's a perv, but because he reluctantly acknowledges it, he's easier to like. Raw sexuality with few limitations on what can be said and done is part of the racetrack culture, welcome or not.

We keep walking toward the track, and my filly, Dodgin' Bullets, is calm in the dark, foggy morning. We've known each other for a while and she's come to depend on my style. She's four and her career is already winding down, but she's made enough money to warrant a nice life in breeding, and she's lucky for it. Because of past and present injuries, she stabs the ground as she walks, and her jolty movements travel up through her broad shoulders and dictate the way my body moves. Her ears are at attention and she's ready to bail if the situation turns ugly.

My mood and my movements are how we communicate. On a loose rein, we walk onto the track and part ways with Larry, who takes off flat out and is out of sight in seconds. Half a mile away, horses gallop toward us through the darkness. Dodgin' Bullets takes me back to the 5/8 pole at a jog, getting more fluent with each step. I can see the dew on her eyelashes, and clouds of steam spew from her nostrils, circle back, and hit my knees. Her black coat is wet from the mist. It's like I'm riding a fish and we're simply swimming along.

Just as I find a moment of peace, here comes Crazy April. She's riding some poor beast that moves like a square wheel. April screams at it to pick up its head and to "quit fucking stumbling!" April's been at the track for a lifetime and it shows in her face. She talks to herself incessantly.

Crazy April comes from a wealthy family, but her life has been a long dance with mental illness. She tries to hide the meth lesions on her face and arms with makeup. Her black eyeliner and thick foundation have partly settled into the lines around her eyes but mostly run from the moisture. She resembles a melted doll spotted with cigarette burns. Her horse patiently carries her along, trying to make the whole experience go by as quickly as possible. Her saddle towel is dirty and worn. Crazy April passes me with an angry glare. Her black eyes, tired but still full of fight, reveal how much she has endured.

My filly and I reach the middle of the exercise track. She's warmed up and knows it's time to gallop. We stop and face the infield, watching the horses coming up on our left pass by, waiting for our chance to merge. It's cool out, my filly's anxious and fresh, and it becomes impossible to keep her still. I finally pull the right rein to let her know it's time, and she pushes off. We're in full stride after three jumps.

I stand up to take my weight off her back, grip her sides with my calves and ankles, and put my hands on either side of her spine at the top of her shoulders. I keep enough tension in the reins to let her know I don't want too much speed, but that she can still let go a bit. She gets looser with each stride, so I let her gallop on for the first quarter of a mile. It's when they're moving slowly that some horses feel like riding a motorcycle on its rims. My filly wants me to let her go. She pulls and shakes her head, trying to break my hold. We do the same dance every day, and after a quarter mile she gives up and gets comfortable. We go a mile and a half at a strong and steady pace.

When I pull up on the far turn she stumbles badly and I nearly go over her head. It takes all my strength to regain my balance while holding up the front end of her body.

"Damn, that was ugly," I hear.

I look up and see that Ava is facing the infield on her horse.

"No shit," I say. "I thought for sure we were going down."

Ava is a gypsy princess from San Diego. Blond haired and blued eyed, her twenty-four-year-old frame has been battered by bad falls on the track and a confusing, lonely life off it. Ava was recruited by a big modeling agency and sent to Italy when she was just fourteen. When I asked her why she traded in the glamour for life on the backside, she told me about the time she saw herself on a billboard.

"I didn't know who that was up there—it wasn't me," she said. It seemed as if someone twenty years older was talking.

Ava's mother was also an exercise rider. She died in 1986 when her horse stepped sideways at full speed, crossed its legs, and fell hard, breaking her neck.

Her mother's death didn't scare off Ava. She proudly shows a four-inch scar across the base of her neck from a surgically repaired collarbone. Her rib cage is adorned with tattoos and another large scar from the time a horse jumped the inside rail and left her with broken ribs and a punctured lung. As she sits forward and stands up on her horse, I see a skeleton riding a bullet with a whiskey bottle in its hand on the inside of her left arm.

"New one?" I ask.

Ava's clothes are dirty and her face is sunburned and dehydrated. Her blond curls hang over her freckled shoulders in braids. She's a rack of fragile bones on top of a burly colt. At five-nine, her frame is long and unbefitting of a rider, yet she looks more at home on the horse than she does on her own two legs.

We jog past the grandstands and see 30,000 empty seats. It's a beautiful structure with 1950s décor dating to racing's golden age. Inside, decorative, vintage vendor signs with big, green-and-yellow letters float above cracked counter tops where drinks were passed to well-dressed patrons back when going to the races was a big deal. The grandstand's checkered floor, unlittered by used tickets and programs, shines from polish. You can almost hear echoes of old announcers calling races, smell popcorn and hot dogs in the dark corners.

The stands are quiet. Soft wind whistles through the high ceilings, bringing the taste of rain. Even at Santa Anita, one of the elite racetracks in the world, the aura of decline is undeniable.

There was a time when racing was the sport of kings; before the Internet and the flight of the railbirds—fans who came just to sit on the rail and watch the horses and riders beat each other out. Online gambling and viewing has put a damper on even the big racing draws. The Internet hook is similar to the complimentary drinks, rooms, and meals offered at Vegas casinos. On big race days, an online gambling-account network offers incentive rebates—basically free money with which to start gambling. That doesn't happen at the track's mutual windows.

The bigger tracks on the coasts, Belmont and Saratoga in the East and Santa Anita and Del Mar in the West, barely manage to survive while smaller tracks continue to close or cut races and purses. While racing's Triple Crown still pops up on sports fans' radar, most people watch only those three races, or just the Kentucky Derby. Smaller tracks in places like Kansas, New Mexico, Arizona, West Virginia, and so many other states now depend on slot machines, casinos, and attached resorts to bring in patrons. Even Hollywood Park in Inglewood is scheduled to close when the economy recovers enough for construction to begin on a massive retail, residential, and hotel complex.

As tracks shut down, riders, trainers, grooms, and hot walkers have to leave or find other work. Many of them have never done anything outside of racing.

I TRAVELED AROUND THE country for years going from job to job in my beat-up Mazda, everything I had stuffed in the back. Loba, my half-coyote, half-something dog, sat in the passenger seat next to me for those long journeys between the East and West coasts. I found her abandoned when she was about a week old, huddled up next to the trunk of an almond tree on a ranch I worked at in Central California. She was calm and patient. All the things I wasn't.

I drove from one town or city to another, one racetrack to another, just to ride as many horses as I could. I never dreamed of becoming a racetracker. I didn't fantasize about living out of my car or in cheap motels, about eating out of a change can and not trusting anyone around me. But the track found me and took me in. It gave me a place to call my own, as it does and has always done for strays and wanderers.

I dropped out of high school two weeks into my freshman year. At fifteen I was rarely home and always high, drunk, or both on the beaches of North Florida. I had been a horseback rider since the age of eight. I gained a rep as a pretty good show jumper. Horses anchored me during the most chaotic periods of my life.

When I was sixteen, my frustrated, exhausted, and broke single mother of three asked me what it was going to take for me to not end up a Daytona Beach burnout. Two weeks later, we packed up the car and left for Maryland, where I would spend a year living on Bonita Farm, a beautiful, old-school, forty-acre training center run by the Boniface family—horse-training royalty.

It was the beginning of a twelve-year tour. I strayed from Maryland to South Carolina, then out to California. I left California and went to Texas, then back again, only to leave and go east to Delaware, New York,

Kentucky, Louisiana. Then I returned to California, where I remain. I knew that as long as I could ride horses and avoid getting seriously hurt, I would be able to go anywhere I wanted.

The track has a theme of its own and characters that recall the weird hunchbacks and sinister villains you see in old cartoons. To most people, it may seem like an oddity to spend every morning with old men who have exercised horses since the days of the Model T, who walk through barnyards with chaps made from leather so old and beat up they look like they came from a Civil War collection in the Tennessee hills. But watching a man who's been broken into a thousand pieces a hundred different times stride along like an old cat, and wondering how the hell he gets around on those bowed legs and has the strength to wrestle giant beasts for six hours every morning is strangely compelling.

MOST TRAINERS AREN'T TAN, healthy, and debonair like Bob Baffert. Most are like the guys at Clocker's Corner at Santa Anita's quarter pole, right at the head of the stretch: hand-to-mouth journeymen eking out livings training cheap horses. On Clocker's sunny patio, old timers sit around a big plastic table with piles of racing forms, coffee cups, and overnights, telling hard-bitten war stories. Years of sun, drink, and stress have turned their faces red and blotchy, their noses gin blossomed.

Horse trainers live on the edge. Sometimes business is legit, but things do slide, and talking about what's been seen in the barns is always political. As tracks decline, conversations grow increasingly cynical. The use of drugs and other performance enhancers have become commonplace in the training business. Everyone knows the tricks, but no one really knows which tricks others are using.

The old men don't understand the Internet and the complications of the modern game, or the lack of respect the younger generation has for the sport's traditions. Their crisp cowboy hats and greasy comb-overs can't hide the sadness behind jokes about the exercise girl with the fat ass or tales of scotch-and-cocaine-fueled mayhem at the 100 to 1, a watering hole across the street from Santa Anita. They're the broken heroes from another time still wearing their uniforms in a world that doesn't care anymore.

Hungry-looking jockeys mill around a table. The group teases one jock about his latest blond lady friend, and he takes it with an impatient but good-natured sigh. He's more concerned with getting a horse that can win.

Jockeys are tiny, bionic men who possess the same air of competence seen in the best athletes. But in truth they are little worriers perched atop giant war hounds. They wear faded, blue Wranglers with perfect creases running down the front and back of each leg. The outline of a snuff can is worn into the back pockets of older jocks' jeans. The younger jocks love to represent their native homes of Puerto Rico and Mexico with bling and custom, kick-ass ostrich-leather boots.

Most start out as street kids from the poorest places and come to the states to be apprentice jockeys, also called bug boys because of the asterisks next to their name on racing programs. They are usually penniless when they show up in the U.S. Some go on to make a million in their first year of riding. But after losing the bug, it gets much harder for a rider to make such a good living because he no longer has the advantage of being a lighter weight than the journeymen—by that time fancy cars and easy women have quelled the hunger pains.

Jockeys come out to the track in the mornings and breeze horses for as many trainers as they can for free in the hopes that they'll get the mount in the afternoon. But just because a jock shows up to work a horse doesn't mean he'll get to ride it in a race. There's no contract or written deal, just odds and dreams.

Agents circle around the tables with their cellphones and papers and leather-bound organizers tucked under their arms. A tan, blue-eyed dude, about forty-five years old, laughs into his cellphone. It's the laid-back chuckle of a Louisianan. He's been one of the best jockey agents in the country for decades and is now established in the West. In a white fedora, worn-out fitted jeans, and an undersize Banana Republic tee, he looks like a simple woman's 1970s South Beach dream. A gold chain hangs over a burnt-orange, hairless chest, and a thick gold band with a single diamond sits on his pinkie finger.

He is one of thousands circling the country on a giant merry-go-round, trading jocks and moving from one track to another, hustling horses. A rider's ability to win races and make money depends largely on his agent's connections. This agent has worked for jocks everywhere.

He's also dated many a backside woman. He tried with me once and never spoke to me again after I turned him down. He's a traveling racetrack pimp who peddles horses and humans for a living. He has to eat, too, and he knows that in this business you can pit a mediocre rider and a fast horse that didn't run its numbers last time against seven or eight other teams, and at 5-to-1, money can be made. Purse money is one thing, but a decent-size bet at a good price can really turn shit around.

A sense of disgust rushes through me as I realize I have been staring for too long, so I turn back to the horses winging by on the track behind the tables. They come around the turn in full gear, spindly legs splaying out in every direction. Jesus Christ, some are such bad movers. It looks like they'll blow the turn, jump the outside rail, and land in your bacon and eggs. It's happened.

Plus, the track itself isn't what it once was, which only darkens an already grim situation for California racing. Rocks the size of lemons from the track's foundation are floating to the surface through the synthetic material put down some years ago to replace dirt. It was supposed to be easier on the horses' legs. Horses still break down, maybe not at the rate they did, but now there's an epidemic of soft-tissue injuries instead of broken bones. Those injuries can end a horse's career just as quickly and indefinitely.

ON THE BACKSIDE, WHERE the very poor and very rich brush shoulders every day, grooms and hot walkers are at the bottom of the pecking order. They get paid the least but spend more time with the horses and know them better than anyone. Depending on the outfit or barn a groom works for, if he or she doesn't have a "big horse"—one that provides that extra check from winning or placing—they probably can only afford to live in one of the small, cement quarters in the barn called tack rooms. These rooms are supposed to be for storing saddles, bridles, and equipment.

There are community showers, a kitchen, a chaplain, and a medical trailer on most backsides. Children are raised in the barns. They go to school from them and come home to them. In the evenings, the smell of tortillas and onions fills these little corridors, where hot plates and microwaves warm up dinner for families and neighbors. Anyone is welcome.

When I lived in New York and worked at Belmont Park, I exercised horses for John Kimmel, one of the wealthiest trainers on the grounds. I was galloping the nicest horses in the barn, including an Argentine filly named Miss Linda, who ran in the Breeders' Cup that year, right after September 11. I was nineteen and living in an attic full of junk and broken furniture in a Queens ghetto.

Since Miss Linda had not yet won a qualifying race, Kimmel and the owners had to supplement the filly (put up extra money—tens of thousands of dollars) so she could run. I was struggling to feed myself. I didn't understand how I was being exploited because I was in love with what I was doing. I was in love with riding magnificent horses and I helped make rich men and their lazy wives thousands if not millions while I ate hot dogs from the corner gas station.

It's hard for outsiders to understand how we live on the backside, playing parts in a serial drama that even dedicated racing fans rarely witness: long mornings on tough racehorses, hung over and in need of hair o' the dog, exhausted from hard work and low wages.

Racetrackers always come back, though, no matter how tired they get of watching horses snap their legs, of waking up at 4:30 in the morning seven days a week to be serfs to sheiks and millionaires. On the backside, you are a slave until you learn how not to be one, especially if you're a woman. I've seen many beaten down by the harassment and degradation. Some of them even come to depend on it as they slowly lose their own identities and allow the track life to mold them.

"One little kiss, Liz?" Dilip would say, sitting outside on my porch, drunk and smiling.

"Hell no!" I'd snap back with attitude and a smirk.

"Come on…please?" he'd beg with a sweet smile that stretched the skin on his face, making his cheeks suddenly appear darker.

Dilip Amarsingh was a jockey in Trinidad as a boy, or so he told me once. He came to the States for fame and fortune. It was hard to make friends moving from place to place so much, and Dilip was one of the few I had found in a very long time.

I first saw Dilip in the parking lot of Golden Gate Field by the San Francisco Bay on a dark, cold, and foggy morning. He was a tall, bird-boned young man getting out of his car with his helmet, flak jacket, and heavy leather chaps. He put on a light jacket that wouldn't scare the horses by flapping in the wind when he breezed around the sloppy racetrack at thirty-five miles per hour.

Dilip was looking to join legends like Angel Cordero Jr. and Laffit Pincay Jr., who were also once poor nobodies in the tropical ghettos of Puerto Rico and Panama, respectively. Height and size are important for a jockey, but nothing matters more than a rider's balls. Dilip, no doubt, thought he had them all beat.

To make it big, a rider has to prove to the racing establishment—whose opinions could put him in the Hall of Fame or right back on the streets—that the horses will run for him. Horses did run for Dilip, but unfortunately some horses can only run so fast.

We worked together for a while in the same barn for trainer Greg Gilchrist at Golden Gate Fields. Gilchrist, who recently retired, was in a bad war at one point in his life and never fully came back. Clean shaven, with white hair and a temper that would make Godzilla cower, Gilchrist was one of those men who could survive anything but come to terms with nothing.

We were Gilchrist's only two riders for a while. Dilip was good on a horse's back, but he still hit the ground on occasion like the rest of us. One morning before taking my horse onto the track, I caught Dilip in my peripheral vision flying through the air and landing on three full buckets of water. The splashing and the crashing of the buckets sent horses and people scattering.

Dilip would visit with me and we'd get drunk and make fun of fellow trackers, particularly ones we thought of as inferior.

"Gotta watch out for those no-ridin' sons-a-bitches," was our refrain after a couple of bottles of good California wine.

Eventually, I left Golden Gate and lost touch with Dilip. But at the track everyone remains connected even if they don't talk and are thousands of miles apart. I wasn't surprised when I learned that he, too, had gone to New York. We missed each other by only a few months. Dilip picked up a job working for the same trainer I had been working for. He might have taken my spot.

Dilip, I heard through the grapevine, was doing well, riding a few races here and there, determined as ever to make his presence known. Still, he survived mostly by exercising horses, because whoever handpicks the greats hadn't gotten to him yet. But he was confident, and I'm sure he passed the time trying to con kisses from women he wore down with his sense of humor and persistence.

Then, one day in September six years ago, Dilip was getting his morning coffee at the racetrack kitchen at Belmont. Not the nice kitchen where the highfalutin trackers hang out, but the roach-motel kitchen where the track's tranny hookers sell themselves at night.

443

Another Trinidadian man was in line with Dilip. It was 5 in the morning and the track was almost in full swing. Dilip and the man had a beef that had been festering for a while, about a woman, I heard.

The two had words. Dilip walked out of the rat-infested cafeteria and into the morning to get on his first horse. He was so lanky and narrow he must have looked like Woody the Cowboy, island style, crossing the parking lot. He didn't know that the other man had followed him and was holding a steak knife he had been hiding in his backpack. Dilip fell onto the cold concrete outside the tranny hangout, with the knife in his chest. Thirty-one years is not long to live.

I was at Santa Anita getting coffee from the track kitchen when a mutual friend gave me the news. I was there because even after walking away nearly three years ago, I need to get on the horses. I will always belong to the track, to my former life. I can't help myself. I know you can love the track, but it will only love you back for as long as you're useful.

LONG SHOTS

Anne Fishbein

Shot at Santa Anita Park and Hollywood Park
between March and August 2010.

LIBERTAD

Sandow Birk

He stood at the curbside, one small duffle and two new surfboards bubble-wrapped in their own bags. The planes looked huge behind the terminal—shiny, smooth, and glowing under the floodlights as the fog drifted in from El Segundo. It still didn't seem like he was going anywhere. An hour earlier, he'd been with a couple of friends, joking about how crazy it was to go surfing in the middle of a war. Now here he was, slightly buzzing, watching the Lakers game at a bar in the international terminal. He ordered another beer and then another, paying for each round with a fresh twenty so he could collect small bills before he boarded the plane.

Across the expanse of the terminal, he saw the departure board flashing destinations in the middle of the hall. There were three flights that night bound for San Salvador. Three flights a day to a war zone. It must be like that every day, he thought, every war. While you sat watching TV, flights were booked full of people and crying babies headed to a war in droves.

A sip of Heineken and the Miss World Pageant, live from Las Vegas, came on. It always started like this, he thought; it always started like nothing was going to start at all.

He was going surfing because he wanted to, he told himself, because it mattered. Because the waves in

El Salvador are some of the best in the world and he wanted to get out of his life in L.A., get away from his lousy delivery job and his long drives to the beach, away from the crowds in the surf and the news and the radio and from everything he knew. He wanted to get away from the daily trips to the hospital where he'd watched his younger brother fade away, tired and yellow. He wanted to get away from the feeling of helplessness and the months of fickle hope. Away from his parents' grief, the weight of sadness and scattered ashes.

He had been surfing since he was a kid. It was what he did best and what was familiar. And now he needed to be alone with great waves and the right boards, pushing himself. When he thought about it like that, it seemed the best thing to do. But now, sitting alone with the Heineken warming in his palm and a ticket to a war zone, it also seemed foolish and unimportant and he was afraid.

A flash popped out of the corner of his eye. Four Japanese men were posing for pictures in front of the departure board, smiling and clean.

Two weeks earlier he had knocked on the door of the boss's hot, carpeted office during an afternoon coffee break and asked for two weeks off. The boss looked up.

"You already had a vacation this year."

"Not vacation," he explained, thinking of the two new boards he'd had made for the occasion. A 6'0" three-fin for most days, and a 6'4" for when the surf gets big. "Just time off. No pay."

"No pay?" The boss raised his eyebrows and looked at him for a moment. He wasn't sure if the boss knew about his brother, but he didn't want to explain. "Sure, okay. Put it on the calendar," the boss said and went back to the papers on his desk.

It was that easy. He bought his ticket that same afternoon at the TACA office on Wilshire and Normandie. "Caca," they had called it after the first trip.

He had been to El Salvador five years ago, before his brother got sick. It had been great then, a month of adventure—the two of them surfing all morning, trading waves with no one else around. Afternoons swinging in hammocks reading tattered paperbacks, muscles sore, skin sunburned, hair dry and salty. The war was little more than a ghost story at their campfire, a distant sound in the night. They were used to feeling safe, especially together.

He got up from the bar and wobbled down an escalator that had stopped running. In the restroom, he swayed and pissed in a toilet stall, and as he stood there it occurred to him that everyone else in the bathroom had black hair. It crept over him then, that feeling of sliding into Latin America, and the nervousness came as his memories of other trips drew closer. The dirt-floored bars and mosquitoes, the taxis with holes in the mufflers, the sweat and heat. And guns. Machine guns hung over shoulders, and the sounds of them in the night. That's what he remembered now.

He took out his wallet and put it into his old, worn money belt and strapped it on low under his Levi's. It felt familiar. He squeezed out a few more beer dribbles while thinking of black hair. He caught a glimpse of his blond hair in the mirror and he knew then he was going away.

On the departure board, the announcements began to read longer as the last of the European flights left, and when they read "Mexico, Guatemala, Salvador, and other Central American locations," he knew that meant Nicaragua.

11:03. The Qantas flight left for Sydney, and from then on all the announcements were made in Spanish first. There was still too much time to kill, and he walked slowly down the corridors of the terminal, bored. Everywhere there were babies and cardboard-box suitcases tied with string; there were big, black mustaches, boom-box radios, and cowboy hats, and he was sinking into it all, getting there before he had even left. Snakeskin boots and huge belt buckles, infants in pinafore smocks, and women in dresses with slips showing. He was drunk.

Shit, he thought, and closed his eyes.

HE WOKE WITH THE bump and the shudder of the landing gear in Mexico City. Out the window, the sky was light purple in the dawn and the waning moon hung dead center above a gray building. It looked like LAX, like they hadn't gone anywhere. He watched the ground crew in the growing light as passengers bustled in the aisle. He dozed again until the plane's takeoff woke him for an unexpected view of miles and miles of cement-gray houses and dirt streets and crumbling walls, getting smaller as they rose but spreading out bigger and disappearing at the edges in a brown haze along the mountains.

He slept and woke and had powdery eggs and orange juice and his head hurt. Outside it was just a sea of white clouds. When they started descending he tried to keep his eyes open, waiting for the swing over the ocean and a glimpse of the town and the point and the waves. Looking over the mountains with tiny villages between the green of the trees, he couldn't imagine there was a war down there. Torture and death squads and bombs seemed more like TV. Below just looked like mountains. And heat.

And then the ocean and the beach and the pier. He strained to see if the waves were good but couldn't tell before they disappeared from view, and he waited to feel the bump of landing.

Three thudding stamps in his passport and he was standing against a pillar waiting for his boards. Above his head was a poster of a girl in a dress, on crutches. She had only one leg. "Another victim of FLMN bombs," it read in Spanish. As he looked down, a family walked by, and there was a girl in the same dress but with both legs, and he had to look up at the poster again to make sure.

"¿Que hora es?" he asked as he climbed in the taxi's front seat.

The leatherette was hot and he began to sweat. Driving along, there was nothing and it was brown; the green of the jungle he remembered was gone and it was all open and flat and dead. He thought there must have been a fire but the taxi driver said it was just the dry season. There were clusters of dirt-and-stick shacks along the road close to the asphalt. There were people and cattle now and then walking along in the sun, but the taxi driver never slowed down. Everything was poorer and worse than he remembered. The town seemed smaller, too, and the streets were crowded.

"How have things been here?" he asked the driver.

"Tranquilo."

He got a room in the cement motel across from the beach, and the woman at the desk remembered him and asked where his brother was.

"He's not coming this time," he said.

"What a pity," she said.

The heat grabbed him, hugging him heavy and wet, and he knew it wouldn't let go until he was gone.

The trade winds were blowing already in the late afternoon and the surf was choppy and weak, so he walked through the town looking for a cold drink. Everything was the same as before, but different: the short, narrow streets of cobblestone and low, adobe houses with worn, shuttered doors opened to cool, hammock-crossed interiors and tiled floors lost in deep shadows. Old, toothless women lounging in fraying beach chairs, mongrel dogs slinking away under cars, ribs showing. Babies sitting in paint-chip-flecked dirt, dusty trucks with flat tires in dirt lots, and young girls in plastic sandals walking with Tupperware bowls on their heads.

In the main street before the church plaza, people were drawing huge pictures on the pavement in white chalk and others were filling in the colors between the lines with rice and tree bark. At a corner in front of a pupuseria he watched them finish a drawing of Jesus with a sawdust face and toilet paper rolls for hair and seashells for eyebrows. Good Friday.

In the afternoon, he walked out along the point and watched the wind blow the waves sloppily over the reef. He decided to go for a surf anyway, to get in the water and out of the sweat and get a feel for the new board before the real waves came. The board rode well, loose and solid, light under his feet, and he surfed until the sun was too much and his lips stung from the salt.

He walked back into the town after a shower. The moon came up late, almost full, low and red beyond the pier. He watched trucks running over the designs on the pavement, rice and flowers and sawdust scattering to the gutters. Red-and-blue political posters for the ARENA party were plastered on doors and walls and light poles, its logo painted on the sidewalk and benches and fences. In his sparse room at the motel he tried to read but there was a distant, echoing boom and then the light flickered and went out, and he knew it was the guerillas bombing the power lines.

"¿CUANDO? ¿CUANDO? ¿CUANDO?"

He woke under the single sheet. It was almost dawn.

"¿Cuando? ¿Cuando? ¿Cuando?" squawked the parrots from their cages in the restaurant across the street.

Standing at the window, he could see the sun just topping the ridge of volcanoes in the east. The sound of the unseen surf cracked sharp in the air.

"¿Cuando? ¿Cuando? ¿Cuando?"

Fifteen minutes later, he was up at the point, balanced on a rock, barefoot—his flip-flops buried under stones—timing the incoming waves to scramble out a few yards over the rocks before the next one hid them from view. He could smell the zinc oxide smeared on his cheeks, and his T-shirt was tight across his stomach, knotted behind his back. The waves were bigger and the water was smooth and orange in the sun and he was alone.

He surfed for hours while the sun got higher and hotter, until his lips cracked and his face burned. The set waves were head high and long and fast and sucking off the shallow rocks so that he had to watch his outside rail as he pumped his way across the wall, the speed building for the turns, the water smooth and fast.

When he finally came in, he was so hungry that his legs were weak and he walked slowly along the point to the motel and stood in the cool flow of the shower in the cement room. At the restaurant across the way, he sat at an outdoor table and watched families play on the sand and in the waves. The waiter recognized him from before.

"¿Café?" the waiter asked, surprised. "¿No cerveza?" and brought him a plastic cup of hot water and a jar of Nescafé. "¿Y tu hermano?"

"Él no viene este vez," he said, and they talked about the town and how the restaurant was doing.

"Not many surfers come through here anymore," said the waiter. "Sometimes an American and his girlfriend from the capital."

After that there was a fried fish with its eyes charred black. A mariachi band played over the blare of the jukebox. Children laughed and begged for food with upturned palms until the waiters shooed them away. Dogs hid beneath chairs. The sun got hotter and hotter and the waves looked fun in the glare.

The days melted along, hot and humid, the streets filthy with trash and sleeping drunks sprawled in the dirt; oyster shells and bottle caps glinted in the sun, flies and filthy dogs, scraps of paper blowing off dry, cracked posters on whitewashed walls. Sometimes it was fine and he was just there, tired, but then suddenly it became too familiar, and he couldn't stop remembering, and as he walked and picked his way along broken sidewalks and around stinking trash piles he felt as if he were being pressed under a thumb, and there was a panic inside his chest and he wanted to escape. Soldiers lounged behind sandbags at every street corner, rifles swaying. Dogs hid from the sun in deep shadows and the heat was heavy until he was back in the shade of the cement room, lying before the fan with eyes closed, breathing.

Slowly the surf got bigger, building a foot or two a day, rolling in from some unseen storm beyond the white-blue of the horizon. It was eight feet on the sets and still building and he could hear the crack and roar beyond the slats of the louvered glass windows of the motel, where waves rolled and barreled along the point in the dark.

On the fourth day, the surf was ten feet in the early dawn as he balanced barefoot on the rocks. Then the pressure was gone and he knew why he had come. The waves rose slowly in the distance like hills. He would feel them lifting from behind as he paddled hard, and then the slide, and the drop, and him jumping to his feet cleanly and the board falling out beneath him, the speed building up in his knees at the bottom and leaning into the turn, the board coming around solid and fast and the wall of water before him, huge and moving toward the town and the fishing boats bobbing far away beside the pier. He surfed from first light until the trade winds rose before noon, until his stomach ached and his arms were weak and rubbery. There was always the afternoon in the shade of a restaurant, sore shoulders and his skin tight and hot from the sun. Coke bottles that fit perfectly into his palm.

And every morning he was on the rocks again at dawn, the takeoffs coming later, the drops getting deeper, the turns harder, pushing his surfing, always alone.

On the sixth day, as he picked his way cautiously over the rocks, he could see another surfer was already in the water. He was a journalist down from the capital, the American. Floating in the water between waves, the journalist talked about being caught in a shootout between the army and the guerillas in a village in the mountains, and how a photographer near him had stood to take pictures and been shot in the stomach.

The journalist caught the next wave, and when he paddled back he explained how he had tried to get the photographer to a hospital but had been forced off the road by mortar shelling. They'd hidden in the wreckage of a house where the photographer had lain there bleeding and died.

They talked about surfing and other things, and traded waves and everything was all right. The journalist caught a good wave and was far down the beach. He looked down the coast, past the journalist walking on the shore, past the pier and the town, to the distant volcanoes, and thought about getting shot in the stomach.

AT DAWN, THE TOWN was calm and quiet and still cool before the sun. The waves continued to rise and he spent his mornings in the water and afternoons at lunch: fish and rice, or a bowl of seafood soup with tortillas and goat's milk cheese before a nap in front of the fan in the motel. After Easter, the crowds had gone back to the capital and the town settled down, but the heat lingered, not caring that the holiday had ended.

During those quiet afternoons he walked the streets and tried to reconcile things, the town as he remembered it from years before and the way he saw it now. He thought about his brother and everything seemed worse than before: dirtier, smellier, more broken, rotting, rusting, destroyed—older, roasting itself in the heat. He couldn't imagine it going on like it was, just squeaking by, just holding together.

He wandered in the cemetery between the hotel and the point, stepping in the shade between hundreds of crumbling cement crosses and graves the size of shoe boxes. Or in the town plaza, where every surface was plastered with posters—green, white, red, and blue, fighting for space on the walls, torn and shredded like the town. Or he walked across the beach toward the pier, where stinking open sewers trickled black across the sand. Or around soccer games and sand fights between school kids. Pillars collapsing, tiles broken, bent and rusting rebar protruding from every corner and cement wall, and palm-frond roofs tumbling in on families of ten.

ON THE SEVENTH DAY, the sets moved in from deep water and exploded off the outside reef. He went quickly from rock to rock in the gray dawn, glancing up to watch the waves as he went, and almost stepped on the headless body of a chicken covered with flies. It startled and nauseated him and he couldn't get it out of his head as he paddled out to the surf, the water warm.

The journalist showed up later and they egged each other on, taking risks and paying for their mistakes, getting dragged underwater over the rocks, cutting their feet, water up their noses. The surf was enormous and smooth, with power and speed that wound up like a spring in his legs. Paddling hard and forcing himself over the edge of the biggest waves, the wall of water long and fast and moving ahead, driving for speed and the whole thing throwing out blue and wide with the town at the end against the base of the hills, dry and yellow, everything racing and nothing else mattering.

By the eighth day, the peak of the swell was over and the surf began to drop, slowly, almost begrudgingly. The lull between sets got longer and it seemed the sun would boil the water as they waited. But then, suddenly, the horizon would darken and catch them off guard. By the tenth day, there was almost nothing left of the swell and the sun was too hot to bear during the long waits between waves.

Once the surf was gone the whole town changed for him. The days now dragged. The afternoons were endless, the streets oppressive, the sea as lifeless and flat as the cloudless sky. The journalist was gone and he wondered if he'd see him again.

He slept twelve hours a day in the full blast of the three-speed fan and his mind continually calculated the time remaining before his flight out, first by the number of meals, then by how many trips to the bakery or pages yet to be read in his book, turning over the problem of unwanted time, trying different ways to satisfy the desire to make a fixed amount appear less than it actually was.

One late afternoon, after the electricity went off and the fan died and a nap was aborted, he walked out past the cemetery and along the point. The sea was listless and the tide was out. He hopped aimlessly from stone to stone and came to a large pool of water captured between the rocks and sat to watch a single fish, shimmering blue and yellow in the sun, circling rhythmically from the shadows of one rock ledge to another. It was a beautiful fish, as large and flat as the palm of his hand, and it was soothing to watch it gliding in spurts around the pool. The day was ending, slowly, and he thought how the fish would still be trapped long after dark, before the tide rose.

That evening he sat down on a bench in the café and his beer was set before him with a thud, the bottle sweating as much as he was. Moths fluttered around the lantern and the stove griddle sizzled, the sound mingling with the slap of the tortillas and a cassette of cumbia music on a boom box. The night melted. He read the beer label carefully to delay it, but the first pull was always the best. Everything was okay: the night, the heat, the flies. A scurry of yellow chicks flitted under the table. A bus bounced past and growled on the highway, glowing with green and yellow and red running lights, and he watched the soldier on the street corner follow it with his eyes, lazily, his rifle slung backward over his shoulder. The chicks peeped and scattered erratically when he shifted his feet, stopping to peck at something unseen on the cement floor.

The girl brought him two hot pupusas on a blue plastic plate, the chicks fleeing desperately before her plastic sandals. The first bite was too hot. He watched the discs on the griddle and the movements of the woman slapping them out and he pulled off the beer, still cold, and saw the soldier outside light a cigarette. Everything was okay. Everything was good as he waited for the pupusas to cool. Distant booms echoed in the dark.

THE WHIR AND COOL air from the fan woke him and a moment later the radio at the restaurant across the street erupted in a full-orchestra version of "Guantanamera." The electricity had come on again. He rolled over, sticky on the bed sheet, the side of his face wet with spittle. It was 2:15 in the afternoon and outside it was scorching. That morning, while he sat in the shade of the restaurant, drinking Sprite in big, cold swallows, another loud, deep-throated boom sounded low across the hillsides and through the town like thunder. He scanned the hills for a rising puff of smoke. Los muchachos were getting closer.

He splashed his face with water from the tiny sink. It smelled bad, but as he stood before the fan to dry it was cool, if only for a moment. He looked through the window and the street was yellow with heat and dust. He found his shoes on the tile floor and slipped them on and went out to the motel office for a gaseosa, his tenth of the day, sugary and sickening, but cold and wet.

It had been five days since the waves died and the suffocating pressure of boredom had finally left him. He no longer had the need to escape, the oppression of idleness that had clawed in him, growing larger as the surf dwindled. He had been lulled into the tropics, worn down by apathy. Now the town was feeling like he remembered it. He lay down on the bed and switched off the flashlight, listening to the sound of the sea and the ramble of soft Spanish from a conversation down the street. He was okay and everything was good, and as another echoing boom sounded from the hills he closed his eyes.

SWEAT RAN DOWN HIS temples and seeped through his eyebrows, stinging his eyes. He wiped it away with the back of his hand. He was walking along the road out of town, shirtless, in the afternoon. Ahead of him, the asphalt boiled in the sun and the end of the road blurred invisible in the heat waves.

The outing had started with a trip to the bakery, and as he walked, he ate fresh, warm pastries and turned down a side street to the highway. Now he was walking out along the coast, the beach unseen behind a row of cement houses on the left. Dry, brown hills sloped up on the right. Somewhere ahead, not more than an hour by car, was Guatemala, cooking too, he thought, and he imagined the soft asphalt beneath his tennis shoes, running to the border and into another country. He wished it were just around the next bend.

He walked along and sweated, eyes burning, going nowhere. Trash littered the roadside and he stopped and picked up a dirty scrap of paper. It was a pamphlet from the FLMN, los muchachos. As he walked farther, he began to notice them everywhere, scattered along the roadway. They must have been thrown from a car in the night. The text demanded the release of three prisoners held by the government. After he read it, he let it slip to the ground and looked around uneasily.

Farther up the road, he stopped at a small cement house with a roof of corrugated metal. Comedor was lettered erratically on the green wall beside a picture of Scrooge McDuck and he stepped inside. The walls and rafters were black with years of soot from indoor cooking fires. A young girl with slightly askew, dark eyes sat at a table with a baby on her lap. He asked for a Coke but she said there weren't any, so he took a Fanta orange instead, glad to be out of the sun, the bottle warm and the drink almost hot. The electricity was off again. He drank it all in long swallows and left the bottle on the table. On the wall by the door was a dusty poster advertising Alka-Seltzer.

Out in the sun again he began to walk back toward the town, his feet crunching on the roadside. Cement crosses in the weeds by the side of the road marking accidents. A horn from behind startled him and a rusty blue school bus rattled past, slowing down to see if he wanted a ride. Inside, the bus was packed with people wearing long sleeves and dresses and there were more people standing on the rear bumper and perched on the roof with the spare tire. He kept walking and the bus clunked into gear and wheezed onward, leaving a dark-brown ball of exhaust floating above heat waves.

HE SAT BAREBACK ON the wooden benches of the restaurant in the night, sipping a warming pilsner in the yellow glow of a single bulb. Out in the darkness, beyond the porch, the waves washed weakly in the blackness, but gradually, as he forked his way steadily through a plate of rice and beans, he felt it change. At first it might have just been wishful thinking, or a slight change in the sound in the darkness, but once the table was cleared and he sipped his third beer he was almost sure. The surf was building in the night.

As he crossed the street back toward the motel, there was a crack in the distance and the power flickered and went out, so he sat on the steps of the motel office in the blackness. He couldn't sleep without the fan and he sipped at another bottle of warm beer from the motel fridge. By then he was certain—a new swell was arriving. It was good just sitting there in the dark, feeling it coming.

He slept uneasily, tossing and dreaming, and he woke early and stood before the window. Dawn was just the furthest edge of night and he brushed his teeth with bottled water in the dark and stretched himself awake.

He slipped out quietly across the patio of the motel, past the sleeping watchdogs and out the back way, up the rickety wooden steps and across the dry, crunching leaves to the road, his board light and familiar under his arm. The horizon was pink then, soft and glowing, and the pier was outlined in yellow lights, gleaming against the dark water.

He took the shortcut through the cemetery, ducking through the crumbled wall and into the darker shadows of the trees, moving quickly to get to the surf. A shout startled him and he pulled up, listening. There were four figures in the darkness, one of them crouching, and the sound of metal clicking.

"¿Que demonios es esto? What the hell is this?!" one whispered, and he sensed others nearby. He was confused, not fully awake, and it was too dark. One of them, short and stocky, came toward him carrying a shovel. He felt someone behind him, too, heard the footsteps and then felt something touch the back of his head, behind his left ear, hard like a broomstick, but he knew it was a gun.

So that's what it feels like, he thought, and he heard them gathering around him and the clanging of equipment and the sound of a shovel hitting the dirt. In the darkness he could see one was wearing army pants but the others were in jeans. Three of them wore baseball hats and pointed rifles at him. He knew at once it was los muchachos. There was a hushed conversation and his brain was empty, listening as they argued, puta madre, puta madre, and a louder whisper saying "¡Cállate, cállate! ¡Cierra la puta boca!"

"Where are you fucking going, gringo?" someone asked, softly.

"To the beach," he said. "To surf."

His board was too white in the dark and he could feel the wax sticking to the hairs on his forearm. He was cold. The pressure on the back of his head was just enough to push his face down a little, and he saw that they were all wearing boots.

Then, a voice from behind. It was the waiter's voice, the waiter from the restaurant across the street.

"Está bien," he heard. "Está bien. Solamente un surfeador. He's cool. Permitele a ir."

He wanted to turn around but he didn't. He kept his head down.

The arguing started up again until one voice, louder, whispered over the others, "¡Calma, calma, calma—cállate!"

There was whispered swearing and then a pause and the one in front of him, with the army pants, looked him up and down. "Está bien, gringo? You cool?"

"I'm just going surfing," he said, trying to raise his head to meet his eyes, but the pressure pushed his head down and he looked at the dirt and the boots around him. A rooster crowed, and then another.

He waited. They waited. The surf sounded loud in the dark beyond the trees.

"Get the fuck out of here," the short one said.

"Muchas gracias," he said and walked toward the beach, his mind a blur, stepping around the tombstones and into the trees until he reached the edge of the sand. He could feel them watching and he waited for the impact in his back and wondered how much it hurts when a bullet hits you, and he remembered the story of the photographer, shot in the stomach, bleeding to death. I should run, he thought, I should dive behind a tree, but he just kept walking until the sand became the cobblestones of the point, and then hopped from rock to rock to the water's edge. As he leapt from the last rock into the sea, he heard a sharp, short crack and then the rooster's crow.

"A HIGH-RANKING POLITICAL FIGURE was sitting in the back of his Jeep Cherokee at a red light in San Salvador when a boy ran out through traffic and placed a bomb on the hood of the car," said a voice on the radio.

Placed, he thought as he sat in his pickup truck listening to the news at a red light. It was a nice day in L.A., with the smog not so thick for a late-summer morning and the sun not too hot yet on the leatherette of his truck. He rolled the word around in his head. Placed. Not thrown or tossed or hurled, but placed, as if softly, as if with care.

He could see it well, the man in the backseat of a black SUV and a boy running out into traffic with something in his hand, the driver startled and them both seeing it then, wrapped in duct tape and reflecting in the sun and the dust on the hood and the traffic light and them now realizing it was a bomb. It stayed with him, all the way down the freeway, after the news was over. He saw the boy running, the heat rising from the hood, the dust on the windshield glass. He got stuck at the bottleneck near the shopping center on La Cienega Boulevard. He reached over and rolled the radio station knob between his fingers, and the morning sun glanced off his side mirror and over his hood, and he could almost see a bomb.

A red Toyota rolled up alongside him, idling. He crumpled the 976 phone-sex card that he had found stuck in his side window when he went to work in the morning. He flattened it out against his thigh and looked at the sexy blond in a negligee in the dot-screen photo. "Llamame," it read. He remembered the night he came out of a bar and found his window smashed, tiny chunks of glass all over the inside of his car, his glove box and maps and cassette tapes thrown around with old Sip-n-Drive coffee lids. When he went to have the window fixed the next day, they opened up the door panel and a mass of phone sex cards in different colors were piled in the bottom of the door.

Sitting at another stoplight, he looked over at a woman in a Hyundai and watched the stream of cars crossing the intersection and thought of all the phone sex cards piled inside all those car doors.

A MAN'S BAPTISM IN
A TOWN CALLED JESUS CARES

John Waldman

I moved here at my daughter's urging
to spend my remaining days
living a churchgoer's life. Here
where dawn is a wicker couch
shod in boiled wool slippers.
Where the purple martins and Mexican fruit bats
loiter in octagonal homes
perched on a single stilt in each yard.

Within the week of my arrival
a man from the Pop-a-Lock changed my flat
when the sidewall on one of my Goodyears
split like the peel on an ornamental orange.
On my way home I saw my son-in-law
teetering on the porch of Billy's Bar
or was it La Kantina?
surveying the ragged lawn like a shepherd.

At my daughter's urging I am here
to tie up the strings on a life of advocacy,
outrage, infidelity, and dereliction.
To live at half-mast
under an empty billboard
on a porch of green metal chairs
and a monthly recipe of medication
costing the same as the mortgage, twofold.

In this grave time that is no time for sleep
that is no time for the ledger of one's life to be rendered illegible
I stare like the boy who saw a thousand eclipses
projected on the sidewalk
when the light from a single passing scattered
through a jigsaw of cedar leaves
or close my eyes to count the paper boats of my dreams
drifting like moths on a surface of blue light.

THE GREAT WISCONSIN SOLIDARITY EXPERIMENT

Natasha Vargas-Cooper

I DRIVE OUT OF Madison, Wisconsin, through a winter-scrubbed landscape of brown trees and frozen waterways. Dusk approaches as I skirt Loon Lake, not far south of the state line, and head toward Gurnee, Illinois, home of Six Flags Great America. The entrance to my hotel, the Gurnee Grand, is just 984 feet from the park's main gate. Tourists also like the hotel's Jacuzzi-equipped theme rooms (Pharaoh's Den, Lions' Lair, Romans' Romp). I am on the trail of a missing state senator.

Over the past twenty-four hours, I've exchanged numerous text messages with Wisconsin's Chris Larson. He is one of fourteen Democratic state senators who refused to show up and vote on Governor Scott Walker's budget proposal to take collective-bargaining rights away from unionized public employees. They left Wisconsin's capital to deny Republicans the legislative quorum needed to pass the bill. In return, Walker ordered Wisconsin state troopers to arrest the senators. During the course of our cellphone negotiations, Larson tells me that he's moved several times to avoid media helicopters hovering over his ever-changing hideaways. His last text instructing me to come to Gurnee, out of the reach of Wisconsin's state troopers, is my best clue yet.

I feel the early-March chill outside the Gurnee Grand as I gather my things from my rented Chevy

Aveo. Before I reach the lobby, a new text beeps on my phone: "Still in caucus. Standby. No Guarantees."

I answer that I'm willing to wait all night, as long as it takes.

Inside my hotel room (no Jacuzzi or romping Romans), I plop down in a puke-green recliner, grab the remote, and turn the TV to MSNBC. Right there, in plain sight on *The Ed Show*, is the man I have been searching for. Just more than two months into his first term, Larson is the most junior of the Wisconsin Fourteen, and with his boyish good looks, the most photogenic. Now he, Walker, and all of Wisconsin's governing establishment have been thrown into the middle of a national political drama. Before I return to Los Angeles, I will attend heated town hall meetings, see a recall movement gain momentum, and watch a hundred thousand people, led by a line of farm tractors, descend on the capital and call for class war. These are the images ricocheting through the heartland during the early spring of the tea party-fueled putsch.

Right now, Gov. Walker is on TV. He's ridiculing a letter from Wisconsin Senate Minority Leader Mark Miller calling to end the legislative stalemate with a peace summit of sorts near the Wisconsin-Illinois border, perhaps here in Gurnee; the governor also claims he has information that some of the missing senators are willing to break ranks and vote with the Republicans. Walker's attempt to embarrass and divide the Wisconsin Fourteen seems to have had the opposite effect. Three weeks after the start of their exile, Larson and the other thirteen senators have already stayed away much longer than anyone predicted. Their steadfastness is like a rejuvenating tonic for the pent-up frustration of a Democratic base exhausted by a feckless national leadership that seems to be ceding ground on every major issue from tax cuts to gun control and Gitmo.

But as I sit in my motel room and impatiently wait for the green light from Larson, an underlying dilemma plagues me: is this revolt in the heartland, finally, the beginning of a new era for unions and labor? Or is it merely the death rattle of a movement on the brink of its afterlife?

Modest civil disobedience may have earned the Wisconsin Fourteen instant lionization in many quarters, but my six years of union experience, first as an organizer and then as regional coordinator for the million-member Service Employees International Union (SEIU), tells me to be wary.

After all, it is Republican overreach rather than Democratic leadership that has led to this showdown. A critical tactic in the conservative drive to build a permanent majority in Wisconsin and other Rust Belt states is to bust the unions under the guise of "emergency" austerity measures. Walker's plan cuts right to the marrow of a labor movement that he, and just about everybody else, thinks is tottering on its heels. If it dies, one of the last major funding sources for Democrats dies, too. But Walker might have messed with the wrong state. Wisconsin has too much blue-collar cultural memory to go down without a fight. And now, public school teachers, state clerks, nurses, cops, and firemen are holding the line against an attack that was born in Madison but is quickly spreading to a dozen or more other states.

IT'S 11 P.M. WHEN Larson at last agrees to meet me in the lobby of the Hampton Inn, next door to the Gurnee Grand. He's just come out of a marathon closed-door meeting with his fellow exiled senators.

Tall, gap-toothed, and handsome, but with a squished, broad nose, Larson appears in a fitted black overcoat, a sedate suit with a Wisconsin flag lapel pin, and an athletic backpack. He looks shockingly young, younger than his thirty years, and seems to be relieved that I am even a few years younger myself.

We jump in my Chevy and head for the town's late-night diner: Denny's. By the time we settle into a booth, Larson has dropped the routine political affectations— the measured language, the approved talking points, the inauthentic humor. We're cracking up comparing Republicans to evildoers on *South Park* and shit-talking mutual acquaintances in Milwaukee.

And then, just as Larson is about to take a bite of his veggie burger, I ask the freshman senator if he is scared.

"What would I be scared about?" he replies.

How about stumbling unprepared into the national spotlight and making a compromise that appeases Republicans but pisses off the other half of Wisconsin? Perhaps losing reelection based on what the Wisconsin Democratic leadership decides to do? Maybe not being up to the task of helping to lead an uproarious force for social change?

Larson takes a breath, purses his lips, and says firmly, "No. I'm not scared. I just want to do stuff. Doing stuff, like solving problems and crises, is more important to me than staying in office."

When I ask if the fourteen Democrats have handlers or Democratic strategists helping them in this fight, he laughs and says no. In fact, they hadn't even jelled as a group when they decided to flee the state.

My stomach churns. Larson strikes me as an earnest guy, but I still don't trust he's up to this task. For one thing, he has no real roots in labor. His parents are conservative business owners. The reason he was motivated to run for office, his real passion, is the environment. But the moral math of saving seals and restoring wetlands is easy compared to the much more complicated, often sordid, and certainly more treacherous world of human beings, not to mention labor-management conflicts.

"I came out of the Orwellian snake pit of politics and personality," Larson tells me. "Everything felt so outrageously high-stakes and everyone was cutthroat because we thought we were doing the most important things in the world."

Larson is, of course, talking about his undergraduate days with the College Democrats at the University of Wisconsin–Milwaukee, where he and his classmates spent most of their time agonizing over the group's mission statement.

Given the fight he's in, Larson's melodramatic memories of something as squishy as a college Democratic club worry me. When he gives me a line about how the best way to make the biggest impact is from within the establishment, I wonder: have the Dems brought daisies to a knife fight? In this current battle between labor and capital, in which Gov. Walker has broken all the rules, and funding for antilabor pols comes from the likes of the oil-and-toilet-paper-billionaire Koch brothers, a radical, militant stance seems necessary just to avoid getting pulverized. It's bare-knuckles time—no time for milquetoasts.

But after Republicans successfully demolished the Dems' core leadership in last year's midterms, those who remain are mostly lower-profile Democrats. Many of the Wisconsin Fourteen are either newbies or backbenchers now pushed to the epicenter of an unprecedented moment in state and national politics.

Larson, though, seems to enjoy being under national and international scrutiny, with Al Jazeera and Italian TV crews jostling with the locals on Madison's Capitol steps.

"I like working with all the lights on," he says, smiling.

By 2 A.M., Larson, perhaps out of exhaustion, or maybe because of our mutual appreciation for foul-mouthed cable-animation shows, begins to tell me things that start to change my mind about him.

He enrolled in college as a film major to be closer to a girl he was in love with. Once she rejected him, he packed up and drove out to California, where he lived out of his car in Santa Monica for close to six months. He had notions of wanting to be a novelist but was unable to write anything of worth. The next few years were sketchy, but Larson alludes to doing odd service jobs to fund his way back to Wisconsin.

When he was nineteen and broke, Larson was arrested for shoplifting food. He worked out a deal with the judge: he'd reenroll in college in exchange for dropping the charges. Once he was back on track, the girl he originally made a play for showed renewed interest. ("You'll find that most men end up where they are because they were chasing a girl," Larson tells me, a bit bashfully.) He decided to get involved with campus activities and ended up with the College Dems, who were organizing around a local environmental issue.

At one of the Dems' functions he met Robert Kennedy Jr., who took a liking to Larson and encouraged him to run for office, something local at first. He persuaded the girl he'd been chasing to marry him and decided to run for Milwaukee County supervisor in 2008, a race he won.

As it turns out, Gov. Walker was the Milwaukee County executive when Larson was county supervisor. And so, despite his junior position in the state Senate, Larson has more experience working directly with Walker than his Democratic colleagues.

"He always had the board to rein in his extreme ideological propositions," Larson says. Walker would drastically slash programs that had any liberal bent, even if they were successful, and then the rest of the board would scurry to repair what damage it could. "I've seen his tricks. I'm like the ex-girlfriend at the wedding," he jokes.

My begrudging admiration for Larson ratchets up another notch when he tells me he decided to run in the state senate Democratic primary last year against an incumbent, Jeff Plale, because Plale was a "sellout" for holding up legislation aimed at fighting climate change in favor of business interests. Larson built a grass-roots campaign from scratch in a left-leaning district of Milwaukee that has become younger and hipper in the past few years. A tireless, young staff of volunteers ran operations out of his basement.

Wisconsin Democratic Party chairman Mike Tate called Larson and told him to quit or else the party would effectively end his career in politics. Larson won the primary and then defeated Republican candidate Jess Rip in the general election for the Seventh District.

This story beats the hell out of the one about his College Dem angst. A Democrat who beat both the Democratic establishment and the Republican challenger might be the real thing, precisely the sort of pol who can work with a labor movement that must battle its own listless legacy.

493

MADISON IS IN A lull between political storms when I arrive a few days before I meet Larson, but the drumbeats haven't stopped. State troopers put a big dent in the throngs that initially occupied the Capitol when they cleared the building so it could be cleaned, and subfreezing nighttime temperatures cut in half the forty or so who dragged their sleeping bags and tents to the bottom of the Capitol steps and established an overnight encampment called Walkerville. But all around the rotunda, posters and banners still denounce Walker and call for taxing the rich. About a half-dozen protestors have Saran Wrap tied around freshly tattooed arms after spending part of the night in the warmth of a nearby tattoo parlor getting the word solidarity permanently inked into their skin. And once allowed back inside the state building, many take up their principal duties: sitting in a drum circle, pounding on empty buckets, and chanting for "a general strike." An interesting notion for some kids who probably have no jobs, let alone a union.

Outside the Capitol, maybe ten yards from Walkerville, firefighters from Local 311 hold a midafternoon rally with more than a thousand followers. Their message is simple and direct: recall the Republican legislators supporting Walker's bill and return a Democratic majority to the narrowly GOP-controlled Senate.

With the fight over the budget bill stalemated by the Wisconsin Fourteen's flight to Illinois, the recall is being brandished to galvanize the mounting negative sentiment toward the governor and his allies. It emerges two weeks after demonstrations that have energized public opinion but achieved little else. There's been almost no formal coordination among the Democratic

Party, labor unions, and the various progressive groups that have popped up. Organizers openly fret that protest fatigue could be setting in. This new recall tactic could bolster the movement.

At sunset I head to the Capitol steps for a jazz funeral to commemorate "the death of the middle class." It would be impolite not to show up. And yet the spectacle is a reminder of some of my worst moments in the labor movement because this party is being thrown by the California-based National Nurses United (NNU), rival union to the SEIU. The two unions spent a bloody decade fighting for turf, and I was an SEIU frontline foot soldier. The turf war encapsulated everything that was sick and twisted about the American labor movement, as the two organizations fought pitched battles hospital by hospital, state by state.

The behavior of my old union could hardly be considered saintly, but among my SEIU colleagues it was widely believed that the NNU grew its ranks by organizing, almost exclusively, elite registered nurses by exploiting their fears of mixing with other lower-ranked and often immigrant health care workers. When the SEIU tried to organize large for-profit health care corporations, attempting "wall to wall" organizing that would bond all hospital employees into one big union, the NNU would show up days before a union vote and ask the registered nurses, "Do you really want to be in a janitor's union?" Left unsaid was that the janitors were not white.

But the NNU wasn't the only problem. My disenchantment with the labor movement peaked just after I watched President Obama's swearing-in at a Milwaukee union hall, known locally as a "labor temple," with fellow SEIU staff.

The new president and the Democratic Congress had promised something called the Employee Free Choice Act, or EFCA, that would make organizing a union infinitely easier than any time since the New Deal. It could have changed the course of a battered American middle class. A nice idea, but Congress punked out and labor, even in the notoriously union-friendly state of Wisconsin, had no urgency, no stomach for the fight.

Back in D.C., I was stunned by the level of dysfunction in the national "war room" the SEIU had set up to fight for the Free Choice Act. What should have been a street-level mobilization of the rank-and-file was being handled like one more top-down Washington political project—outsourced to consultants from Hillaryland, out of touch with the ground-level realities of union locals I had visited in a half-dozen states, miserably failing after pissing away millions of dollars. I had enough. Two weeks later I quit the labor movement.

I carry that baggage onto the steps of the Capitol at sunset, where a New Orleans-style jazz band plays a funeral dirge. Predictably, the nurses union overplays its hand and turns an opportunity to dramatize a serious issue into a fringe clown show. Instead of addressing the nuts-and-bolts strategy needed to defeat Walker, the event veers off into political la-la land with a gaggle of Green Party activists trashing Obama and nameless corporations, chanting over and over, "There is no middle class! Only the rich and the people!"

What had been buried under this pile of rhetoric was any tangible, visible strategy that might actually resonate with Wisconsin middle-class families threatened by an immediate rollback of salaries and their bargaining rights.

The Great Wisconsin Solidarity Experiment

IF THERE'S ANY HEAT, any real traction, to this outrage, it will have to radiate beyond the bounds of liberal Madison. So I go looking.

It's a dark, cold Sunday afternoon when I make it to the small town of Reedsburg, a hamlet of 7,800 hardy souls seventy miles north of Madison. As foreboding as the sky looks, it's an even darker moment for Republican state Senator Dale Schultz.

A balding, avuncular pol from a local middle-class family, he's spent more than half of his fifty-eight years in the state Legislature and built a solid reputation as a totally reasonable across-the-aisle consensus builder.

But that ain't working this afternoon in the local Pineview Elementary School gym, where 300 people, many clad in Badger red, have turned out for a town hall meeting on the Walker budget bill.

I am as delighted as Schultz is perplexed by the scene in front of us. I had expected, rather cynically, to find the usual stage-managed media event that I had witnessed (and helped organize) countless times— twenty workers bused into a rally, holding up placards and armed with talking-point handouts peppered with slogans. Instead, we see an authentic expression of anger, mobilization, and a tangible yearning for action beyond rhetoric and polemics. It's the first glimmer I see of some sort of a movement that is surging upward and outward. These aren't protest people. Here, in the bleachers, are Pineview's teachers, some students, moms and dads, shop owners, retirees. All corn-fed and Wonder Bread white. It's a PTA/AARP/Boy Scouts meeting on steroids. And you can bet there are way more Republican voters in this gym than Green Party voters. But that's not stopping them from giving hell to one of their own.

Schultz is trying to forge some sort of a bridge, but there are no takers even though some or a lot of those present reelected him just a few months ago with 65 percent of the vote. "No!...No!...No!" reverberates off the gym walls as Schultz patiently and calmly lays out what he thinks is a reasonable compromise.

He says he wants to amend the bill so that public-employee collective-bargaining rights are only temporarily suspended and then restored in two years, allowing the state a bit of breathing room to solve its immediate economic crisis. He's hoping this will end the standoff in Madison, allow the Wisconsin Fourteen to return home, and ease the way for a bipartisan legislative kumbaya.

"I believe it could head off a passionate explosion," Schultz tells the grumpy crowd.

"That won't do!" someone shouts out. Others follow suit. Nobody is in favor of the compromise solution.

Several audience members who take the microphone during the three-hour program remind the senator that public employees are already making a compromise by offering to freeze their wages and pay a larger share of their benefits. Schultz replies that other public-employee unions, such as the police and firefighters, have restrictions such as a prohibition on strikes, and, consequently, he reasons, teachers, nurses, and social workers should not think of themselves as exempt from state restrictions on their bargaining rights. Schultz then, unwittingly, uncorks a zinger that might instantly kill off a less well-liked pol in a less polite state. "All the animals in the barnyard need to be equal," he says.

In a gesture of Wisconsin Nice, no one throws anything, not even an epithet, at Schultz for his unintentional Animal Farm metaphor.

Retribution, though, is likely to come through the polls. I don't know about Schultz's future, but this flop of a town hall meeting in Reedsburg portends poorly for Wisconsin Republicans in general. This town has its share of public school teachers and maybe some other state workers who commute to Madison. But this gentle, rural, relatively affluent, and almost entirely white burg is no hotbed of radicalism.

The whole scene is a code-red indicator that the upheaval in Madison is no mere university-based aberration. The blowback against Walker and the GOP is reverberating loudly out here where the hottest topic is usually the local Little League team.

After Schultz patiently takes questions for about an hour, I speak with Judith Boe, a music teacher at Pineview who recently retired after thirty-five years. Now in her sixties, short and shrunken, wearing a red Reedsburg sweatshirt, Boe credits Schultz for pushing back against his party, but she's in no mood for half measures.

"I don't think he can be effective unless he joins the fourteen Democrats" in openly opposing the Walker-backed bill, she says. Boe, like many at the town hall, says she believes that the Wisconsin Fourteen will not compromise on the collective-bargaining issue for fear of being voted out of office by their own whipped-up base.

Near the end of the program, a heavy-set Asian man, about sixty, dressed in a floral, rose-colored shirt, approaches the microphone. He is the head of the only nonwhite family in the gym. Without rancor, he calculates that Walker's bill would cost eight local teachers their jobs. And their lost salaries, he says, would suck that much more capital out of the local economy.

Before this meeting, he tells Schultz, he considered himself strictly an independent voter.

"After hearing you speak," the man says, "I've decided to become a Democrat."

A FEW DAYS AFTER our meeting in Gurnee, I reach Senator Larson by phone, and he is brimming with optimism. Word among the Wisconsin Fourteen is that momentum on their side is snowballing and that the protracted struggle is eroding the position of the Senate Republicans. The Walker gambit is backfiring and those recall petitions that I had originally laughed off now loom ominously in front of their targets.

What's thought to be confirmed intelligence convinces many that enough moderate Republicans are ready to make a deal that will allow the fourteen to come home and vote on a bipartisan bill that will protect the bargaining rights of the unions in return for salary concessions (which labor has already publicly agreed to). Larson tells me he's confident that a "watershed" moment is at hand. The general feeling is that labor is about to score a rare and significant victory in pushing back Walker and, by extension, the entire national Republican agenda. After all, this battle is flaring in the Rust Belt swing states.

What nobody bargains for is that the desperation setting in among Republicans will not lead to a capitulation, but rather to a shocking political blitzkrieg. On Wednesday, March 9, with only three hours' notice and the fourteen Democratic senators still in exile, the Senate Republicans announce that a vote will be held on the budget-repair bill, with or without a quorum.

In a meeting room, packed with witnesses, local media, staffers, and anxious Democratic legislators who've remained in Madison, the nineteen Republican senators take their seats at a conference table. Thousands of protesters gather outside and chants of "SHAME! SHAME! SHAME!" penetrate the chamber room.

As the roll call begins, the typically mild-mannered Democratic Assemblyman Peter Barca, who has been furiously taking notes during the session, interrupts and begins to read a memo from the attorney general that states meetings of this sort must have at least twenty-four hours' public notice.

The Republicans ignore Barca, refusing to even glance at him. The "yes" votes are called out one by one, with Barca on his feet pointing to the memo pleading with Senate Majority Leader Scott Fitzgerald to stop the vote: "Mr. Chairman, this is a violation of law! This is not just a rule, this is law."

The rest of the action takes less than ten seconds. Fitzgerald slaps the gavel on the table and the Senate Republicans vote eighteen-to-one to strip unionized public employees of their rights to collective bargaining. Boom, just like that it's all over.

The only dissenting vote is Republican Senator Dale Schultz from Reedsburg. The absent fourteen Democrats are recorded simply as "not present." The Republicans quickly scurry out of the Senate chamber and witnesses to the vote start to loudly chant in dismay, with one spectator crying out, "What have you done?"

There is video of the vote on YouTube (posted by Larson's staff), and I've watched it repeatedly because it sends a shiver through my body. It shows the Republicans sitting toadlike, murmuring their yeas over Barca's protests, with the thunderous chanting rolling through the rotunda and into the meeting room.

The Republican leadership claims that by separating out the collective bargaining ban from other economic rollbacks included in Gov. Walker's budget austerity plan, the larger quorum denied by the Democratic boycott was no longer necessary, because that only applied to legislation dealing with the budget itself (a rather curious contention and contortion given that the union-bashing measure was supposedly central to Walker's "budget-repair" bill).

Walker immediately takes a victory lap following the Senate vote, issuing a statement saying, "I applaud the Legislature's action today to stand up to the status quo and take a step in the right direction to balance the budget and reform government."

In a counterstatement, Senate Minority Leader Mark Miller says, "In thirty minutes, eighteen state senators undid fifty years of civil rights in Wisconsin. Tomorrow we will join the people of Wisconsin in taking back their government."

It doesn't take until tomorrow. The reaction is immediate. Thousands of protesters push past police and storm into the Capitol minutes after the vote. Calls go out among union members and activists to organize the biggest demonstration yet on the coming Saturday. Student activists stage a walkout the next day. Walker has brilliantly maneuvered to win a key battle, but the war is only escalating. I am astounded by the scene that unfolds in Madison the day after he signs his radical legislation into law.

As promised, the biggest demonstration since this battle erupted brings 100,000 or more protesters into the streets of the capital. I am awestruck by the almost socialist realist tableau of organized labor and its supporters that materializes that ice-cold Saturday. It isn't Petrograd. Not quite. But it's something we haven't seen in America since the days of Ludlow or Homestead or the great Seattle General Strike of 1919.

The Great Wisconsin Solidarity Experiment

A cavalcade of tractors from the Wisconsin Farmers Union, flanked by a brigade of snow mobiles, leads the hour-long protest procession to the Capitol. Detachment after detachment of unions and their families defiantly march toward the seat of state power. Lining the perimeters are a battery of "recall stations" manned by volunteers gathering a bonanza of signatures. Near the front of the march, a phalanx of firefighters from Local 311 puts a platoon of bagpipes at their vanguard. Tall, white men wearing blue sweatshirts emblazoned with the words "Cops for Labor" march alongside.

Police officers and firemen leading a militant labor march? Who is going to argue that these guys are the pampered and spoiled public employees that Walker has so adamantly demonized? And while Republicans may have taken their conservatism for granted, someone forgot they have generational roots in the old-line industrial unions that have been decimated by decades of antiunionism. Messing with unions is like messing with their families. Their anger and horror at the sensation of feeling the bottom fall out is almost primal.

The drum-circle crew can barely be heard as union banners and placards are lofted high into the air as the crowd roars over and over again, "This is what democracy looks like!"

"WE ACHIEVED OUR GOALS of engaging the public and drawing attention to the Republicans' war on working people," Larson tells me after he returns home to Wisconsin. "We did everything short of changing the actual Republicans in the Legislature. Now that's up to the people."

Democrats, at the time of this writing, have managed to at least temporarily block Walker's bill in the courts.

503

Four Republican state senators seem headed for recall and five more are in the crosshairs. In a by-election three weeks after the signing, a Democrat won back Walker's old seat as Milwaukee County executive by a two-to-one margin. It's not impossible that Democrats will win back a legislative majority and expunge the anti-union bill. And an incumbent Republican-backed Supreme Court Justice, who had been ahead by thirty points two months previous, narrowly defeated an obscure union-backed challenger only after 14,000 "misplaced" votes were mysteriously produced by a Republican county official days after the voting.

The example of the Wisconsin unions reverberates through neighboring states as tens of thousands of workers rally in Columbus, Lansing, and Indianapolis to fight similar antiunion measures. In Ohio, an even more draconian version of Walker's bill seems headed for reversal in a popular referendum this fall. As one union official tells me, "Without collective-bargaining rights, we're not a union, we're a club with bumper stickers."

This is how I see Wisconsin: neither a beginning nor an end but, primarily, an example. An example of what is possible when the narrow bounds of everyday politics and the humdrum of business unionism is disrupted by a visceral and radical fight for what is right.

We are in the midst of a national, strategic assault on organized labor being carried out by a cadre of zealous Republican governors. More than 740 pieces of antiunion legislation total have been introduced into almost every statehouse in the country this year, all of them taking aim at public-employee unions—the final rampart, perhaps the Alamo, of American labor.

I have also seen the only effective way to resist this onslaught. I saw it in the streets of Madison and in that gymnasium in Reedsburg, in the stoic determination of the cops and the firemen fighting for something bigger than themselves, and I sensed it in the defiance of young Senator Larson, who was pushed into a fight he could not imagine only weeks before.

ON THE GODLESSLY COLD March morning that I leave Madison, a taxi driver named Dennis picks me up. I know the taboo about reporters using taxi drivers as oracles but, sorry, there's something notable about Dennis and his fellow Wisconsin cabbies. Unlike their immigrant counterparts in most American cities, they're mostly middle-aged or older white men. Climb into the back of one of their smoke-scented Crown Vics, as I do for the umpteenth time as I am heading to the airport, and you immediately understand what the fight is all about.

A pink-faced, broad-shouldered Vietnam vet with a bulbous nose, Dennis encapsulates the history of a Middle America that used to be. Thirty years ago, you could enlist into the American Dream, like he did, with a 9-to-5 job at Hormel, or maybe at an IBP slaughterhouse. Rapacious deindustrialization and the accelerated export of jobs thanks to bipartisan free-trade policies, however, knocked the unionized working class down the ladder into low-paying service jobs.

This was Dennis's story and also the one of just about every other hack I chatted up in Wisconsin.

When Dennis worked on the floor of a now-defunct, unionized assembly plant, he was able to buy his family a house and put away some savings with a dignified salary. By the late seventies, "done taking orders," he ventured into his own air-conditioning business. He did okay for a few years, but Wisconsin industry was hollowed out, as was the rest of the heartland's, and his business faltered. Soon, he didn't have the coin to pay for college for his two daughters.

With no meaningful retirement income, here he is in his early sixties, driving a cab to make ends meet. Dennis, for sure, is on the down slope, but still hanging on to the last tattered threads, or at least the memories, of what was once a rock-solid, blue-collar culture.

I can't help but compare him with the cabbies I knew when I lived in Washington, D.C. They were almost exclusively from war-torn Sierra Leone and lived in fear of ever returning to their homeland. But I could imagine they could at least dream of a future.

Back in Madison, Dennis and his native-born co-workers, bundled in parkas and driving those beastlike gas guzzlers, only remember a future that is getting ever more grim and dim. Several decades of lethargy and aimlessness have come home to roost in a rather devastating way for American workers. Wisconsin showed labor the hard work it has to do to tread water.

I leave Wisconsin with what the great Victor Serge called "pessimism of the intellect, optimism of the will." As inspiring as the Wisconsin action was, I also know it will not be easy to replicate or sustain, let alone nationalize. And even if the unions do succeed there, they will have restored the situation only to the status quo. Not one new worker will be in a union. Not yet, anyway.

EASTSIDERS PROJECT: LITTLE VALLEY

Gregory Bojorquez

I LIVED IN MONTEBELLO, Boyle Heights, and then El Sereno until 2002. I started shooting the bulk of the "Eastsiders" project in 1997. I knew I had to shoot the project while everyone had their youth and involvement in the Eastside. One of my frequent subjects was Miguel Acosta. I've known him since I was ten. We played Little League in Monterey Park, and after high school graduation in the early nineties he moved to his grandparents' house on Fifth Street in Little Valley.

Little Valley is roughly one square mile in East L.A. between Rowan Avenue and Downey Road. Its northern border is the 60 Freeway and its southern border is Whittier Boulevard.

I had another friend, Roy Garcia, who brought me to Little Valley, too. Roy moved next door to ELA fixture Beto, or "Stomper," on South Brannick Avenue. We would see each other at parties and at Cypress Hill and Psycho Realm shows, and we started hanging at Miguel's on Fifth Street to watch football games and drink beer and joke around.

A lot of the social life in Little Valley revolves around the dead ends created by the freeway, and also its markets. Ramirez Market, on Princeton Street and South Record, has been in Little Valley for decades. The market's facade and pay phone are riddled with bullet holes from gang-related conflicts, but the neighborhood kids continue to hang out there.

Yoly's Market, at Sixth and Bonnie Beach, has a vibrant mural that used to include the inscription "Barrio Lil Valley." The Sheriff's Department made the owners remove the phrase because of its association with the gang named after Little Valley. But generations of blue-collar workers have grown up in Little Valley, too.

Though these pictures from Little Valley, taken between 1997 and 2001, are just part of a larger project I call Eastsiders, comprising hundreds of photos, they are a good example of everyday life in an East Los Angeles neighborhood whose residents usually go unnoticed.

Consider a guy like Felix, who I photographed with his bike in front of Ana's market. Felix is a mentally disabled man whose family moved to Palmdale years ago. I was told he walked all the way back to Little Valley from Palmdale. When Felix showed up, the people in the neighborhood took care of him. Felix would hang out with the guys, and one of them, Bob, let Felix live in his garage. Felix got shot in the leg by someone from a rival neighborhood. I wonder if people in an upper-middle-class neighborhood would take care of a person like Felix the way those in Little Valley did.

Three generations of a Little Valley family stand beside Yoly's Market on Father's Day. The little girl, who is the granddaughter, daughter, and little sister of the three males, stares at Chino (RIP) in his wheelchair.

A friend of Beto's and his son in a very
clean, root-beer-brown 1957 Chevy Bel Air
on an autumn day on Bonnie Beach Place.

I went by Fifth Street on New Year's Day and Wolf
and Pato were hanging out with some others in
front of a condemned house having some beers.

Muzzles (second from left) lived above
Little Valley's Ramirez Market on
Princeton Street and South Record.

I walked up to this party crew, who called themselves
the Freaky 1's, and when I asked if I could take their
photo they immediately got into this pose.

Hanging out on a Sunday afternoon with (left to right) Beto, Pablo, Mario, Danny, Pecas (RIP), Jalapeño, and Chuey (father of Bam Bam and Jalapeño). We were drinking Coronas and shots of Presidente at Bam Bam's house on Bonnie Beach and Sixth Street.

Larry, the cousin of my friend Miguel Acosta,
messes around with an unplugged guitar. He
was talking about Jimi Hendrix.

Enorio (RIP) was walking his pit bull terrier on Fifth Street when I snapped this photo. Not long after, Enorio, a father of two, was found dead of an apparent suicide, hanging from a tree in the backyard of a house he lived in on Fifth Street.

SOMEWHERE SOUTH OF NORTH ALVARADO

Lucy Engelman

He came from Oregon way back
before he knew curiosity
or ransom.
Lightly he traced tools in the sandlots,
wiped broad sweat openly.

But then it changed.
He saw sweetwater at night
and sang lullabies to blackbirds, and
started speaking languages not yet heard.
These times had been long passed in the waning.

Yet ever so slightly, he turned,
looked over his shoulder,
seeing not the brassy billboards glowing,
but instead
the yawning entrance to the freeway.
Waltzing toward it,
he disappeared.

IN BLOOM

James Greer

EVEN IMPATIENT PEOPLE WON'T get bored watching the Damask rose, and sick people will find its blossoms cheering. The location of the flower depends on where you are physically and the politics of self-destruction. When Routledge Ruut stood, alone and smoking in the middle of the desolate battlefield, he could not see the parts of bodies or writhing and groaning recently human* forms. He could not see or hear anything, in fact, blind from the blood caked over his eyes and deaf from the cannon's shout, but he could see in his mind the Rosa damascena he had grown in a small clay pot on his windowsill earlier that year.

Who was Routledge Ruut kidding? That rose was long bloomed, and the clay pot shattered or consumed by fire when enemy troops ravaged the town near six months ago. And yet. If a thing can be held in the mind and regarded with precision, passionately held by force of will as if the eye were present, he had been taught, then no separate reality existed that could overthrow the one so constructed.

What you wouldn't do to get there. The carnage before you: a drop of elderberry jam on a snowy mountaintop. Routledge Ruut, you are a killer. Probably** makes you feel better to say warrior, soldier, but that's a sham. The roses you seek: nothing will stand in your way. No one can or will. You start wars, and you end them, all for the sake of a rose. More precisely: for the attar that can be obtained by steam distillation in copper tubs of crushed petals and sepals, the olive-green, malodorous oil from roses harvested before dawn and extracted the same day.

After which, what happens? More roses grow. You can't stop them from growing. When they grow, you go after them and slaughter anyone who stands in your way.

EVERYBODY WANTS MY BLOOD. The helicopters shooting diamonds above the low hills at night, the Russian nurses, the white coats, the sloppy sailors with buckets of fish guts, preening*** on the wharf. Or perhaps I should say: there's no one who does not want my blood. That is why I am covered in bruises, from needles, from constant poking with needles. That is why I am so bloody anemic.

Routledge Ruut has pig snot for brains. What runs through his arteries I wouldn't even guess, but nothing good. Nothing pure. Once I saw him pricked with a small sword and something olive green spurted from the wound. I will admit that I wounded him. For what reason he does the ravaging and so forth. For what reason at all. The countryside is stupid, infested with stupidities, plied every day with more stupidities, through various means, some popular**** and open and free. Routledge Ruut knows all that, but he doesn't care a damn except for the well-being of his roses. In the meantime I am running short on blood, and there are only so many stupidities I can reasonably stand.

I need to stop Routledge Ruut. Well, not stop him but instead turn his attention[a] to the stupidities. From the roses to the stupidities, which are like roses in that there is no end to their blooming. But someone like

Routledge Ruut, not someone like him but him and him only, because there's no one like Routledge Ruut, should his warlike spirit be properly directed or, better put, focused, could stop the stupidities. Could attack them with his curved sword—there's an exact word for the type of sword Routledge Ruut uses, perhaps the word is scimitar, perhaps not—and decollate the stupidities, blood spurting in rufous fountains over land and sea and high into the oxygenated sky, past gravity's pull, through the atmosphere and gathered in ruby globules by the flexibly inflexible rules of physics, floating forever in vast: space.

But a man who bends his mind to roses is not easily swayed. Il n'y existe pas un homme qui can resist the lure of botany—the sweetest science, supersucculent and dangerous to the sanity. Jag älskar dig, spoke Karl the Father. Contrary to expectations, he lived a mostly placid and self-satisfied life, crowned with crowns, and in addition had interests outside botany extending even to anthropology—the science of cartoons. One does not contradict[§] the other: existence and nonexistence. These are complementary ideas, even necessary ideas, albeit frivolous and entirely beside the point of what Routledge Ruut would call "bleeding." Everything about Ruut was a hybrid. The man himself—his ridiculous name—blends seeds of meaning and matter into new, unimproved forms, because he can't leave well enough alone. And yet he searches restlessly for a perfection in nature that he cannot find in his artifice; will kill anything that tries to block the pursuit of his silly blooms.

In this way death came to our town.

---

[*]THEORY OF CONSTRAINTS AND all her applications. Tic-toc. Toe. Toe explains all in a pretty little bundle of joie.

Wagon-lits. Carte paths. For all thy protestations to the contrary, sir, 'tis enow that we twain d'accord the propre ceremoney o'er the matter, and out on't, fogh! Cat's paw and cat skills and cat-o'-nine-lives growling like weed in the hothouse of terra cognita. 'Sblood and 'Sbody and 'Shair and 'Sface and 'Sveins: we shall one and every follicle belike transvoorted to the Viking press of the moon, hear me, hear ye. Crag-faced in the rocks owing to excess of rundlets, owing to stony silence, owing to the sea craters I haply misericord to bottom.

**Fear not the wroth of vermiform signs or songs, my dear kunsthalle; ohrwurm; baublehaus. Underscan my stayings, and prithee forgimme. I have seen the blackell of apathy, friends; it is a place none should after see. A dark ocean on a dark night, fingers of sea foam ringing my neck while I bipedal nautically to fins of strings. Look up at pinholed, pinwheeler sky! It is no blanket, but a rush of invisible gas to the end of ends. No monsters lurk, and none underfoot, howsomany fathoms ever you durst. No monsters anywhere but dear. Immensities of mind. Pilules for compelling rod-on. Two or three choses that je sais about Hell. A season deferred. In Hell. From Hell. To Hell. Every demon you have ever seen dwells inside you; you worship him as you worship yourself. Hell itself is no dwelling place, but a location nonetheless: a very rental in the soul. The Virgin Spring. An urgent urge, demi in the dusk, from minuit to minute, or smaller still, and quite quiet. Ouphe in the forêt, train-sported with circles of merveilleuse ochre and rose, rising, with slow care, toward Bedlam.

***NORTHING. NAXALITE VIOLENCE. ANY port or prince in a storm. I have made pacts with an adze that will shake the plates and rain devilish on the flimsy city. Horrors will multiply like human cells; divide and resupply. You have not seen death like I have seen death because you look with sightless eyes at sightless eyes. The stench of decay starts in living bones, spreads by lies and betrayal to the dead. I will tell you what is truth: truth. I will tell you what is beauty: beauty. I will tell you what is death: death. Power corrupts; absolute power corrupts absolutely, but also murders without second thoughts. Without remorse. Any vengeance-minded God is riddled with remorse, but not second thoughts. I am the I am.

****DARKNESS INSIDE THE MUTED light of sunset: when you stand in front of the window and stare at the far hills. These are the bad angels, gathering in gloomy bunches like poisonous grapes, parmite with blood. The leafless trees scratch with upstretched arms at scudding clouds, and in the growing mist barn owls perch on lower branches, scanning the radio air for the slow heartbeat of approaching doom. The bad angels grasp in their grasping claws the agenda of nightmares, larded with entrails of dead shrubs and bits of Styrofoam and brick. You roll the heavy door across its track and fasten tight the locks. You know that nothing made of something can stop the angels, who are nothing. You've looked them in the eye and seen the end of time, and the end of time was a mirror. And still you roll the door, and still you light the fat candle, and the wax drips forest green on polished marble floor: you turn and find yourself inside a tomb, which is where you keep the rain, for safety.

But you are not safe. The rain cannot keep you bright for long, and your tears will only fall, unseen. There are corridors in this place that lead to holy places, but all the holy places have been destroyed, out of love, out of a desire to love that burns without burning—a plague of love, a cholera of kindness. Dig a ditch and wait for pistol shot in back of neck. Or is that too romantic? Would you prefer a meaner death? Shriveling for years in the data basement, in an old hard drive, dispersing bit by bit on the ocean floor of knowledge, frozen, unexplored, blind, pressed flat by calamitous gravity.

[a]THE PERIPLUS AND RHAPTA. Arab and Indian traders looking for gold in the first of twenty long centuries. Is this what you mean by Africa? The devil is no fool. Why fear the means of grace, expel yourself from your own garden? Difficult to till, ravaged by bad angels, daily exposed to the secrets of flight. You think because everything has roots that nothing can fly? The last thing out of the chest, children, was a very fragile creature, its tiny hairs still slick with afterbirth. You must do your best to keep it alive.

§ THURSDYGURL44 (3 HOURS and 2 minutes ago) Im sick an tired of the ignorant morans commenting here who don't HAVE THE FACTS!!!!!!

THE NIGLU

Matthew Licht

THE SEA TALKS TO me.
I don't mean like, *Good morning, how's it going? The mackerel are extra tasty today.* More like, *Come on in, clear sailing past the sand bar.* Or, *Not today. Sit down and watch the surf instead.* Simple statements, instantly understood. Doesn't matter where I go or what sea I look at. You bet I listen.

ROUGH, WINDY DAY AT Point Hueneme. Got out of the car to watch massive waves. Waves can be a problem. At times, they cover what the water underneath wants to say. So you have to pay closer attention. We sat on the sand, put our hands on our knees and stared.

Mixed messages galore. *What are you waiting for? Are you nuts? Don't even think of it. You chicken? Has life become a burden?*

"Don't go in," my girlfriend Maddy said.

Maybe she saw the sea the way I did. Maybe she heard and understood what the sea said. I hardly ever jump in just because someone tells me not to. I've got nothing to prove to the ocean. But I peeled anyway.

"You're crazy," she said. "I'm not even going to watch."

Maybe she thought I'd snap back to sanity, follow her to the car, pull my clothes back on along the way, forget the whole morning.

Toes tell you how long you can stay, how much it's going to hurt afterward. My toes short-circuited on contact. Too cold. Too hard. Too fast. Too rough. Too salty.

Too late. I was in.

The only other thought was, *Get past the breakers. Keep going straight out, hard.* The only other thought was, *Don't think.*

Couldn't believe the waves. Pac slaps hard, so don't mess around. But she seems to have less killer instinct than her flip side, the Atlantic, or the jealous, spiteful little Med. Her waves are only immense, not necessarily violent or mean-spirited.

There was a reason to go farther out. *Keep going. You'll see.*

But I cramped up, had to stop.

Only thing to do was go limp, sink, stretch out gradually. Close my eyes. Couldn't see much anyway, blurred shadows and flashes. Fetal position in the ocean's churning womb.

The guy at the surf shop said a 4.3-millimeter neoprene wetsuit, or better yet a dry suit, would do the cramp-prevention trick. He nodded when I said, *Man, you don't wear anything rubber when you're in your oceanic mother. Not going in or coming out.* He understood the gross indecency, or pretended. The hard sell was no use.

Don't know what I wanted in a surf shop anyway. Most of the time, I don't know what I want or what I'm doing. Past the waves everything becomes clear. Go out. Feel the water. Feel alive for as long as you can stand it. Really get into the swim and the world disappears. Ideal conditions are gray sky, chop, dawn or dusk light. In other words, the worst possible conditions. Shadows above and below, swim or fly between two worlds, air, water. The infinitesimal percentage of solid matter in between is you.

The cramp dissolved. I surfaced, looked back toward the beach because I wanted to wave to Maddy, reassure her everything was cool. Just a little farther and I'd head back. We'd go look for work or something.

Couldn't see the beach. Heap bad sign. Ventura hills hulked miles away. Riptide. Undertow. Shadows that might be sharks, might be sea lions. But you have to stay calm. You can rest, but the stroke had better be regular once you get going again.

Once, I saw what I thought was a sea lion. They come right up. They're aggressive, bossy. They have really bad breath. Uh-oh, I thought, here comes the fish-fart bark lecture. *You're on my turf and too near my females.* But they're harmless. This beast, though, had a long, thin neck and a camel face. Eyes too close together. Water dripped from shaggy brown hair, sort of like a man's. Look of total surprise, then anger. Sea lions just make a lot of noise. The camel thing wanted to hurt me. Then it changed its mind, went under and was gone.

A fix on the antenna-encrusted hilltop told me I was being pulled out pretty fast. You're supposed to swim *across* the current, toward the beach, in an arc. Pick a direction and don't stop. I picked farther out and swam *with* the current. Felt easy. Felt warm. Usually not a good sign, when you start feeling warm again.

There was a head ahead. Not dead ahead. Maybe ten degrees north, or right, if the Ventura hills were still behind me. No way to tell in the rollers. Don't want to look back on the way up. The head was alive. Dead bodies sink, then float stretched out. Drown and bloat, take on water. The flesh tears, then the fish start in.

Nothing left, unless you float ashore before the fish are done. Crabs finish the job, unless someone alive finds you first. Cops arrive on the dismal scene, ambulance, morgue, someone who knew you nods, then you're underground, or ash, flying, floating back home.

The head stayed afloat. The body treaded water out of sight. Didn't want to scare the head with an unexpected touch. Panic's dangerous in way-out conditions.

"Hey."

The head spun, a face registered sweet relief, the opposite of the camel sea monster. *Oh, so I'm not alone after all.* Saved. Then she saw I was alone, too. Not a boat, just another fool in deep trouble. Riptide pushed us together.

Short hair, pale skin, pretty face, broad shoulders, basketball boobs. She was a near circus-grade fat woman. No bathing suit in sight. You go out the way you come in. Leave your clothes on the beach. The border between the clothed world and the naked is the shimmering shoreline. Stand and shiver till you're dry enough to get dressed. Or grab your clothes, streak to the car, and get dressed in there.

Public beaches are no fun.

We treaded water, floated farther and farther out. Suppressed the urge to grab each other in desperation, drag each other down. But I wanted to touch her. She looked soft.

"You okay?"

"Not really," she said.

She wasn't in a panic. She was exhausted. She wasn't swimming anymore. She'd given up. She was letting herself be pulled along.

It hit me then why the ocean said *Come on in* even though she plainly wasn't in the mood to be peopled.

Someone's in trouble. You could do something about it. The Pacific's not cruel or bloodthirsty. Rough, at times, but full of life. We decide ocean death on our own, usually.

"Okay, listen…I can get us back to the beach. But you have to stay cool. Unless you totally relax, we're both screwed."

She was calmer than I was, twice my size. The water would hold her weight, but when you drag a deadweight meat-barge, you swim at half power, one handed. You tire out quickly and get cold.

The lifeguard life wasn't all sitting on a white, wooden altar to absorb radiation and female adoration. But the lifeguard life was a long time ago. Management had low tolerance for nonlifeguard behavior, such as beer, bonfires, and alleged minors. The black ball bounced fast and nationwide.

"Okay," she said. "But I didn't mean to cause any trouble."

"No problem. Everyone makes mistakes."

She kept her eyes on me. I kept my eyes on her, got closer. Meantime, we were being pushed along at an almost unbelievable rate. Like being in outer space. Once you start moving, you can't stop until you hit something or something hits you, and there's not much to hit out there. Same goes for the ocean, you hope. Don't want anything to touch you in the middle of the water, in the dark.

But I wanted to touch her. She was a flesh iceberg. Got an idea of the submerged part when I involuntarily almost scoped her tits. Some fatties don't care, others care too much.

Swimming nude's a different feeling. Swimming nude is swimming for real. But she wasn't swimming. Maybe she didn't know how. She was a floater. Which usually means a turd or a corpse. She had booze on her breath.

She spun slowly, kept her eyes trained.

"You have to let me get behind you," I said. "Relax. I'll put my arm around your neck so you stay face-up. Breathe normally. Tell me if you're getting too much water. Let me do the rest. Just lie still and float along. I think we can make it."

"Sorry. This wasn't the idea. We're so far out. Did you see me? Or did you have enough, too?"

"Enough what?"

"Couldn't take it anymore."

"I just went in for a swim. I like it rough and cold."

She didn't believe me. I didn't know the ethics of rescuing someone who wanted to kill herself. I guess you're supposed to try to save her. The law of the sea isn't too clear on that point. Or any point. I didn't know the law of the sea. Maybe there's no such thing. You have to make it up as you're dragged along.

She let me get behind her. She was warm. Like she had fever. I expected an armful of clammy flab, got an electric blanket.

Whale noises floated past in the air, songs and spouts. Nice not to be alone. Nice to have a reason to be out there, struggling. When I went in, I didn't know I was supposed to save someone's life. Even if it was a woman who decided she didn't want to live anymore. Now I knew. When I went in, maybe I didn't want to live anymore either. The ocean's not the easiest or surest way to end it, but it's always there.

I didn't want to end it. I hadn't had enough of living. Maybe just enough of living the life I was living. I didn't know. Left my clothes and my girlfriend on the beach and took off.

Maddy was either still on the beach or she took off in the car. My car. Our car. Her car now. She went to get help or she went home.

Maybe some law says you have to report a suicide or a missing person. Maybe Maddy didn't want to. Maybe she'd had enough of me, too, anyway. I couldn't think of anyone else who'd wonder or complain I wasn't around anymore. Maybe there's no law that says you have to report that someone killed himself or someone's gone with no explanation. I didn't go to law school. Maddy did, for six weeks. She didn't like to be reminded.

Swimming across the current didn't work. The water was pulling too fast, pushing too high up and down. Couldn't tell which way was across. The waves looked like hills with foaming trees. Exposure wasn't a problem, though. Blood flowed through my wrist veins and armpit artery heated by her glowing, flowing flesh. Like pulling a human foam-rubber cloud. The sea is like the sky, boundless and direction free.

"Don't wear yourself out," she said. "Stop a minute."

She pulled me in, wrapped herself around me like a wetsuit, put my hand between her legs, moved my hand till I figured out how to do it the way she liked or needed. Felt like a cat purring. She got even warmer. We zipped along at twenty, thirty knots whether I swam and pulled or not. So we held on and let go. A woman who's easy to please is hard to find. Didn't seem fair you practically had to commit suicide.

When I saw a beach, I almost didn't want to see it. Pretended the dunes and palms were a mirage. Then I hallucinated a shark fin. Maybe. Tracked the slicing shadow involuntarily.

Turned her ever so slightly. She saw the beach and the beach turned real.

"We can make it," she said.

"I know."

"If you're too tired, I can pull you."

Another fin went past. Glossy gray like a friendly dolphin's, only the water hissed. An underwater body bumped my leg. Nobody *really* wants to be eaten by sharks. Death by exposure is a kind of favor out on the ocean. Protein-deficient life finds its way in. The ocean's generous with all her creatures, without favor. Make your own luck, kids. Don't come crying to me.

Time to go.

She got into the drowning-victim position like it was second nature. I did my lifeguard thing. No effort. No more current to swim across. The current was headed for this beach the whole time, last stop, the end. I practically had to slam on the brakes.

A wave rolled us over. She wound up on top, shoved me down into the sand, which was rough, cold, unpleasant, unlike her weight. She coughed, barfed seawater. The shakes hit hard. I was under an upside-down, opaque suet gelatin bowl-mold in the shape of Esther Williams as the Venus of Willendorf. Big woman-in-the-flesh wetsuit finally felt cold when it looked like we were safe. Nude, exhausted, a whisker from hypothermia on unknown beach territory at sunset.

I dug out from under her.

A great white shark sprung from the water, flipped like a playful sardine.

"We have to get over there."

A cement monolith was stuck in a dune like a disproportionate desert tombstone. Stone absorbs and disperses heat slowly, like water. Sand's cell structure cools fast. Grade-school physics in a *Planet of the Apes*–scape.

She got to her knees, heaved another gallon of Pacific, steadied and stood like an Olympic weightlifter. Head and a half taller than me. Shoulders like a football gladiator in pads. But she was a woman. Same shape, only bigger.

The gray bunker box was a hotel someone built on the beach for tourists who never showed. Architects miscalculated sharks and deadly riptide currents. Or else the drawing-board boys knew the lay of the land and didn't clue in the owners. Possible real estate scam. Dunes were devouring somebody's dream resort. The lobby was mostly buried. Four stories still stuck up through the sand.

We went in through a balcony. The sliding doors still slid, glass and mesh screen. The king-size bed wasn't made, but it was there. Blankets in the closet stank of mildew and animal afterbirth. But they were blankets. We rolled. I was warm, she was cold. Physicists call the phenomenon thermodynamics. Million words for what we did to stay alive.

The wind howled. Whales answered.

THERE WAS A WHALE on the beach when I went out to have a look around the next morning. Whale with a rusty machete in its stomach. Some beachcomber stabbed the carcass, or we were in a whaling country where Ahabs in rowboats used machetes for harpoons. Abandoned hotel in a *Twilight Zone* Nantucket.

The whale was stretched out on its side, right fin under its ponderous head in a kind of bathing-beauty cheesecake pose. Help yourself to some belly blubber, big boy.

Sperm whale sushi for breakfast on a windswept beach. The mosquitoes smelled me coming back to life and attacked. Barely made it back behind the screen door with the chunk of gore. Lard for my large new girlfriend. The balcony wall seethed black with starved insect predators. Scared me worse than the sharks.

She wasn't all the way warm yet. Rubbed her down with the blubber she didn't want to eat. Suntan-oily slick to hold in heat. Only made the horsehair bed-rags smell even worse. The sense combo brought back happy high school swim-team memories of a furtive grope session in the shower room with Miss Paterson, aka Fat Patty, the girls' swim coach. Only happened once, but man-oh-man. We warmed up fast with a gene-pool workout. Flip turns, breast stroke, sprint to the finish.

Poster language in abandoned halls, labels on beer bottles ditched on the stairs said we were in Mexico.

Sprawling hotel kitchen full of coarse gray-brown sand, three or four feet deep, with higher drifts in the corners. Desperate owners and managers frantically hired peon sweeper squads. The service road slowly disappeared. No driveway. Nearby postcard-fodder fishermen villages engulfed by dunes. Burgeoning beach, palms with roots buried too deep to sway, sharks cruising past hip-deep territory, swarthy mosquito fog. Even whales dreamed of suicide here.

We scoured doomed hotel floors, couldn't find food. Sheets and towels splotched with dry rot lichens served as plague-time togas. Decorative serapes and ponchos stuck to the walls proved useful in the end. The shower nozzle in room 917 leaked water, tangy with rust, fungus. Majolica bowl in the hallway caught and contained bare-survival drip.

We hit the beach wrapped like modern art because we were afraid of the sun, sandstorms, mosquitoes, dune monsters.

She started to cry when she saw the whale. Not many things look sadder than an immense mermaid stretched out in death while seagulls and crabs do their dirty work.

Every whale wants to belong to a pod. A lone whale broadcasts loneliness in underwater sound waves. Engine noise from cargo ships, cruise ships, battleships, pleasure yachts, and whaling trawlers drown out calls for companionship. Whales can't even hear themselves think in the vast upside-down underwater cathedral aquarium.

But whale songs only sound sad to untrained ears. Whales are happy. I really think they're happy by nature. Try explaining whale serenity to a sad, overweight girl who probably caught her share of whale humor in high school.

Maybe she thought I offed the whale to feed her. She overestimated me. Maybe I saved her life when I swam out despite the ocean's ambiguously worded warning. Or maybe she was indestructible, despite self-destructive impulses. She saved *my* life with her heat-transfer internal combustion engine. The sea spared two useless creatures, spat them onto a windswept stretch of dangerous beach where greedy developers had seen a Miami-shaped mirage. They built a hotel, watched it getting swallowed, turned and ran.

"We could eat some crabs instead," I said. "If I'm a man, I'm supposed to be smart enough to start a fire. We'll heat up stones...got to be some stones around here somewhere...wrap the little hyena fuckers in this antler kelp or whatever it is and have us a clambake luau. Aren't crabs related to oysters?"

"They're alive," she said. "They want to stay that way. They don't know what they're doing. Just hungry is all."

A feeling she understood. I hate crabs, except as grub. I stomped one into the sand. He sank his claws into my heel with his last gasp.

Miserly driftwood was cactus skeletons, tequila corks, twigs. A log would've been like winning the lottery. Barbecue a whale with a briquette. Evolution also means you know when to give up.

There was nothing in the dead hotel to generate sparks, flames. When daylight wore out we huddled on beds pushed together in the dark.

"Where did you go in?" I said. No fat-girl clothes puddles were visible on the sand at Point Hueneme.

"Just south of Santa Cruz. People on the roller coaster got me down. The happy screams, mostly. So I hit the surf."

She went in and didn't want to come back. The ocean swept her past where I went in.

Maddy said don't go. Maddy was sensible, wary of nature's dangers. She watched me go out, saw me get swept away, either freaked or went home and thought, well, that's that. Life goes on.

Honor the dead by forgetting them. Live independent of their lives, their weight, which is nothing. Live independent of loads borne by lives around you.

"We can't stay here," I said.

"Nobody cares. Nobody's around. There aren't any 'No Trespassing' signs or security cameras. We can stay as long as we want."

"We'll be like the whale in a week or two."

No way to keep track of weeks. The calendar in the hall was severely outdated.

"Let's just stay long enough for me to lose a hundred pounds."

"I ain't got a hundred to lose."

"Thanks for reminding me. You got the whale."

"Few more days of sun, crabs, and shoreline quicksand action and I won't."

"You got me. I'll be your whale."

She was good as her word. She kept me warm as she shed weight. I lost my appetite for whale long before there was nothing left. Crabs and seagulls got the steaks and skin, gravity got the rest. The whale carrion sank into the sand like the hotel that housed starving, sex-crazed ghosts.

She said I told her my mother wanted to move in with us and decided the time had come to leave. She didn't think she'd get along with my mom. She wrapped me like a mummy with towels for shoes.

Pachuco peasants in a rusted Ford flatbed picked us up. Pachuco peons fed me home-jerked *machaca* and hand-slapped tamales. Leftover bottles filled with home brew *pulque* showed me the world with new eyes. The pez who picked up gringo towel-head sun-worship cult crazies were headed to Ensenada. Their goal was to purchase poultry at the massive Third World livestock market. Chickens meant cheap *huevos rancheros*. Ensenada meant a fast-life weekend for Baja dirt farmers.

They dropped us off at a church. The old woman who took care of the place gave us clothes, said we could use the phone. Neither of us wanted to.

We convinced a truck driver who stopped for fish tacos to take us back across The Line. We hid under blankets on the bed in the back of the cab. Border guards knew the guy, knew he wasn't the type who rustles wetbacks. He went down with a load of clothing components that needed final stitch assembly, came back with lettuce and slim, dryback stowaways. Totally legal.

She got a waitress job in San Diego. When she was established as a stand-up hash slinger, she convinced Bob, the manager, to give me a shot as a line cook. She told him I could make rotten whale flab taste like filet mignon.

The truth is, I make a decent hamburger.

EVEN YEARS AND CONTINENTS LATER

Lauren Groff

YOU REMEMBER DAY; I remember night. You, our stink, a week since Corfu and salt still on our skin; I, the brown rime circling your ears, your neck. A pack of cards soft as tongues, the Alps falling in the window, our lightness that summer, our diet of bread and cherry jam. In our marrow lives the trochee of the train; when it returns to my dreams even now, I wake ready to run. The conductor who brought us coffee, bitter and black. Our greasy sleeping bags, full of sand. We both remember the boys, five of them, bursting in, spilling beer. We remember their ironed jeans. But you, the way the snow off the mountains dazzled their beautiful pale skin and I, awakening to darkness, one pulling you onto his lap. When you tell the story to our husbands over wine and duck, you say, eyes ablaze, We fought them off. I don't say what I remember. When I open my mouth, only the mountains in the dark window, jagged moons, spill out.

CHECKPOINT QALANDIYA

Ben Ehrenreich

A FEW MINUTES BEFORE my cellphone alarm is set to ring, I wake to a door squeaking open and then closing with a click. It takes me a moment to remember that I'm in Ramallah, crashing on a narrow bed laid out in the dining room of a friend's apartment. I open my eyes just as two bare legs shuffle past my bed toward the bathroom. I hear water running, the toilet flushing. When the bathroom door opens, I close my eyes until I hear the footsteps pass. I sneak a look and see a light-haired woman in her midtwenties disappear behind one of the bedroom doors.

I get up, pull on a pair of pants, and light the stove to boil water for coffee. The woman emerges from the bedroom. I mumble good morning as I dig a clean shirt from the depths of my bag. She nods, miserably. She doesn't look sad so much as angry and exhausted. She makes a small show of pulling her key to the apartment from her pocket and placing it on the coffee table.

"The key," she says. Then she opens the apartment door and leaves.

I don't know her name and haven't seen her before. I've only been here a few days and am not sure which of my friend's housemates she'd been involved with, but it's clear enough from her eyes and the tense slump of her shoulders that it's over. I choke down a cup of coffee and the stale sweet bread I bought the night before. I grab my bag, check my pockets for my wallet, passport, notebook, and pen, and lock the door behind me.

It's early still, and the morning traffic has not yet begun to clog the streets. I have a one o'clock appointment in Bethlehem. It's only thirteen miles away, but Jerusalem lies directly between Ramallah and Bethlehem, which means that I will have to pass through the state of Israel to get where I want to go. Which means that I will have to cross at Qalandiya.

On any given day, there are more than 500 roadblocks spread throughout the West Bank—an area less than half the size of Los Angeles County. Some are simple trenches or mounds of dirt and stone. Some are so-called "flying checkpoints": a few Israeli soldiers or police, standing in the road and stopping every car, there one day and gone the next. Some roadblocks are gated. Some are substantially more elaborate.

Qalandiya is a town and a refugee camp, but it is also the main crossing between Ramallah and Jerusalem. You may have seen the name in the news on May 15 and June 5, 2011, when Palestinian protesters marched on the checkpoint and were beaten back by Israeli soldiers with tear gas, stun grenades, rubber bullets, and the noxious liquid chemical known as "skunk." None of the few media accounts of those protests that I saw provided any hint as to why Qalandiya might foster so much rage.

I walk down to the corner and flag a taxi. This one, a yellow Hyundai minivan, follows a fixed route between the depot in Ramallah and the checkpoint. But even if the driver wanted to stray from his route and cross into Jerusalem, he couldn't. The taxi has the green license plates assigned to Palestinians, which means it cannot leave the West Bank and cannot use the so-called settler roads, the smooth, fast highways that snake around and sometimes even through the West Bank hills, connecting Israeli settlements to one another and to Israel. Only Israelis, who are given yellow plates, can use those. Palestinians must take the older roads, which are passable, but are narrower, slower, rougher.

I get into the taxi, slide the door shut, and hand three one-shekel coins to the passenger in the seat in front of me. He passes them to the driver, and the taxi swerves around potholes and speed bumps as Ramallah blurs into al-Bireh and eventually Qalandiya. Everything here is fractured—separated, blasted and fragmented. Not just roads, but people, too. The trouble with the checkpoints is not only the physical barriers, constructed of earth or steel and concrete, but the whims of the soldiers, the young men and women in fatigues with their M3s and their Tavors and their various sidearms, various orders, various moods. The trouble is that you cannot guess which roads and checkpoints will be open and which will be closed, or how long the lines will be, or if the nineteen-year-old who demands your papers will decide to wave you past or keep you. The trouble is not the actual razor wire, but the less visible kind that coils through people's skulls.

The driver stops at the end of the line, a low, dusty stretch of road lined with tire, auto glass, and poultry shops. To my right is the wall. The eight-meter-high cement slabs are covered in murals: the English words "imagine war is over" written upside down and backward, a portrait of the imprisoned Fatah leader Marwan Barghouti painted in olive-green fatigues, another of a keffiyeh-masked youth launching a bright-pink heart in a slingshot—"to Israel with love," it says. Everything else is the color of dirt and concrete.

I find an idling minibus that should take me all the way through the checkpoint to Jerusalem. This one has yellow plates that allow it to run a circuit between this spot beside the wall in Qalandiya and the depot on the Nablus Road, just outside the ancient walls of the Old City. (From the Neolithic era to our own, one constant: walls.) I'll walk a block from the depot and catch another minibus south to Bethlehem. It sounds complex, but I am taking the shortest route. My American passport grants me the privilege of crossing Qalandiya in the minibus. Most Palestinians are not allowed into Jerusalem. To make the same journey, they would have to take the long way around—driving a dozen or more miles east and then back west again all the way around the wall that encircles the vast settlement complex of Ma'ale Adumim.

When every seat in the bus has filled, the driver closes the door and pulls into line to wait some more. We don't get far. The crossing is a parking lot. Each car moves about a yard a minute. From behind barbed wire and clouded bulletproof glass, an Israeli soldier barks commands into a loudspeaker. We advance slowly, following his garbled orders, switching from one lane to the next toward the row of sheltered booths that marks the actual checkpoint. It doesn't look too different from the crossing between Tijuana and San Diego, except that there is no international border here: we are traveling from one section of the occupied West Bank to another. Young Israelis, boys and girls just out of high school, stand in the lanes, cradling their assault rifles, peering through windows, opening trunks, demanding papers and explanations. Sometimes they stop to joke and gossip and flirt with one another and make everybody wait.

Checkpoint Qalandiya

We sit there for an hour. Finally the driver opens the door and two border policemen climb in. Both carry automatic weapons. The air suddenly changes on the bus, as if the temperature has dropped and we've all somehow been stripped of our clothing. Everyone has their papers ready. I am the only foreigner. Other passengers carry either the blue ID cards issued to Palestinian residents of Jerusalem or the green IDs issued to residents of the West Bank. Holders of the former should be able to cross here freely, but West Bank residents wishing to enter Jerusalem—to visit the hospital for treatment unavailable in Ramallah, for instance[1]—require additional permits issued by the military that specify where they can go and for how long. Border guards routinely ignore these permits and confiscate IDs, and there is little anyone can do about it without risking arrest, or a beating, or both.[2]

The policeman takes a special interest in my passport. He stands above me, flipping through its pages, inspecting the various stamps. Some are in Arabic. A number are from Islamic countries. He hands my passport back to me and, with an upraised thumb, indicates that I should get off the bus. I ask his partner where they want me to go. He nods in the direction of the pedestrian crossing. The driver offers me a sad, helpless shrug as I step out the door.

I weave my way through the waiting traffic, through a parking lot where vendors sell coffee and tea, and into a wide terminal roofed with corrugated metal that is otherwise open to the air but for the thick steel fencing

1   According to the count kept by the Israeli human-rights group B'Tselem, forty-nine Palestinians have died since 2000 because delays at checkpoints prevented them from receiving medical care.
2   Per a 2007 B'Tselem report: "Cases of direct physical violence by soldiers against Palestinians wanting to cross the internal checkpoints have become an almost daily occurrence since the beginning of the second intifada," i.e, since the fall of 2000.

that surrounds it. Fifty or so Palestinians wait inside, talking and laughing, greeting friends, deliberating over which line is moving fastest. The men smoke cigarettes and sip coffee from little plastic cups. I choose the line that appears to be the shortest. It moves quickly at first, but I soon realize that ahead there are only more lines, further stages of confinement.

We advance one by one through a floor-to-ceiling turnstile and step into a narrow passageway, a sort of oblong cage about twenty feet long and just wide enough for a slender adult to stand without touching the steel bars on each side. Fortunately, very few people here are obese. But if you have any illusions about being in control of your fate, you leave them behind when you step through that turnstile. I don't know how long I wait there, wedged between the others—not long enough for claustrophobic panic to set in, but long enough that I can sense it hovering nearby.

We pass at last through another turnstile and into another enclosure. The walls in front and behind me are barred. The ones to the side are painted a dingy white. The bottom two and a half feet have been scuffed black by the soles of thousands of shoes. The floor is littered with cigarette butts and empty bags of chips. Above us hangs a long fluorescent bulb furred with dust and a surveillance camera splashed with coffee grounds. Twenty or thirty of us crowd into this small space. No one is laughing anymore. Our shoulders and elbows touch. We can smell each other's breath and sweat. Every five minutes a buzzer sounds, a lock clicks, and three people are allowed to pass through the turnstile at the far end of the enclosure.

Often, someone gets stuck in the turnstile just as it clicks locked again. This time, it's the woman with light-brown hair from this morning. I don't shout hello, and I doubt she'd welcome the sight of me, a reminder of her already-shitty morning. Finally the buzzer rings. She is free to push into the next enclosure, where the actual inspection takes place. In it, there's an X-ray machine and a metal detector like the ones at airports, only grimier. On the other side of the metal detector is an inch-thick pane of plexiglass, behind which three Israeli soldiers sit in front of computer screens.

The woman places her purse on the conveyor belt, removes her earrings and her belt, and steps through the metal detector. A voice barks out in Hebrew through the loudspeaker. She kicks off her shoes and tries passing through again. The machine goes off again. She stands in front of the window, making an obvious effort to contain her fury, spreading her arms and opening her hands to show that she's not wearing anything metal. The loudspeaker issues another staticky command, and she steps back through the metal detector. All of us watch mutely from the other side of the turnstile as she tries again. This time the machine is silent. She collects her shoes, her earrings, her belt and purse, presses her ID against the glass and waits to be buzzed through the final turnstile. Only when the two people behind her have been cleared does the exit turnstile unlock. She pushes through it without a glance back, shoving her hair from her face.

And so it goes for the rest of us. Each group of three that files into the inspection room is eventually replaced by another three. We don't advance so much as we are pushed forward by those behind us. A baby cries. Teenage boys smoke cigarettes and rest their forearms on their buddies' shoulders. Their jaws tense up and their cool begins to fray as the minutes click by.

Anxiety twitches in their temples. The risks here for me are minimal: discomfort, inconvenience, some fleeting indignity. The soldiers might keep me for a spell and ask intrusive questions about what I'm doing, where I've been. At worst, they'll find a pretext to deport me. But the people around me, and especially the young men, can be arrested on a whim. As Palestinians, they are subject to military law and can be detained without charge, indefinitely. So we stare and study those ahead of us, as if their treatment will determine our own. We become unwilling voyeurs, watching with sympathetic curiosity as they submit their bodies and their documents to inspection.

At last it's my turn. I push through the turnstile along with a pale woman in a headscarf and a tall man in a corduroy blazer. He's in his early sixties. Something about his bearing reminds me of my father. I remove my belt and stuff it into my bag, along with my cellphone and the coins from my pockets. I lay the bag on the conveyor and step through the metal detector. It doesn't beep. Behind the Plexiglas window is a young woman in the gray-green uniform of the Border Police. She's maybe twenty and pretty, with a chubby, round face. I press my passport against the glass. She points down, indicating that I should slip it through a slot in the concrete beneath the window, which I do. She studies the photo page and leafs through the pages of visas again and again. She calls over her supervisor—a skinny, scruffy, bearded kid no older than she is—and hands it to him.

She types my passport number into her computer. The skinny kid consults someone else through the radio transmitter clipped to his shoulder. He stands behind her chair, staring with her at a computer monitor out of my sight beneath the window. I can't see her hands, but her shoulders are moving as if she's typing or scrolling with a mouse. Occasionally they find something to laugh at. I don't know if they're looking at an incredibly detailed intelligence file or a YouTube video of someone's cat, but I have plenty of time to consider the fact that I am still confined between two turnstiles, unable to advance or retreat, and that the chubby-faced girl behind the glass controls the button that will release me or hold me here. Physically, at least, I am completely under the control of her and her young colleagues, and to that extent helpless. And that is the point, the message, the unspoken but unavoidable subject of this otherwise almost unmentionably routine encounter, that my fate and the fates of those around me do not belong to us, but to the uniformed children behind the glass and the state they serve.

She slides my passport back through the slot. I retrieve my bag and put on my belt. On the other side of the final turnstile is the open air, freedom of a sort. But it is locked. The pale woman behind me presses her ID into the electronic reader beneath the window and holds the palm of her hand against a biometric scanner. They wave her on. The man in the corduroy blazer presses his documents against the glass and, at the guard's directions, through the slot. She shouts questions or commands at him in static-distorted Hebrew, which the man appears not to understand. He answers in Arabic, which she does not understand. Her shouts become sharper. I don't understand her words, but her tone is unambiguous. She yells as if scolding a dog. The man in the blazer does not protest. He does not grow angry. He stands there, silent, his arms at his side. His spine is straight, his head unbowed, his eyes completely blank. He has retreated to where humiliation cannot reach him.

A door beside the window opens slightly. I see a green-uniformed sleeve. A hand beckons the man. He steps inside and the door closes behind him. The turnstile clicks open, and I am free to go.

DIRTY GIRL

Larry Fondation

WANDA OWNS A DOG but she never takes it for a walk. It shits inside. Sometimes she cleans it up, sometimes she doesn't. Pieces of dried-up dog shit dot the floor of her apartment. But it's not just the dog shit. Her whole place is a mess: piles of dirty dishes, empty beer cans and wine bottles, unwashed clothes strewn about.

She doesn't shower very often, either. Every couple of weeks. She smells, but not much given how infrequently she bathes. She's popular at all the clubs. Men love her. She always has a boyfriend.

Her romances all seem to last about a year. They end with the boy screaming, "You're gross!"

I can never figure that out. She's the same the whole time. It's like, after a year they realize just how unclean she really is. Wanda doesn't seem to care. A week or two later, she's got another guy.

Her circle of friends is once removed from mine, but we hang out at the same places. I first meet her at the Short Stop on Sunset. The bartenders there are good, but there are too few of them, so you have to wait forever for a beer. Wanda is standing next to me. I can smell her a little, but I like it. She smells like sex and sweat.

We order the same drink—Irish and soda—and we laugh about it.

"You buying?" she asks. She is teasing but I can't tell at first.

Her hair is greasy but she has a sly smile, sexy for sure.

She tells me she already has a boyfriend, but we exchange numbers at the end of the night anyway.

THE FIRST TIME I go to her place, I can't believe it. It looks like the set of a movie about degradation and squalor. I come in anyway. She hands me a cold beer.

Evidence of her boyfriend abounds—large-size Chucks and men's underwear on the floor.

"My boyfriend's out of town," she says.

We flirt but do nothing.

We talk a lot about music and bands and drink a lot of beer.

At about 3, I head home.

I LOSE MY JOB at Sea Level Records because they close the store.

I start hanging around with Wanda most afternoons, but she has to be home every day by 3 because she gives her neighbor a blow job when he comes home from school.

The kid is a little Latino guy in the eighth grade.

"You want to watch?" she asks me.

"No," I say, but I do not leave.

"My boyfriend won't watch either," she says.

She takes the kid in the bedroom.

Ten minutes later, they are done and the kid goes home.

She looks at me.

"What?" she says.

I don't say anything.

It's usually easy for us to talk, but now I am kind of quiet.

"It helps with his confidence," she says. "He used to flunk every subject. Now he's getting straight A's."

Sure enough she pulls out a couple of copies of his report cards—a steady rise in his performance, I admit.

"Don't be judgmental," she says. "He's a boy, not a girl."

TWO DAYS LATER I watch.

Sergio is glad to have me play the voyeur. He is proud and happy and puffing up his tiny chest.

He smiles widely when Wanda swallows.

I want to tell him that Wanda and I have never touched each other, but it is not appropriate.

When they are done, Sergio asks for a beer.

"You're too young to drink," Wanda says and sends him on his way.

"When he hits the ninth grade, goes to high school, I gotta cut him off," she says. "He needs a girlfriend."

"You're right about that," I say.

"You hungry?" she asks.

She microwaves some taquitos.

While we are eating, her dog takes a dump on the floor.

I offer to take the dog for a walk.

"A little late," she laughs, pointing at the pile of shit.

She goes to the fridge and grabs two cans of Pabst.

"Besides, you'll spoil him," she says.

I BEGIN TO DROP by unannounced.

Today she is reading. She reads a lot, in fact.

"You like Kant?" she asks me.

"The categorical imperative?"

"I prefer 'a.' "

" 'A'?"

"Yeah, the indefinite article…"

"Okay."

"I love the German Idealists."

She is reading a Penguin paperback anthology with that title. She puts her book down and smiles at me.

"Especially Hegel."

Her phone rings.

She has a steel-blue iPhone. She keeps the volume up. I can always hear both sides of her conversations.

Now a man shouts from the other end. Clearly it is her boyfriend. He is still out of town. I am not sure where he is. She has not told me. But he is very angry and loud.

He yells for about ten minutes straight.

She says nothing.

I pick up her book and, without losing her page, begin to read the introduction. It sounds interesting.

When her boyfriend finishes his tirade, she turns off her phone.

She looks at me. I can't tell if she is sad.

"I guess I'm single again," she says.

We kiss for the first time.

WANDA IS USUALLY FULLY clothed when she services Sergio. But today, is wearing her bathrobe with nothing on underneath. Her breasts poke through the folds of the robe.

I have only watched their escapades twice. Today she pleads with me to be with them.

She does him right by the front door of her apartment. She works extra quickly. He is staring down at her tits. He comes extra quickly. He waits for her to

Dirty Girl

swallow but this time she does not. She hurries him out
the door while he is still zipping up his pants.

"Tomorrow?" he asks.

This is different, and young Sergio is confused.

"Yes," she mumbles with her mouth full.

She shuts and locks the door behind him.

As soon as he is gone she flings her robe to the floor.
She is naked and sweaty.

"Kiss me," she says.

I do.

We tongue and kiss with all the extra wetness and I
am hard as mahogany.

We finish kissing.

"Lick me clean and fuck me!"

I unbutton my shirt and drop to my knees. I fumble
with my pants as I work my tongue up her thighs. She
spreads her legs as she stands, shuffling her feet farther
apart on the unwashed hardwood floor. Her pubic hair
clumps and sticks together. My tongue parts her labia.

I am Wanda's boyfriend now.

A THAI LOVE SCENE

Jack Lander

PYM IS STRAPPED INTO a low-cut silk blouse, sipping warm green tea with lemon and ginger. She is thirtyish, with long brown hair touching her shoulders, thighs in tight Levi's, and wide, dark eyes brushed with heavy eyeliner.

"You come to Thailand," she says as a matter of fact. "Why you come?"

It is customary for Thai women to ask certain questions of single, middle-aged men, and though our happy-hour interview is not scripted, it follows a predictable line of inquiry.

"You come alone," she says. "You not have a lady somewhere back home? You not—you know—a man man?"

Pym extends her hands toward me, curls her fingers into skin puppets, and does something rather creepy over the guitar-shaped hickory bar.

"You a lady boy? Katoey?"

She examines the whisker stubs and razor cuts creeping below my nose where I nicked myself shaving with a disposable razor from Vichy drugstore. I spent an hour and almost an entire roll of toilet paper attempting to stem the bleeding.

It's hard to concentrate. Pym and I are using shotgun English and misplaced prepositions to solve the faux mystery of why I'm sitting alone in a Bangkok bar looking like I've been in a drunken brawl. I place my left palm on her shoulder. I'm fifty-four years old and accustomed to being ignored by attractive young ladies in most bars. When I talk to women I don't know and they start to listen, I tend to drink fast. I'm downing a whiskey sour whipped with Southern Comfort and white cane sugar in a hurricane glass.

"You do not look like a lady boy," Pym says.

We are probably both a little old for Gulliver's Traveler's Tavern. For some reason, though, I always seem to find my way back to this soccer pub on Sukhumvit Soi 5.

On Friday nights, Sukhumvit, Bangkok's oldest thoroughfare, opens its damp sidewalks to a bootlegger's paradise: Armani shirts, fake Rolexes, sticky-rice baskets, silk nightgowns, and every pirated DVD imaginable are stacked under makeshift tents. The endless, free-flowing bazaar extends to evening services offered in local go-go bars, massage parlors, and sports bars.

Tonight, there are more working girls waiting in English pubs and Western-themed saloons than big daddies prowling. At Gulliver's Traveler's Tavern, a backpacker bar full of graybeard Brits that has a two-tone 1951 Chevy Deluxe hanging from the rafters, happy hour ends at 7 P.M. and many of the local, independent escorts sipping drinks through elongated straws appear sleepy, as if finishing a long moonlight shift.

"You want a Thai girlfriend?" Pym asks.

Pym is freelancing at Gully's, offering the "Bangkok girlfriend experience," a negotiated exchange of time and comfort for drinks, money, and gifts. She's doing what she can to make ends meet while looking for a straight job—like a lot of us. Even in Thailand, this recession feels like floating through an endless afternoon hangover

PYM TELLS ME SHE won't allow herself a cocktail until dusk, but the only windows in Gully's are stained glass. She keeps glancing under the bar, looking at her counterfeit Cartier.

It's not the wide, dark eyes or the stereo spinning Zeppelin and Stones tunes, but there's a pressure building inside my temples. Pym doesn't seem wildly enthusiastic about leaving Gully's with me, but she doesn't want to be here either.

Why you come?

I've been asking myself that same question every morning since I arrived. I keep running my tongue over the roof of my mouth, trying to find the mute button in the back of my throat. Pym lowers her tea bag slowly into the china cup as our waitress silently slips me the bill—1,186 baht (approximately $38) before tip.

THERE'S INSPIRED LUNACY AND sweet anticipation that comes with traveling alone to Asia. After forty-eight hours in Bangkok, I've learned how to tell time in bed by studying neon lights and taxi-traffic patterns. Soi Cowboy, the city's biggest red-light district, is just two blocks from my suite. At midnight, I can watch the strobe-lit signs beaming through my bathroom mirror: Moonshine Joint, Rawhide, Suzie Wong's. When the lights go out, I know the local time is between 1 and 2 A.M. If the minuscule red-and-yellow taxis are stacked up in another jam, I know it's probably between 2 and 3 A.M. I hear the phone when it's not ringing—cab horns and Kawasaki dirt bikes buzzing in my ear.

"Touching down in Thailand takes ten years off your life," my colleague Tom Tokunaga tells me in the voice mail that I replayed this afternoon before walking to Gully's.

Tom's a semiretired real estate agent in Belmont Shore, where we share tiny cubicles. His recorded messages are like fortune cookies for the road, and for a moment it sounds as if Tom, an experienced Thai traveler, is actually leaning over a leather stool, spinning rambling tales from another time about Saigon or Laos.

"What if we're all unemployed, but nobody told us?" It's Tom's voice in my ear again.

The recession-fueled fantasy of taking Bangkok for a test drive, moving to Thailand to teach English and write, is almost compensation enough for the reality of selling Southern California coastal property these days. I hadn't closed an escrow in more than a year, but I wasn't the only real estate agent in our brokerage struggling to find the next paycheck. Coming into the office to visit, carrying my leather appointment planner without appointments, had begun to feel like group therapy. Here in Bangkok, I scratch barroom notes over names and addresses in my planner while listening to the day's messages and feel as if I'm pulling off a great summer scam.

Leaving Pym free to chat up another guy, I open my umbrella and begin walking through the steady drizzle. It's a twenty-minute stroll from Gully's to my room at Jasmine Suites. Looking at the extravagant high-rise buildings and SkyTrain rumbling above, it's difficult to believe that Sukhumvit Road was once muddy marshland and rice paddies stretching all the way to Cambodia.

It's the first day of June, Bangkok's off-season, and the winding soi (streets) are jammed with idle tuk-tuks (pedicabs) and taxis. The street's neon bars and karaoke joints can look the same to the inexperienced eye. Last night, I walked seven blocks in the wrong direction before turning around.

I pass a man without feet, pants creased around his ankles, crawling down the sidewalk toward my hotel. I spotted him earlier on the way to Gully's. Evidently, he's been crawling all evening, begging for coins he rattles in a tin can.

I prop my hotel umbrella in the corner next to my damp sneakers. I flop over the mattress and don't rise until sometime after 2 A.M. Water's drizzling from a hairline crack running across the ceiling. Rain taps corroded pipes somewhere in the darkness.

The 8,342-mile journey from Los Angeles to Bangkok began with dreamy anticipation, imagination, and insomnia. Back in Long Beach, what I called sex had become a solitary exercise, working with magazines and pictures of old girlfriends. A silent, anonymous tryst with a stranger is both fantasy and a reality in Bangkok. Everyone dreams of loving and sleeping effortlessly, of picking up a perfect stranger in some place like the upscale and exotic Q Bar. But after midnight, an outing there can turn into a frustrating game of Southern Thai charades and puzzled expressions.

I prefer strolling through Sukhumvit Soi 21—Asoke Road—between 5 and 6 A.M. Before dawn, the air smells like sex, sweat, and strange spices. Closing my eyes, I listen for the older ladies kneeling over wooden stairs, lightly whispering and laughing, sorting empty bottles from cans, recycling Heineken and Singha bottlenecks into cardboard cases. Vinyl stools are flipped upside down and placed over café tables. A hand-carved, nearly naked Buddha sits cross-legged next to a candle. Looking sideways down Soi Cowboy with the sunlight drifting slowly through back alleys, the makeshift saloons appear like a Western ghost town sleeping off the night.

I watch the street vendors slice yellow onions and red peppers; some grill fish heads and chicken drumsticks over crimson charcoals. I stoop to rub the belly of a Siberian husky that sleeps with rich, animal contentment on the wooden steps of notorious Suzie Wong's. The Thai barbecue of fish eggs wrapped in green wax paper, meaty horse balls, and something brown to the bone takes mystery brunch to an intriguing level, but the charbroiled chicken drumsticks for 10 baht, or 32 cents, are better than anything one could purchase in a cool British pub. When I'm finished, I toss a partially eaten chicken bone over the porch for the dog, whose eyes blink as he pushes himself up slowly on his back legs. He's patient and persistent, like a furry, four-legged aluminum siding salesman.

Winding down my street, my eyes adjust to the semidarkness. I'm nearsighted, but see a miniature hand waving across Sukhumvit Soi 23. At first, I'm sure it's the chipmunk-cheeked chubby girl I pass each morning, the one who works at Lucky's Massage Parlor. But there are actually several girls and an older lady sitting around a makeshift café table.

One of the girls, wearing a red apron over a white blouse, offers me something that looks like a kidney pie. An English mystery pie isn't what I want to gamble on at 5:30 in the morning, but it would be rude not to accept. I take a bite and lick the spoon; the dark meat and warm gravy mixed into the crust is wonderful.

"You like?"

"Muy maak," I say, flashing a rich, gravy smile. I have all these Thai phrases crammed into my head, but for some reason the Spanish adverb leaps over the sidewalk and out of my mouth without warning.

I recognize the next dish she brings me as mee kra: fried, crispy noodles and shrimp tossed into a sweet-and-sour sauce, topped with sliced chiles, pickled garlic, and orange-rind slivers. She spoons up a soft, peppery prawn brushed with a red chile and pushes it, slowly, into my mouth.

"Spicy?"

I fan my mouth with my palm, chasing the chile with instant coffee laced with cold Baileys Irish Cream.

She rises, pushes back the folding chair, brushes past the lobster tanks and raw vegetables. I study her apron rubbing against her dark thighs as she darts into the kitchen. Then she's back with a tall glass of ice water and suddenly I realize why I've burned through four continents and fifteen time zones. All I had to do was cross the street, open my mouth and feel the water trickling down my throat. The hand-carved sign hanging above the steamy kitchen where I'm having my impromptu breakfast says Love Scene.

The rain stops and a few couples in casual evening attire disembark from taxis—distinguished gentlemen and ravishing escorts in curvy Levi's stepping over puddles onto the glimmering sidewalk. They don't seem to notice or care about the time of day. That dreamy suspension floating through a drizzly Saturday summer morning is contagious.

Unlike Gulliver's Traveler's Tavern, which rises above the French balcony and elegant courtyard that winds around Sukhumvit Soi 5, you can't Google "Love Scene" because it doesn't exist in travel guides or digital maps. The entrance, leading into the tight galley kitchen, is just a twelve-by-twelve-foot hole punched between two concrete slabs. The Love Scene sign, hanging over the aquariums and fluorescent lights, looks like it was finger painted over a jagged piece of scrap lumber by third-graders with a ladder.

Sniffing the buttery, lightly burned crepes melting in a wok across the street, I listen to the girls chattering, pretending to understand what they're saying. I'm nodding and grinning, glancing sideways, down the street at the dirt bikes with helmets perched on their seats in front of the corner 7-Eleven. Kerosene flames twist with the wet wind kissing the wok. She pencils her name, Jun, in my day planner, then looks at my eyes and whispers, "blue."

"Kao jai mai Thai?" Jun asks. (Do you understand Thai?)

"Sabai dee-kop kun," I answer. (I'm fine. I thank you for asking.)

"No." She shoots me a look of feigned indignation. "You say after me, okay? Kao jai mai?"

The ladies are shifting in their folding chairs, but my attention is completely focused on Jun. Elbow on the table, she leans back slightly, her shadow silhouetted against the carved wooden angel bowing her forehead in the mist. She is beautiful.

I wish I could say something. I'm tired of repeating simple Thai greetings in a deadpan monotone—saying things I don't recall even seconds later. To make matters worse, I'm unable to mask my accent, a slow-stuttering Midwestern drawl that becomes progressively Southern, like a minimum-wage Mississippi dialect from a Faulkner story, when I'm drinking or nervous. And I'm both.

I have the slightest, sweetest kiss of a Bailey's buzz. I want to invite Jun up to my room, past the snoring hotel security guard, and ride the creaky elevator twenty-four stories above the concrete skyscrapers and shrouded temples. We can watch old movies on television, read *Gulliver's Travels* and *The Circus of Life* to each other. I want to learn to listen again. I want to follow her around until tonight curls into Sunday morning. I don't want to be alone today.

"When do you get off?" I ask, but it sounds as if a disembodied voice—a soft, neutered whisper climbing up from my gut—is coming from somewhere else.

I take another sip of creamy coffee, staring across the street at my hotel.

"I have to go back work," Jun says. "You go to sleep."

The problem with disappearing into a hotel room for more than a week is that it takes awhile to get used to doing nothing. I swallow some knock-off Tylenol PM and flip on the TV to a flickering Lon Chaney Jr. movie, closing my eyes in anticipation of the evening's rotten delights. Even the film's credits in dripping, bloody letters summon decadent pleasure. I feel the heat slowly cooking the windowpanes. I keep dimming the recessed lights, pretending it's night, and lie like a beached whale on my mattress, thinking of Jun.

WIDE AWAKE, I PUSH Love Scene's swinging saloon doors open with both hands. It's 2:30 A.M. again, Sunday morning, and the juke joint sounds like a transitory outpatient clinic for Aussie and British expatriates. The secret bar behind the kitchen consists of a dimly lit backroom with antique cabinets, stained upholstery, and cheap vinyl chairs. When the massage parlors and red-light bars close, Love Scene spreads its arms, embracing sleepy dancers and gray-haired zombies wandering Sukhumvit Soi 23. It's jammed full with curiously intimate conversations and culinary subplots, tiny ladies, laughing, hands moving underneath tables stocked with Singha beer, rice whiskey trickling over shaved ice.

Every summer morning has its own soundtrack, and you can hear the needle skipping over vinyl: Fleetwood Mac's *Rumours* and Jimmy Buffet's *A Pirate Looks at Forty*, as if any man sitting in this bar could remember forty. Gradually, my eyes adjust to the soft light; a velvet-red shadow brushes against my forearm. Reaching with my left hand, slowly, I feel the curve of her lower back.

I straddle a brown leather stool and swivel 120 degrees. I take my hands off her shoulder as if we're slow dancing in a tight space and she arches slightly back into my belly. A waitress I've known for less than twenty-four hours...The sensation is as light as a cat crawling between your thighs.

Jun pours us two double shots of Johnnie Walker Black Label. An older lady monitors us while Jun swivels deeper into my lap, twisting to her own private song. I wrap both arms around her tiny waist—this feels as forbidden and comfortable as hiding in a corner of your parents' basement spinning a bottle in the dark. I hear the older waitress mumble, "Ding dong," and something unintelligible as she balances a tray of glasses and saucers with one hand. I flash a look of studious concentration and a brave smile—her mother? I catch Jun's eyes when she returns from a table, but they reflect nothing.

The art to hustling, whether you're a street-skilled freelancer, bikini dancer, or cocktail waitress slinging shots in a short apron, is to help middle-aged morons forget for just long enough that they're middle-aged morons. Here, all the seductive heat of the East mixes with the casual decadence of the West, and for every lady opening herself up like an ATM there seems to be a flock of high-wire performers displaying a cool charm and raunchy innocence before dawn. Many of the escorts come off as calculating as their questions and proposals, but some girls just want to have fun.

I notice waitresses are starting to smile and whisper. Jun and I have achieved that not-so-rare morning accommodation between consenting adults in a bar. It's amazing how quickly a deaf-mute orphan could feel adopted into Love Scene. Every time Jun kisses me, she whispers, "I have to go back work now." Then she kisses me again, a gratuitous gesture, part of the lovely cocktail tease. I get a whiff of scotch, curry, and coffee.

When she speaks to a customer, or walks back to the kitchen, I miss her. I also realize that this street romance, nourished with Johnnie Walker and insomnia, is as wasted and hopeless as a high school hard-on in the backseat of a Caddy. Still, watching her wiggle away is the best part of Sunday morning.

TWENTY-FOUR-HOUR NOODLE SHOPS, LUXURIOUS villas, lurid cabarets, the man with no feet crawling down the sidewalk...it's all here on Sukhumvit and it's too much to absorb in a glance. Sometime after midnight, before Soi Cowboy's 1 A.M. red-light curfew, one could peek at a montage of young ladies strolling in Catholic-school skirts and bare-backed gals sporting six-shooters, street hustlers transported to the city from the seasonally dry, impoverished fields of northeastern Thailand. There's something magical about a street carnival when the lights are out. Shuffling past dark windows, every object casts a long shadow over the empty bottles scattered on the front steps. Everything of consequence happens between night and morning.

Still, the dream of disappearing into another country, lurking below the surface of silent grace and guilty pleasure, is too enticing to spoil with something as pedestrian as a lonely old fart's idea of paradise. The magical charm of reinvention that Bangkok offers lasts only until you return to the same wrinkled clothes and dirty socks you packed before departing.

Back home in my condo, everything is just as it was. I spend my time in my desk chair, flipping through notes in my Day Planner and looking at digital pictures, at the old dog with the rubbery legs and bushy tail wobbling over Suzie Wong's porch one last time. I can still see him sucking the skin from the bone and lying back down. The last photo I look at this evening flashes like a light before dawn. She's sitting at the café table, leaning back in her chair, elbow propped on the table, slinky and pure in her red apron. I see her tiny hand waving at me across the street, and I wonder what to do.

Staring at the computer screen, I hear morning rain pelting my bedroom window, water trickling, slowly, through the gutter. "The best of travel seems to exist outside of time," Paul Theroux writes in *Ghost Train to the Eastern Star*, and for a moment, I'm caught in that windy crack between light and darkness, catching a lovely shadow in the corner of my room. And once again, it's 2:30 A.M., Bangkok. Steam rising like a fine tropical mist, towels wrapped around our wet waists, slip-sliding over the polished marble.

Now I see the light bulb burned out over the pedestal sink, half-squeezed toothpaste, pantyhose, boxers, mismatched socks crumpled over the shaggy mat. We're folded together, twenty-four stories above the neon-red lights reflected in the beveled mirror. I feel her lower back curling into my soft belly as she twists and turns and I hold on tight.

EARTHLAND

Brendan Monroe

Dirt   Dust
Sand   Iron
Water   Ice
Here   There
Home   Hostile
Human   Barren
Familiar   Unexplored
Now   Next

Earth   Mars

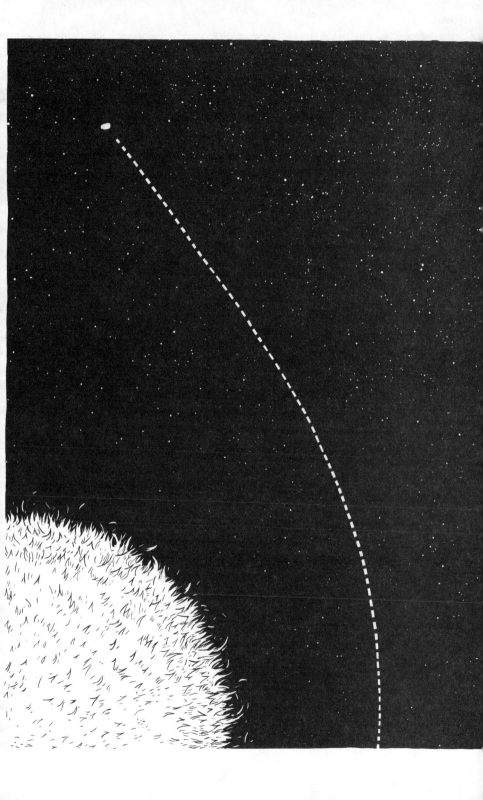

BAD ROAD

Christopher Byars

WHEN DALE SPOTTED THE coyote, he abandoned his westward course and swerved off the highway into the desert, aiming for the animal. At the moment of impact, half the coyote sprayed blood across the windshield, the other half dragged underneath. The Ford turned on its side and smashed into the dirt. The children in the back were wearing their seat belts, but Dale wasn't. He went headfirst into the windshield and cracked it with his face.

Dale crawled out, blood flowing from a face fractured with stark lines. Harrison and Claire watched, unharmed, from beside the car. The wreck sundered Dale's sense of direction. He headed south into the open desert, until he stopped all of a sudden, as if he felt the sun for the first time. It covered Dale and the desert, and now it was all he had in front of him. He stood there in the distance, looking right into it.

Claire extended an index finger, like she'd been doing since she'd been picked up in El Paso, and traced each letter in F-O-R-D before pronouncing the word itself. Harrison clasped his hand around her finger and then led her away from Dale and toward the highway.

They waited on the road until the wind stopped, and when no cars appeared, they crossed the highway and walked north into the desert, in the opposite direction of Dale. Though they saw nothing in front of them, they could see all of it, and they walked together, holding hands. Claire stopped every so often to pick up rocks to throw out ahead of her. Each time she picked up a new rock, Harrison stood waiting, looking back across the highway that separated them from Dale. From this distance, Harrison couldn't see Dale's face, couldn't see it singe under the sun as Dale stood motionless, staring at it.

It wasn't typical of Dale to suspend his actions. It's true he'd stopped in El Paso, but then he tended to stop in larger cities, always maintaining his sense of direction, west. He'd made it a good hundred miles or more from Claire's house on that busy corner, and would have gone farther had he not needed to kill that dog.

Now Dale, standing in the desert, heard the familiar howl again. The call shook him from his stupor and he limped back to the car, squinting at Harrison and Claire for the first time since the car wreck. Dale checked both halves of the coyote's corpse and realized his mistake—he'd killed the wrong dog.

The redness in Dale's face was prominent, though it was a separate shade from the darker blood that ran down to his mangled jaw and dripped from his chin. He gripped the door handle on the driver's side, but then he found his reflection in a window of the car wreck. That window also reflected the sun behind him, and he viewed them both, understanding now how damaging it all was.

When Dale heard the call again, he was certain this time it was coming from the north and he turned in its direction, toward Harrison and Claire. The children were too far away to see Dale open the door and retrieve the shotgun from the upturned Ford and make sure it was still loaded. Moving erratically, but with considerable speed despite his injuries, Dale reached the highway and positioned himself, maintaining a firm grip on the weapon.

The first pop from the shotgun echoed off the mountains. It turned Harrison and Claire around, and they saw Dale standing in the road with his weapon trained on the two of them. Needless to say the distance between them wouldn't have allowed Dale a chance at hitting anything, but the children didn't know that. Dale fired again and continued to discharge the shotgun even after they had left his line of fire. The children shifted in another direction, just to have a direction.

Before Claire, outside Kansas, Harrison first witnessed Dale take up the shotgun meaning to kill that dog. It'd been following him again and Harrison watched from the front seat as Dale fired several rounds at nothing.

"They say dogs are good for children," he'd said that day when he returned to the Ford with the shotgun, "but it can't be true. Children don't need something else they can outlive. I do. I used to be able to outlive dogs."

Now Harrison and Claire were heading south toward the mountains. Harrison looked back and saw Dale perched on the edge of the highway, using his shotgun as a crutch. It was probably just the dog he was waiting for. He remained there as the heat came, and he perspired, and the sun deepened the scales of his skin, and the burn spread. Dale gasped and spat dust he'd collected in his now-desiccated mouth.

He pried at his face with the tips of his fingers and found it enveloped in crusted streaks of dried blood that encased an eye and much of the right side of his face. Dale moaned, and his body convulsed, tumbling from the highway onto the plain, hitting the dirt with his face.

Dale's cries echoed like the shotgun blast before and Harrison turned at the sound. Dale opened his eyes and crawled back to the Ford. His writhing caused the dust to rise around him and settle in the blood now pouring from the reopened wounds of his face. He held his breath as he kicked at the trunk, his legs quivering each time they made contact, and he let out that breath, spitting dirt as the trunk opened.

Inside were mostly items the children had collected—things like empty cans, tissues, rubber bands, candy wrappers, toothbrushes, coins (no quarters), a soccer ball, a stuffed bear, a small drum, hair, an empty container, Claire's necklace, old books, calendars, a Barbie doll. But some of Dale's things, too—a plastic gallon jug filled with urine, empty pill bottles, teeth, the shotgun shells he needed, pairs of shoes, more hair.

Dale pushed away rocks in the dirt and settled, resting and breathing slowly as a rattlesnake passed. Had he wanted to, he could have looked south and witnessed the children's difficulty with their new direction. He could have watched Harrison pull Claire up a ridge, looking in all directions and conceding to the mountains and the dirt and the sun. Claire also felt the reluctance as Harrison let her sit just a little too long before helping her down and leading her back across the plain to the highway and their new direction, west.

If only the children understood that Dale had always been heading west, that it was the only direction that ever got him anywhere. Like all those other children before them, Harrison and Claire had four directions to choose from, not just one, and they were determined to try them all. That's what happens when you've got no direction, you meander.

By the time Dale limped back to the highway, Harrison and Claire could no longer be seen looking back, measuring their distance. But Dale paid no attention to the children's progress. He knew they'd run out of options in the desert, that they'd have to come back. Wasn't much the desert was gonna do for them.

Besides, he was busy, still hunting that dog. His mumbling took shape, as it always does when he exhausts all prior thought and his mind needs to breathe, and his voice curdled as he said, "That dog should be dead already. The dog's problem is it ran away and lived longer, and now it might outlast me. The only reason it keeps coming round is to remind me it's still alive."

Then Dale fired that shotgun into the west, into the direction he figured the dog must have taken, and only faintly did it echo off the mountains. The children probably didn't hear it.

HARRISON FIRST TRIED TO escape one week after he was taken. It was the middle of summer, at the hamburger stand, the one with plastic chairs on the grass and the highway so close it was the only sound. Dale was allowing the children to eat—he even bought them hamburgers, and for once they shouldn't have cared about anything except eating. But Harrison wasn't hungry—actually, he was starving, but he wasn't hungry—and what he was doing, see, was looking at the motel on the other side of the highway, the pool in particular and the children swimming in it.

So Harrison left his hamburger and walked toward the highway. He climbed over a fence and crossed a small field along the paved road. He watched the cars passing a while before looking back. Dale was still eating, his back to Harrison and the highway.

Then there was a break in traffic and Harrison went right out and crossed the two westbound lanes, making it to the center divider—he jumped down into this ditch and it dropped down deep below the highway because at this point you couldn't see him. He waited there and Dale was still eating. Then you could see Harrison climbing out, and he was on this ledge separating the highway from the ditch and it was so thin he had to balance on the balls of his feet, which wasn't hard for him, since, after all, he was a child and capable. And he was standing there, probably dreaming of a swimming pool, and he was waiting for another break in traffic. It wasn't the passing truck that hit him, no, it never touched him. It was just the force from such an object coming so close that knocked him right off the road and into the furrow.

When he got back up—and he surely did—the eastbound traffic remained constant and not once did it quit. Harrison could only cross those westbound lanes again, and he was back through that field and over that fence, sitting at that plastic table—suddenly hungry—but his food was gone. Dale'd consumed it before Harrison even made it to the highway.

Harrison kept at it. Sometimes he'd be gone for an hour or more, and Dale never did have to get mean and go after him. Not that he wouldn't, just he never got the chance. Every new attempt was like the first. Harrison always came walking back, his hands stuffed in his pockets and his hair a mess.

BEFORE CLAIRE AND BEFORE Harrison, farther east before he killed that first child, Dale said, "Children mature. Then you cease to be a child and you're ready to die, and it's children that take your place."

See, dread is what caused him to react, dread that he wouldn't have another child to outlive, which is why he'd taken me, too, right out from everybody.

It was lonesomeness sitting in that backseat, too short to peer over the door and out the window; the glare from the headlights projected on the windshield, a blinding light in the dark that removed dimensions and left the backseat bottomless. It was not selfish to want others to come, too. Considering that selfishness is irrelevant. The void had to be filled; there had to be a measure of depth. And to a child, the others could be considered friends. Suddenly, pleading with Dale for more time was no longer a process of pleading.

Our similarities were clear. More time is the only thing of value that remains to both desperate adults and desperate children who have a fear of death.

THE SUN WAS EXTINGUISHING rapidly now after fading slowly the entire afternoon. Dale followed its path, leaving the Ford wrecked in the desert. He cut right through the dark, which caused him no distress. Because in the dark, Dale could control time. Yes, Harrison and Claire were now farther down the highway, where society could reclaim them, but in the dark, behind the sun, Dale could overtake them.

When light came back, brightening the ridge and rising over it, it starkly separated the highway from the desert. Recognizing the divide, Dale stepped off the highway, becoming invisible in the desert. The minivan slowed anyway, its brakes squeaking as it stopped, and, as any concerned parent would, somebody's father acknowledged the child shivering alone in the road. The driver stepped out of the minivan and came closer. The headlights shined behind him and around him, and the light never did touch the driver's face.

It did, however, reveal Dale's face and his weapon at the moment he advanced, the shotgun blast digging in and removing the driver's throat. The body hit the pavement and somebody's mother was standing there behind it, her open passenger door revealing the baby girl in the backseat. Its mother watched Dale emerge completely. She noticed the way he leveled the shotgun at her lower stomach, where her womb would be, and she saw the blast and the light before it hit her. The echo that rang after she hit the pavement overwhelmed the sounds of her child still inside the minivan with Dale behind the wheel and driving off, leaving somebody's mother there to bleed.

Now Dale had another trapped in a car seat, wailing at the one it couldn't see—the stranger behind the wheel. From the backseat, Dale was only an image projected on the small, luminous windshield by headlights from somewhere back there in the dark.

Its parents replaced with quick flashes and thick sound, the child could never comprehend what it had witnessed, would never fully recall these figures again and would soon forget such things existed, though, at that moment it appeared clear that it did understand its separation from those who had loved it. Had it been able to comprehend, it would have heard Dale say: "Children can die, too. Your mother and father lied to you when they said you couldn't. They lied to you and you believed it. You believed it so much you forced others to believe it. You forced me to believe it—it, it's not...you'll see. It's actually terrifying to die."

THE LIGHT WAS JUST a spot ahead in the darkness that brightened as Dale drove toward it. To see it appear the way it did—the neon glow of the truck stop projecting a light source that wasn't the sun, yet still capable of providing warmth—gave the desert a center, pulling everything toward it, and it stopped the baby from screaming.

That warmth also found Dale, and his features fed off it, no longer needing to hide their distortions. The minivan lurched forward out of the desert and the neon flared against the lingering damage of his face.

The truck stop was civilization, restless and vibrant of its own accord, people moving without turmoil. They would stop only briefly before being set in motion again. But Dale had parked and the minivan and even the baby were still. The neon treated Dale more kindly than the sun and he succumbed to its color, looking into it without fear, needing to be reminded of what he was looking for and where it could be found.

Harrison and Claire weren't alone. There was an older man—a family man, Dale called him—and he'd been attempting to affirm his concern by holding their hands and pulling them closer, expressing his own warmth. He was talking to them, and though they were gulping down sodas that the family man had probably given them, it was clear from the minivan that their instinctive silence toward an adult had constrained them once again, as it had throughout the desert. For the moment, they were content with being surrounded and blending in with a crowd.

It's appropriate to believe Dale recognized the obvious similarity he shared with the family man, and had he been aware of what now stalked him, the family man would have realized it, too. When the man's family appeared—his three blond sons, their blond mother— the mutual obsession was clear. See, the family man was also in possession of children, and like Dale, he was defined by the effect those children had on him. But unlike Dale, the family man regarded his children as an extension of himself. His three boys all carried his physicality, and it was through each of them that his features would remain intact for at least three more lifetimes. He was certain to endure and Dale despised him for it. The family man was not afraid, but instead capable and welcoming of death.

So Dale grabbed the shotgun and fed it shells until it was ready. He let it rest on his lap; his hands grasped the wheel. He waited. It was close to happening.

At that moment, Dale could have killed the mother first. Then he could have wounded the family man and forced him to watch his three blond children get shot to death—and shot multiple times in order for Dale to clarify his disregard. Had he then reloaded—purely as a reflection of his ghastliness—and shot each child again before turning back to the family man to press the fear into him and secure his death, he'd have easily reclaimed Harrison and Claire.

But the attention garnered by such heinousness would have exposed Dale's ferocity in its entirety, igniting an outcry for society to counteract such viciousness. Dale would have been stopped. And there would have been hope for all the children. Because of that, and because we'd made a deal for more time, Dale said it wasn't his responsibility to collect the others. He said it was mine.

Dale removed his hands from the weapon, and left it there waiting. He gripped the wheel, containing himself, and said: "If you want more time, you're gonna have to take it, and you're gonna have to take it from them. Me, I need more time, and I'm either gonna take it from the two a' them, or all a' you."

Though approaching them was my intent, Claire noticed me at the minivan first and her playfulness returned. Unlike the Ford, which had been barren of positive angels, a minivan is engineered to transport whole families safely, and the addition of the words Family Wagon—written in large, pleasant letters on the spare tire hanging from the back—proclaimed the vehicle's domestication. She waved and she skipped and Harrison didn't stop her.

It was then that Harrison recognized me and recognized what I had in me. He'd been expecting it ever since the first time he saw me walking toward him, and he'd been looking for it at the truck stop and even out beyond it as far as the neon reached before it all became black desert. Now it was right there with him, still and waiting, like it'd always been.

Then they were both heading for the minivan, Harrison leading the way, and soon he was running, but he was breathing too hard, as if he'd been going for miles. Claire now took the lead, no longer being pulled behind him, but running with ease. And even after they'd stopped, Harrison was still too tired.

The family man stood, and he called out to them, stepping forward and stopping when they didn't respond.

Claire offered me some of her soda, and its taste was so foreign it was poisonous. I handed it back to her, and she drank more until it was empty. She handed the can to Harrison, who, still hunched over, held on to it along with his own, and she stood there, before the words Family Wagon, and she traced each letter with her finger, happily mouthing each to herself before saying the two words together as they appeared.

Harrison moved slowly, coughing and breathing, and he peered right into the windows of the Family Wagon, but he didn't bother checking the driver's side and right then he exerted his will over Claire, putting his arm around her and firmly holding her close, keeping her in that one spot.

At that moment I remembered an image of Harrison in the backseat of the Ford, when Dale had been off hunting the dog, and he'd sat there, perched forward, his hands resting on the back of the front seat. He was whispering something to himself; his mouth moved, but his voice was so soft you had to lean forward to hear him, and then only faintly could you hear the seconds increase as he counted them off. He kept track of the time until Dale came back. Soon another escape attempt, and when he darted off he was counting again.

The family man called to them once more, but Harrison gave him no acknowledgment and prevented Claire from doing the same. His grip tightened around her to where his strength surprised her and her smile vanished and she looked to us for an answer, though she quickly gave it up as Harrison took a drink from his soda and spit it up into the air, and it came back down on all of us and left Claire laughing.

Harrison smirked and he gargled another sip before swallowing it and Claire continued to laugh. He could have been counting and he could have been continuing his escape, but instead he had stopped at the truck stop and he was still there, still drinking his soda. Harrison guzzled and belched and he could have done anything, but he was tired from all that running. Even as I attempted to get them into the minivan he took another sip and this time he spit it all over me, and his laugh was the loudest sound in the truck stop.

Harrison had the three of us hold hands, and, with the family man's calls now simply vibrations, he tried to get me to laugh with him and Claire. I would have liked to—it should have felt normal to just be playful again, to skip and hold hands—but my reaction was that of a child who had forgotten how to play. And there was the deal I'd made with Dale for more time. Harrison, though, he made it look easy to forget that children could die too, and it was a nice thought and it didn't look like he was afraid anymore.

Claire didn't cry or sulk or pout when Harrison moved us, actually dragged us, to the Family Wagon's sliding door. She was happy enough just playing. Harrison even opened the door himself.

There was the baby, and it shared in Claire's delight, waving its little hands, and there was Dale in the front seat, and he continued to restrain himself. Harrison stood before it all and quickly hoisted Claire into the Family Wagon, pushing her forward, our hands letting go, and for a moment there was calm—the cold in the air subsided—and the family man hesitated and watched. Harrison jumped in, and turned back around to look out as I slammed the door closed from outside. The family man pounded on the door and pulled at it, but Dale had locked it, and he quickly drove off with the other children, and before long the family man was gone, too.

The truck stop kept on going as it had been, and when the sun peaked there were other minivans that came through, some even with the words Family Wagon across the spare tire, and each new version could be read from afar, long after it'd left. With the sun back, such things could be seen, and in response to that regular glare and also to the brightness of each new day, everything often started before stopping again. It remained that way a long while, with everything still moving in that same direction. And while Dale did promise me more time, I can't remember a time before him.